EGON RONAY'S GUINNESS

PUB GUIDE

1985

Food and accommodation

First published by Egon Ronay Organisation Ltd 1985
Greencoat House, Francis Street, London SW1P 1DH, in association with
Mitchell Beazley London, Mill House, 87–89 Shaftesbury Avenue, London W1V 7AD
Copyright © Egon Ronay 1985
All rights reserved

The contents of this book are believed correct at the time of printing and every
effort has been made to ensure the information is correct. Nevertheless, the
Publisher can accept no responsibility for errors or omissions or for changes in the
details given.

Printed and bound in Great Britain by Cox & Wyman Ltd, Reading
Filmset by JH Graphics Ltd, Reading
Produced by Egon Ronay Organisation Ltd
Cartography revised by Intermap P.S. Ltd
All road maps are based on the Ordnance Survey Maps, with the permission of the
Controller of H.M. Stationery Office, Crown Copyright Reserved.

Layout and typography by Barbara Ronay

THE EGON RONAY ORGANISATION

Our researches have included the whole field of catering, from de luxe hotels and restaurants to inns, pubs, transport and motorway cafés, hospital meals, international airlines, European airports, car ferries, theatres, the British Armed Forces, etc. Our four annual Guides are the present one, as well as

Egon Ronay's Lucas Guide 1985 to Hotels and Restaurants.
Just a Bite, Egon Ronay's Lucas Guide 1985
for Gourmets on a Family Budget
Egon Ronay's TWA Guide 1984 to Good Restaurants
in Major Cities, Europe & United States.

Our researches are carried out by full-time professional inspectors with catering backgrounds and proven knowledge of international cooking, which we test before training them for many weeks in the Organisation to achieve common standards of judgement with as much objectivity as this field allows. Their professional identities are not disclosed until they seek information from the management after paying their bills.

To find establishments for our Guides, we normally rely partly on re-inspection of current listings and a research programme drawn up from many sources, such as readers' recommendations and requests for visits from proprietors of establishments (these latter two categories being subject to careful vetting).

The Organisation maintains complete independence in its editorial selection and judgements. It is sustained, in addition to sales, by sponsorship and advertising, without which the price of our Guides would be prohibitive, but we do not accept advertising, payment or free hospitality from any of the establishments we cover.

CONTENTS

WE CORDIALLY INVITE

establishments not in this Guide

to write to us if they would like to be considered for inclusion next year
— provided their standard of food *served in the bar* is exceptionally
high, or their bedrooms clean and very pleasant, or both.

**Write to Egon Ronay's Guinness Pub Guide, Greencoat House,
Francis Street, London
SW1P 1DH**

We do not accept advertising, payment or free hospitality from any of the
establishments we recommend.

Continuing success

After the success of our first joint venture in 1984, we look forward to further developing the role of Egon Ronay's Guinness Pub Guide, which reflects all that is best about British pubs.

The Guide's relentless search for pub food of the highest quality has, we hope, contributed to the improving standards achieved in recent years. Guinness has been synonymous with beer of the finest quality for more than two centuries.

And it is no coincidence that pubs featured within these pages for the food they prepare have an equally high reputation for the beer they serve.

Good food and good beer make natural partners. Similarly, the Egon Ronay Organisation and Guinness Brewing make an ideal team in their pursuit of excellence.

Ernest Saunders
Group Chief Executive
Arthur Guinness & Sons plc

Egon Ronay

HOW TO USE THIS GUIDE

GOOD BAR FOOD
We include establishments where our team of professional inspectors found excellent-quality bar food. Such pubs are indicated by *'Food'* following the locality. We did not cover pub restaurants, as they fall within the scope of *Egon Ronay's Lucas Guide 1985 to Hotels and Restaurants.*

Two typical dishes are listed, with prices valid at the time of our visit. However, prices may well have risen since our researches. We also indicate any restrictions on availability of food, for instance, only sandwiches at Sunday lunch time. Additionally, it is advisable to check the hours at which food is served. Last order times refer to bar food where it is served in the evening.

Those establishments serving outstanding – 'Much Above Average' – food are shown with a star.

GOOD ACCOMMODATION AT PUBS
We also tried the accommodation and we list the number of bedrooms for those pubs we can recommend for an overnight stay, such pubs being indicated by *'B & B'* following the locality. When looking for accommodation, bear in mind that the publican's free time is traditionally in the afternoon, when he or she is usually not available.

The accommodation is rated Grade 1 or Grade 2 (if the rooms vary, we use Grades 1 & 2), and we indicate where dogs are not allowed in bedrooms. The symbol £A+, £A, £B or £C shows the price of bed and a cooked English breakfast in a double room for two occupants:

£A+ over £37
£A from £31 to £37
£B from £24 to £30
£C under £24
(including VAT)

Some hotels included for their bar snacks do not offer pub style accommodation but are recommended in *Egon Ronay's Lucas Guide 1985 to Hotels and Restaurants*. This is indicated in their write-up.

ATMOSPHERIC PUBS

These pubs are recommended as pleasant or interesting places for a drink rather than for their bar food or accommodation. Entries are denoted by the figure to the right:

SUITABLE FOR FAMILIES

Those pubs we suggest as suitable for families are ones that have a room or indoor area where children are allowed whether eating or not. Many pubs welcome children if they are eating bar food and some pubs make a feature of outdoor play areas, but readers should note that these are not the qualifications on which we base our **Family pub** category. Restrictions on children staying overnight are mentioned in the entries.

BEERS AND CIDER

We print whether an establishment is a free house or brewery-owned. After the 🍺 symbol are listed the names of a number of beers, lagers and cider on draught. *Real ale* appears if one or more of the beers offered can be defined as such.

continued

OPENING TIMES
Opening hours vary throughout the country. Some pubs have a six-day licence. As many pubs close at some time during Christmas and the New Year, it is advisable to check. Also, some pubs choose to close one or more days a week.

ORDER OF LISTING
In London, listings are in alphabetical order by the establishment's name. Out of London listings are in alphabetical order under the names of localities within the regional divisions of England, Scotland, Wales, the Channel Islands and the Isle of Man.

MAP REFERENCES
Entries contain references to the map section located in the middle of the Guide.

SYMBOLS

Food   Recommended for bar food

B & B   Recommended for accommodation

★   Bar food much above average

▯   On draught

Family pub   Suitable for families (see also preceding page)

SUMMING UP

We wrote to the 950 pubs in our 1984 Guide asking about the importance of their food sales. *85% of the replies stated that they could not survive without them!* A quarter have increased their food turnover by more than 50%, half by more than 25% — all in the last two years. The speed with which this change has occurred is surprising.

Even though these statistics refer to only a small proportion of pubs in Britain, the significance of the findings cannot be overestimated. The pubs they mirror represent the best in the country — those which set the trend.

Dramatic changes
Snack-type bar food is rapidly giving way to full meals. Three-course meals, tables laid and waitress service bring to mind the atmosphere of German-type brasseries or, in many cases, French bistros.

The number of what we call 'family pubs' has increased, and they have improved their facilities for children. There is a dramatic change in publicans' attitudes to welcoming — as opposed to tolerating, let alone barring — children. 88% of landlords said that they favour serving food to families with children; about a third would welcome children even under four years old! (Results of our survey on licensing are on page 15.)

All this points to a more radical and faster change in the traditional face of the British pub and its social function than is realised. Within ten to fifteen years traditional British pubs, as we know them, may well be reduced to a fraction of their former number.

So much for the changing face of pubs. How about the food they offer?

continued

The chips are down

Though food keeps improving, the progression is slower and still has a long way to go. Certainly numerous pubs are a very satisfactory answer to bistros in France. There is more home-made food and fewer commercial pies. There are often more interesting dishes than the predictable prepacked fare. But there are still far too many houses with dull, carelessly prepared food, seas of peas, mountains of smothering cress, artificial-looking salads to match mock beams and plastic ferns, and *practically no good chips to be found.* The phenomenon of British inability to produce a modest dish of decent chips instead of the undercooked, frozen, greasy, flabby, stuck-together, reheated stuff purveyed by 'cooks' who ought to be ashamed of themselves is absurd.

Fetish of microwave

Naive brewers exemplify the British delusion that money poured into improved kitchens, into stainless steel, and the fetish of microwave ovens, will result in improved quality. If a quarter of the investment had gone into the training of kitchen staff, if brewery-owned pubs employed cooks half as skilled as those turned out by the Armed Forces schools of catering, pub food could be a joy almost everywhere.

But breweries do deserve praise for the way they maintain and keep improving accommodation. Free houses, too, have been conspicuously investing in creating very good bedrooms and bathrooms. Annexes are being built, and rooms at the inn have now become much more than a romantic notion.

Creature (dis)comforts

Yet there are still at least as many rooms crying out to be refurbished. While automatic breakfast kettles (somewhat incongruous with the country inn image) are universal, they are often a source of frustration when it comes to locating the electrical socket. And – please – could more and warmer blankets, as well as something better than depressingly battered coat hangers, be provided?

Television is by no means general in rooms – and long may it remain blissfully absent as a matter of policy: people who seek out a lovely country inn for spending a night or two and yet want to stay in their room to watch snooker may well have a split personality.

Clearly, rooms at the inn are entering the phase of serious business. What puzzles me is that no one has yet thought of popularising them through cooperative marketing groups.

Changes in the licensing laws: what the publicans think

Results of our researches conducted in October 1984, compiled from nearly 700 answers received from landlords in our 1984 Guide

86% are in favour of changes

14% are against changes

74% do *not* want *all* restrictions abolished

93% favour the landlords deciding their own opening hours

73% think that greater flexibility in hours would *not* result in greater consumption of alcohol

27% think that greater flexibility *would* result in greater consumption of alcohol

67% think flexibility in hours would increase the consumption of food

58% think the increase in food consumption would be about 20%

PUB
OF THE YEAR

Our annual award is a Pewter Plate, a floating trophy engraved with the winner's name and retained until next year. Since it would be impossible to name 'the best pub in the land', we are choosing one from the short list below, and the final choice is announced on the day of publication. As previously, the main criteria are a very high standard of bar food and a congenial atmosphere fostered by the appealing personality of the landlord. The short list is as follows: *Henley-on-Thames, Little Angel; Shipton-under-Wychwood, Lamb Inn; Staddle Bridge, McCoys; Tetbury, Gentle Gardener; Yattendon, Royal Oak; Llanfihangel Crucorney, Skirrid Inn.*

1985

PUB OF THE YEAR AWARD

?

FOOD MUCH ABOVE AVERAGE

Dulnain Bridge

Wester Howgate

Tarbert

Kirkby Stephen Stapleton
Moulton Staddle Bridge

Stamford Stow Bardolph

Huntingdon

Whitney-on-Wye Shipston-on-Stour Fowlmere Little Walden
Llowes Saffron Walden
Llanfihangel Crucorney Broad Oak Brightwell Great Waltham
Stanton Harcourt Baldwin Chenies
Tetbury Fawley
Burton Maidensgrove Henley-on-Thames
Box Yattendon Stanford Burham
Dingley

Langley Marsh Rockbourne Biddenden
Staple Fitzpaine Stuckton Fulking
Ansty

FOR LIST SEE OVER

17

★ PUB FOOD
MUCH ABOVE AVERAGE

ENGLAND
Ansty, Dorset: Fox Inn
Biddenden, Kent: Three Chimneys
Box, Wilts: Chequers
Brightwell Baldwin, Oxon: Lord
  Nelson Inn
Broad Oak, H & W: Broad Oak Inn
Burham, Kent: Golden Eagle
Burton, Wilts: Plume of Feathers
Chenies, Herts: Bedford Arms Thistle
  Hotel
Fawley, Bucks: Walnut Tree
Fowlmere, Cambs: Chequers Inn
Fulking, W Sussex: Shepherd & Dog
Great Waltham, Essex: Windmill

Henley-on-Thames, Oxon: Little
  Angel
Huntingdon, Cambs: Old Bridge
  Hotel
Kirkby Stephen, Cumb: King's Arms
  Hotel
Langley Marsh, Som: Three
  Horseshoes
Little Walden, Essex: Crown Inn
Maidensgrove, Oxon: Five
  Horseshoes
Moulton, N Yorks: Black Bull Inn
Rockbourne, Hants: Rose & Thistle
Saffron Walden, Essex: Saffron Hotel
Shipston-on-Stour, Warwicks: White
  Bear
Staddle Bridge, N Yorks: McCoy's at
  the Tontine
Stamford, Lincs: George of Stamford
Stanford Dingley, Berks: Old Boot Inn
Stanton Harcourt, Oxon: Harcourt
  Arms
Staple Fitzpaine, Som: Greyhound
  Inn
Stapleton, Co. Durham: Bridge Inn
Stow Bardolph, Norfolk: Hare Arms
Stuckton, Hants: Three Lions Inn
Tetbury, Glos: Gentle Gardener
Whitney-on-Wye, H & W:
  Rhydspence Inn
Yattendon, Berks: Royal Oak

SCOTLAND
Dulnain Bridge, H'land: Muckrach
  Lodge Hotel
Tarbert, S'clyde: West Loch Hotel
Wester Howgate, Lothian: Old
  Howgate Inn

WALES
Llanfihangel Crucorney, Gwent:
  Skirrid Inn
Llowes, Powys: Radnor Arms

THE ENGLISH CHEESE PUB AWARD 1985

With new names like Lymeswold, Melbury and Ash Barrow appearing regularly on the market, it's clear that the art of English cheesemaking is a constantly developing one. The public continue to show great interest in both the established and the new varieties, and pubs have long played a major role in popularising this fine, nourishing product.

English cheese and English beer are natural companions, and the traditional lunchtime fare of cheese, bread and pickles with a glass of ale remains a favourite throughout the land.

Our inspectors have again taken a close look at pub cheeseboards, taking note of quality, variety and presentation. Our recommendations for good English cheeseboards follow.

We award an annual trophy to the pub with the best English cheeses and are pleased to announce this year's winner:

RHYDSPENCE INN
WHITNEY-ON-WYE

An impressive range of perfectly kept cheeses – at least ten in the prime months – is offered at this fine old Welsh Border inn.

Previous winners
1981 The Park, Bedford
1982 The Plough, Rusper
1983 Lamb & Flag, London WC2
1984 Black Bull, Moulton

GOOD ENGLISH CHEESEBOARDS

LONDON
Admiral Codrington, SW3
Lamb & Flag, WC2

ENGLAND
Bedford, Beds: Park
Biddenden, Kent: Three Chimneys
Bowdon, Ches: Griffin
Braintree, Essex: Retreat
Bridge Trafford, Ches: Nag's Head
Brockton, Shrops: Feathers Inn
Brome, Suffolk: Oaksmere
Burtonwood, Ches: Fiddle i'th Bag Inn
Byworth, W Sussex: Black Horse
Chenies, Herts: Bedford Arms Thistle Hotel
Chiddingfold, Surrey: Swan
Constable Burton, N Yorks: Wyvill Arms
Cottesmore, Leics: Sun Inn
Cumnor, Oxon: Bear & Ragged Staff
Dorchester-on-Thames, Oxon: George Hotel
East Haddon, Northants: Red Lion
Etton, Cambs: Golden Pheasant
Faugh, Cum: String of Horses Inn
Fenay Bridge, W Yorks: Star
Fulking, W Sussex: Shepherd & Dog

Grantchester, Cambs: Green Man
Harpenden, Herts: Silver Cup
Hildenborough, Kent: Gate Inn
Horley, Surrey: Ye Olde Six Bells
Hungerford, Berks: Bear at Hungerford
Kenley, Surrey: Wattenden Arms
Kingsclere, Berks: Crown
Kinver, Staffs: Whittington Inn
Lacock, Wilts: Red Lion
Ledsham, Ches: Tudor Rose
Lickfold, W Sussex: Lickfold Inn
Longparish, Hants: Plough Inn
Mark Cross, E Sussex: Mark Cross Inn
Marsh Gibbon, Oxon: Greyhound Inn
Millthorpe, Derbys: Royal Oak
Moulton, N Yorks: Black Bull Inn
Murcott, Oxon: Nut Tree Inn
Nassington, Northants: Black Horse Inn
Naunton, Glos: Black Horse
Nottingham, Notts: Lord Nelson
Nunney, Som: George Inn
Peppard Common, Oxon: Red Lion
Perranarworthal, Corn: Norway Inn
Philleigh, Corn: Roseland Inn
Rushlake Green, E Sussex: Horse & Groom
Sambourne, Warwicks: Green Dragon
Semley, Wilts: Benett Arms
Shalfleet, I of W: New Inn
Shelley, W Yorks: Three Acres Inn
Shepperton, Surrey: Thames Court
Slaithwaite, W Yorks: White House
Sonning-on-Thames, Berks: Bull Inn

continued

Staple Fitzpaine, Som: Greyhound Inn
Stapleton, Co. Durham: Bridge Inn
Testcombe, Hants: Mayfly
Timperley, Ches: Hare & Hounds
Waltham St Lawrence, Berks: Plough Inn
Washbrook, Suffolk: Brook Inn
Westbury, Bucks: Reindeer Inn
Weston, Ches: White Lion
Whitney-on-Wye, H & W: Rhydspence Inn
Wilson, Derbys: Bull's Head Inn
Wincham, Ches: Black Greyhound Hotel
Yattendon, Berks: Royal Oak Hotel

SCOTLAND
Canonbie, D & G: Riverside Inn
Killiecrankie, Tayside: Killiecrankie Hotel

WALES
Abergavenny, Gwent: Crowfield Inn
Llowes, Powys: Radnor Arms

Traditional Country Cheeses

For further information about English cheeses, contact the English Country Cheese Council, 5–7 John Princes Street, London W1M 0AP

The
Schweppes®
Family Pub Guide

SELECTED BY THE
EGON RONAY ORGANISATION

Below is a list of pubs which the Egon Ronay Organisation has selected as being particularly suitable for families. All have an *indoor* area or special room where children are allowed whether eating or not, and all of them serve Schweppes soft drinks.

These and other pubs in the Guide which have facilities for children are denoted by the words **Family pub**. Many pubs welcome children if they are eating bar food and some pubs make a feature of outdoor play areas, but readers should note that these are not the qualifications on which our **Family pub** category is based.

In recent years, the Egon Ronay Organisation has drawn attention to the trend towards more family pubs. The demand for making pubs more and more suitable for the whole family is growing and special facilities for children are improving all the time.

LONDON
Albion, N1
Cock Tavern, EC1
City Barge, W4
Hand in Hand, SW19
King's Head & Eight Bells, SW3
Paxton's Head, SW1
Prospect of Whitby, E1
Shepherd's Tavern, W1
Ship, SW14 (until 7pm)
Ye Olde Cheshire Cheese, EC4

ENGLAND
Avon
Tormarton, Compass Inn (lunchtime)
Berkshire
Ascot, Stag (lunchtime)
Chaddleworth, Ibex
Great Shefford, Swan
Highclere, Yew Tree Inn
Hungerford, Bear at Hungerford
Upper Basildon, Beehive Inn
Wickham, Five Bells
Yattendon, Royal Oak Hotel

Buckinghamshire
Cheddington, Rosebery Arms
Fawley, Walnut Tree
Fingest, Chequers Inn
Forty Green, Royal Standard of England
Hambleden, Stag & Huntsman Inn
Hartwell, Bugle Horn
Skirmett, King's Arms
Stewkley, Swan
Stony Stratford, Cock Hotel
Westbury, Reindeer Inn
Winslow, Bell Hotel
Cambridgeshire
Elsworth, George & Dragon
Fowlmere, Chequers Inn
Grantchester, Green Man
Holywell, Ye Olde Ferry Boat Inn
Huntingdon, George
Huntingdon, Old Bridge Hotel
Keyston, Pheasant Inn
Madingley, Three Horseshoes
Molesworth, Cross Keys
Needingworth, Pike & Eel
Newton, Queen's Head

These and other pubs in the Guide which have facilities for children are denoted by the words **Family pub**.

It can only be...
Schhh...you-know-who

St Neots, Chequers Inn
St Neots, Stephenson's Rocket
Wansford, Haycock Inn
Whittlesey, Falcon Hotel
Wisbech, Rose & Crown Hotel
Cheshire
Burtonwood, Fiddle i'th Bag Inn
Congleton, Lion & Swan Hotel
Disley, Dandy Cock Inn
Goostrey, Olde Red Lion Inn
Parkgate, Ship Hotel
Weston, White Lion
Wincham, Black Greyhound Hotel
   (lunchtime)
Cleveland
Guisborough, Fox Inn
Cornwall
Boscastle, Wellington Hotel
Helston, Angel Hotel
Lanreath, Punch Bowl Inn
Manaccan, New Inn
Marhamchurch, Bullers Arms
Perranarworthal, Norway Inn
Philleigh, Roseland Inn
St Mawes, Rising Sun Inn
St Mawgan, Falcon Inn
Sennen Cove, Old Success Inn
Trebarwith, Mill House Inn
Cumbria
Askham, Queen's Head Inn
Barbon, Barbon Inn
Bassenthwaite Lake, Pheasant Inn
Boot, Woolpack Inn
Calderbridge, Stanley Arms
Cartmel Fell, Mason's Arms
Casterton, Peasant Inn
Elterwater, Britannia Inn
Faugh, String of Horses Inn
Hawkshead, Queen's Head
Levens, Hare & Hounds Inn
   (lunchtime)
Loweswater, Kirkstile Inn
Lowick, Farmers Arms (lunchtime)
Metal Bridge, Metal Bridge Inn
Sandside, Ship Inn
Talkin, Hare & Hounds Inn
Wasdale Head, Wasdale Head Inn
Winster, Brown Horse Inn

Derbyshire
Bamford, Rising Sun Hotel
Fenny Bentley, Bentley Brook Inn
Hope, Poachers Arms
Devon
Alswear, Butchers Arms
Beer, Anchor Inn
Branscombe, Masons Arms
Brendon, Stag Hunter's Inn
Christow, Artichoke Inn
Croyde, Thatched Barn Inn
Eggesford, Fox & Hounds Hotel
Georgeham, Rock Inn
Hatherleigh, George Hotel
Haytor Vale, Rock Inn
Hexworthy, Forest Inn
Lifton, Arundell Arms
Lydford, Castle Inn
Lynton, Crown Hotel
Moretonhampstead, White Hart
   Hotel

These and other pubs in the Guide which have facilities for children are denoted by the words **Family pub**.

Greater Manchester
Hawk Green, Crown (lunchtime)
Hampshire
Beauworth, Milbury's
Damerham, Compasses Inn
Ibsley, Old Beams Inn
Ovington, Bush Inn
Ringwood, Original White Hart
Rotherwick, Coach & Horses
Stockbridge, Vine Inn
Hereford & Worcester
Abberley, Bell at Pensax
Bewdley, Black Boy Hotel
Bromyard, Hop Pole Hotel
Carey, Cottage of Content
Chaddesley Corbett, Talbot Inn
Fownhope, Green Man Inn
Hereford, Cock of Tupsley
Kingsland, Angel Inn
Knightwick, Talbot Hotel
Ledbury, Ye Olde Talbot Hotel
Leominster, Royal Oak Hotel
Malvern, Foley Arms Hotel
Mamble, Sun & Slipper
Pembridge, New Inn
Ross on Wye, Rosswyn Hotel
Sellack, Loughpool Inn
Weobley, Red Lion Hotel
Woolhope, Butchers Arms
   (lunchtime)
Hertfordshire
Ashwell, Three Tuns Hotel
Chenies, Bedford Arms Thistle Hotel
Flamstead, Three Blackbirds
Great Chishill, Pheasant Inn
   (lunchtime)
Puckeridge, White Hart
Humberside
Bishop Wilton, Fleece Inn
Driffield, Bell Hotel
Howden, Bowmans Hotel
Market Weighton, Londesborough
   Arms
Pocklington, Feathers Hotel
Skidby, Half Moon Inn
Sutton upon Derwent, St Vincent
   Arms

Isle of Wight
Chale, Clarendon Hotel
Kent
Biddenden, Three Chimneys
Chilham, Woolpack
Fairbourne Heath, Pepper Box
Harriestsham, Ringlestone Inn
Hawkhurst, Royal Oak Hotel
Hawkhurst, Tudor Arms Hotel
Ickham, Duke William
Marshside, Gate Inn
Newenden, White Hart
Smarden, Bell
Tenterden, White Lion Hotel
Wingham, Red Lion Inn
Wye, Kings Head Hotel
Wye, New Flying Horse Inn
Lancashire
Forton, New Holly Hotel
Mellor, Millstone Hotel
Newton-in-Bowland, Parkers Arms
   Hotel
Slaidburn, Hark to Bounty Inn
Whitewell, Inn at Whitewell
Leicestershire
Cottesmore, Sun Inn
Empingham, White Horse
Kegworth, White House (lunchtime)
Langham, Noel Arms
Old Dalby, Crown Inn
Waltham-on-the-Wolds, Royal
   Horseshoes
Lincolnshire
Boston, New England Hotel
Grimsthorpe, Black Horse Inn
Lincoln, Wig & Mitre
Newton, Red Lion Inn
Silk Willoughby, Horseshoes
Stamford, Bull & Swan Inn
Stamford, Crown Hotel
Stamford, George of Stamford
Middlesex
Isleworth, London Apprentice
Shepperton, Anchor Hotel
Shepperton, Thames Court
Teddington, Clarence Hotel
   (lunchtime)

These and other pubs in the Guide which have facilities for children are denoted by the words **Family pub**.

It can only be...
Schhh...you-know-who

Twickenham, White Swan
Norfolk
Blickling, Buckinghamshire Arms
Briston, John H. Stracey
Great Ryburgh, Boar Inn
Hunworth, Bell Inn
Scole, Scole Inn
Stow Bardolph, Hare Arms
Winterton-on-Sea, Fisherman's
  Return
Northamptonshire
Blakesley, Bartholomew Arms
Collyweston, Cavalier
Fotheringhay, Falcon Inn
Nassington, Black Horse Inn
Weedon, Crossroads Hotel
Weldon, George Hotel
Northumberland
Cornhill-on-Tweed
  Collingwood Arms Hotel
Seahouses, Olde Ship Hotel
Wall, Hadrian Inn
Wooler, Tankerville Arms
Nottinghamshire
Bottesford, Red Lion
Newark, Robin Hood Hotel
Oxfordshire
Ashbury, Rose & Crown Hotel
Asthall, Maytime
Charlbury, Bell at Charlbury
Chipping Norton, Crown & Cushion
Clanfield, Clanfield Tavern
Cumnor, Bear & Ragged Staff
Dorchester-on-Thames, George
  Hotel
Duns Tew, White Horse Inn
Faringdon, Bell Hotel
Fifield, Merrymouth Inn
Frilford Heath, Dog House Hotel
  (lunchtime)
Fyfield, White Hart
Henley-on-Thames, Victoria
Oxford, Turf Tavern
Peppard Common, Red Lion
Pyrton, Plough Inn
Shenington, Bell

Shiplake, Baskerville Arms
South Leigh, Mason Arms
Stanton Harcourt, Harcourt Arms
Towersey, Three Horseshoes
Weston on the Green, Chequers Inn
Witney, Butchers Arms
Woodstock, Black Prince
Woodstock, Marlborough Arms
Woodstock, Punch Bowl Inn
Shropshire
Bridgnorth, Falcon Hotel
Brockton, Feathers Inn
Hopton Wafers, Crown Inn
Market Drayton, Corbet Arms Hotel
Pulverbatch, White Horse
Somerset
Brendon Hills, Ralegh's Cross Inn
Burtle, Ye Olde Burtle Inn
Croscombe, Bull Terrier
Glastonbury, George & Pilgrims
  Hotel

These and other pubs in the Guide which have facilities for children are denoted by the
words **Family pub**.

It can only be...
Schhh...you-know-who

Knapp, Rising Sun
Leigh on Mendip, Bell Inn
Long Sutton, Devonshire Arms
Montacute, Kings Arms Inn
North Petherton, Walnut Tree Inn
North Wootton, Crossways Inn
Nunney, George Inn
Stoke St Gregory, Rose & Crown
Williton, Egremont Hotel
Wincanton, Hunters' Lodge Inn
Woolverton, Red Lion

Staffordshire
Alrewas, George & Dragon
Leek, Three Horseshoes Inn
Onecote, Jervis Arms
Sandon Bank, Seven Stars Inn
Stafford, Swan Hotel
Tutbury, Ye Olde Dog & Partridge

Suffolk
Brome, Oaksmere
Bromeswell, Cherry Tree
Cavendish, George
Long Melford, Crown Inn Hotel
Mildenhall, Bell Hotel

Needham Market, Limes Hotel
Newton, Saracen's Head
Pin Mill, Butt & Oyster
Southwold, Crown Hotel
Stoke-by-Nayland, Crown
Woodbridge, Bull Hotel

Surrey
Alford Crossways, Napoleon Arms
Chiddingfold, Crown Inn
Cobham, Plough
Downside, Cricketers
Farnham, Spotted Cow
Gomshall, Black Horse Inn
Holmbury St Mary, Royal Oak
Oakwoodhill, Punchbowl Inn
Ockley, King's Arms

East Sussex
Bexhill, Wilton Court
Brightling, Fullers Arms (lunchtime)
Burwash, Bell Inn
Framfield, Barley Mow
Hartfield, Anchor
Mark Cross, Mark Cross Inn
Offham, Blacksmith's Arms

These and other pubs in the Guide which have facilities for children are denoted by the words **Family pub**.

It can only be...
Schhh...you-know-who

Schweppes family pub guide

Old Heathfield, Star Inn
Winchelsea, Winchelsea Lodge
  Motel
West Sussex
Ashington, Red Lion
Clayton, Jack & Jill Inn
Lancing, Sussex Pad
Lickfold, Lickfold Inn
Lurgashall, Noah's Ark
Midhurst, Angel Hotel
Petworth, Angel
Stopham Bridge, White Hart
Warwickshire
Coleshill, Coleshill Hotel
Dunchurch, Dun Cow Hotel
Priors Hardwick, Butchers Arms
Sambourne, Green Dragon
Shipston on Stour, White Bear
Stratford-upon-Avon, Slug & Lettuce
Wellesbourne, King's Head
Wilmcote, Swan House Hotel
West Midlands
Stourbridge, Talbot Hotel
Wiltshire
Box, Chequers
Bratton, Duke
Broad Hinton, Crown Inn
Burton, Plume of Feathers
Castle Combe, Castle Hotel
Chiseldon, Patriots Arms
Corsham, Methuen Arms Hotel
Devizes, Bear Hotel
Fonthill Bishop, Kings Arms
Ford, White Hart
Fovant, Cross Keys Inn
Holt, Old Ham Tree
Lower Woodford, Wheatsheaf
Malmesbury, Suffolk Arms
Mere, Old Ship Hotel
Pewsham, Lysley Arms
Ramsbury, Bell at Ramsbury
Salisbury, Haunch of Venison
Salisbury, High Post Hotel
Semley, Benett Arms
North Yorkshire
Appletreewick, Craven Arms
Arkengarthdale, C. B. Hotel

Askrigg, Kings Arms Hotel
Bainbridge, Rose & Crown Hotel
  (lunchtime)
Constable Burton, Wyvill Arms
Coxwold, Fauconberg Arms
East Layton, Fox Hall Inn
Elslack, Tempest Arms
Gargrave, Anchor Inn
Great Ayton, Royal Oak Hotel
Harome, Star Inn
Horton in Ribblesdale, Crown Hotel
Hovingham, Worsley Arms Hotel
Hubberholme, George Inn
Kettlewell, Bluebell Hotel
Kettlewell, Racehorses Hotel
Malham, Buck Inn
Malton, Green Man Hotel
Middleham, Black Swan Hotel
Osgodby, Barn (summer)
Oswaldkirk, Malt Shovel Inn
Pickhill, Nags Head
Richmond, Castle Tavern
Rosedale Abbey, Blacksmith's Arms
Rosedale Abbey, White Horse Farm
  Hotel
Sleights, Salmon Leap
Snainton, Coachman Inn
Staddle Bridge, McCoy's at the
  Tontine
Starbotton, Fox & Hounds
Staveley, Royal Oak
Terrington, Bay Horse Inn
Wath in Nidderdale, Sportsman's
  Arms Hotel
West Witton, Wensleydale Heifer
South Yorkshire
Sutton, Anne Arms
West Yorkshire
Darrington, Darrington Hotel
Holywell Green, Rock Hotel
Linton, Windmill Inn
Shelley, Three Acres Inn
SCOTLAND
Borders
Eddleston, Horse Shoe Inn
Melrose, Burts Hotel
Melrose, George & Abbotsford

These and other pubs in the Guide which have facilities for children are denoted by the
words **Family pub.**

It can only be...
Schhh...you-know-who

Central
Killin, Clachaig Hotel
Killin, Queen's Court Hotel (till 9pm)
Kippen, Cross Keys
Strathblane, Kirkhouse Inn
Dumfries & Galloway
Castle Douglas, King's Arms Hotel
Moffat, Balmoral Hotel
New Abbey, Criffel Inn
Fife
Anstruther, Craw's Nest Hotel
Grampian
Elrick, Broadstraik Inn (till 7.30pm)
Fochabers, Gordon Arms Hotel
   (lunchtime)
Highland
Dulnain Bridge, Muckrach Lodge
   Hotel
Glenfinnan, Stage House Inn
Invergarry, Inn on the Garry
Invermoriston, Glenmoriston Arms
Lewiston, Lewiston Arms Hotel
Lybster, Bayview Hotel
Muir of Ord, Ord Arms Hotel
Onich, Onich Hotel
Portree, Rosedale Hotel (lunchtime)
Spean Bridge, Letterfinlay Lodge
   Hotel
Spinningdale, Old Mill Inn
Uig, Ferry Inn
Ullapool, Argyll Hotel
Lothian
Balerno, Marchbank Hotel
Edinburgh, Rutland Hotel
Linlithgow, Champany Inn
Wester Howgate, Old Howgate Inn
Strathclyde
Airdrie, Staging Post
Busby, Busby Hotel
Loch Eck, Coylet Inn
Tarbert, West Loch Hotel
Tayvallich, New Tayvallich Hotel
Tayside
Killiecrankie, Killiecrankie Hotel
WALES
Clwyd
Bodfari, Dinorben Arms Inn

Holywell, Stamford Gate Hotel
Llanarmon DC, West Arms Hotel
Mold, Arches Inn
Dyfed
Cardigan, Black Lion Hotel
Cenarth, White Hart
Henllan, Henllan Falls Inn
Llanarthney, Golden Grove Arms
Llandovery, King's Head Inn
Wolf's Castle, Wolfe Inn
Gwent
Llanfihangel Crucorney, Skirrid Inn
Monmouth, Queens Head Hotel
Raglan, Beaufort Arms Hotel
Whitebrook, Crown at Whitebrook
Gwynedd
Beaumaris, Ye Olde Bull's Head
Penmaenpool, George III Hotel
Mid Glamorgan
Nottage, Rose & Crown
Powys
Crickhowell, Nantyffin Cider Mill Inn
Hay-on-Wye, Old Black Lion
Llanfrynach, White Swan
Penybont, Severn Arms (lunchtime)

CHANNEL ISLANDS
Pleinmont, Guernsey, Imperial Hotel
St Aubin's Harbour, Jersey, Old Court
   House Inn

ISLE OF MAN
Peel, Creek Inn

These and other pubs in the Guide which have facilities for children are denoted by the words **Family pub**.

Schweppes®
The First Name in Fruit Juice

RESTAURANTS

RECOMMENDED IN OUR HOTEL & RESTAURANT GUIDE

AT PUBS

ENGLAND
Chenies, Herts: Bedford Arms Thistle Hotel
Chipping Campden, Glos: Kings Arms Hotel
Coggeshall, Essex: White Hart Hotel
Corton, Wilts: Dove
Cumnor, Oxon: Bear & Ragged Staff
Grimsthorpe, Lincs: White Hart
Harome, N Yorks: Star Inn
Hildenborough, Kent: Gate Inn
Hungerford, Berks: Bear at Hungerford
Huntingdon, Cambs: Old Bridge Hotel
Kintbury, Berks: Dundas Arms
Lifton, Devon: Arundell Arms
Llanfair Waterdine, Shrops: Red Lion Inn
Moulton, N Yorks: Black Bull Inn
Ockley, Surrey: King's Arms
Orford, Suffolk: King's Head Inn
Pett Bottom, Kent: Duck Inn
Ramsbury, Wilts: Bell at Ramsbury
Ripponden, W Yorks: Old Bridge Inn
Saffron Walden, Essex: Saffron Hotel
St Mawes, Corn: Rising Sun Hotel
Scole, Norfolk: Scole Inn
Shipton-under-Wychwood, Oxon: Lamb Inn
Staddle Bridge, N Yorks: McCoy's at the Tontine
Stamford, Lincs: George of Stamford
Stanton Harcourt, Oxon: Harcourt Arms
Stapleton, Co. Durham: Bridge Inn
Tarrant Monkton, Dorset: Langton Arms
Tetbury, Glos: Gentle Gardener Restaurant
Timperley, Gtr Manch: Le Bon Viveur
Troutbeck, Cumb: Mortal Man Hotel

continued

Tunbridge Wells, Kent: Royal Wells Inn
Winkleigh, Devon: King's Arms
Yattendon, Berks: Royal Oak Hotel

SCOTLAND
Canonbie, D & G: River Inn
Dulnain Bridge, H'land: Muckrach Lodge Hotel
Dysart, Fife: Old Rectory Inn
Linlithgow, Lothian: Champany Inn
Tayvallich, Strathclyde: New Tayvallich Inn
Wester Howgate, Lothian: Old Howgate Inn

WALES
Crickhowell, Powys: Nantyffin Cider Mill Inn
Three Cocks, Powys: Three Cocks Hotel

CHANNEL ISLANDS
St Aubin's Harbour, Jersey: Old Court House Inn

WATERSIDE PUBS

LONDON
Anchor, SE1
Angel, SE16
Bull's Head, W4
City Barge, W4
Dickens Inn, E1
Dove, W6
Grapes, E14
King's Head & Eight Bells, SW3
Mayflower, SE16
Prospect of Whitby, E1
Samuel Pepys, EC4
Ship, SW14
Trafalgar Tavern, SE10
Yacht, SE10

ENGLAND
Armathwaite, Cumb: Duke's Head
  Hotel
Beaulieu, Hants: Montagu Arms
  Hotel, Spats Bar
Bedford, Beds: Embankment Hotel
Beer, Devon: Anchor Inn
Bewdley, H & W: Black Boy Hotel
Bexhill, E Sussex: Wilton Court
Bidford-on-Avon, Warwicks: White
  Lion Hotel
Bledington, Glos: King's Head
Brendon, Devon: Stag Hunter's Inn
Buckler's Hard, Hants: Master
  Builders House Hotel
Burnham-on-Crouch, Essex: Ye Olde
  White Harte
Calderbridge, Cumb: Stanley Arms
Chappel, Essex: Swan Inn
Eskdale, Cumb: Bower House Inn
Felixstowe, Suffolk: Fludyer Arms
  Hotel
Fiskerton, Notts: Bromley Arms
Ford, Wilts: White Hart
Fossebridge, Glos: Fossebridge Inn
Gargrave, N Yorks: Anchor Inn

Great Shefford, Berks: Swan
Helford, Corn: Shipwright's Arms
Holywell, Cambs: Ye Olde Ferry Boat
  Inn
Horley, Surrey: Ye Olde Six Bells
Hubberholme, N Yorks: George Inn
Hungerford, Berks: Bear at
  Hungerford
Huntingdon, Cambs: Old Bridge
  Hotel
Ightham, Kent: George & Dragon
Isleworth, Middx: London Apprentice
Kegworth, Leics: White House
Kettlewell, N Yorks: Bluebell Hotel
Kettlewell, N Yorks: Racehorses
  Hotel
Kintbury, Berks: Dundas Arms
Knightwick, H & W: Talbot Hotel
Lamberhurst, Kent: Chequers Inn
Lamberhurst, Kent: George &
  Dragon
Langdale, Cumb: Pillar Hotel,
  Hobson's Pub
Llanfair Waterdine, Shrops: Red Lion
Loweswater, Cumb: Kirkstile Inn
Marshside, Kent: Gate Inn
Metal Bridge, Cumb: Metal Bridge
  Inn
Needingworth, Cambs: Pike & Eel Inn
Newbridge, Oxon: Maybush
Newenden, Kent: White Hart
North Cerney, Glos: Bathurst Arms
Onecote, Staffs: Jervis Arms
Ovington, Hants: Bush Inn
Parkgate, Ches: Ship Hotel
Piercebridge, Co. Durham: George
Pin Mill, Suffolk: Butt & Oyster
Pooley Bridge, Cumb: Crown Hotel
Porlock Weir, Som: Anchor Hotel &
  Ship Inn
Port Gaverne, Corn: Port Gaverne
  Hotel

continued

Waterside pubs

Pulborough, W Sussex: Waters Edge
Ripponden, W Yorks: Old Bridge Inn
St Mawes, Corn: Rising Sun Inn
Sandside, Cumb: Ship Inn
Sennen Cove, Corn: Old Success Inn
Shepperton, Middx: Thames Court
Sleights, N Yorks: Salmon Leap
Smarden, Kent: Chequers Inn
Stockbridge, Hants: Vine Inn
Stopham Bridge, W Sussex: White
  Hart
Testcombe, Hants: Mayfly
Trebarwith, Corn: Mill House Inn
Twickenham, Middx: White Swan
Umberleigh, Devon: Rising Sun Inn
Wansford, Cambs: Haycock Inn
Wasdale Head, Cumb: Wasdale Head
  Inn
Whitewell, Lancs: Inn at Whitewell
Whitney-on-Wye, H & W:
  Rhydspence Inn
Winkton, Dorset: Fisherman's Haunt
Withington, Glos: Mill Inn
Woodstock, Oxon: Black Prince

SCOTLAND

Canonbie, D & G: Riverside Inn
Catterline, Grampian: Creel Inn
Edinburgh, Lothian: Cramond Inn
Inverbeg, S'clyde: Inverbeg Inn
Killin, Central: Clachaig Hotel
Killin, Central: Queen's Court Hotel

Loch Eck, S'clyde: Coylet Inn
Onich, H'land: Onich Hotel
Portree, H'land: Rosedale Hotel
Spean Bridge, H'land: Letterfinlay
  Lodge Hotel
Tarbert, S'clyde: West Loch Hotel
Tayvallich, S'clyde: New Tayvallich
  Inn

WALES

Aberaeron, Dyfed: Harbourmaster
  Hotel
Brockweir, Gwent: Brockweir Inn
Dolgellau, Gwynedd: Gwernan Lake
  Hotel
Felindre Farchog, Dyfed: Old
  Salutation Inn
Llanarmon Dyffryn Ceiriog, Clwyd:
  West Arms Hotel
Llangorse, Powys: Red Lion
Menai Bridge, Gwynedd: Gazelle
  Hotel
Penmaenpool, Gwynedd: George III
  Hotel

CHANNEL ISLANDS

Pleinmont, Guernsey: Imperial Hotel
St Aubin's Harbour, Jersey: Old
  Court House Inn

ISLE OF MAN

Peel: Creek Inn

LONDON

LONDON
PUBS BY AREAS

BAYSWATER & NOTTING HILL
Victoria, 10a Strathearn Place, W2
Windsor Castle, 114 Campden Hill Road, W8

BLOOMSBURY & HOLBORN
Lamb, 94 Lamb's Conduit Street, WC1
Museum Tavern, 49 Great Russell Street, WC1
Ye Olde Mitre Tavern, Ely Court, Ely Place, EC1

CHELSEA
Admiral Codrington, 17 Mossop Street, SW3
King's Head & Eight Bells, 50 Cheyne Walk, SW3

CITY
Black Friar, 174 Queen Victoria Street, EC4
Cock Tavern, Poultry Market, Central Markets, EC1
Crowders Well, Fore Street, EC2
Dirty Dick's, 202 Bishopsgate, EC2
Fox & Anchor, 115 Charterhouse Street, EC1
Hand & Shears, 1 Middle Street, EC1
Railway Tavern, 15 Liverpool Street, EC2
Samuel Pepys, Brooks Wharf, Upper Thames Street, EC4
Three Compasses, 66 Cowcross Street, EC1
Ye Olde Dr Butler's Head, Masons Avenue, Coleman Street, WC2
Ye Olde Watling, 29 Watling Street, EC4

COVENT GARDEN
Lamb & Flag, 33 Rose Street, off Garrick Street, WC2
Maple Leaf, 41 Maiden Lane, WC2
Nag's Head, 10 James Street, WC2
Nell of Old Drury, 29 Catherine Street, WC2
Salisbury, St Martin's Lane, WC2

EAST LONDON
Black Lion, 59 High Street, Plaistow, E13
Dickens Inn, St Katharine's Way, E1
Grapes, 76 Narrow Street, E14
Prospect of Whitby, 57 Wapping Wall, E1

FLEET STREET
Old Bell Tavern, 95 Fleet Street, EC4
Printer's Devil, 98 Fetter Lane, EC4
Seven Stars, 53 Carey Street, WC2
Ye Olde Cheshire Cheese, 145 Fleet Street, EC4
Ye Olde Cock Tavern, 22 Fleet Street, EC4

KNIGHTSBRIDGE
Grenadier, 18 Wilton Row, SW1
Paxton's Head, 153 Knightsbridge, SW1

MAYFAIR & MARYLEBONE
Prince Regent, 71 Marylebone High Street, W1
Red Lion, 1 Waverton Street, W1
Shepherd's Tavern, 50 Hertford Street, W1
Thistle, 11 Vigo Street, W1
Ye Grapes, 16 Shepherd Market, W1

NORTH & NORTH-WEST LONDON
Albion, 10 Thornhill Road, N1
Bull & Bush, North End Way, NW3
Eagle, 2 Shepherdess Walk, N1
Flask, 77 Highgate West Hill, Highgate, N6
Jack Straw's Castle, North End Way, NW3
Spaniards Inn, Spaniards Road, NW3

ST JAMES'S
Red Lion, 23 Crown Passage, Pall Mall, SW1
Two Chairmen, Warwick House Street, off Cockspur Street, SW1

SOHO & TRAFALGAR SQUARE
Sherlock Holmes, 10 Northumberland Street, WC2
Tom Cribb, Panton Street, SW1

continued

SOUTH-EAST LONDON
Anchor, 1 Bankside, Southwark, SE1
Angel, 101 Bermondsey Wall East, SE16
Fox & Firkin, 316 Lewisham High Street, SE13
George, 77 Borough High Street, Southwark, SE1
Mayflower, 117 Rotherhithe Street, SE16
Trafalgar Tavern, Park Row, SE10
Yacht, Crane Street, SE10

SOUTH-WEST LONDON
Hand in Hand, Crooked Billet, Wimbledon Common, SW19
Ship, 10 Thames Bank, Riverside, SW14
Sun Inn, 7 Church Road, Barnes, SW13
White Horse on Parsons Green, 1 Parsons Green, SW6
Ye Olde Windmill Inn, Clapham Common Southside, SW4

VICTORIA & WESTMINSTER
Albert, 52 Victoria Street, SW1
Orange Brewery, 37 Pimlico Road, SW1
St Stephen's Tavern, 10 Bridge Street, SW1
Two Chairmen, 39 Dartmouth Street, SW1

WEST LONDON
Bull's Head, Strand-on-the-Green, W4
City Barge, Strand-on-the-Green, W4
Dove, 19 Upper Mall, W6

Admiral Codrington *(Food)*

17 Mossop Street, SW3 · Map 12 B1
01-589 4603

Brewery Bass
Landlords Melvyn & Sue Barnett
T-bone steak £5.25 Steak & mushroom pie & vegetables £2.75 (Last order 10.45pm. No bar food Sun)
🍺 Bass; Charrington's IPA; Stones Bitter; Guinness; Carling Black Label; Tennent's Extra; Taunton cider. *Real ale*

The gas-lit bar and flower-filled covered patio are equally delightful settings for enjoying the excellent food served at this sociable Victorian-style pub. Steaks are always very popular, grilled to a T over charcoal, and other hot dishes might include curries, pies and lemon sole. Cold cuts and well-kept cheeses widen the choice further, and to round things off there's a refreshing fruit salad.

Albert

A handsome and much photographed Victorian survival in a street largely taken over by modern office blocks. The Albert opened as a pub in 1867, having been bought five years earlier from the Dean and Chapter of Westminster, and there are many period features to admire, including carved woodwork and fine engraved glass windows.
52 Victoria Street, SW1 · Map 12 C1
01-222 5577
Owner London Host   *Landlords* Mr & Mrs E. Jones
🍺 Watney's Stag Bitter, Special; Combe's Bitter; Websters Yorkshire Bitter; Ben Truman; Guinness; Holsten; Foster's. *Real ale*

Albion *(Food)*

10 Thornhill Road, N1 · Map 10 C1
01-607 7450

Owners London Hosts
Landlords Michael & Shirley Parish

Steak & kidney pudding £2.85 Steamed syrup pudding 80p (Last order 10.30pm)
🍺 Ruddle's County; Webster's Yorkshire Bitter; Watney's Special; Ben Truman; Guinness; Holsten; cider. *Real ale*

Lunchtime crowds flock to this charming Victorian pub to enjoy some splendid traditional home cooking. Hot salt beef is the treat on Monday and Friday, steak and kidney pudding on Thursday; other delights include hearty soups, bangers and mash, succulent roast lamb and fried fish, with sandwiches and ploughman's for lighter snacks and always a good old-fashioned English pud. Less evening choice. Garden.   **Family pub**

Anchor

Customers watched the Great Fire of London from the original Anchor, which was later replaced by a Georgian building. The famous Clink Prison and Globe Theatre stood nearby, and Russian Imperial Stout, Dr Johnson's favourite drink, originated at the neighbouring brewery. Superb river views from the terrace.   **Family pub**

1 Bankside, Southwark, SE1 · Map 11 C2
01-407 1577
Brewery Courage   *Landlord* Gary Lloyd
🍺 Courage Director's Bitter, Best Bitter; John Smith's Bitter; Guinness; Kronenbourg; Hofmeister; Taunton cider. *Real ale*

Angel

Views of the Thames come no better than those enjoyed by this popular pub, whose prominent patrons down the years have included Samuel Pepys and Captain Cook, Judge Jeffreys and Laurel and Hardy. There was a tavern here in the 15th century, and the Angel of today is a brick-built pub with an open-plan interior.

101 Bermondsey Wall East, Rotherhithe, SE16 · Map 10 D2
01-237 3608
Owner Imperial Inns & Taverns   *Landlord* Mr Derek Davies
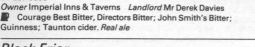 Courage Best Bitter, Directors Bitter; John Smith's Bitter; Guinness; Taunton cider. *Real ale*

Black Friar

A 13th-century Dominican priory formerly occupied the site of this 300-year old pub, re-decorated at the turn of the century. Five types of Italian marble, mosaics, and bas reliefs of jolly friars are an antiquarian's delight. Closed Sat lunch (in winter), Sat eve, all Sun & Bank Holidays.

174 Queen Victoria Street, EC4 · Map 11 C1
01-236 5650
Free House   *Landlord* Mr Doug Walls
Tetley's Bitter; Morrell's Bitter; Guinness; Oranjeboom; Holsten; cider. *Real ale*

Black Lion   (Food)

59 High Street, Plaistow, E13. Map 10 D1
01-472 2351

Brewery Courage
Landlord Mr R. Hales
Prawn omelette & chips £1.50 Steak & kidney pie or pudding £1.50 (Last order 7.30pm. No bar food Sat eve & all Sun)
Courage Directors Bitter, Best Bitter; Guinness; Kronenbourg; Hofmeister; Taunton cider. *Real ale*

The steak and kidney pudding is a must at this friendly, down-to-earth pub. Light, well-cooked suet crust, plenty of tender meat and lovely rich gravy make a dish to remember. Other super snacks include home-made bubble and squeak, hearty chicken and vegetable soup, freshly cut sandwiches and fluffy omelettes served with lovely chips. Blackberry and apple pie for a splendid finish. Less evening choice. Beer garden.

Bull & Bush

Immortalised in the old music hall song 'Down at the Old Bull & Bush', this plush pub lined with prints and photographs of show-biz personalities attracts lively crowds in the evening. Set on the edge of Hampstead Heath, the former 17th-century farmhouse was once the home of painter William Hogarth. Beer garden.

North End Way, NW3 · Map 9 B1
01-455 3685
Brewery Taylor Walker   *Landlord* Graham Dove
Taylor Walker Bitter; Burton's Bitter; Guinness; Löwenbräu; Oranjeboom; Skol; cider. *Real ale*

Bull's Head

Right on the towpath on a delightful stretch of the Thames at Chiswick, this 350-year-old pub gained fame as the headquarters of Oliver Cromwell during the Civil War. The comfortable panelled bar affords pleasant views of the river.

Strand-on-the-Green, W4 · Map 9 A3
01-994 1204
Owner London Host *Landlords* Mr & Mrs Ward
🍺 Watney's Stag, Combes Bitter; Webster's Yorkshire Bitter; Guinness; Carlsberg; Foster's; Holsten. *Real ale*

We have raised our standards considerably since last year. The omission of some houses that appeared in last year's Guide is no reflection on their standing.

City Barge

This popular tavern on the Thames towpath was named after the Lord Mayor's official barge which used to be moored nearby. Largely rebuilt after World War II, the pub still features some fine antiques, beams and brassware. There are two comfortable bars, one in period style and the other smartly up to date.   **Family pub**

Strand-on-the-Green, W4 · Map 9 A3
01-994 2148
Brewery Courage *Landlord* Mr J. MacDonald
🍺 Courage Directors Bitter, Best Bitter, JC; Guinness; Kronenbourg; cider. *Real ale*

Cock Tavern *(Food)*

The Poultry Market, Central Markets, EC1
Map 11 C1
01-248 2918
Free House
Landlord Mr A. Burrows
Salt beef, pease pudding & potatoes £4.50
Sirloin steak & vegetables £6.50 (No bar food eves)
🍺 Courage Best Bitter; Young's Special; John Bull Bitter; John Smith's Bitter; Guinness; Hofmeister. *Real ale*

Succulent salt beef brisket is the speciality at this cheerful pub under Smithfield poultry market: served generously with potatoes, carrots and pease pudding, it's an outstanding pub dish. Steaks, game and roast turkey provide further lunchtime choice, and soup, sandwiches and salads are available for lighter snacks till 3pm. From 6am there's a good breakfast selection. Closed Saturday, Sunday & Bank Holidays.
          Family pub

Crowders Well *(Food)*

Fore Street, EC2 · Map 11 C1
01-628 8574

Brewery Vintage Inns
Landlord Mr A. D. Cregg

Lasagne £2.20 Chilli con carne £2.20 (No bar food eves)
🍺 Bass; Charrington IPA; Worthington 'E'; Guinness; Carling Black Label; Tennent's Extra; Taunton cider. *Real ale*

Lunchtime in the comfortable pantry bar of this popular city pub sees a good choice of tasty, well-prepared snacks. Lasagne and calf's liver veneziana are two of the Italian chef's homeland specialities, and there are also salads and sandwiches, smooth pâté, quiches and chilli. The bar opens on to a terrace and the Barbican's lake complex. Closed Saturday and Sunday.

Dickens Inn *(Food)*

St Katharine's Way, E1 · Map 10 C2
01-488 9936

Free House
Landlord Michael Harwood
Ploughman's lunch £1.45 Steak & kidney pie with vegetables £2.95 (Last order 10pm)
🍺 Dickens Own, Special; Ruddle's County, Ordinary; Fuller's London Pride; Sam Smith's Old Brewery Bitter; Guinness; Tennent's Extra; Carling Black Label; cider. *Real ale*

Tiered wooden balconies create a distinctive frontage at this modern conversion of a dockland warehouse, and a terrace overlooking the river makes it very popular with tourists. The busy bars offer a wide variety of simple, tasty pub food, from pâté and quiche to steak and kidney pie, casseroles and meatballs.

Dirty Dick's

Nathaniel Bentley, who became landlord in 1761, earned the nickname Dirty Dick when he renounced cleanliness – both personal and territorial – after the death of his prospective bride. Genuine period atmosphere remains in the stone-floored cellar, while the main bar is in Victorian style. Closed Sat and Sun eves.

202 Bishopsgate, EC2 · Map 10 C2
01-283 5888
Free House *Landlord* Mr J. Clapham
🍺 Charrington's IPA; Greene King IPA; Courage Director's, Best Bitter; Guinness; Skol, Tennent's; Taunton cider. *Real ale*

Dove

Turner is said to have painted the Thames from here and James Thomson, who wrote the words of 'Rule Britannia', occupied a room at the inn in 1725. The pub stands in a group of fine Georgian houses beside the river, with a vine-clad terrace from which to admire the view.

19 Upper Mall, W6 · Map 9 A2
01-748 5405
Brewery Fuller, Smith & Turner *Landlord* Mr Lovrey
🍺 Fuller's ESB, London Pride. *Real ale*

Eagle

The comedienne Marie Lloyd made her debut at the Eagle in the days when it was one of London's best-known variety theatres. Perhaps an even greater claim to fame of this popular pub off the City Road is its mention in the lyrics of 'Pop Goes the Weasel'.

2 Shepherdess Walk, N1 · Map 10 C1
01-253 4715
Brewery Charrington   *Landlord* Mr Lajune
🍺 Charrington's IPA, Bass, Toby Bitter; Guinness; Carling Black Label; Tennent's Extra; Taunton cider. *Real ale*

Flask

Named after the flasks of spa water which could be bought here or at the nearby spring, this 18th-century Highgate pub is especially popular in summer for its hedge-rimmed forecourt. The interior is beamed and cosy. Among famous former patrons was the painter William Hogarth.

77 Highgate West Hill, N6 · Map 9 B1
01-340 3969
Brewery Taylor Walker   *Landlord* Mrs G. Light
🍺 Taylor Walker Bitter; John Bull's Bitter; Ind Coope Burton Ale; Guinness; Löwenbräu; Oranjeboom; Skol; cider. *Real ale*

Fox & Anchor   *(Food)*

115 Charterhouse Street, EC1 · Map 11 C1
01-253 4838

Brewery Taylor Walker
Landlord Mr P. Zeid

Lamb chump chop £4.25 Mixed grill £5.50
(No bar food eves)
🍺 Taylor Walker Bitter; Ind Coope; Burton Ale; Friary Meux; Guinness; Löwenbräu; Skol; cider. *Real ale*

Grills feature strongly on the menu at this friendly, well-run pub that's open from 6am for huge breakfasts. Lamb chump chop – charcoal-crisp outside, pink and tender within – is typical of the high-quality fare available till 2.30pm, and lighter snacks include sandwiches and salads. Apple pie or good Stilton to finish. Closed evenings, weekends, 1st 2 weeks August & 1 week Christmas.

Fox & Firkin   *(Food)*

316 Lewisham High Street, SE13 · Map 10 D3
01-690 8925

Free House
Landlord Mr John Barlow

Roast beef & vegetables £3 Home-made quiche & salad £1.25 (Last order 10.30pm)
🍺 Fox Best Bitter; Dogbolter; Vixen; Murphy's Stout; Kronenbourg; Hofmeister; John Young's Lager; Taunton cider. *Real ale*

They brew their own beer at this large, sociable pub furnished with old church pews and a pulpit. The real ale's not the only attraction, though, because the food is tasty, nourishing and largely home-prepared: filled baps, well-baked quiches, good fresh salads, crusty pies and a lunchtime hot special like pork chop, curry or roast beef. Live music at night. Patio.

George Inn

The only surviving galleried inn in London, the George is built round a courtyard where Shakespeare's plays were once performed. It was probably known to the Bard, being no more than 500 yards from the site of the Globe Theatre. It's certainly one of the capital's most interesting pubs, manifesting a sense of history throughout.

Family pub

77 Borough High Street, Southwark, SE1 · Map 11 C2
01-407 2056
Brewery Whitbread   *Landlord* Mr & Mrs Davis
Flower's Original; Wethered's Bitter; Fremlins Tusker; Guinness; Stella Artois; Heineken; cider. *Real ale*

Grapes

There's plenty of character in this peaceful little 16th-century pub tucked away by the river in the heart of dockland. Once a popular literary haunt, it is said to have been the model for the 'Six Jolly Fellowship Porters' in Charles Dickens' *Our Mutual Friend.*

76 Narrow Street, E14 · Map 10 D2
01-987 4396
Brewery Taylor Walker   *Landlord* Mr Frank Johnson
Taylor Walker Bitter; Ind Coope Burton Ale; Friary Meux Bitter; Guinness; Löwenbräu. *Real ale*

Grenadier   *(Food)*

18 Wilton Row, SW1 · Map 12 C1
01-235 3074

Owners London Hosts
Landlord Mr Ken Woodhams

Steak & kidney pie £1 Cauliflower cheese 95p
(Last order 10pm)
Ruddle's County; Watney's Special, Stag; Combes Bitter; Webster Yorkshire Bitter; Guinness; Carlsberg; Holsten; cider. *Real ale*

A military theme runs through the bars of this famous pub that was once the mess for the Duke of Wellington's officers. Regulars troop in nowadays to enjoy the convivial company, the good beer and the simple, sustaining bar fare. Sandwiches are freshly cut to order, there's quiche with a salad garnish, and hot dishes include tasty cauliflower cheese and home-made steak and kidney pie. Patio.

Hand & Shears

Dating back to Tudor times, this pub just off Cloth Fair gets its name from the emblem of the Guild of Merchant Tailors. A less happy association is that in the 19th-century, condemned prisoners from the notorious Newgate prison nearby were allowed to take their last drink here. Closed Sat & Sun.

1 Middle Street, EC1 · Map 11 C1
01-600 0257
Owner Imperial Inns   *Landlord* Mr Latimer
Courage Directors Bitter, Best Bitter; Guinness; Hofmeister; Kronenbourg; Taunton cider. *Real ale*

Hand in Hand *(Food)*

7 Crooked Billet, Wimbledon, SW19 · Map 9 A3
01-946 5720

Brewery Young's
Landlords Mr & Mrs D. A. Miles

Chilli con carne £1.50 Pizza £1.95 (Last
order 8.30pm)
🍺 Young's Bitter, Special, Winter Warmer;
Ruddle's Rutland Bitter; Guinness; Young's
Lager; Taunton cider. *Real ale*

Standing in a row of little houses on the
southern edge of Wimbledon Common,
this sociable pub is a very popular place for
lunchtime snacks. Ploughman's platters
come in four varieties, and other favourites
include shepherd's pie, salads, pizzas and
various things with chips. The last two are
the only items available in the evening.
There's a cosy panelled bar, as well as a
patio for pleasant weather.   **Family pub**

Jack Straw's Castle

Perched on the heights of Hampstead Heath, this weatherboarded
pub is a famous tourist attraction. Said to be named after Wat Tyler's
second-in-command during the Peasants' Revolt of 1381, it later
succoured highwaymen and was also the haunt of Dickens and
Thackeray. Rebuilt in 1964, the pub retains many original fittings.

North End Way, NW3 · Map 9 B1
01-435 8374
Brewery Charrington   *Landlord* Brian Hillyard
🍺 Charrington's IPA, Bass; Stones Bitter; Guinness; Carling Black
Label; Tennent's Extra; Taunton cider. *Real ale*

King's Head & Eight Bells *(Food)*

50 Cheyne Walk, SW3 · Map 12 B2
01-352 1820

Brewery Whitbread
Landlord Mary Timmons

Turkey, ham & cranberry pie £1.85 Fridge
cake 85p (Last order 9.30pm)
🍺 Flower's Original; Whitbread Bitter;
Wethered's Bitter; Fremlins Tusker; Guinness;
Stella Artois; Heineken; cider. *Real ale*

Savoury pies take top billing at this delightful Victorian pub by the Thames. Ham,
turkey and cranberry, Huntingdon fidget,
all-vegetable harvest – these and others are
appetisingly displayed at one end of the
comfortable bar, together with cold cuts,
pâtés and big bowls of good fresh salads.
There are simple hot snacks, too, such as
baked potatoes and beef roll, plus cheese
and usually a pudding or two.   **Family pub**

Lamb

Charles Dickens lived just around the corner from this inviting little
pub. Victorian cut-glass snob screens are a noteworthy feature and
hundreds of sepia photographs of stage and music hall personalities
gaze down upon the busy throng at the bar.

94 Lamb's Conduit Street, WC1 · Map 11 B1
01-405 0713
Brewery Young   *Landlord* John Jeffery
🍺 Young's Bitter, Special Bitter, Winter Warmer (winter only);
Guinness; John Young's London Lager; Taunton cider. *Real ale*

47

Welcome to the Guinness section of this Guide. The following ten pages are intended to tell you a little about our famous dark brew and suggest, through recipes, drinks ideas and some travel tales how you can enjoy some of the good things in life with Guinness. Cheers!

GUINNESS WITH FOOD

Cooking with Guinness

"The flavour and body of Guinness make it an excellent ingredient in a wide variety of dishes" says cookery expert, Sonia Allison *(right).*

True aficionados of the dark brew already know that the addition of Guinness to a hearty stew does wonders for the end result.

But there are scores of other dishes, both savoury and sweet, which can be enhanced by the subtle use of Guinness.

Here are some hints to guide you along the way to better cooking with Guinness. Try them and surprise your palate!

All the better with Guinness

To bind a better *Pastry,* especially shortcrust or wholemeal, Guinness is great – for both savoury and sweet dishes. *Casseroles of Meat or Poultry* – one part Guinness to three parts stock really enhances the flavour.

Rich Soups such as oxtail, mixed vegetable or fish really deserve their Guinness. They're never quite the same without it. And if you take your game seriously, Guinness as a base ingredient makes superb gravy too. Tastier *Pasta?* Try a tablespoon of Guinness in the cooking water.

What else? *Marinades* for meat and poultry and *Desserts* such as Coffee Cheesecake – versatile Guinness adds flavour and all-round improvement to both with equal aplomb. *Batters* made with Guinness turn out beautifully crisp and tasty.

How to avoid wasting Guinness

Never put Guinness into casseroles destined for the freezer – add it when you reheat for serving. That way you get the full benefit. *Neat* Guinness on its own is not recommended as stock for casseroles or sauces. Even the best ideas can be carried too far. Full-strength Guinness is best served separately – in a glass.

GUINNESS
COUNTRY
QUICHE

Wheatmeal Pastry
6oz wholemeal flour
6oz self raising flour
3oz margarine
3oz lard
10 tblsp GUINNESS
pinch of salt

Filling
8oz cheddar cheese (grated)
8oz streaky bacon (diced)
4 spring onions (diced)
6 eggs
¾pt milk or cream
salt & pepper
4oz cheddar cheese (grated)

Make the pastry by rubbing the fats into the flours.
Bind to a pliable dough with the GUINNESS.
Knead lightly – roll out on a floured board and use
to line a 12″ flan ring or dish. Prick the base lightly.
Place the 8oz of cheddar cheese over the base of
the pastry. Fry the bacon with the onions for 3
minutes and place on top of the cheese. Beat the
eggs and add the milk or cream – season – pour
over the flan. Top with the remaining cheese and
bake 400°F, 200°C, gas mark 6 for 35/40 minutes.

Serve either hot or cold.

Serves 10

GUINNESS
CARBONADE
FLAMANDE

6 large onions (finely sliced)
2 cloves garlic crushed – optional
4 tblsp beef dripping or vegetable oil
3lb stewing beef (cut into 1″ wide strips)
4 tblsp flour
1pt GUINNESS
3 tsp vinegar
salt & pepper
2 tblsp brown sugar
bouquet garni

Serves 10

Cook the onions with the garlic and half the sugar in the
dripping or oil until soft. Dust the beef with the seasoned flour
and brown with the onions. Blend in the remaining flour, add the
GUINNESS and vinegar. (If meat is not covered add extra beef
stock). Season, add the bouquet garni. Cover closely and cook
gently for 1½ hours. For extra flavour toast slices of french
bread spread with french mustard on top of the casserole.

BARBECUE MARINADE

½ pt GUINNESS
4 tblsp oil
2 tblsp honey
2 tblsp tomato purée
juice and rind of 2 large oranges

Blend all the ingredients together and marinate 2lb of cubed meat or 10 steaks in this for a minimum of 2 hours, but preferably overnight. Drain from the marinade. Thread the cubes on kebab skewers with a selection of vegetables or fruit before cooking on the grill.

Sufficient for 10 kebabs or 10 steaks

GUINNESS
STEAK & KIDNEY PIE

2lb stewing steak
(cut into ½" cubes)
10 lamb's kidneys
(skinned, cored and diced)
3 medium size onions
(finely chopped)
1pt beef stock
2 tsp Worcestershire Sauce
¼pt GUINNESS
8oz mushrooms (finely sliced)
salt & pepper
cornflour to thicken
chopped parsley
2lb puff pastry
beaten egg to glaze

Serves 10

Put the meat, kidney and onion into a saucepan and brown well. Add beef stock, Worcestershire Sauce and GUINNESS. Cover, and simmer gently for about 1 hour until meat is tender. Add mushrooms and seasoning, cook for a further 15 minutes. Remove a little of the stock and blend with about 2 tblsp cornflour. Add the blended cornflour to the steak and kidney. Bring to the boil, stir and cook for 1 minute. Place into one large pie dish or 10 individual dishes. Roll out the pastry and use to cover the cooled steak and kidney, brush with the beaten egg and bake in a hot oven 425°F, 220°C, gas mark 7 for 20 minutes until the pastry is golden brown.

GUINNESS
MIXERS

The art of Guinness-mixing is as old as the famous brew itself and it seems that there's scarcely a drink that hasn't shared the same glass at one time or other. Many of the mixtures have provoked cries of delight. We suggest you experiment with these three first, then move on to more adventurous combinations.

Black Velvet

Guinness mixed fifty-fifty with champagne. This famous drink was invented in 1861 at Brooks's Club on the day Prince Albert died. The steward of the Club, with due decorum, ordered the champagne to be put in mourning and proceeded to mix it with Guinness with unexpectedly delicious results.

Guinness Shandy

Guinness mixed with lemonade. Rumoured to have been invented by the New Zealand rugby team during a British tour. Ordering Guinness and lemonade (instead of bitter), they found the drink extremely refreshing. An appropriate drink for the All Blacks!

Try Guinness mixed with ginger beer too. That's called a Top Hat.

Longship

Guinness halved with lager. A long, refreshing thirst-quencher, favoured by the Danes who find it makes their own pale brew more interesting.

It could make a Viking of you too!

GUINNESS
PUB PSYCHOLOGY

The British pub may *seem* like a quiet haven for relaxation, and cracking a joke or two, but is in fact a maze of subtle gestures, guarded postures and secret conflicts. These are some of the findings of a psychologist and sociologist who were commissioned by Guinness to unravel what really goes on in pubs.

The researchers visited pubs up and down the country inviting groups of drinkers to talk about themselves and their drinks. They spent a year collecting thoughts and impressions on the subject of pubs and drinks – here are some of the results.

What you drink is an expression of who you are: 'you are', they found, 'what you drink'. Each drink carries with it subtle messages about the sort of person you are, your mood and the way you drink.

For example the Guinness drinker sees himself as mature and self-confident – a man who knows what he wants and with the inner security to take time out to enjoy it. He sees other drinks as less distinctive in every way, and lager drinkers in particular as immature whizz kids.

The pub is seen as a man's 'playground'. It offers an escape from the hassles of everyday life, and a chance to recharge batteries, spiritually and physically, and partake of male camaraderie.

GUINNESS TRAVELLERS

Thankfully, there are few places in the world, except perhaps the most far flung, where the desire for a pint of the dark brew cannot be met.

Here are a few interesting possibilities:

Visit *The Guinness Tavern* near the Pompidou Centre in France. The sensible *patron* is reputed to sell little else, with the possible exception of the odd dram of Irish Whiskey.

When further afield, a sojourn in the *La Toc Racquet Club of St Lucia* will improve more than your forehand drive. The tennis professional, a man of sound principles and boundless common sense, appreciates the pleasure a cool Guinness brings after a hard game of mixed doubles.

In America, head for the *Epcot Centre,* the result of a visionary dream by Walt Disney to create a world brotherhood. Guinness is available here in the British pub, just the thing after a hectic tour around this astounding complex.

If night-clubbing is more your style then the *Café des Sports* in Douala, Cameroon serves a mean glass of Guinness to refresh you after the exertions of the dance floor.

Finally, the betting man will be fascinated to know that a visit to the *Cock and Bull Tavern* in Sydney, Australia will answer two needs. You can quench your thirst for a Guinness *and* place a bet on the horses without losing your place at the bar. If you win a modest amount, you'll be paid there and then from the till. A major windfall, on the other hand, will necessitate a visit from a security van to award you your winnings!

GUINNESS
200 YEARS ON...

Still the Perfect Pint of Guinness

The original brewery was opened by Arthur Guinness in 1759 in Dublin on a 9,000 year lease.

Nearly two centuries later, in 1936, the brewery at Park Royal, London opened its doors. Today Guinness is the biggest-selling brand of beer in the British Isles, and indeed 7 million glasses a day are consumed by discerning drinkers, in over 110 countries.

The brewing of Guinness has changed little over the years; barley, water, hops and yeast are the four ingredients used. But it takes more than wholesome, natural ingredients to create the perfect pint. The craftsmanship of the Guinness brewer and his team is of paramount importance.

At each stage of the lengthy brewing process, the brewers and tasters measure, assess and improve. Only when the brewer is satisfied that the distinctive taste, aroma and appearance are perfect is his job complete. The quality control chain is then completed in the pub when the Guinness salesman visits to test samples, check serving temperatures, and help the landlord to get the best from his Guinness.

This route to a perfect Guinness is followed meticulously. The reward comes at the end in that superb pint of cool creamy Guinness.

WHAT THE FAMOUS THINK OF GUINNESS

The list of people — famous or otherwise — who enjoy a glass of Guinness is endless and each has his or her own special reason.

Actor Terence Brady recently divulged in a Daily Mail article his recipe for Sorbet à la Guinness. He is also quoted there as saying: "Just as every oyster eater will tell you the only drink to take with the mollusc is Guinness, the serious curry consumer never takes wine with spice."

Cyril Ray, prolific author and authority on food and wine, says: "What do I love more than anything else in the world? Guinness! What else can you drink in the middle of the morning? With your lunch? As an aperitif before dinner? With your dinner? Before you go to bed? Guinness."

Sporty lady Jane Furniss, who ran in the women's 3000 metres at the Los Angeles Olympics, often drinks Guinness in the evening on the advice of her Irish coach Jim Madigan "because of the goodness in it and I enjoy it".

Star Recipe

Terence Brady's
Sorbet à la Guinness

Dissolve 1lb sugar in 2 pints water to make syrup, and boil to reduce by one third. Allow to cool. Add 1 pint of Guinness and taste. Bitterness of Guinness must come through taste of syrup. Place in ice cream machine or simply freeze.

Lamb & Flag   *(Food)*

33 Rose Street, Covent Garden, WC2
Map 11 B2
01-836 4108

Brewery Courage
Landlord Loraine Baldwin
Stilton ploughman's £1.25 Hot pasty 70p (Last order 10.30pm)
🍺 Courage Directors Bitter, Best Bitter; John Smith's Bitter; Guinness; Kronenbourg; Hofmeister; Taunton cider. *Real ale*

Dickens, Dryden and Samuel Butler are among the literary luminaries linked with this famous little pub, whose selection of English cheeses really is something to write home about. Cheddar and Red Leicester, Sage Derby, Blue Shropshire and other prime varieties are served with pickles and either crisp baguettes or wedges of hot bread. There are other lunchtime dishes, but it's definitely the cheese that takes the biscuit.

Maple Leaf   *(Food)*

41 Maiden Lane, WC2 · Map 11 B1
01-240 2843

Brewery Grand Met
Landlord Mr Noel Healy

Roast beef £2.95 Beef & ale cassoulet £2.95 (Last order 10pm. No bar food Sun eve)
🍺 Webster's Yorkshire Bitter; Ruddle's County; Eldridge Pope Royal Oak; Guinness. *Real ale*

Portions are hearty at this friendly pub with a Canadian theme. Granary-bread sandwiches packed with roast beef or lean, succulent ham are just the thing for aspiring lumberjacks, and hot dishes include lasagne, Suffolk hot pot and tourtière – thin pastry enveloping tasty minced beef and served with fresh vegetables or a salad. The servery is at one end of the cheerful, well-furnished bar.

Mayflower

In 1611 the *Mayflower's* captain was enjoying a pint at this riverside pub when he received his assignment to transport the Pilgrim Fathers to America. The 17th century is faithfully recalled in the black-beamed bars, and there's an interesting collection of nautical memorabilia. A jetty affords super views of the Thames.   **Family pub**

117 Rotherhithe Street, SE16 · Map 10 D2
01-237 4088
Brewery Vintage Inns   *Landlord* Mr Benson
🍺 Charrington's IPA; Bass; Guinness; Carling Black Label; Tennent's Lager. *Real ale*

Museum Tavern

Karl Marx is said to have taken breaks from his studies to visit this popular pub, which stands opposite the British Museum. Today's students and tourists can enjoy an excellent range of well-kept real ales in smartly revamped Victorian surroundings, with carved wood, frosted and stained glass, gilded columns and ceiling fans.

49 Great Russell Street, WC1 · Map 11 B1
01-242 8987
Owner Clifton Inns   *Landlord* Mr Price
🍺 Greene King IPA; Brakspear's Special; Ruddle's County; Guinness; Carlsberg; Foster's; Taunton cider. *Real ale*

Nag's Head

This 18th-century pub has seen many different faces over the years. Once an early-morning haunt of workers from Covent Garden Market, it now attracts a lively pre-theatre crowd. The decor is plush Edwardian in style, with etched mirrors catching the eye along with opera and ballet playbills.

10 James Street, WC2 · Map 11 B1
01-836 4678
Brewery McMullen   *Landlord* Mr M. P. Conway
 McMullens Coventry Bitter; Guiness; Steingold; Hartsman; cider. *Real ale*

Nell of Old Drury

Nell Gwyn, later to become mistress of Charles II, used to sell her oranges on the steps of the Theatre Royal, across the road from this old tavern. Playbills line the walls of the simply furnished bar, and Richard Sheridan is said to have been a patron. Closed Sunday.

29 Catherine Street, WC2 · Map 11 B1
01-836 5328
Brewery Courage   *Landlord* Mr M. P. Dunphy
 Courage Directors Bitter, Best Bitter; John Smith's Bitter; Guinness; Kronenbourg; Hofmeister. *Real ale*

Prices given are as at the time

of our research and are

comparative indications rather

than firm quotes.

Old Bell Tavern

Sir Christopher Wren's workmen were the first customers of this busy Fleet Street inn during the building of the church of St Bride's next door. An earlier house on the same site was used as a workshop by one of Caxton's assistants. Closed Sat eve and all Sun.

95 Fleet Street, EC4 · Map 11 C1
01-353 3796
Free House   Landlord Mrs N. Healy
 Morrell's Bitter; Adnams Bitter; Courage Directors Bitter; Guinness; Oranjeboom; Löwenbräu; Carlsberg. *Real ale*

Orange Brewery   *(Food)*

37 Pimlico Road, SW1 · Map 12 C2
01-730 5378

Owners Clifton Innkeepers
Landlords John & Avril Fletcher

Hot roast pork sandwich £1.50 Beef
bourguignon £2.50 (Last order 10.30pm)
🍺 Orange Brewery SW1, SW2, Pimlico
Porter; Guinness; Holsten; Foster's; cider.
Real ale

A popular Pimlico pub with two bars, its
own range of real ales and a daily changing
selection of tasty snacks. Sandwiches with
fillings of freshly cooked roasts are the
favourite lunchtime choice, and other
offerings include soup and ploughman's
platters, salads and hearty hot specials like
chilli con carne or beef bourguignon.

Paxton's Head

This busy Knightsbridge pub is named after Sir Joseph Paxton, a man
of many talents who is best remembered as the designer of the
Crystal Palace, which originally stood not far away in Hyde Park. The
Victorian-style bar with its central serving area features some delightful etched mirrors in mahogany frames. There's also a cellar bar.

Family pub

153 Knightsbridge, SW1 · Map 12 B1
01-589 6627
Owners H. H. Finch & Co   *Landlord* George Redgewell
🍺 Ind Coope Burton Ale, Special Bitter; John Bull; Double
Diamond; Guinness; Löwenbräu; Skol. *Real ale*

Prince Regent

Portraits and caricatures of the Prince Regent abound in this smartly
refurbished and ever-popular corner pub. There are also royal
warrants, medals and many other memorabilia, and another interesting feature is a collection of little brass plaques engraved by a former
landlord with the names of his staunchest regulars. Patio.

71 Marylebone High Street, W1 · Map 11 A1
01-935 2018
Brewery Charrington   *Landlords* Mr & Mrs P. Lewis
🍺 Charrington's IPA; Mitchells & Butlers Springfield Bitter;
Guinness; Carling Black Label; Taunton cider. *Real ale*

Printer's Devil

Printing workers from nearby Fleet Street crowd into this busy pub,
named after the traditional nickname for a printer's errand boy. The
main bar features a splendid display of woodcuts, old books and
models of printing presses. Rare for the City, there is also a public bar.
Closed Sunday.

98 Fetter Lane, EC4 · Map 11 C1
01-242 2239
Brewery Whitbread   *Landlord* Mr A. Fletcher
🍺 Wethered's Bitter; Flower's Original; Whitbread Best Bitter,
Trophy Bitter, Mild. *Real ale*

Prospect of Whitby

Foreign visitors flock to this old waterside inn, once a den of thieves and smugglers. Turner painted the river from here, and Judge Jeffreys reportedly watched the execution of pirates from a balcony while dining. The one large bar has a beamed ceiling and flagstone floor.   **Family pub**

57 Wapping Wall, E1 · Map 10 D2
01-481 1095
Owner Sovereign Host   *Landlord* Mr Trevor Chapman
🍺 Watneys Stag, Combes Bitter; Ben Truman's Bitter; Ruddle's County; Guinness; Carlsberg; Holsten; Foster's; cider. *Real ale*

Railway Tavern

Train enthusiasts should schedule a stop at this mid-Victorian pub near Liverpool Street Station. Photographs, models of steam locomotives and crests of 19th-century railway companies revive memories of pre-diesel days. Closed Sat, Sun & eves from 9pm.

15 Liverpool Street, EC2 · Map 10 C2
01-283 3598
Brewery Whitbread   *Landlord* Mr Hanley
🍺 Flowers Original; Wethered's Marlow Bitter; Whitbread Trophy; Brakspear's Bitter; Greene King Abbot Ale; Guinness; Stella Artois. *Real ale*

Red Lion   *(Food)*

23 Crown Passage, Pall Mall, SW1 · Map 11 A2
01-930 8067

Brewery Watney Combe Reid
Landlords Gerard & Michael McAree

Steak & kidney pie, salad or jacket potato £3.50
Roast turkey £3.15 (Last order 10.30pm)
🍺 Ruddles County; Webster's Yorkshire Bitter; Combes Bitter; Guinness; Foster's; Carlsberg. *Real ale*

Tucked away in a passage off Pall Mall, this snug little pub does a roaring trade in tasty, home-cooked bar snacks. Pride of place undoubtedly goes to the splendid hot meat pies – steak and kidney, beef and ale, chicken with gammon and mushroom – served with a jacket potato or crisp salad. Sandwiches (choose from ten fillings) are made to order, and there are excellent cold meat salads.

Red Lion

Built in 1723 to accommodate builders working on Chesterfield House, this cosy pub has a delightfully British atmosphere, with dark panelling, wooden settles and tables, leaded windows and prints of old London. In fine weather chairs and tables made out of barrels are set out on the little patio. Closed 1 week Christmas.

1 Waverton Street, Mayfair, W1 · Map 11 A2
01-499 1307
Owners London Hosts   *Landlord* Mr David Butterfield
🍺 Webster's Yorkshire Bitter; Watney Stag Bitter; Ruddle's County; Combe's Bitter; Guinness; Foster's; Cider. *Real ale*

London

St Stephen's Tavern

Beside Westminster pier, this old tavern is a favourite with civil servants and political journalists. The cellar bar was once connected to the Houses of Parliament by a tunnel said to have been used by Guy Fawkes; the upstairs bar sports an ornately carved bar counter and fine engraved glass. Closed Sunday evening.

10 Bridge Street, SW1 · Map 11 B2
01-930 3230
Brewery Whitbread   *Landlord* Mr Christopher Gent
🍺 Webster's Yorkshire Bitter; Watneys Stag Bitter; Combes Bitter; Guinness; Carlsberg; Foster's; Holsten; cider. *Real ale*

Salisbury

This handsome Victorian pub has a style and atmosphere very much in keeping with its location in London's theatreland. It's long been a favourite pre-performance rendezvous and is also popular with the acting profession and its acolytes. The lavish decor is authentic 1890s, with plush velvet, engraved glass screens and moulded ceilings.

90 St Martin's Lane, WC2 · Map 11 B2
01-836 5863
Owner Clifton Inns   *Landlord* Mr Gerry Wynne
🍺 Ind Coope Burton Ale, Double Diamond; Taylor Walker Bitter; John Bull Bitter; Guinness; Oranjeboom; Löwenbräu; cider. *Real ale*

Samuel Pepys

At the end of a narrow alley, this Thames-side pub is a skilful reconstruction of a 17th-century inn. A nautical theme in the cellar bar recalls Samuel Pepys' service as a naval secretary, and extracts from his diary line the walls. The verandah provides splendid river views.
Family pub

Brooks Wharf, Upper Thames Street, EC4 · Map 11 C2
01-248 3048
Owners Vintage Inns   *Landlord* Mr Spencer
🍺 Charrington's IPA; Bass; Stones Bitter; Guinness; Carling Black Label; Tennent's Pilsner, Export; Taunton cider. *Real ale*

Seven Stars

Between the Law Courts and Lincoln's Inn Fields, this tiny pub first licensed in 1602 is a favourite haunt of lawyers and accountants. The ever-busy little bar is enlivened by Spy cartoons of eminent members of the legal profession. Closed Sat, Sun and Bank Holidays.

53 Carey Street, WC2 · Map 11 B1
01-242 8521
Brewery Courage   *Landlord* Mr J. A. Crawley
🍺 Courage Best Bitter, Directors Bitter, JC; Guinness; Hofmeister; Kronenbourg; Taunton cider. *Real ale*

| O.G. 1031·5° | O.G. 1032·6° | O.G. 1033·7° | O.G. 1035·9° | O.G. 1035·9° |
| Brewed in Salford | Brewed in Faversham | Brewed in Marlow | Brewed in Cheltenham | Brewed in Sheffield |

| O.G. 1043·7° | O.G. 1042·6° | O.G. 1038·42° | O.G. 1041·5° | O.G. 1030·4° |
| Brewed in Cheltenham | Brewed in Cheltenham | Brewed in Castle Eden | Brewed in Faversham | Brewed in Salford |

When travelling, be sure to observe local customs.

While you're drinking in some of the local atmosphere, try drinking in some of the local brew.

Chesters, for example, if you're visiting Greater Manchester.

Pompey Royal or Flowers Original, when you're heading towards the West Country.

All over England we brew cask conditioned ales to regional recipes. (A selection is shown above.)

We believe the extra effort involved is worthwhile.

Recently, three of our beers were singled out for praise by no less an authority than CAMRA themselves.

But not only do we satisfy their demanding tastes. We satisfy local tastes, too.

WHITBREAD
Our reputation has been brewing since 1742.

Shepherd's Tavern

A fine old corner pub between Park Lane and Piccadilly. Bull's eye window panes add a period touch to the mellow, pine-panelled bar, and a notable feature upstairs is a sedan chair that once belonged to the Duke of Cumberland. It's now used as a telephone booth.

Family pub

Hertford Street, W1 · Map 11 A2
01-499 3017
Owners London Hosts   *Landlord* Mr Ken Woodhams
Ruddle's County; Watneys Stag; Mann's IPA; Webster's Yorkshire Bitter; Guinness; Holsten; cider. *Real ale*

Sherlock Holmes

A must for devotees of the dauntless detective, this well-known pub is filled with Holmesiana; there's also a fascinating collection of early forensic equipment. Sir Arthur Conan Doyle was a regular visitor here when it was the Northumberland Arms and mentions it in *The Hound of the Baskervilles.* Outside drinking in summer.

10 Northumberland Street, WC2 · Map 11 B2
01-930 2644
Brewery Whitbread   *Landlord* Mrs J. R. Hardcastle
Fremlins Tusker; Flower's Original; Whitbread Winter Royal; Guinness; Stella Artois; Heineken; cider. *Real ale*

Ship

A position right opposite the finishing post makes this pleasant riverside pub one of the most popular places in London on Boat Race day. A long history goes back to Elizabethan times. **Family pub** (until 7pm)

10 Thames Bank, Riverside, SW14 · Map 9 A3
01-876 1439
Owner London Host   *Landlord* Roger Smart
Combes Bitter; Ruddle's County; Webster's Yorkshire Bitter; Guinness; Foster's; cider. *Real ale*

Spaniards Inn

Close to Hampstead Heath, this famous old pub stood beside a tollgate over which Dick Turpin leapt on horseback while fleeing from London. Keats, Byron and Shelley all frequented the inn, which still has its weatherboarded frontage and beamed bars.   **Family pub**

Spaniards Road, NW3 · Map 9 B1
01-455 3276
Brewery Charrington   *Landlords* Mr & Mrs Culver
Charrington's IPA; Bass; Guinness; Carling Black Label; Tennent's Extra; Taunton cider. *Real ale*

Sun Inn

Legend has it that Drake and Walsingham taught Elizabeth I to play bowls on the green in front of this popular pub opposite Barnes Pond. The cellar bar is modern, but ground-floor rooms retain their traditional style.

7 Church Road, Barnes, SW13 · Map 9 A3
01-876 5893
Brewery Taylor Walker   *Landlords* Mr & Mrs J. Fisher
Taylor Walker Bitter; Ind Coope Burton Ale; John Bull; Guinness; Löwenbräu; Oranjeboom; cider. *Real ale*

Thistle   *(Food)*

11 Vigo Street, W1 · Map 11 A2
01-734 1947

Brewery Younger
Landlords Mr & Mrs B. K. E. Banyai

Honey roast gammon & salad £3.50 Fruit pie 75p (No bar food eves)
Younger's IPA, Tartan; McEwan's Export; Guinness; Cavalier; Becks. *Real ale*

A popular place for escaping the bustle of Regent Street, this comfortable pub has an outstanding cold table. Succulent honey-roast gammon, beautifully tender beef, turkey pie and quiche are served with a selection of simple fresh salads, and sandwiches are available for a quicker snack. The fruit pie is delicious, too, and there's a hot special on Saturdays. Closed Saturday evening, all Sunday and Bank Holidays.

Three Compasses   *(Food)*

66 Cowcross Street, EC1 · Map 11 C1
01-253 3368

Brewery Trumans
Landlord Mr W. I. Hutchinson
Shepherd's pie 99p Quiche & salad £1.25 (Last order 11pm)
Trumans Bitter, Best Bitter; Sampson Hanbury Strong Ale; Ben Truman Export Lager; Guinness; Foster's, Holsten; cider. *Real ale*

Seven-day opening is a rarity among City pubs, and the constant availability of excellent home-cooked snacks is a further bonus at the Three Compasses. In the attractively restored panelled bar you can enjoy freshly prepared sandwiches and salads, the quiche of the day – crisp, light and full of flavour – or a splendid shepherd's pie packed with lots of lean, tasty mince.

Tom Cribb

Once barefist boxing champion of England, Tom Cribb became landlord of this busy corner pub upon retiring from the ring in 1811. Posters and prints still recall his and others' pugilistic exploits. Tables with parasols are set out on the pavement in fine weather.

36 Panton Street, SW1 · Map 11 B2
01-839 6536
Brewery Charrington   *Landlords* Mr & Mrs A. M. S. Talbot
Charrington's IPA, Bass; Stones Bitter; Guinness; Carling Black Label; Tennent's Extra; Taunton cider. *Real ale*

61

London

Trafalgar Tavern

Built in 1837 and restored in 1965, this smart riverside pub in Greenwich has a distinctly nautical flavour. Bars are named after Nelson's admirals, and the Hawke and Howe is strikingly designed to resemble the forecastle of an 18th-century man-o'-war. Bay windows provide panoramic views of the river. **Family pub**

Park Row, SE10 · Map 10 D2
01-858 2437
Owner Gateway Hosts *Landlord* Mr Frederick Davies
Young's Special Bitter; Ruddle's County; Webster's Yorkshire Bitter; Guinness; Carlsberg; cider. *Real ale*

Two Chairmen

A colourful sign depicting two sedan chairmen hangs outside this handsome pub in a dignified Westminster Street, and the theme is continued inside with delightful murals of bucks and grandees being carried in sedan chairs. Darkwood panelling and an open fire contribute to the period charm. Closed Sunday.

39 Dartmouth Street, SW1 · Map 11 B2
01-222 8694
Owner Clifton Inns *Landlord* Miss P. Allcorn
Ruddles County; Webster's Yorkshire Bitter; Watney's Stag Bitter; Combe's Bitter; Guinness; Carlsberg; Foster's. *Real ale*

Two Chairmen

Tucked away in a narrow street near Trafalgar Square, this congenial little pub was built in 1683 and reconstructed 200 years later. Its name refers to the sedan chairmen who plied their trade about the city in the 17th and 18th centuries. The intimate, simply furnished bar is a congenial place for a good pint of real ale. Closed Sunday.

Warwick House Street, off Cockspur St, SW1 · Map 11 B2
01-930 1166
Brewery Courage
Courage Best Bitter, Directors Bitter; Guinness; Hofmeister; Kronenbourg. *Real ale*

Victoria

Built in 1835, this splendid pub still features etched glass, mahogany panelling and a moulded plaster ceiling, while fittings from the old Gaiety Theatre adorn the upstairs bar. Queen Victoria, after whom the pub was named, visited here when she opened nearby Paddington Station.

10a Strathearn Place, W2 · Map 9 B2
01-262 5696
Brewery Charrington *Landlords* Mr & Mrs Byrne
Charrington's IPA; Bass; Stones Bitter; Guinness; Carling Black Label; Harp; cider. *Real ale*

Let TWA be your guide to the USA.

TWA helps you see America on wheels.

It may seem strange for a great airline to offer you travel by car.

But TWA offers you terrific car hire deals in America.

TWA knows that flying is a fine way to get from place to place. But as every good guide-reader knows, you have to get around by car to see it all properly. Find the little-known places. Take in the spectacular scenery.

TWA's Getaway Fly/Drive programmes are among the best in the business. All part of our guide to America.

Enjoy it.

See your

TWA
Main Agent

You're going to like us

London

White Horse on Parsons Green *(Food)*

1 Parsons Green, SW6 · Map 9 A3
01-736 2115

Free House
Landlord Mrs Sally Cruickshank
Fish pie & vegetables £2.60 Eggplant
Parmesan £2.20 (Last order 9pm. No bar food
Sat & Sun eves)
🍺 Bass; Charrington's IPA; Springfield
Bitter; Tennent's Extra; Stones Bitter;
Guinness; Taunton cider. *Real ale*

The menu is long and varied at this attractive, spacious pub, where the crowds testify to Sally Cruickshank's skills in the kitchen. Standard favourites – quiche, jacket potatoes, cold meats and salads – are supplemented by imaginative choices like fish and banana pie, liver casserole and stuffed vegetarian pancakes. Rare roast beef in a bun is a popular Saturday lunchtime snack. **Family pub** (lunchtime)

Windsor Castle

Built on the site of what was once Kensington spa, this friendly little pub brings a breath of country air to city streets. Oak and elm panelling and wooden settles add to the old-fashioned charm.

114 Campden Hill Road, W8 · Map 12 A1
01-727 8491
Brewery Charrington   *Landlord* Mr Gavriel
🍺 Charrington's IPA; Bass; Guinness; Carling Black Label;
Tennent's Extra. *Real ale*

Yacht

Dating back to the 17th century and rebuilt after World War II bomb damage, this pleasant Thames-side pub stands near Greenwich's major tourist attractions. The mahogany-panelled bar has a strong maritime theme, with portholes, ship's instruments and yachting photographs. The terraces command splendid views along the river.
Family pub

Crane Street, SE10 · Map 10 D2
01-858 0175
Owner Gateway Hosts   *Landlord* Mr T Ryan
🍺 Ruddle's County; Webster's Yorkshire Bitter; Guinness; Holsten;
Foster's; cider. *Real ale*

Ye Grapes *(Food)*

16 Shepherd Market, W1 · Map 11 A2
01-629 4989

Free House
Landlords A. F. Wigram & P. L. Jacobs

Cottage pie £1.85 Tandoori chicken £2.15 (No
bar food Sun & eves)
🍺 Fremlin's Tusker; Wethered's Bitter; Ind
Coope Burton Ale; Arkell's BBB; Guinness;
Stella Artois; Heineken; cider. *Real ale*

On the corner of Shepherd Market, this well-preserved Victorian pub is a delightful spot for a lunchtime bite. The carvery is the centre of attraction, with excellent cold meats and fresh salmon to accompany crunchy coleslaw and other super salads. There's a good selection of sandwiches, too, plus seasonal oysters and winter warmers ranging from vegetable soup to chilli con carne. Patio.

Ye Old Dr Butler's Head

Dr William Butler, physician to James I and a great believer in the medicinal properties of ale, founded this hostelry in 1610. Today, City workers throng the sawdust-strewn bar with its black beams and old brewery mirrors. Closed Sat, Sun and evenings from about 8pm.

Mason's Avenue, Coleman Street, EC2 · Map 11 C1
01-606 3504
Free House   Landlords Nigel & Carolina Field
Bass; Courage Best Bitter; Guinness; Tennent's Extra; Carling Black Label. *Real ale*

Ye Olde Cheshire Cheese

Rebuilt in 1667 after the Great Fire of London, this famous Fleet Street pub looks much as it did when Dr Johnson used to pop in from his house round the corner, with panelling, scrubbed tables, and sawdust on the floors. Congreve, Pope and Voltaire are among other famous patrons. Closed Sat and Sun.   **Family pub**

145 Fleet Street, EC4 · Map 11 C1
01-353 6170
Free House   Landlord Mr L. Kerly
Marston's Pedigree, Burton Bitter, Pils Lager. *Real ale*

Ye Olde Cock Tavern

Built in 1549 and a narrow survivor of the Great Fire of London, this famous tavern is rich in history. Two features of special note are a superb Tudor chimney piece and a handsomely carved and gilded cock. Its literary links are impressive, too, with Samuel Pepys, Dickens and Tennyson familiar faces in their day. Closed Sat and Sun.

22 Fleet Street, EC4 · Map 11 C1
01-353 3454
Owners London Host   *Landlord* Mr P. M. Kelly
Truman's Best Bitter, Bitter, Mild; Guinness; Holsten; Carlsberg; Foster's. *Real ale*

Ye Olde Mitre Tavern

This little gem of a pub is tucked away down an alley between Hatton Garden and Ely Place. Originally built in 1546 for the Bishop of Ely, it later saw service as a prison and Civil War hospital. The present 18th-century building has a great deal of old-world charm, with dark-wood panelling and fine old seating. Closed Sat, Sun & Bank Hols.

1 Ely Court, Ely Place, Holborn, EC1 · Map 11 C1
01-405 4751
Brewery Ind Coope   *Landlord* Mr F. Rix
Ind Coope Burton Ale, Double Diamond; Friary Meux Bitter; Guinness; Skol. *Real ale*

London

Ye Olde Watling

This richly historic pub in the oldest street in London provided food
and lodgings for the builders of St Paul's. Little has changed in 300
years – massive beams, arched doorways and leaded windows
remain in the bars. Closed Sat eve, all Sun, evenings from about 8pm
and Bank Holidays.

29 Watling Street, EC4 · Map 11 C1
01-248 7524
Owners Vintage Inns   *Landlord* Mr R. G. Wale
 Charrington's IPA; Bass; Guinness; Carling Black Label;
Tennent's Extra; Taunton cider. *Real ale*

Ye Olde Windmill Inn   (B & B)

Clapham Common Southside, SW4
Map 9 B3
01-673 4578

Brewery Young
Landlords Mr & Mrs Tobin

BEDROOMS 13   Grade 1   £B   (No dogs)
 Young's Special Bitter, Ordinary, Young
John's Ale, Winter Warmer (winter only);
Guinness; London Lager. *Real ale*

Standing by the edge of Clapham
Common, this large, sturdily built pub is
well placed for travellers to the south of
London. The spacious bars have a solid
Victorian feel, with their rich decor,
mahogany tables and stained glass, and
there's a pleasantly secluded beer garden.
Bedrooms are smartly modern, with neat
fitted furniture, attractive matching fabrics,
colour TVs and tea-makers. One has a full
bathroom, the others shower units.

ENGLAND

Abberley *(Food)*   *Bell at Pensax*

Near Worcester · *Hereford & Worcester*
Map 7 D1
Great Witley (029 921) 677

Free House
Landlords Robert & Pamela Eaton
Pâté £1.25 Sausage & parsley pie £2 (Last
order 10pm)
📖 Hook Norton Best Bitter; Taylor's
Landlord; Wood's Special; Guinness;
Tuborg; cider. *Real ale*

Pamela Eaton does all the cooking at this
smart red-brick pub, which lies between the
villages of Abberley and Pensax. Her pâté is
a popular starter or light snack, along with
soup and garlic mushrooms, and for
heartier appetites there are things like chilli
con carne and beef goulash. Anyone with
space to spare should try the toothsome
treacle tart. Patio.   **Family pub**

Abbots Bromley *(B & B)*   *Crown Inn*

Market Place · *Staffordshire* · Map 4 C4
Burton-on-Trent (0283) 840227

Brewery Bass
Landlords Mr & Mrs Finch

BEDROOMS 6 Grade 2 £C (No dogs)
📖 Bass; Mitchells & Butlers Mild;
Worthington 'E'; Guinness; Carling Black
Label; Taunton cider. *Real ale*

This friendly half-timbered pub stands
facing the village market place where a per-
formance of the ancient Horn Dance is a
traditional attraction every September.
Paintings and antlers adorn the comfortable bar which offers a fine selection of
malt whiskies. Simply furnished bedrooms
have TVs and share a single public bathroom. Local sausages are a feature of Mr
and Mrs Finch's home-cooked breakfasts.
Garden.

Abingdon *(Food)*   *Ox Inn*

15 Oxford Road · *Oxfordshire* · Map 6 A3
Abingdon (0235) 20962

Brewery Morland
Landlord Mr J. P. Conway

Steak & mushroom pie £2.80 Chicken in white
wine sauce £3.45 (Last order 10pm)
📖 Morland's Ordinary Bitter, Best Bitter,
Dark Mild, Artist; Guinness; Stella Artois;
Heineken; cider. *Real ale*

Steaks delivered straight from the next-
door butcher top the popularity charts at
this welcoming roadside inn. Mrs Conway
also provides a good choice of home-
cooked dishes such as steak and mushroom pie or pork chop in cider sauce.
Steaming apple crumble makes a satisfying finish. The choice is smaller on
Sundays. Patio and garden.

Ainsworth *(Food)*   *Duke William*

Wells Road, Near Bolton · *Greater Manchester*
Map 3 B3
Bolton (0204) 24726

Brewery Whitbread
Landlords Ann & Basil Collier-Brown
Roast lamb £2.50 Steak & kidney pie £2
(No bar food eves or lunch Sat–Mon)
📖 Whitbread Trophy; Dutton's Light;
Chester's Best Mild; Heldenbrau; Stella
Artois; Heineken; cider.

Customers come from far and wide to
enjoy the splendid lunchtime bar snacks
that have made this cosy Georgian pub so
popular. Home-made savoury pies are
great favourites, along with pâté, grills and
daily specials like roast lamb or poached
halibut with shrimp sauce. Good fresh
vegetables accompany main courses.
Book, and remember that the early bird has
the widest choice. Terrace.

Aldenham *(Food)* — *Game Bird*

Hartspring Lane · *Hertfordshire* · Map 6 B3
Watford (0923) 25826

Brewery Benskins
Landlord Mr L. Mortiss

Game Bird pie £2.50 Filled potatoes £1.95 (Last
order 7.30pm. No bar food Sun eve)
🍺 Ind Coope Burton Ale; Benskins Bitter;
John Bull Bitter; Guinness; Löwenbräu; Skol;
Oranjeboom; cider. *Real ale*

The heart of this zippy pub with intimate
alcove seating is a large island bar dispensing world-wide lagers. A cold buffet
offers a self-service selection of cooked
meats and salads, while hot choices
include filled jacket potatoes (Sultry
Sophia comes with a tangy bolognese
topping), special duckling pie and daily
dishes like cauliflower cheese. Freshly cut
sandwiches, too – perhaps sausage and
sauerkraut.

Alfold Crossways *(Food)* — *Napoleon Arms*

Near Cranleigh · *Surrey* · Map 6 B3
Loxwood (0403) 752357

Free House
Landlords Wilf & Mary Forgham

French onion soup £1.30 Curry with rice &
vegetables £2.75 (Last order 10pm)
🍺 Fuller's London Pride; Webster's
Yorkshire Bitter; Wilson's Great Northern
Bitter; Carlsberg; cider. *Real ale*

Tables outside and an ornamental pool
make this low-built roadside pub particularly attractive in summer. The wide choice
of snacks available in the bar ranges from
French onion soup to baked potatoes with
various fillings and an expertly prepared
herb omelette. More substantial dishes like
beef curry cater for the truly hungry, and
there's ice cream to finish. **Family pub**

Alfriston *(B & B)* — *George Inn*

East Sussex · Map 6 C4
Alfriston (0323) 870319

Owners Hotels of the Cinque Ports
Landlord Mr Robin Harriott

BEDROOMS 8 Grade 2 £C (No dogs)
🍺 Watneys Stag Bitter, Special, Special
Mild; Usher's Bitter; Ben Truman; Guinness;
Carlsberg; cider. *Real ale*

Steeped in history and once notorious as a
haunt of smugglers, this 15th-century
timber-framed inn stands in the main street
of a pretty Sussex village. Oak beams
abound, and a blazing fire keeps winter at
bay in the comfortable main bar. The mood
is similar in the bedrooms, most of which
have fine old furnishings. There's a
pleasant garden. **Family pub**

Allensmore *(Food, B & B)* — *Three Horseshoes*

Near Hereford · *Hereford & Worcester*
Map 7 D2
Wormbridge (098 121) 329
Free House
Landlords Mr & Mrs Sloggett
BEDROOMS 4 Grade 2 £C (No dogs)
Home-made soup 95p Chilli con carne £3
(Last order 10pm. No bar food Sun lunch)
🍺 Mitchells & Butlers Brew XI; Bass,
Allbright; Younger's Tartan; Guinness;
Tennent's; Carling Black label; cider. *Real ale*

A cordial welcome awaits visitors to the
Sloggetts' whitewashed country pub near
the junction of the A465 and B4348. Bar
snacks are a popular feature, ranging from
made-to-order sandwiches and ploughman's platters to delicious French onion
soup, chicken and chips, curries and a
gorgeous treacle tart. The four spotless
bedrooms (no children accommodated)
have attractive floral decor and sturdy furnishings. Excellent breakfasts.

England

Alresford   *(Food)*   *Horse & Groom*

Broad Street · *Hampshire* · Map 6 B3
Alresford (096 273) 4809

Brewery Whitbread
Landlords Mr & Mrs P. Clements

Steak & kidney pie £2.45 Chicken & tomato
casserole £2.50 (Last order 9.30pm)
🍺 Flower's Original; Whitbread Strong
Country Bitter; Guinness; Heineken; Stella
Artois; cider. *Real ale*

The mood is friendly and relaxed at the
Clementses' popular pub, whose exterior is
adorned with colourful flower tubs and
hanging baskets. Inside, in the brick-walled
bar, a good choice of snacks is always
available, the pick perhaps being hearty
daily specials like spiced lamb, pasta
italienne or flavoursome chicken and
tomato casserole served with nicely
cooked fresh vegetables. Garden.

Alrewas   *(Food, B & B)*   *George & Dragon*

Main Street, Near Burton-upon-Trent
Staffordshire · Map 4 C4
Burton-on-Trent (0283) 790202
Brewery Marston, Thompson & Evershed
Landlords Mr & Mrs R. G. Stanbrook
BEDROOMS 13   Grade 1   £A
Steak & kidney pie £1.50 Pork & liver pâté £1.20
(Last order 10pm. No bar food Sun)
🍺 Marston's Pedigree, Albion Mild, Lager;
Guinness; Heineken; cider. *Real ale*

The Stanbrooks are charming hosts at this
pleasant country pub, which offers plenty
of atmosphere along with good food and
comfortable accommodation. In a setting
replete with Royal Family souvenirs you
can enjoy bar snacks ranging from a super
roast beef sandwich to burgers, salads and
pies, both savoury and sweet. Neatly fitted
bedrooms have tea-makers and colour TVs.
Garden. Accommodation closed 1 week
Christmas.   **Family pub**

Alsager   *(Food, B & B)*   *Manor House*

Audley Road, Near Stoke-on-Trent · *Cheshire*
Map 3 B4
Alsager (093 63) 78013
Free House
Landlords Mr & Mrs A. Cottingham
BEDROOMS 8   Grade 1   £A+ (No dogs)
Hot seafood platter £2.25   Beef & onion
batch 90p (Last order 10pm)
🍺 Ansells Bitter; Double Diamond; Tetley's
Bitter; Burton Bitter; Guinness; Skol;
Löwenbräu; cider. *Real ale*

Only five minutes from the M6, this striking
red-brick inn offers a good selection of tasty
snacks in its characterful main bar. Seafood, both hot and cold, is a popular choice,
along with sandwiches, pâtés, cold meats
and a daily roast. The oak-beamed bedrooms with handsome fitted units are
splendidly comfortable, having central
heating, TVs, well-appointed shower
rooms as well as lots of extras. **Family pub**

Alswear   *(B & B)*   *Butchers Arms*

Near South Moulton · *Devon* · Map 8 C3
Bishop's Nympton (076 97) 477

Free House
Landlords Peter & Jean Gannon

BEDROOMS 3   Grade 2   £C
🍺 Usher's Best Bitter, Triple Crown;
Whitbread Trophy; Guinness; Carlsberg;
cider. *Real ale*

Once a flour mill, this pleasant village inn
on the A373 is a good, welcoming place.
The rustic public bar and quiet lounge bar
provide a choice for the thirsty, and there's
a popular games room with pool and
skittles. Three prettily decorated bedrooms
have washbasins and tea-makers, and
guests can watch TV in the Gannons'
lounge. Garden.   **Family pub**

Alton   *(Food)*   *Eight Bells*

Church Street · *Hampshire* · Map 6 B3
Alton (0420) 82417
Free House
Landlords Mr & Mrs Moxley
Home-made soup & French bread 85p Filled
jacket potato with side salad £1.60 (Last order
10pm)
🍺 Hall & Woodhouse Badger Best Bitter;
Bass; Courage Best Bitter; John Smith's
Bitter; Kronenbourg; Guinness; Taunton
cider. *Real ale*

Rosemary Moxley's wholesome, freshly
prepared bar snacks make this rustic roadside inn an ideal stopping place. Specialities include jacket potatoes with tasty
fillings like chilli con carne, and there is a
wide choice of plain and toasted sandwiches. You can also have pizza, a burger or
a seafood platter. Garden.

Anslow   *(Food)*   *Brickmakers Arms*

Beamhill Road, Near Burton upon Trent
Staffordshire · Map 4 C4
Burton-on-Trent (0283) 813799

Brewery Marston, Thompson & Evershed
Landlord Mr K. W. Woolley

Pâté with toast 75p Farmhouse grill £1.90
(Last order 8.45pm. No bar food Sun)
🍺 Marston's Pedigree, Low C, Lager. *Real ale*

Real ale makes a welcome accompaniment
to Mrs Woolley's excellent home-made
snacks, and the two combine to keep this
yellow-brick pub constantly busy. Pastry is
particularly recommended, whether in a
meat pie or a delicious blackberry and
apple pie. The menu also offers steak,
heaped mixed grills, salads and ploughman's. Sandwiches only on Monday–
Thursday evenings. Swings in the Garden.

Ansty   *(Food, B & B)*   *Fox Inn*

Near Dorchester · *Dorset* · Map 8 D3
Milton Abbas (0258) 880328
Free House
Landlords Peter & Wendy Amey
BEDROOMS 10   Grades 1 & 2   £B
Cold table £4 Barbecued steak £4 (Last
order 10pm)
🍺 Ansty Ale; Fox Ale; Hall & Woodhouse
Badger Best Bitter, Tanglefoot; Hector's Bitter;
Guinness; Carlsberg; Brock; Taunton cider.
Real ale

An outstanding village pub, whose spectacular cold buffet is known far and wide. A
dozen or more delicious cooked meats,
including seasonal game, are served with
amazing variety of super salads, and there
are appetising filled jacket potatoes, too.
The convivial bars are also notable for a
fine collection of plates and Toby jugs.
Comfortable bedrooms, most with private
facilities, have TVs and tea-makers.
Garden.   **Family pub**

Appleby   *(Food, B & B)*   *Royal Oak*

Bongate · *Cumbria* · Map 3 B2
Appleby (0930) 51463

Free House
Landlord Colin & Hilary Cheyne

BEDROOMS 8   Grade 2   £C
Crofter's pie £1.75 Prawns St Jacques £1.50
(Last order 9pm)
🍺 Younger's XXPS; McEwan's Mild, Export,
Lager; Guinness; Taunton cider. *Real ale*

This attractive old black and white inn
stands on the southern edge of Appleby.
Meat dishes are a good bet among the bar
snacks, thanks to an excellent local butcher,
and other choices include salads and
sandwiches, shellfish and home-made
lasagne. Bedrooms (three with TV) offer
simple comforts, and there are two welcoming bars and a pleasant terrace.

England

Appletreewick   (Food)   *Craven Arms*

Near Skipton · *North Yorkshire* · Map 4 C2
Burnsall (075 672) 270

Free House
Landlords Paul & Jane Emsley
Gammon & eggs £3.25 Steak & kidney
pie £2.75 (Last order 9.30pm. No bar food Sun
& Mon eves in winter)
🍺 Tetley's Porter; Theakston's Old Peculier,
Best Bitter; Younger's Scotch Bitter;
Guinness; Carlsberg; cider. *Real ale*

Paul Emsley takes care of the cosy bar while
his wife Jane does the cooking at this
charming creeper-clad inn which lies
between Burnsall and Bolton Abbey. Tasty,
wholesome snacks range from soups and
pâté to ploughman's, salads, sandwiches,
fried haddock and an excellent steak and
kidney pie. There are some delicious
desserts, too. Garden.   **Family pub**

Arkengarthdale   (B & B)   *C. B. Hotel*

Reeth, Near Richmond · *North Yorkshire*
Map 4 C2
Richmond (0748) 84265

Free House
Landlords Mr G. Gilbraith & Mr W. Dixon

BEDROOMS 8   Grades 1 & 2   £C (No dogs)
🍺 Webster's Pennine Bitter, Yorkshire Bitter;
Guinness; Carlsberg; cider.

Scenically situated in the heart of the
Yorkshire Dales, this friendly, welcoming
inn is a popular base for walking holidays.
Good-sized bedrooms are bright and
cheerful, with plenty of cupboard space.
One has its own bathroom, two others
shower cubicles. The beamed bar has a
warm, traditional appeal, and there's an
ample lounge with a section for tele-
viewing. No under-threes overnight. Patio.
                                 Family pub

Armathwaite   (B & B)   *Duke's Head Hotel*

Near Carlisle · *Cumbria* · Map 3 B1
Armathwaite (069 92) 226

Brewery Whitbread
Landlords Mr & Mrs D. B. Taylor

BEDROOMS 8   Grade 2   £C
🍺 Whitbread Mild, Trophy; Heineken; cider.

Trout and salmon fishing are popular
pastimes at this peaceful pub by the banks
of the river Eden. There's a lot of angling
talk in the pleasant lounge bar, which
features a grandfather clock and some
splendid antique chairs and tables. Eight
neatly kept little bedrooms, all with tea-
makers and washbasins, provide simple
comforts for an overnight stay. Garden.

Ascot   (Food)   *Stag*

63 High Street · *Berkshire* · Map 6 B3
Ascot (0990) 21622

Brewery Friary Meux
Landlords Mr & Mrs T. McCarthy

Chicken & ham hot pot £1.70 Vegetarian jacket
potato £1.10 (Last order 10.45pm)
🍺 Friary Meux Bitter; Ind Coope John Bull,
Double Diamond; Guinness; Skol. *Real ale*

Enjoy Ann McCarthy's daily blackboard
specials in the main bar or, in summer, at
one of the pavement tables at this welcoming main street pub. The choice might
range from pizza or a pasta dish to beef
Stroganoff, fish pie or Chinese chicken.
Home-made granary bread makes a good
accompaniment, and there are also sandwiches and burgers, as well as homely
desserts to round things off.
                          Family pub (lunchtime)

Ashburton *(B & B)* — *Exeter Inn*

26 West Street · *Devon* · Map 8 C4
Ashburton (0364) 52559

Free House
Landlords Mr & Mrs A. Shepherd

BEDROOMS 3 Grade 2 £C (No dogs)
🍺 Palmer's IPA, Bitter; Badger Best Bitter;
Usher's Best Bitter; Tetley's Bitter; Guinness;
Skol; cider. *Real ale*

Built more than 800 years ago to accommodate the builders of the village church,
this friendly inn retains a great deal of its
original charm. The beamed bar is delightfully old-fashioned and the comfortable
bedrooms are equally appealing, with
sloping floors and ceilings and odd little
corners. The bathroom they share is
modern and spotless. Patio. **Family pub**

Ashbury *(Food, B & B)* — *Rose & Crown Hotel*

Near Swindon, Wiltshire · *Oxfordshire*
Map 6 A3
Ashbury (079 371) 222

Free House
Landlord Mr Marcel Klein
BEDROOMS 10 Grade 2 £B
Steak & kidney pie £1.70 Ploughman's £1.35
🍺 Charrington's IPA; Stones Bitter;
Worthington 'E'; Guinness; Carling Black
Label; Tennent's Extra; Taunton cider. *Real ale*

Bar food is a popular feature at this sturdy
whitewashed village inn, which lies about
four miles from junction 15 of the M4.
Baked potatoes with various fillings provide tasty quick snacks, and more substantial items include bangers with bubble and
squeak, Cotswold hot pot and turkey curry.
Centrally heated bedrooms (all with TVs
and tea-makers) are in simple modern
style. Patio. **Family pub**

Ashcott *(Food)* — *Ashcott Inn*

Near Bridgwater · *Somerset* · Map 8 D3
Ashcott (0458) 210282
Free House
Landlords Peter, Allison & David Milne
Stuffed fillet of sole with salad £3.50 Oriental
ginger ice cream 75p (Last order 10pm. No bar
food Sun lunch)
🍺 Flowers Original; Eldridge Pope Dark
Brown; Dorchester Bitter; Guinness;
Heineken; Stella Artois; Taunton cider.
Real ale

There's no shortage of choice on the bar
menu of this trim 17th-century pub.
Starters include soup, ratatouille and
garlicky baked mushrooms, and besides
main courses like rainbow trout and lamb
cutlets there is a tempting range of daily
specials such as lasagne with herb bread or
pork chop with barbecue sauce. Garden.

Ashington *(Food)* — *Red Lion*

West Sussex · Map 6 B4
Ashington (0903) 892226

Free House
Landlords Nigel & Cathy Evans

Country casserole £2.45 Fish & meat salads
from £2.50 (Last order 10pm. No bar food Mon)
🍺 Hall & Woodhouse Badger Bitter,
Tanglefoot; King & Barnes Festive; Guinness;
Carlsberg; Foster's; cider. *Real ale*

Children are especially well catered for at
this large friendly pub on the A24, with a TV
room and light snacks like mini-burgers on
the bar menu. There are also sandwiches,
ploughman's, jumbo sausages, and more
substantial choices like grilled gammon,
savoury pancakes or steak and cider stew.
Closed Monday 1 Oct–1 May. Garden.
Family pub

Ashwell   *(Food)*   *Bushel & Strike Inn*

Mill Street, Near Baldock · *Hertfordshire*
Map 5 B2
Ashwell (046 274) 2394

Brewery Wells
Landlords Sandra & Tony Lynch
Cold roast rib of beef £2.75 Lamb & pork
brochette £2.50 (Last order 10pm)
🍺 Wells Eagle Bitter, Bombardier, Silver
Eagle; Guinness; Red Stripe; Kellerbräu.
Real ale

The garden is delightful in summer at this
charming village inn and the two cosy bars
provide a warm welcome on colder days.
Food from the buffet bar includes starters
like home-made soup, avocado with
prawns, salads, fried chicken and lamb
brochettes, as well as daily specials such as
a hot pot or pork in cider. Sandwiches too.

Ashwell   *(B & B)*   *Three Tuns Hotel*

6 High Street · *Hertfordshire* · Map 5 B2
Ashwell (046 274) 2387

Brewery Greene King
Landlord Mrs E. M. Harris

BEDROOMS 11   Grade 1   £B
🍺 Greene King Abbot Ale, IPA, Light Mild;
Guinness; Harp; Kronenbourg; Taunton
cider. *Real ale*

This two-storey brick-built hotel is the
social hub of a village that is both attractive
and historic. The quarry-tiled public bar is a
favourite local meeting place, and there's a
lounge bar with old lamps and prints.
There's some fine period furniture in the
comfortable bedrooms, four of which are in
a nearby Victorian house; all have TV.
Family pub

Askham   *(Food, B & B)*   *Punch Bowl*

Near Penrith · *Cumbria* · Map 3 B2
Hackthorpe (093 12) 443

Brewery Whitbread
Landlords Aubrey & Diana Zalk

BEDROOMS 5   Grade 2   £C   (No dogs)
Chicken curry £2.75 Rump steak £4.65
(Last order 9.30pm)
🍺 Whitbread Best Mild, Trophy Bitter;
Guinness; Heineken; cider.

Not far from the M6, this village pub is
winning friends with some very good
cooking. In the cottage bar or out on the
patio you can enjoy anything from sandwiches and steaks to a pancake tastily filled
with ham, chicken and mushrooms. The
home-made ice cream is delicious, too.
Five tidy bedrooms offer simple overnight
comforts.   **Family pub**

Askham   *(Food, B & B)*   *Queen's Head Inn*

Near Penrith · *Cumbria* · Map 3 B2
Hackthorpe (093 12) 225

Brewery Vaux
Landlords John & Anne Askew
BEDROOMS 6   Grade 1   £B   (No dogs)
Cottage pie with red cabbage £2 Oriental pork
& rice £3.50 (Last order 9pm)
🍺 Vaux Sunderland Bitter, Samson, Mild;
Lorimer's Scotch; Guinness; Tuborg; Taunton
cider. *Real ale*

Set in a peaceful village, this smartly kept
pub retains plenty of character in its old
beamed bars. Sandwiches, generous
salads and hot dishes like cottage pie are
always available and there are steak
suppers in the evening. The bedrooms are
pleasantly furnished and six of them have
their own well-fitted bathrooms. Children
under seven not accommodated overnight.
Family pub

Askrigg *(B & B)*   *King's Arms Hotel*

Market Place · *North Yorkshire* · Map 4 C2
Wensleydale (0969) 50258

Free House
Landlords Ray & Liz Hopwood

BEDROOMS 11 Grade 1 £B
Scottish & Newcastle Exhibition;
Younger's Scotch Bitter; McEwan's 80/-,
Export Lager; Taunton cider.

Scenes for a popular TV series were filmed
at this 17th-century coaching inn, where
the public bar with its huge fireplace and
cosy settles, and the panelled lounge with
ancestral portraits and a grandfather clock,
are full of character. Bedrooms, off steep
stairs and quaint passages, are handsomely furnished with antiques and quality
fabrics; all have TVs, tea-makers and good
private bathrooms.   **Family pub**

Asthall *(Food)*   *Maytime Inn*

Near Burford · *Oxfordshire* · Map 5 A2
Burford (099 382) 2068

Free House
Landlords Tim & May Morgan

French onion soup £1.50 Breast of chicken in
lobster sauce £5.25 (Last order 10.30pm)
Wadworth's Special Bitter, 6X; Morrell's
Varsity Bitter; Webster's Yorkshire Bitter;
Younger's Tartan; Foster's. *Real ale*

All ages and appetites are catered for at this
plush old stone pub, where the Morgans
present a bar menu of exceptional variety.
Smooth, creamy chicken liver pâté makes
an excellent starter or snack, and there
are pizzas and pasta, ploughman's and
omelettes, plus vegetarian specials and
substantial main-course dishes served with
good fresh vegetables. Simple sweets, and
a special children's menu. Garden.
Family pub

Aston Cantlow *(Food)*   *King's Head*

Near Stratford-upon-Avon · *Warwickshire*
Map 5 A2
Great Alne (078 981) 242

Brewery Whitbread
Landlords Di & Joe Saunders
Fisherman's pie £2.30 Red cherry cheesecake
roll £1 (Last order 9.45pm)
Flower's IPA, Best Bitter; Whitbread Best
Bitter; Guinness; Heineken; Stella Artois.
Real ale

The welcome could not be warmer at the
Saunders' black and white half-timbered
inn, where Shakespeare's parents held
their wedding breakfast in 1557. The food is
still a very popular feature, with snacks in
the beamed bars including soup and
ploughman's, cod bake and a well-
seasoned chilli con carne with rice. Red
cherry cheesecake roll makes an unusual
and delicious dessert. Garden.

Aswarby *(B & B)*   *Tally Ho*

Near Sleaford · *Lincolnshire* · Map 4 D4
Culverthorpe (052 95) 205

Free House
Landlords Mr & Mrs C. Davis

BEDROOMS 6 Grades 1 & 2 £B
Adnams Bitter; Bateman's Bitter;
Guinness; Ayingerbräu; Samuel Smith's Diät
Pils; cider. *Real ale*

Generations of eager feet, including those
of the Belvoir Hunt, have worn down the
stone steps leading into the cosy beamed
bar of this characterful 17th-century stone
inn. Bedrooms, in a converted stable block,
are contrastingly modern, with pretty
fabrics, tea-makers, colour TVs and neat
tiled bathrooms or showers. Standards
of housekeeping are impressively high.
Garden.

England

Bainbridge   *(B & B)*   *Rose & Crown Hotel*

Leyburn · *North Yorkshire* · Map 4 C2
Wensleydale (0969) 50225

Free House
Landlord Mr B. C. C. Thorpe

BEDROOMS 13   Grade 2   £A
🍺 Younger's No. 3 Ale, Scotch Bitter;
Newcastle Exhibition; McEwan's Export;
Kestrel; Taunton cider. *Real ale*

Yorkshire is renowned for its hospitality,
and you'll find it in abundance at this fine
old village inn. The famous Bainbridge
horn – traditionally blown to guide lost
travellers – is one of many curios that adorn
the entrance hall and bars. Spotlessly clean
bedrooms, furnished in a variety of styles,
modern to traditional, have colour TVs and
six have their own neat little shower rooms.
Patio.   **Family pub** (lunchtime)

Bamford   *(B & B)*   *Rising Sun Hotel*

Hope Road, Hope Valley · *Derbyshire*
Map 4 C3
Hope Valley (0433) 51323

Free House
Landlords John & Teresa Ellis

BEDROOMS 11   Grade 1   £B
🍺 Webster's Yorkshire Bitter, Dark Mild;
Guinness; Foster's; Carlsberg.

Outside Bamford on the A625, this low half-
timbered pub enjoys breathtaking views of
the surrounding Peak District. You can sit
out on the terrace in fine weather and there
are two cosy, relaxing bars. Attractively
furnished bedrooms have central heating,
fitted carpets, colour TVs and tea-makers.
Five have neatly fitted private bathrooms,
the rest shower cabinets. Good breakfasts.
Family pub

Bantham   *(B & B)*   *Sloop Inn*

Near Kingsbridge · *Devon* · Map 8 C4
Kingsbridge (0548) 560489

Free House
Landlord Mr Neil Girling

BEDROOMS 5   Grade 2   £C
🍺 Bass; Usher's Best Bitter; Worthington
Best Bitter; Guinness; Carlsberg Hof; Carling
Black Label; cider. *Real ale*

Once associated with the smuggling trade,
this welcoming old inn is just a short stroll
over the dunes from the beach. Black
beams and wooden benches add old-world
charm to the bar, where locals like to chat or
have a game of crib. Pretty bedrooms (four
with well-equipped bathrooms) have
simple contemporary furnishings and tea-
makers. Accommodation closed Christmas.
Patio.   **Family pub**

Barbon   *(Food, B & B)*   *Barbon Inn*

Near Kirkby Lonsdale · *Cumbria* · Map 3 B2
Barbon (046 836) 233

Free House
Landlord Mr K. Whitlock
BEDROOMS 11   Grade 1   £B
Morecambe Bay potted shrimps £1.85 Grilled
sirloin steak £4.95 (Last order 9pm.
No bar food Sat eve)
🍺 Theakston's Real Ale, Best Bitter, Old
Peculier; Foster's; cider. *Real ale*

This old whitewashed coaching inn enjoys
a quiet rural setting between the Lakes and
the Dales. The little residents' lounges are
cosy and intimate, and the bar offers some
enjoyable fare, from good thick mushroom
soup to salads, steaks and a delicious fruit
pie, plus a roast for Sunday lunch. Comfortable, prettily papered bedrooms are
attractively furnished and equipped with
tea-makers. Garden.   **Family pub**

Barnard Castle   *(Food)*   *Red Well Inn*

Harmire Road · *Co. Durham* · Map 4 C2
Teesdale (0833) 37002
Free House
Landlords Mr & Mrs M. J. Rudd &
Mr & Mrs K. M. Thompson
Mussels in white wine & garlic butter £1.90 Fried
beef in hot pepper sauce with rice £3.20 (Last
order 9.30pm. No bar food Sun & Mon eves)
🍺 John Smith's Bitter, Magnet; Theakston's
Best Bitter; Guinness; Hofmeister; Harp;
Taunton cider. *Real ale*

Standards remain high in the pleasant
lounge bar of this creeper-clad pub. Staff
cheerfully dispense substantial main
courses, grills and salads – perhaps braised
ham florentine, richly flavoured steak and
kidney pie or stuffed Whitby lemon sole.
Smooth chicken liver pâté, filled seafood
pancake or a quiche salad for a lighter bite.
Family pub

Bassenthwaite Lake   *(Food, B & B)*   *Pheasant Inn*

Near Cockermouth · *Cumbria* · Map 3 B1
Bassenthwaite Lake (059 681) 234

Free House
Landlords Mr & Mrs W. E. Barrington-Wilson

BEDROOMS 20   Grade 1   £A+   (No dogs)
Pâté £1.45 Cumberland pork, ham & egg
pie £1.60 (No bar food eves)
🍺 Theakston's Best Bitter; Bass; Guinness;
Carlsberg. *Real ale*

Open fires and well-polished furniture
make the three lounges of this peaceful
lakeside inn very inviting and the cheerful
bedrooms provide homely comfort. Simple
lunchtime snacks available in the cosy bar
range from potted shrimps, pâté, and
savoury quiche to smoked trout, a
Cumberland sausage platter or a hot daily
special. Garden.   **Family pub**

Bath   *(Food)*   *Park Tavern*

3 Park Lane · *Avon* · Map 8 D3
Bath (0225) 25174

Brewery Courage
Landlords Mr & Mrs D. Collins

Chicken livers £1.85 Devilled kidneys £1.85
(Last order 9.30pm)
🍺 Courage Best Bitter, Directors Bitter, JC;
John Smith's; Guinness; Hofmeister; Taunton
cider. *Real ale*

Mrs Collins' tasty and imaginative bar
meals draw the crowds to her simple pub
with its own garden. Choices on a hugely
varied menu might include mussels in
white wine, pasta dishes, curries, an assortment of pizzas and the ever-popular
devilled kidneys. For a lighter snack, there
are jacket potatoes, ploughman's and
salads. No sweets, however.

Bawburgh   *(Food)*   *Kings Head*

Harts Lane, Near Norwich · *Norfolk*
Map 5 D1
Norwich (0603) 744977

Free House
Landlords Mr & Mrs A. A. Wimmer
Beef chasseur £3.60 Crab quiche & salad £2.20
(Last order 10.30pm)
🍺 Wethered's Bitter; Adnams Bitter;
Stewart & Paterson Bitter; Whitbread Mild;
Guinness; Foster's; Carlsberg; cider. *Real ale*

Some very enjoyable snacks are to be
found in the quaint old bars of this charming pub opposite the village green. For a
quick bite there's pâté and various ploughman's, and you can also tuck into beef
chasseur, spicy lamb casserole and crab in
a wine sauce. There's a squash court and
bowling green for the energetic, and a
garden for fine weather.   **Family pub**

Beaulieu   *(Food)*   *Montagu Arms Hotel*

Hampshire · Map 6 A4
Beaulieu (0590) 612324

Free House Greenclose Hotels
Landlord Mr J. Talbot
Venison sausages & vegetables £2.25
Curry £1.75 (No bar food eves)
🍺 Wadsworth 6X; Flower's Original Bitter;
Whitbread Best Bitter; McEwans's Export;
Guinness; Heineken; Löwenbräu; cider.
Real ale

Spats Bar is a lively, popular spot for lunchtime snacks at this comfortable former
monk's hostelry and coaching inn. Start
with the day's soup – our broccoli was
really delicious – and go on to roast
chicken, venison sausages, perhaps a curry
in winter. Other choices include open
sandwiches, interesting salads and yummy
sherry trifle. *For accommodation see Egon
Ronay's Lucas Hotel & Restaurant Guide
1985.*

Beauworth   *(Food, B & B)*   *Milbury's*

Near Cheriton · *Hampshire* · Map 6 B4
Bramdean (096 279) 248

Free House
Landlords Greg & Jaqueline Gregory
BEDROOMS 6   Grade 2   £C
Crab salad £2.95 Chilli con carne £2.65
(Last order 10.30pm)
🍺 Wethereds Bitter; Flowers Original;
Marston's Pedigree; Gale's Horndean Special
Bitter; Wadworth's 6X. *Real ale*

Standing on the Cheriton-Bishops
Waltham road on the site of an old mill, this
listed building boasts many fascinating
features, including a huge treadwheel and
a 300-foot-deep well. Tasty bar fare ranges
from French onion soup to salads, grilled
trout and sirloin steak, and sweets include
a scrumptious lemon and sultana
cheesecake. Recently restored bedrooms
have pretty decor and solid traditional
furnishings.   **Family pub**

Beckley   *(Food)*   *Abingdon Arms*

Near Oxford · *Oxfordshire* · Map 6 A3
Stanton St John (086 735) 311

Brewery Halls
Landlords Mr & Mrs Greatbatch

Spiced game pie with port sauce £2.65
Roast beef £4.65 (Last order 10.15pm. No
bar food Sun eve)
🍺 Halls Harvest Bitter; Ind Coope Burton Ale;
Double Diamond; Guinness; Skol. *Real ale*

Mrs Greatbatch's excellent home cooking
attracts a loyal following to this delightful
converted house with a large and pretty
garden. Rare roast rib of beef is a perennial
favourite, along with ploughman's, prawns
in creole sauce, quiche lorraine and
chicken, ham and mushroom pie. Fish soup
is a popular winter warmer, seafood salad a
summer treat for two. Puds include a nice
raspberry torte.

Bedford   *(B & B)*   *Embankment Hotel*

The Embankment · *Bedfordshire* · Map 5 B2
Bedford (0234) 217791

Brewery Charrington
Landlord Mr J. Bradnam

BEDROOMS 20   Grade 1   £A
🍺 Charrington's IPA, Stones Bitter,
Worthington 'E'; Carling Black Label;
Tennent's Extra. *Real ale*

Built in Victorian times, but with a mock-
Tudor facade, this recently refurbished
hotel stands near the centre of town overlooking the river Ouse. Bedrooms of
various sizes provide accommodation of a
high standard: modern fitted units, direct-
dial telephones, remote-control TVs,
trouser presses. Nearly all have their own
neat bath or shower rooms. Public rooms
include a smart reception area and comfortable bar.

Bedford   *(Food)*   *Park*

98 Kimbolton Road · *Bedfordshire* · Map 5 B2
Bedford (0234) 54093

Brewery Wells
Landlord Mr E. Cheeseman
Choice of 3 cheeses, pickles, bread £1.65
Pâté, pickles, bread £1.35 (No bar food eves or
Sun)
🍺 Wells Eagle Bitter, Bombardier, Noggin;
Guinness; Kellerbräu; Red Stripe; cider.
Real ale

A selection of more than 20 fine English
cheeses is the strong point of this smart
beamed pub. Served with pickles and fresh
granary bread, they make a splendid lunchtime snack. If you're not in the mood for
cheese, there are also home-made pies,
quiche, soup and warming winter specials
like Lancashire hot pot. Simple sweets to
finish. Patio.

Beer   *(B & B)*   *Anchor Inn*

Fore Street · *Devon* · Map 8 C3
Seaton (0297) 20386

Free House
Landlords Mr & Mrs D. Boalch

BEDROOMS 9   Grade 2   £C   (No dogs)
🍺 Eldridge Pope Royal Oak, Dorset IPA;
Flowers Original; Guinness; Carling Black
Label; Faust Export; Taunton cider. *Real ale*

This handsome gabled inn stands near the
sea in a pleasant fishing village once
notorious for smugglers. Public rooms
include two traditionally furnished bars
and a little reception-lounge, and there are
nine neat, attractive bedrooms. All have
tea-makers and colour TVs and some enjoy
lovely sea views. Bathrooms are modern.
No children under seven overnight.
Accommodation closed 1 week Christmas.
Garden.   **Family pub**

Beetham   *(Food, B & B)*   *Wheatsheaf Hotel*

Near Milnthorpe · *Cumbria* · Map 3 B2
Milnthorpe (044 82) 2123

Free House
Landlord Mrs F. Miller

BEDROOMS 8   Grade 2   £B
Cottage pie £1.40 Hot pot £1.30 (Last order
10pm)
🍺 Slater's Bitter; Stones Bitter, Mild;
Guinness; Carlsberg; Taunton cider. *Real ale*

Mrs Miller's welcoming corner pub, just
across the road from the church, makes a
useful halt for travellers on the A6. The
beamed bar is a cosy place to enjoy homely
snacks like sweet and savoury pies, freshly
made sandwiches, hot pot and appetising
cold meat salads. Eight neatly furnished
bedrooms all have washbasins and electric
blankets and there are four well-kept
bathrooms.

Belsay   *(Food)*   *Highlander Inn*

Hygham Dykes · *Northumberland* · Map 4 C1
Belsay (066 181) 220

Owners Newcastle Inns
Landlord Barrie Dixon

Game pie with salad £2.25 Haggis with potato
& turnip £1.70 (Last order 9.30pm)
🍺 Younger's No. 3 Ale; Scottish & Newcastle
Exhibition, Newcastle Bitter; Guinness; Harp;
Carlsberg Hof; Taunton cider. *Real ale*

South of Belsay on the A696, this handsome converted farmhouse attracts the
crowds with a good range of hot and cold
bar snacks. You can help yourself from the
buffet of pies, salads and home-cooked
meats, or choose from a menu of daily
specials like sweetbreads with rice, a roast,
or an excellent steak and kidney pie. Good
home-made sweets, too. Courtyard.

England

Benenden   *(Food)*   ### King William IV

The Street · *Kent* · Map 6 C3
Benenden (0580) 240636

Brewery Shepherd Neame
Landlords Nigel & Hilary Douglas

Duck liver pâté £1 Supreme of chicken
Wellington £3.45 (Last order 9.30pm. No bar
food Sun)
🍺 Eldridge Pope Master Brew, Mild;
Guinness; Hurlimann; Taunton cider. *Real ale*

The Douglases are the affable hosts at this
pleasant village pub, whose lounge bar
sports oak beams and a fine old fireplace.
Snacks are a popular feature, and the blackboard menus offers a good variety, from
simple ploughman's or garlic mussels to
onion tart, chicken curry and full-flavoured
beef and red wine casserole. Leave room
for a delicious sweet like our lovely strawberry confection. Garden.

Berkeley Road   *(B & B)*   ### Prince of Wales Hotel

Near Berkeley · *Gloucestershire* · Map 7 D2
Dursley (0453) 810474

Free House
Landlords David & Jane Taylor

BEDROOMS 8   Grade 1   £A
🍺 Marston's Pedigree; Theakston's Best
Bitter; Whitbread's West Country Pale Ale;
Guinness; Harlech Lager; cider. *Real ale*

Housekeeping and maintenance are both
excellent at this efficiently run hotel alongside the A38. The bedrooms are comfortable and well equipped, with smart modern
furnishings, colour TVs, direct-dial telephones and tea-makers. All rooms have
attractively tiled private bathrooms with
modern suites. Public areas include a
spacious bar and neat reception-lounge,
and there's a very pretty garden. Good
breakfasts.   **Family pub**

Bewdley   *(Food, B & B)*   ### Black Boy Hotel

Kidderminster Road · *Hereford & Worcester*
Map 7 D1
Bewdley (0299) 402119
Free House
Ladlords Mr A. R. Wilson
BEDROOMS 28   Grade 2   £B
Cottage pie £1.15 Braised oxtail & vegetables
£1.95 (No bar food eves & all Sun)
🍺 Mitchells & Butlers Springfield Bitter,
Bitter, Mild; Guinness; Tennent's Pilsner;
Carling Black Label. *Real ale*

The club-like bar of this fine old inn is a
popular place at lunchtime, when honest,
homely fare ranges from rich, nourishing
turkey soup to salads, sandwiches and a
splendid casserole of lamb's liver and
onions. Tangy lemon cheesecake to finish.
Bedrooms vary from spacious and handsomely furnished to smaller and simpler.
There's a comfortably traditional lounge
and a quiet writing room.   **Family pub**

Bexhill   *(Food)*   ### Wilton Court

Wilton Road, Marina · *East Sussex* · Map 6 C4
Bexhill (0424) 210208

Free House
Landlord Mrs Frances M. Burt

Cottage pie £1.50 Sherry trifle 85p
(Last order 10pm)
🍺 Courage Directors Bitter; Bass; Fullers
London Pride; Whitbreads Tusker; Guinness;
cider. *Real ale*

Mrs Burt's seaside pub is just the place to
go for a tasty and sustaining lunch. Daily
roasts like shoulder of lamb or beef sirloin
top the bill, and dressed crab, whether
served in a salad or a sandwich, is another
popular choice. Home-made soup, steak
and kidney pie, and some delicious
desserts are also on offer. Evening fare
consists of soup and sandwiches only.
                                  Family pub

Bibury *(Food, B & B)*

Catherine Wheel

Near Cirencester · *Gloucestershire* · Map 6 A3
Bibury (028 574) 250

Brewery Courage
Landlord Mr Bill May
BEDROOMS 2   Grade 2   £C
Bibury trout £3.50 Olde English sausages £1.80
(Last order 10pm)
 Courage Best Bitter, JC; Simonds Bitter;
Guinness; Hofmeister; Kronenbourg; Taunton
cider. *Real ale*

With its massive walls, oak doors and low
beamed ceilings, this Cotswold-stone pub
possesses considerable period charm. The
menu revolves around simple snacks, well-
prepared and generously served; soups
and pâté, home-cooked beef, plump, herby
bangers, winter casseroles, trout from the
farm down the road. The two bedrooms –
sturdily furnished and smartly maintained –
share a splendidly equipped bathroom.
Garden. **Family pub**

Biddenden *(Food)*   ★

Three Chimneys

Kent · Map 6 C3
Biddenden (0580) 291472

Free House
Landlords Christopher & Pippa Sayers

Avocado mousse £1.45 Sherried
kidneys £3.50 (Last order 10pm)
 Adnams Bitter; Marston's Pedigree;
Harvey's Best Bitter; Godson's Black Horse;
Guinness, Stella Artois; cider. *Real ale*

Real ale, cosy beamed bars and charming
hosts are just some of the assets of this old
country pub. There's also an enormous
garden for fine weather, and excellent bar
food ranging from warming soups to
dishes like leek gratin, cheese and onion
flan, stuffed shoulder of lamb and home-
baked ham. Apple charlotte and date and
walnut pudding are among the irresistible
desserts. **Family pub**

Biddestone *(Food)*

Biddestone Arms

Near Chippenham · *Wiltshire* · Map 7 D2
Corsham (0249) 714377

Free House
Landlords Roy and Pam Chippendale

Chilli con carne £1.50 Stilton
ploughman's £1.25 (Last order 10pm)
 Wadworth's 6X; Usher's Best Bitter, PA;
Flowers Best Bitter; Whitbread West Country
Bitter; Guinness; cider. *Real ale*

Familiar bar fare is offered in good variety
at this attractive stone pub standing at one
end of the village. Sandwiches, ploughman's and pâté are popular choices for
quick snacks, with other items running the
gamut from soup and tasty Cornish pasties
to omelettes, seafood and sirloin steak. For
Sunday lunch there's a four-course menu
or a basket meal. Garden.

Bidford-on-Avon *(Food, B & B)*

White Lion Hotel

High Street · *Warwickshire* · Map 5 A2
Bidford-on-Avon (0789) 773309

Free House
Landlord Mr John McDonald
BEDROOMS 15   Grades 1 & 2   £B
Savoury baked egg with salmon £2.10 Baked
cheesecake 85p (No bar food eves or Sun)
 Everards Old Original; Newcastle Bitter;
Younger's Shire Mild; Tuborg; McEwan's
lager; cider. *Real ale*

A riverside terrace is a summertime bonus
at this cosy old hostelry by an ancient stone
bridge. Lunchtime snacks are simple and
satisfying: warming soups, filled jacket
potatoes, ploughman's platters, savoury
baked eggs, with some old-fashioned puddings to fill any gaps. Good-sized bedrooms
(six with well-appointed private bathrooms)
range from traditional to modern in style; all
have tea-makers and TVs. There's a comfortable residents' lounge.

England

Bierton   (Food)   Red Lion

Near Aylesbury · *Buckinghamshire* · Map 5 B2
Aylesbury (0296) 24453

Brewery Aylesbury
Landlords Mr & Mrs L. Bishop

Chicken & ham pie £1.25 Fillet of plaice £3.60
(Last order 9pm. No bar food Sat & Sun)
🍺 ABC Bitter; Benskins Light Mild; Bass;
Ben Truman; Guinness; Carlsberg.

Run by the Bishop family for several generations, this friendly pub offers a different
menu in each of its bars. The simple public
bar is the place for homely snacks like cauliflower cheese, shepherd's pie or lasagne,
while the plush lounge bar features more
elaborate choices like grilled gammon
steak and veal escalope with ginger wine.
Try a lemon meringue pie or raspberry flan
for dessert. Patio.

Binfield   Stag & Hounds

A historic hunting lodge, from which Elizabeth I watched maypole
dancing on the green. In addition to the cosy, characterful lounge bar
with sturdy old settles and pews, there are several little beamed
snugs in the converted stables. Just outside stands the stump of an
ancient elm which marked the centre of Windsor Great Forest.

Forest Road · *Berkshire* · Map 6 B3
Bracknell (0344) 483553
Brewery Courage   *Landlords* Mr & Mrs B. Howard
🍺 Courage Best Bitter, Directors Bitter, John Courage Bitter;
Guinness; Hofmeister; Kronenbourg 1664; Taunton cider. *Real ale*

Bircham   (B & B)   Kings Head

Near King's Lynn · *Norfolk* · Map 5 C1
Syderstone (048 523) 265

Free House
Landlords Sutton family

BEDROOMS 5   Grade 1   £C
🍺 Adnams Bitter; Bass; Marston's Owd
Rodger (winter only); Stones Bitter; Carling
Black Label; Tennent's Extra; Taunton cider.
Real ale

Guests receive a warm, friendly welcome
from the Sutton family at this rambling pub
on the edge of the Sandringham estate. The
homely lounge bar and traditional public
bar are popular with those wanting a tipple;
there's also a cosy TV lounge. Sturdily
furnished bedrooms with attractive soft
furnishings provide excellent comfort; all
have tea-coffee making facilities and
modern bath/shower rooms. Accommodation closed Christmas week.   **Family pub**

Bishop Wilton   (B & B)   Fleece Inn

Near York · *Humberside* · Map 4 D2
Bishop Wilton (075 96) 251

Free House
Landlords Allan, Barbara & Irene Hawcroft

BEDROOMS 4   Grade 2   £C (No dogs)
🍺 Theakston's Best Bitter; John Smith's
Bitter; Tetley's Bitter; Guinness; Skol;
Carlsberg Hof; Taunton cider. *Real ale*

The red-brick facade of this village pub
blends in well with its peaceful surroundings. Darkened beams give a rustic
appeal to the pleasant lounge with TV.
Tissues and books strike a homely note in
the bedrooms, which are cheerful, spotless
and beautifully warm; they share a sparkling bathroom. Simple, hearty breakfasts
are served in the tiny dining room. No
children under 12 overnight.   **Family pub**

Bishop's Lydeard   *(B & B)*   *Lethbridge Arms*

Near Taunton · *Somerset* · Map 8 C3
Bishop's Lydeard (0823) 432234

Brewery Whitbread
Landlords Mr & Mrs A. J. Wilkins

BEDROOMS 6   Grade 2   £C   (No dogs)
🍺 Flowers Original; Whitbread Best Bitter,
IPA, Trophy; Bass; Guinness; Heineken; Stella
Artois; Taunton cider. *Real ale*

Dating back to the 14th century, this cosy
village inn at the foot of the Quantock Hills
is a popular place for a drink and a chat. Pub
games are a feature, and there is a comfortable TV lounge for residents. Simply
furnished bedrooms provide adequate
comforts and the public bathrooms are well
kept. No children overnight.   **Family pub**

Bishop's Lydeard   *(Food)*   *Rose Cottage*

Near Taunton · *Somerset* · Map 8 C3
Bishop's Lydeard (0823) 432394

Free House
Landlords Mr & Mrs P. Dale-Thomas

Fish & prawn mornay £4.25 Vegetarian
moussaka £2.65 (Last order 9.30pm)
🍺 Eldridge Pope Dorset IPA, 1880 Ale;
Carlsberg Pilsner; cider. *Real ale*

Excellent food is a top priority at this
attractive little roadside pub. Mrs Dale-
Thomas's bar menu might include fresh
vegetable soup, quiche, smoked salmon
mousse, sweet and sour chicken with
pasta, and some delicious sweets. There's
also a formal à la carte menu in the evening.
Closed Sun, Mon, 1st two weeks November
and 2 weeks from 24 December. Patio.

Bishop's Waltham   *(Food)*   *White Horse*

Beeches Hill · *Hampshire* · Map 6 A4
Bishop's Waltham (048 93) 2532

Brewery Whitbread
Landlords Arthur & Carol Noot

Rabbit pie £1.60 Tandoori chicken £3 (Last
order 10pm. No bar food Mon in winter)
🍺 Flower's Original; Wethered's Bitter;
Whitbread Strong Country Bitter; Guinness;
cider. *Real ale*

Much loved by the locals, this splendid little
inn provides wholesome, tasty food in the
most convivial and welcoming of surroundings. Carol Noot's homely offerings
could include familiar favourites like steak
and kidney pie and chilli con carne, with an
Indian dish such as lamb biryani to ring the
changes. Sandwiches and salads, too, with
jam roly-poly for a truly traditional finale.
Garden with children's play area.

Blacko   *(Food, B & B)*   *Moorcock Inn*

Gisburn Road, Near Nelson · *Lancashire*
Map 4 C3
Nelson (0282) 64186

Brewery Thwaites
Landlords Peter & Kathy Brandstatter
BEDROOMS 3   Grade 2   £C
Steak & kidney pie & chips £2.20 Savoury
pancake & chips £2.20 (Last order 11pm)
🍺 Thwaites Bitter, Best Mild; Guinness;
Kronenbourg; Stein.

Peter Brandstatter, landlord of this converted farmhouse on the Lancashire fells,
comes from Austria and his bar menu
includes Continental treats like bratwurst
with sauerkraut and rösti potatoes. There's
also a good choice of more familiar items
such as steak and kidney pie, omelettes,
lasagne and steakburger with onion sauce.
Overnight guests have three comfortable
bedrooms with their own TVs and shower
units.   **Family pub**

England

Blackpool (Food)

Grosvenor Hotel

Cookson Street · *Lancashire* · Map 3 B3
Blackpool (0253) 25096

Brewery Bass
Landlords John & Jackie McKeown

Macaroni cheese with ham £1.70 Paella £1.70
(No bar food eves or Sun)
🍺 Bass, Dark Mild; Stones Bitter; Guinness;
Carling Black Label; Taunton cider. *Real ale*

Welcoming landlords John and Jackie
McKeown provide a splendid range of
lunchtime food at this large Victorian pub.
Besides soup, sandwiches and omelettes
for a light bite, you can choose a more
filling hot special like breaded haddock,
mixed grill or hearty minced beef pie with
chips and fresh vegetables. There's also a
cold buffet in summer.

Blakesley (B & B)

Bartholomew Arms

Near Towcester · *Northamptonshire*
Map 5 B2
Blakesley (0327) 860292

Free House
Landlords Mr & Mrs C. A. Hackett

BEDROOMS 5 Grade 1 £C (No dogs)
🍺 Marston's Pedigree; Younger's Scotch
Bitter, Tartan; Newcastle Bitter; Guinness;
Carlsberg Hof; Taunton cider. *Real ale*

Soap-box racing is a star local attraction
and Mr Hackett's delightful little pub is a
great favourite with both drivers and spectators. The three rustic bars are cosy drinking places, and there are five comfortable,
prettily furnished bedrooms, all with TVs.
The public bathroom that they share is tiled
and well kept. Garden.   **Family pub**

Bledington (Food, B & B)

King's Head

The Green, Near Kingham · *Gloucestershire*
Map 5 A2
Kingham (060 871) 365
Free House
Landlords Rita & Graham Smith
BEDROOMS 3 Grade 1 £B (No dogs)
Rack of lamb £5.20 Mushroom & prawn
pancake £2.75 (Last order 10.45pm)
🍺 Wadsworth's 6X, Devizes Bitter; John
Smith's Bitter; Younger's Tartan; Guinness;
Löwenbräu; Heineken; cider. *Real ale*

A delightful 16th-century village inn, complete with landscaped gardens and a little
stream. In the beamed bars, where the
snooker memorabilia are a major talking
point, you'll eat heartily and well off traditional English fare like ploughman's
platters, home-baked pies and enormous
racks of lamb. Pretty bedrooms are comfortable and well equipped, with TVs, tea-
makers and neat bathrooms.   **Family pub**

Bletchingley (B & B)

Whyte Harte

High Street · *Surrey* · Map 6 C3
Godstone (0883) 843231

Brewery Allied Breweries
Landlords Mr & Mrs Derek King

BEDROOMS 9 Grade 2 £A (No dogs)
🍺 Burton Ale; Friary Meux Bitter; John
Bull Bitter; Guinness; Skol; Löwenbräu; cider.
Real ale

Easy to spot with its striking white-painted
exterior, this popular village pub has a
history that goes back to the 14th century.
The large, convivial bar has a splendid
inglenook fireplace where a welcome log
fire roars in winter. Bedrooms in the old
part have a delightfully cottagey feel, while
others are more modern and have their
own bathrooms. The beamed bar is large
and convivial and there's a tiny TV room.
Garden.

Blickling (Food, B & B)

Buckinghamshire Arms

Near Aylsham · *Norfolk* · Map 5 D1
Aylsham (026 373) 2133

Free House
Landlord Mr Nigel Elliott
BEDROOMS 3 Grade 1 £B
Smoked salmon salad £3.20 Home-made
pâté £2.20 (Last order 10pm)
🍺 Adnams Bitter, IPA; Greene King Abbot
Ale; Ind Coope Burton Ale, John Bull;
Guinness; cider. *Real ale*

Nigel Elliott offers good food and a friendly
welcome in this handsome 17th-century
hostelry. On the bar menu is simple fare
like delicious stockpot soup, a few hors
d'oeuvre platters (our seafood one was
excellent), plus salads, sandwiches and hot
dishes such as toad-in-the-hole. Comfortable bedrooms (one with a four-poster), all
with TVs, share an old-fashioned bathroom. Lots of tables for outdoor eating.
Family pub

Bollington (Food)

Church House Inn

24 Church Street, Nr Macclesfield · *Cheshire*
Map 4 C3
Bollington (0625) 74014
Free House
Landlord Leonard Boyd
Steak & kidney pie with vegetables £2.60
Crab sandwich 65p (Last order 9.30pm. No bar
food Tues eve)
🍺 Tetley's Bitter, Mild; Ruddle's County;
Saxon Cross Bitter; Carlsberg Export;
Guinness; cider. *Real ale*

Tasty home cooking draws the crowds,
especially at lunchtime, to this sturdy pub
furnished with padded church pews. Soup
or mushrooms in garlic butter make an
excellent start, and there are satisfying
main courses like goulash, lasagne and
beef and orange in cider. There are sandwiches (at lunchtime only) and salads, too,
as well as delicious sweets like bilberry pie
or crisp almond torte.

Boot (Food, B & B)

Woolpack Inn

Eskdale · *Cumbria* · Map 3 B2
Eskdale (094 03) 230

Free House
Landlords Mr & Mrs J. G. Pease

BEDROOMS 7 Grade 1 £C
Ploughman's lunch £1.45 Sandwiches 75p
(No bar food eves)
🍺 Younger's Scotch Bitter; Newcastle
Exhibition; McEwan's Lager; Taunton cider.

The Pease family's friendly inn is a welcoming haven for hikers in the Eskdale valley. At
lunchtime hearty soups, generously filled
sandwiches and ploughman's cater for the
hungry in the cosy bar (only sandwiches on
Sundays), and there are seven cheerful,
roomy bedrooms with tea-makers and a
neat public bathroom. Two lounges include
one with TV. Rooms closed 1 Nov-
31 March, when bar is open Fri and Sat eves
only. **Family pub**

Boscastle (B & B)

Wellington Hotel

The Harbour · *Cornwall* · Map 8 B3
Boscastle (084 05) 203

Free House
Landlord Mr G. J. Stedman

BEDROOMS 21 Grade 2 £C
🍺 Flowers Original; St Austell Best;
Whitbread Best Bitter; Usher's Triple Crown;
Guinness; Carlsberg Hof; cider. *Real ale*

This one-time coaching inn close to the
little harbour remains a popular stopping
place for travellers. Drinkers can choose
between the simply furnished lounge bar
and the spacious public bar with its rough-
stone walls and bar billiards; and there's
also a quiet TV lounge. Comfortable,
brightly decorated bedrooms with radios
have mostly built-in units, and compact
bathrooms are up to date. Accommodation
closed November–February. **Family pub**

Boston   *(B & B)*   New England Hotel

49 Wide Bargate · *Lincolnshire* · Map 5 C1
Boston (0205) 65255

Owners Anchor Hotels
Landlords Mr & Mrs W. N. Davies

BEDROOMS 25   Grade 1   £A+ (No dogs)
📭 Old Tom Mild; John Smith's Bitter;
Hofmeister. *Real ale*

Accommodation is first class at this well-maintained, brick-built pub in the centre of town. All the bedrooms have been smartly modernised, with fitted units, tea-makers, colour TVs and radio-alarms. There's plenty of writing space, too, and every room has its own compact tiled bathroom. Note the fine plasterwork ceiling in the spacious bar, which is a favourite local meeting place. **Family pub**

Boston Spa   *(B & B)*   Royal Hotel

High Street · *West Yorkshire* · Map 4 C3
Boston Spa (0937) 842142

Owners Chef & Brewer
Landlords Mr & Mrs William Patterson

BEDROOMS 7   Grade 1   £B
📭 Webster's Yorkshire Bitter, Green Label Best; Guinness; Carlsberg; Foster's; cider. *Real ale*

About a mile east of the A1 on the A659, this smartly painted inn makes a comfortable overnight stop. Bedrooms have good fitted carpets, duvets, tea-makers and radios, and they share a neatly kept public bathroom. Guests can relax with a drink in the cosy beamed bar or watch TV in the residents' lounge. Excellent breakfasts. Garden. **Family pub**

Bottesford   *(Food)*   Red Lion

Grantham Road · *Nottinghamshire* · Map 5 B1
Bottesford (0949) 42218

Brewery Kimberley
Landlords Mr & Mrs M. Kay

Steak & kidney pie £2.25 Apple crumble 70p
(Last order 10.30pm)
📭 Hardy & Hansons Best Mild, Best Bitter; Guinness; Stella Artois; Heineken; cider. *Real ale*

Mick and Jill Kay are friendly, professional hosts at this neat whitewashed pub near Belvoir Castle. The two bars – spacious lounge, snug public – offer a varied menu, from chip butties and cheeseburgers to quiches, salads and tasty pies (cottage, fisherman's, mince with mushrooms and onions). There's often a roast, especially on Sunday. Simple sweets such as apple crumble and cheesecake. Garden. **Family pub**

Bourton-on-the-Hill   *(B & B)*   Horse & Groom

Near Moreton-in-Marsh · *Gloucestershire*
Map 5 A2
Blockley (0386) 700413

Free House
Landlord Mr J. L. Aizpuru

BEDROOMS 3   Grade 2   £C No dogs
📭 Bass, Toby Bitter; Worthington 'E';
Tennent's Lager; Carling Black Label. *Real ale*

Pictures of racehorses adorn the rugged bar walls of this handsome sandstone pub with a pretty garden and nice views of the Cotswolds. Simple comforts for an overnight stay (no children) are provided by three spacious, centrally heated bedrooms, all with shower cubicles and washbasins. There's a good public bathroom. Accommodation closed December–January. Garden.

Bowdon *(Food)*   *Griffin*

Stamford Road, Near Altrincham
Cheshire · Map 3 B3
061-928 1211

Owners Pennine Host
Landlords Tony & June Lee
Prawn & coleslaw barmcake £1.10 Home-
cooked ham salad £2.95 (No bar food
eves & Sun)
🍺 Wilsons Great Northern Bitter, Mild;
Guinness; Carlsberg; Foster's. *Real ale*

The Lees are carrying on a tradition of hospitality that dates back to Georgian times at
this white-painted pub opposite the parish
church. In the bar there's a simple bill of fare
consisting of soup, pâté, ploughman's and
toasted sandwiches. Or try a traditional
barmcake with topside of beef or prawn and
coleslaw. The salad bar offers an excellent
selection of imaginative salads to accompany the choice from the cold table – perhaps turkey pie or smoked mackerel. Patio.

Bowes *(B & B)*   *Ancient Unicorn*

Near Barnard Castle · *Co. Durham* · Map 4 C2
Teesdale (0833) 28321

Free House
Landlords Bob & Jean Saunders

BEDROOMS 11   Grade 2   £B
🍺 Piper Scotch Bitter; Worthington Pale Ale;
Bass Best Mild; Carling Black Label; Taunton
cider.

Dating from the early part of the 16th
century, this sturdy coaching inn has been
brought up to date by Bob and Jean
Saunders. Bedrooms in the converted
stables provide modest comforts for an
overnight stay: all have modern furniture,
TVs, tea-makers and private bath or
showers rooms. A log fire is a welcoming
sight in the convivial beamed bar. Patio.
Family pub

Bowland Bridge *(Food, B & B)*   *Hare & Hounds*

Grange-over-Sands · *Cumbria* · Map 3 B2
Crosthwaite (044 88) 333

Free House
Landlords Peter & Barbara Thompson

BEDROOMS 7   Grade 1   £B
Salmon salad £2.95 Chicken curry £2.50 (Last
order 9.30pm)
🍺 Tetley's Traditional, Bitter, Mild;
Guinness; Skol; Oranjeboom; cider. *Real ale*

Well looked after by its delightful owners,
this fine old inn enjoys a quiet position in a
pleasant valley. The beamed bar is a comfortable place to enjoy tasty snacks, from
sandwiches and salads to pizzas, steak and
chilli con carne. Bedrooms in the old
building have considerable period charm;
the others, with private facilities, are
smartly modern. All have colour TVs.
Garden.   **Family pub**

Box *(Food, B & B)*   ★   *Chequers*

Market Place, Near Corsham · *Wiltshire*
Map 7 D2
Box (0225) 742 383
Brewery Usher
Landlords Ken & Jackie Martin
Beef curry £4 Steaks £4.95 (Last
order 10pm)
BEDROOMS 1   Grade 2   £B   (No dogs)
🍺 Usher's PA, Best Bitter, Founder's Ale,
Country Bitter; Guinness; Holsten; cider.
Real ale

Hospitality is a way of life at this charming
17th-century pub, where Malaysian-born
Jackie Martin produces some outstanding
bar food. Her curries – two days in the
making – are renowned locally, and steaks
are also very popular. More traditional
lunchtime fare – ploughman's and pies –
with a summer cold table. Superb apple pie
to finish. There's a single attractive bedroom with modern shower room.
Family pub

Boxford (Food) | Fleece

Near Colchester · *Suffolk* · Map 5 D2
Boxford (0787) 210247

Brewery Tollemache & Cobbold
Landlords Mr & Mrs F. Crocco

Lasagne £2.50 Fish soup £2.25
(Last order 10pm. No bar food Mon)
🍺 Tolly Cobbold Best Bitter, Original;
Hansa. *Real ale*

Franco Crocco's Italian specialities add
extra appeal to this charming village pub.
Seafood looms large on the menu, with
dishes like fish soup and garlicky prawns,
and there's also expertly prepared pasta, as
well as chicken pancakes and lovely fruit
tarts to finish. During the shooting season,
you might be offered roast partridge or a
pheasant casserole. Garden.

Braintree (Food) | Retreat

42 Bocking Church Street · *Essex* · Map 5 C2
Braintree (0376) 47947

Free House
Landlords Mr & Mrs David Locke

Prawn & mushroom puff pie £2.65 Apple
crumble 50p (Last order 11pm)
🍺 Tolly Cobbold Original Bitter; Trumans
Bitter, Best Bitter; Dortmunder Union;
Holsten; cider. *Real ale*

Skill and imagination go into the cooking at
this fine old inn, whose bars feature
beamed ceilings and a huge inglenook fireplace. The blackboard menu changes daily,
offering soups, pâté and a wide selection of
main courses – from omelettes and grills to
salads and our splendid sole with mushrooms and grapes. Desserts are simple and
delicious, and there's an impressive
cheeseboard. Garden.   **Family pub**

Branscombe (B & B) | Masons Arms

Near Seaton · *Devon* · Map 8 C3
Branscombe (029 780) 300

Free House
Landlord Mrs Janet Inglis

BEDROOMS 22 Grade 1 £A+
🍺 Hall & Woodhouse Badger Best Bitter;
Devenish Bitter, Wessex Best Bitter;
Whitbread Trophy; Guinness; Heineken;
cider. *Real ale*

This 14th-century village inn, with its
beamed bar and tables set out on the
terrace in summer, makes a delightful place
to stay, and Janet Inglis is a welcoming
hostess. Bedrooms, including some in
nearby cottages, are neat and prettily furnished and bathrooms are well maintained.
Residents can relax in the peaceful upstairs
lounge or TV room.   **Family pub**

Bratton (B & B) | Duke

Melbourne Street, Near Westbury · *Wiltshire*
Map 8 D3
Bratton (0380) 830242

Brewery Usher
Landlord Mr K. H. Stolzenberg

BEDROOMS 5 Grade 2 £C (No dogs)
🍺 Usher's Founders Ale, Best Bitter, Pale
Ale; Guinness; Carlsberg; Holsten Pils; cider.
Real ale

Standing on the B3098 about halfway
between Salisbury and Bath, this smartly
renovated pub provides comfortable overnight accommodation for tourists and
travellers. Five spacious bedrooms, all with
modern fitted units, TVs and tea-makers,
are served by two well-equipped bathrooms. The spacious open-plan bar and
lounge area retains a characterful air, and
housekeeping is excellent throughout.
Patio and garden.   **Family pub**

Bray *(Food)*   *Crown at Bray*

High Street · *Berkshire* · Map 6 B3
Maidenhead (0628) 21936

Brewery Courage
Landlords Mr Ashcroft & Mr Whitton

Pâté £1.75 Honey-roast chicken &
vegetables £2.75 (No bar food eves)
🍺 Courage Best Bitter; Guinness;
Hofmeister; Kronenbourg. *Real ale*

Swift, friendly service at neatly laid tables
copes with the crowds who enjoy the
combination of an atmospheric setting –
plenty of old beams – and tasty lunchtime
bar snacks. Popular dishes include tandoori
chicken, roast beef and York ham, all with
salad, and a minced beef hot pot. A gooey
treacle tart is top of the home-made sweets.
Saturday and Sunday lunch consists of a
barbecue in summer and jacket potatoes in
winter. Garden.

Breage *(B & B)*   *Queen's Arms*

Near Helston · *Cornwall* · Map 8 A4
Helston (032 65) 3485

Brewery Devenish
Landlords Mr & Mrs V. M. Graves

BEDROOMS 3 Grade 2 £C (No dogs)
🍺 Devenish Cornish Best Bitter, Bitter;
Whitbread Tankard, Mild; Guinness;
Grünhalle; cider. *Real ale*

The Graveses make visitors feel most
welcome at this tiny village pub dating
from 1854. The two bars are very comfortable, and upstairs there are three quite
spacious bedrooms with simple modern
furnishings and tea-making facilities. The
carpeted public bathroom has a shower
cubicle. Children not accommodated overnight. Garden.

Bredwardine *(B & B)*   *Red Lion Hotel*

Near Hereford · *Hereford & Worcester*
Map 7 D1
Moccas (098 17) 303

Free House
Landlords Mr & Mrs M. J. Taylor

BEDROOMS 10 Grade 1 £C (No dogs)
🍺 Bass, Allbright; Mitchells & Butlers DPA;
Carling Black Label; Taunton cider. *Real ale*

Set in a peaceful village on the B4352
between Hereford and Hay-on-Wye, this
old red-brick inn is a great favourite with
fishing and shooting folk. Bedrooms in the
converted outbuildings have their own
bath or shower rooms, and all are spacious
and well maintained. Guests can relax in
the beamed bar or in the large, comfortable
lounge.

Brendon *(Food, B & B)*   *Stag Hunters Inn*

Near Lynton · *Devon* · Map 8 C3
Brendon (059 87) 222

Free House
Landlords Mr & Mrs J. Parffrey
BEDROOMS 22 Grade 2 £B
Cottage pie £2.50 Apple pie 75p (Last
order 9pm)
🍺 Flowers Original; Whitbread Trophy, Best
Bitter, Poachers; Exmoor Ale; Guinness;
Heineken; cider. *Real ale*

This lovely old inn enjoys a setting of great
beauty and serenity by the banks of the East
Lyn river. The roomy bars and attractive
garden are delightful spots for enjoying
excellent home-prepared fare like French
onion soup, cottage pie, seafood platter
and flavour-packed chicken casserole. The
spacious, comfortable bedrooms are spotless, and there are two peaceful lounges,
one with TV. Accommodation closed
January–end March.   **Family pub**

England

Brendon Hills (B & B) · *Ralegh's Cross Inn*

Near Watchet · *Somerset* · Map 8 C3
Washford (0984) 40343

Free House
Landlords Mr & Mrs P. N. Nash

BEDROOMS 9 Grade 1 £B (No dogs)
🍺 Golden Hill Exmoor Ale; Flowers Best;
Whitbread Best Bitter, Trophy; Guinness;
Heineken; cider. *Real ale*

This isolated pub makes an ideal base from
which to explore the rugged beauty of
Exmoor, and the Nashes welcome visitors
to the area. Three traditionally furnished
bedrooms in the original building and six
extremely comfortable ones in the banga-
low annexe have colour TVs and smart carpeted bathrooms. A log fire warms the
long, narrow bar when it's chilly outside.
Garden. Closed last two weeks November.
Family pub

Bridestowe (Food) · *White Hart*

Fore Street · *Devon* · Map 8 B3
Bridestowe (083 786) 318

Free House
Landlords Owen & Millard families

Local poached trout £2.95 Steak on toast £2.75
(Last order 10pm)
🍺 Palmer's IPA; St Austell Extra;
Worthington Best Bitter; Guinness; Carling
Black Label; cider. *Real ale*

You'll find simple, well-prepared bar food
in this 17th-century pub in a village just off
the A30. You might start with delicious
tomato and vegetable soup or pâté and go
on to some home-cooked ham. Steaks and
fish are cooked to order: we enjoyed a
delicious poached trout with an attractively
presented salad. Pasties, pies and gâteaux
in summer. The beer garden is useful for
children in good weather.

Bridge Trafford (Food) · *Nags Head*

Near Chester · *Cheshire* · Map 3 B4
Chester (0244) 300206

Brewery Greenall Whitley
Landlords Jim & Vera McPeake

Steak & kidney pie with vegetables £1.90
Toasted ham & pineapple sandwich 90p
(Last order 10pm)
🍺 Greenall Whitley Bitter, Festival, Mild;
Guinness; Grünhalle; cider. *Real ale*

A good selection of tasty snacks makes this
roadside pub a popular spot for lunch.
Besides plain and toasted sandwiches,
there are flavoursome home-made soups,
cold meat salads, steaks and hot specials
like lasagne or an excellent chicken casserole. The choice in the evenings and at
weekends is mainly sandwiches and basket
meals. Swings in the garden.
Family pub (till 8pm)

Bridgnorth (B & B) · *Falcon Hotel*

St John Street, Lowtown
Shropshire · Map 7 D1
Bridgnorth (074 62) 3134

Brewery Mitchells & Butlers
Landlord Mr A. R. Owen

BEDROOMS 16 Grades 1 & 2 £C
🍺 Mitchells & Butlers Mild, Springfield
Bitter, Brew XI; Carling Black Label; Taunton
cider. *Real ale*

Just across the Severn bridge from the
main part of Bridgnorth, this white-painted
inn provides comfortable overnight
accommodation. Bedrooms in traditional
or modern style are pleasantly furnished
and bathrooms are well maintained. Relax
in the cosy bar with its antique clocks or in
the TV lounge. The Owens provide very
enjoyable breakfasts. Patio. **Family pub**

Bridport *(Food, B & B)*   *Bull Hotel*

34 East Street · *Dorset* · Map 8 D3
Bridport (0308) 22878
Free House
Landlords Terleski family
BEDROOMS 20   Grades 1 & 2   £C
Grilled whole plaice £2.25 Beef curry &
rice £2.25 (Last order 9.15pm. No bar food
Sun lunch)
🍺 Eldridge Pope Royal Oak; Hall &
Woodhouse Badger Best Bitter; Bass Triangle;
Dorchester Bitter; Guinness; Carlsberg. *Real ale*

The Terleski family take good care of this
16th-century coaching inn in the centre of
town. An extensive bar menu caters for all
tastes, with snacks ranging from grills,
omelettes and salads to hot specials like
curry, goulash, cauliflower cheese and
fresh seafood. Overnight guests will find
the simply furnished bedrooms comfortable. Patio.   **Family pub**

We neither seek nor accept

hospitality, and we pay for all

food, drinks and accommodation

in full.

Bridport *(Food, B & B)*   *George Hotel*

4 South Street · *Dorset* · Map 8 D3
Bridport (0308) 23187

Brewery Palmer
Landlords John & Elizabeth Mander
BEDROOMS 4   Grade 2   £C
Moussaka £1.65 Home-made pies £1.65 (Last
order 9.30pm. No bar food Thurs eve & Sun
lunch, also Sun eve in winter)
🍺 Palmer's IPA, Bridport Bitter;
Guinness; Shilthorn Lager. *Real ale*

The warmth of the welcome is exceptional
at the Manders' appealing stone-built pub,
where the bar provides a delightfully traditional setting for wholesome, freshly
cooked food. Generously filled omelettes
are among the all-time favourites, and other
popular items include pies, salads, quiches
and the day's fish special. Guests staying
overnight in the simple, spacious bedrooms
can look forward to a really good breakfast.
                    Family pub

Brightling *(Food)*   *Fullers Arms*

Oxley Green, Near Robertsbridge
East Sussex · Map 6 C4
Brightling (042 482) 212

Free House
Landlords John & Sheila Mitchell-Sadd
Prawn & halibut pie £2.50 Chocolate brandy
cake 95p (Last order 10pm)
🍺 Wethered's Bitter; Fremlins Bitter;
Whitbread Best; Samuel Whitbread;
Guinness; Stella Artois; cider. *Real ale*

This simple sandstone pub in the rolling
Sussex countryside is a pleasant spot to
pause awhile. In the cosy bar or well-kept
garden you can enjoy light snacks like
quiche or ploughman's, or go for something more substantial – perhaps lasagne
or the popular prawn and halibut pie. Be
sure to leave room for the gorgeous chocolate brandy cake. Closed Monday. Garden.
                    Family pub (lunchtime)

Brightlingsea   (Food)   *Cherry Tree*

29 Church Road · *Essex* · Map 5 D2
Brightlingsea (0206 30) 2713

Brewery Greene King
Landlord Mr A. D. Vowles
Chicken in port sauce £2.95 Omelettes £1.95
(Last order 10pm. No bar food Wed eve &
all Sun)
🍺 Greene King IPA, Abbot Ale, XX Mild;
Guinness; Harp; Taunton cider; Kronenbourg.
Real ale

Looking very smart after recent renovation,
this 19th-century cherry-pink pub has
gained a well-earned reputation for its fine
home cooking. A blackboard menu offers a
daily-changing range of tempting fare,
from simple salads and sandwiches to
delicious omelettes and flavoursome
chicken in port sauce with prawns and
tomatoes. To finish, try the excellent fresh
fruit pies. Patio.

Brighton   (B & B)   *Black Lion Hotel*

London Road · *East Sussex* · Map 6 C4
Brighton (0273) 501220

Brewery Beard & Co
Landlords Mr & Mrs Colin Patey-Johns

BEDROOMS 16   Grade 1   £A
🍺 Harveys Bitter, Old Ale, Mild; Guinness;
Carlsberg; cider. *Real ale*

This smartly maintained brick, stone and
pebbledash pub stands on the A23, providing motorists with easy access to the
north and ring roads as well as the town
centre. Centrally heated bedrooms are
uniform in style, with practical modern furnishings and televisions; all but two have
up-to-date private facilities. There are two
plush bars, one of which leads on to the
spacious garden with plenteous seating.

Brighton   (Food)   *Cricketer's*

15 Black Lion Street · *East Sussex* · Map 6 C4
Brighton (0273) 24620

Brewery Watneys
Landlord Miss W. Sexton

Chicken, ham & mushroom pie £1.35 Crab
sandwich £1 (Last order 10.45pm)
🍺 Watneys Special, Stag Bitter; Ben
Truman; King & Barnes Festive; Guinness;
Foster's; Carlsberg; Harp; cider. *Real ale*

Winnie Sexton is a lively, popular hostess
at this friendly old pub where locals and
visitors like to relax in the plush bar.
Delicious home-made savoury pies are a
feature of the menu, which also offers
sausages, jacket potatoes, and tempting
daily specials like chilli con carne or chicken
provençale. Wide selection of sandwiches,
too.

Brighton   (Food)   *The Greys*

103 Southover Street, off Lewes Road
East Sussex · Map 6 C4
Brighton (0273) 680734
Brewery Whitbread
Landlords Alan & Sarah Gray
Avocado & smoked chicken with walnut
vinaigrette £1.75 Mediterranean fish stew
£2.75 (Last order 9pm. No bar food Sun & Mon)
🍺 Whitbread Strong Country Bitter, Flower's
Original; Guinness; Stella Artois; cider.
Real ale

The local fish market provides many of the
raw materials for Jackie Fitzgerald's splendid bar food at this friendly modern pub
just off the Lewes Road. Fresh sardines,
garlic prawns and whole grilled plaice are
typical seafood specials on a menu whose
delights could also include tortellini served
with a rich basil-flavoured tomato sauce.
For meat eaters there's game pie, steaks
and hearty casseroles.

Brightwell Baldwin *(Food)* ★   *Lord Nelson*

Near Watlington · *Oxfordshire* · Map 6 B3
Watlington (049 161) 2497

Free House
Landlords S. A. Johnson & J. K. Jorgensen

Beef Nelson £4.50 Fresh calf's liver £4.25 (Last
order 10pm)
🍺 Brakspears Pale Ale; Webster's Yorkshire
Bitter; Ben Truman Export. *Real ale*

Jack Jorgensen's cooking steals the show
at this handsome old pub, where the bars
are laid out with carefully set tables. High-
quality ingredients are used throughout,
and favourites on the interesting menu
include creamy-sauced chicken maritime
and the superb beef Nelson – prime fillet in
a memorable port wine sauce. Good vegetables and lovely sweets, too, such as fruit
pies and sorbets. Closed Monday except
Bank Holidays.

Briston *(Food)*   *John H. Stracey*

Near Melton Constable · *Norfolk* · Map 5 D1
Melton Constable (0263) 860891

Free House
Landlord Mr I. Verrando

Lasagne £3 Steak & kidney pie £3.80
(Last order 9pm)
🍺 Greene King Abbot Ale; Adnams Bitter;
Ind Coope Burton Ale, John Bull; Tetley's
Bitter; Guinness; cider. *Real ale*

Isidoro Verrando and his wife are true pro-
fessionals, who run this welcoming roadside pub with real dedication. In the cosy
beamed bar you can tuck into authentic,
flavour-packed minestrone, lasagne and
cannelloni, as well as English favourites
like rich, tender steak and kidney pie,
Cromer crab salad and home-cooked ham
and chips. At lunchtime there are also
French bread sandwiches and several
ploughman's. Patio.   **Family pub**

Broad Chalke *(B & B)*   *Queen's Head*

Wiltshire · Map 6 A4
Salisbury (0722) 780344

Free House
Landlords Robert & Judith Grier

BEDROOMS 4   Grade 1   £B
🍺 Courage Directors Bitter; Wadworth's 6X;
Ringwood Best Bitter; Salisbury Bitter;
Guinness; Hofmeister; Taunton cider. *Real ale*

Beams, rough stone walls and traditional
decor sustain a sense of history in the bars
of this immaculate village pub, run in
friendly fashion by Robert and Judith Grier.
To the rear, in a well-designed annexe, are
the comfortable, spacious bedrooms, with
simple white furniture, tea-makers, telephones and remote-control TVs. Each has
its own spotless modern bathroom. Patio.

Broad Hinton *(B & B)*   *Crown Inn*

Near Swindon · *Wiltshire* · Map 6 A3
Broad Hinton (079 373) 302

Free House
Landlords Mr & Mrs Albert Harris

BEDROOMS 4   Grade 1   £B
🍺 Eldridge Pope Royal Oak, Dorchester
Bitter; Wadworth's 6X; Bass Triangle;
Guinness; Carling Black Label; Taunton cider.
Real ale

The Harrises are conscientious hosts at this
pleasant, mustard-coloured inn. The olde-
worlde lounge bar opens on to the patio
and garden, and there's a simple public bar.
Bedrooms are all well equipped with good
modern furniture, colour TVs and tea-
makers, plus tiled shower cabinets. No
under-sixes overnight; accommodation
closed during Christmas period.
                    Family pub

England

Broad Oak   *(Food)*   ★   *Broad Oak Inn*

Near Garway · *Hereford & Worcester*
Map 7 D2
St Weonards (098 18) 263

Free House
Landlords Clive & Angela Russell-Taylor

Wye smoked salmon £4.50 Broad Oak
casserole £4.95 (Last order 9pm)
🍺 Flower's Original Bitter; Heineken.
Real ale

Standing in open countryside with only a
stately oak for company, this lovely old pub
is a marvellous place for a meal. The menu
is a delight from beginning to end: stuffed
vine leaves with a savoury dip, home-cured
pastrami, seafood pancakes, smoked Wye
salmon and a sensational hot brandy
chocolate cake. Closed Sunday evening
and all Monday (except Bank Holidays).
Garden.

Broadwell   *(Food, B & B)*   *Fox Inn*

Moreton-in-Marsh · *Gloucestershire*
Map 5 A2
Stow-on-the-Wold (0451) 30212
Brewery Donnington
Landlords Dennis & Debbie Harding
BEDROOMS 2   Grade 2   £C   (No dogs)
Chicken casserole with mustard sauce £2.65
Caribbean ham £1.80 (Last order 8.45pm.
No bar food Tues eve & all Sun)
🍺 Donnington's Best Bitter, SPA;
Löwenbräu; cider. *Real ale*

Nestling on the village green, this cosy inn
has a pleasant beer garden where traditional pub games like Aunt Sally are still
played. In the beamed bars robust dishes –
casseroles, roasts, seasonal game – are
served with a good selection of fresh vegetables. Pâté, salads and ploughman's at
Tuesday lunchtime. Two homely bedrooms with TV share the family bathroom.
Hearty cooked breakfasts.   **Family pub**

Brockton   *(Food)*   *Feathers Inn*

Near Much Wenlock · *Shropshire* · Map 7 D1
Brockton (074 636) 202

Free House
Landlords Robbie & Jackie Robinson
Beef & mushroom casserole £2.55 Risotto with
chicken, prawns, crab & peppers £3.95 (Last
order 10pm)
🍺 Simpkiss Bitter; Shire Mild; Wem Bitter;
Younger's Tartan; Guinness; Kestrel; cider.
Real ale

Two converted Elizabethan cottages make
up this charming, heavily beamed pub on
the B4378. Robbie and Jackie Robinson's
bar menu offers ample choice, from
ploughman's jumbo sausages and garlic
mushrooms to fish or chicken with chips
and daily specials like risotto or spiced
lamb's kidneys in wine. Toasted sandwiches, too. Closed Tuesday lunchtime.
                                Family pub

Brome   *(Food)*   *Oaksmere*

Near Eye · *Suffolk* · Map 5 D2
Eye (0379) 870326

Free House
Landlords W. J. & M. P. Hasted

Lowestoft pie £2.95 Prawns provençale £2.25
(Last order 10pm)
🍺 Courage Directors Bitter, Best Bitter, Mild;
Guinness; Kronenbourg; Hofmeister;
Taunton cider. *Real ale*

Built in 1550 and altered in Victorian times,
this fine country mansion stands in 200
acres of parkland and formal gardens.
Tasty snacks served in the beamed bar
range from soup, sandwiches and
ploughman's to herby garlic sausage,
chargrilled Vienna steak and potato-topped
fish pie. Super sweets, excellent cheeseboard. *For accommodation see Egon
Ronay's Lucas Hotel & Restaurant Guide
1985.*   **Family pub**

94

Bromeswell   *(Food)*   *Cherry Tree*

Near Woodbridge · *Suffolk* · Map 5 D2
Eyke (039 47) 310

Brewery Tollemache & Cobbold
Landlords Mr & Mrs Cheek

Shepherd's pie £1.90 Apple pie 60p (Last
order 10.30pm)
🍺 Tolly Cobbold Bitter, Mild; Guinness;
Hansa Lager; Dortmunder; Taunton cider.
Real ale

Mrs Cheek's cooking is a popular attraction
at this former hunting lodge, where on fine
days the customers make good use of the
little garden. Tasty quiches are the centrepiece of the lunchtime cold buffet, which
also features serve-yourself salads and
various sweets. There are filled rolls, too,
and hot dishes include individual cottage
pies and chilli con carne. Garden.
Family pub

Bromham   *(Food)*   *Greyhound Inn*

High Street, Near Chippenham · *Wiltshire*
Map 6 A3
Bromham (0380) 850241

Free House
Landlords George & Mo Todd
Taramasalata £1.15 Chicken Verluccio £2.70
(Last order 10pm)
🍺 Wadworth's IPA, 6X; Bass Special;
Younger's Tartan; Guinness; Carlsberg Hof;
Carling Black Label; Taunton cider. *Real ale*

Jugs and chamber pots hanging from the
ceiling are a trademark of this friendly pub
where George Todd's tasty, generously
served bar meals are sure to satisfy the
hungriest customer. Sauced dishes like
beef with tomato, garlic and red wine are a
speciality, and there are also simpler items
such as soup, ploughman's and curry.
Sweets are good, too.

Bromyard   *(Food)*   *Hop Pole Hotel*

The Square · *Hereford & Worcester* · Map 7 D1
Bromyard (088 58) 82449

Brewery Marston, Thompson & Evershed

Landlords Peter & Anne Robinson
Pasta in walnut sauce £1.50 Honey roast
duckling £4.50 (Last order 9pm. No bar food
Sun eve for non-residents)
🍺 Marston's Pedigree, Lager; Guinness;
cider. *Real ale*

The Robinsons provide a good choice of
enjoyable bar food in this imposing old
coaching inn. Lunch brings simple offerings like hearty vegetable soup, burgers
and tasty steak, kidney and mushroom pie
along with salads and ploughman's. In the
evening there are more interesting dishes
such as Greek-style sardines and lamb's
kidneys casseroled in champagne cider
with mushrooms.   **Family pub**

Buckler's Hard   *Master Builders House Hotel*

The beamed bars were once part of the home of Henry Adams, a
renowned 18th-century shipbuilder. A miniature cannon has pride of
place on a mantelpiece, and the walls are festooned with photographs of sailing ships old and new. Note, too, the list of over 50 ships
built here on the Beaulieu River between 1698 and 1822. Garden.
Family pub

Near Beaulieu · *Hampshire* · Map 6 A4
Buckler's Hard (059 063) 253
Brewery Allied-Lyons   *Landlord* Mr R. Dinnage
🍺 Halls Harvest Bitter, Burton Bitter; John Bull Bitter; Tetley Bitter;
Guinness; Skol; Löwenbräu; cider. *Real ale*

England

Bungay   *Fleece Hotel*

In the centre of a medieval market town near the Norfolk border, the Fleece, originally a coaching house, retains a good deal of atmosphere and charm. Low ceilings, heavy beams and a large inglenook fireplace characterise the bar, which also features delightful touches like the wrought-iron Fleece motif in the partitions. Patio.

8 St Mary's Street · *Suffolk* · Map 5 D1
Bungay (0986) 2192
Brewery Adnams   *Landlord* Mrs G. Haynes
 Adnams Bitter, Old Ale (winter only); Courage Best Bitter; Guinness; Skol; Löwenbräu; cider. *Real ale*

Burcot   *(Food)*   *Chequers Inn*

Near Abingdon · *Oxfordshire* · Map 6 B3
Clifton Hampden (086 730) 7771

Brewery Usher
Landlords Mary & Michael Weeks

Hot pot £2.35 Apple & raspberry pancake £1.35
(No bar food eves)
 Usher's Founder's Ale, PA; Guinness; Carlsberg; Holsten. *Real ale*

A blackboard displays the day's offerings at this recently extended thatched pub dating from 1500. And excellent fare it is, too, from sweetcorn and watercress soup to smoked ham salad, beef Stroganoff and flavoursome creamy fish pie. Also ploughman's and farmer's platters, and, to finish, Mary Weeks' popular chocolaty 'Disaster Cake' with a crunchy biscuit centre. Roast on Sunday. Garden.

Burham   *(Food)*   ★   *Golden Eagle*

80 Church Street · *Kent* · Map 6 C3
Medway (0634) 668975

Free House
Landlords Chris & Chiu Blackmore

Nasi goreng £2.25 Beef & chilli £2.50 (Last order 10.30pm. No Malaysian food Mon eve)
 Wadworth's 6X; Goachers Maidstone Ale; Shepherd Neame Master Brew; Guinness; Hurlimann; cider. *Real ale*

The fresh spicy flavours of Malaysian cooking are the unexpected attraction at this friendly pub. Nasi goreng and creamy chicken curry are popular items in Chiu Blackmore's repertoire, and our beef and peppers with chilli in black bean sauce was as good as you'll find anywhere. The number of locals eating in the beamed bar tells you just how much it's all appreciated. More familiar bar fare also available.

Burnham-on-Crouch   *(B & B)*   *Ye Olde White Harte*

The Quay · *Essex* · Map 6 D3
Maldon (0621) 782106

Free House
Landlords Mr & Mrs G. J. Lewis

BEDROOMS 15   Grade 2   £C
 Tolly Cobbold Bitter; Charrington's IPA; Stones Bitter; Guinness; Carling Black Label; Foster's. *Real ale*

The talk is mainly of yachts and yachting in this delightful riverside pub, where the Lewises are charming and attentive hosts. The panelled bar features some nautical instruments, and there's a TV lounge with a collection of china. Cheerful bedrooms are smaller on the top floor (dormer windows, lovely views), larger downstairs (some with private facilities) and more modern in the annexe. Sit on the jetty in fine weather.

96

Imagine the flavour of the French countryside, in a wine glass. <u>Vin de Pays.</u> The everyday wine of France.

Make friends with the wines of France.

GET TO KNOW

Raffles

ONE STEP AHEAD

LOW TO MIDDLE TA

RAFFLES
Special Virginia

Raffles 100's

TALLER
THAN
KING SIZE

Burnt Hill   *(Food)*   *Nut & Bolt*

Near Yattendon · *Berkshire* · Map 6 A3
Hermitage (0635) 201496

Free House
Landlords Gerry & Jane Campkin

Filled jacket potatoes from £1.20 Curry &
rice £1.50 (Last order 10pm)
🍺 Morland's Best Bitter, Bitter; Ruddle's
Bitter, County; Fuller's ESB, London Pride;
Guinness; Taunton cider. *Real ale*

Outside Yattendon just off the Pangbourne
road, this friendly, red-brick pub is popular
for its tasty and generously served bar
snacks. A regularly changing menu offers
hot specials like moussaka, haddock and
prawn pie and various curries, and there's
always a good choice of sandwiches and
filled jacket potatoes for those in search of a
quick bite. Garden.

Burpham   *(Food)*   *George & Dragon*

Near Arundel · *West Sussex* · Map 6 B4
Arundel (0903) 883131

Free House
Landlord Mr Eric Brookfield

Ham salad £1.60 Plaice, chips & peas £1.95
(Last order 10pm)
🍺 Bass, Toby Bitter; Charrington's IPA, Mild;
Guinness; Löwenbräu; Taunton cider. *Real ale*

Once a haunt for local smugglers, this
16th-century pub offers a cheerful welcome
to present-day customers in search of tasty,
home-cooked food. There's always a daily
special to supplement sandwiches, soup,
steak, well-made omelettes and salads. Or
you may choose a jacket potato filled with
chicken livers or perhaps curried prawns.
There are tempting sweets from the trolley
as well. Patio.   **Family pub**

Burslem   *(Food)*   *Traveller's Rest*

239 Newcastle Street · *Staffordshire*
Map 4 C4
Stoke-on-Trent (0782) 810418
Free House
Landlords John & Janet Pazio
Tourte aux champignons with vegetables £1.50
Old English hot pot & vegetables £1.80 (Last
order 10.30pm. No bar food Sun & Mon eves)
🍺 Ind Coope Burton Ale, Bitter; Ansells Mild;
ABC Bitter; Guinness; Skol; Löwenbräu; cider.
Real ale

Former musicians John and Janet Pazio
deserve applause for the excellent food
served in their modern roadside pub.
Lunchtime brings an appetising buffet of
home-cooked meats and colourful salads,
as well as hot dishes like braised beef with
beans or leek and fish pie. There are sandwiches, too, and perhaps a satisfying bread
and butter pudding to finish. Less choice in
the evening. Garden.

Burtle   *(Food)*   *Ye Olde Burtle Inn*

Near Bridgwater · *Somerset* · Map 8 D3
Bridgwater (0278) 722269

Free House
Landlords Stuart & Valerie Boulton

Steak & kidney pie £1.95 Special mixed
grill £4.30 (Last order 10pm)
🍺 Golden Hill Exmoor Ale; Wadworth's 6X;
Whitbread Trophy; Newcastle Bitter;
Guinness; Heineken; cider. *Real ale*

There's a friendly welcome and a good
choice of bar food at this old whitewashed
pub. Chicken, sausages or scampi with
chips are featured on the menu, along with
more elaborate items like coq au vin or
prawn-stuffed fillets of plaice with mushrooms. The huge Barnsley chop is a great
favourite, and there are baked potatoes and
salads too. Traditional roast on Sundays
(book). Garden.   **Family pub**

Burton *(Food)* ★ *Plume of Feathers*

Near Chippenham · *Wiltshire* · Map 7 D2
Badminton (045 421) 251

Brewery Usher
Landlords Peter & June Bolin

Beef & venison pie £3.25 Curries £2.30 (Last
order 10.30pm)
🍺 Usher's Best Bitter, Founder's Ale, Triple
Crown; Ben Truman; Guinness; Carlsberg;
Taunton cider. *Real ale*

East meets West on the enticing menu of
this 16th-century village pub, whose stone-
walled bars have a cosy, rustic charm. The
landlords spent many years in the Far East,
and deliciously authentic dishes like
Sinhalese chicken curry and Indonesian
beef rendang are real winners. Occidental
options range from American-style hamburgers to seafood provençale and a crispy
apple and sultana pancake. Garden
Family pub

Burtonwood *(Food)* *Fiddle i'th Bag Inn*

Alder Lane, Near Warrington · *Cheshire*
Map 3 B3
Newton-le-Willows (092 52) 5442

Brewery Greenall Whitley
Landlords Don & Jean Roy
Assorted cold platter with salads £2.95
Chicken hongroise with lyonnaise
potatoes £2.35 (Last order 10.30pm)
🍺 Greenall Whitley Bitter, Mild, Festival;
Guinness; Grünhalle; cider. *Real ale*

A wide-ranging menu caters for all tastes at
this smart country pub. Hot dishes might
include beef kebab with chilli sauce or
chicken chasseur, and there are also soups,
filled baps, a variety of ploughman's and an
excellent beef pie. Weekday lunchtimes
you can also help yourself to salads from
the cold buffet. Patio and garden.
Family pub

Burwash *(B & B)* *Bell Inn*

High Street · *East Sussex* · Map 6 C4
Burwash (0435) 882304

Brewery Beard
Landlord Mr & Mrs P. Ingham

BEDROOMS 5   Grade 2   £C
🍺 Beard's Best Bitter, Old Ale (winter
only); Guinness; Carlsberg Hof, Pilsner;
cider. *Real ale*

Hanging baskets in summer add extra
appeal to this pretty pub, which has a
delightful beer garden at the back. The
beamed bar is a friendly place for a drink,
and you can listen to live jazz on Tuesday
evenings. Simple, charming bedrooms
provide good comfort and all have tea-
makers. Guests share the family bathroom.
Family pub

Byworth *(Food)* *Black Horse*

Near Petworth · *West Sussex* · Map 6 B4
Petworth (0798) 42424

Free House
Landlord Harry King

Mussels in garlic sauce £1.55 French apricot
tart 75p (Last order 9.30pm)
🍺 Young's Bitter; Eldridge Pope Dorset IPA;
Guinness; Heineken; cider. *Real ale*

It's best to arrive early at this busy pub,
widely known for an enterprising choice of
bar food. Blackboard specials might range
from gravad lax and mushrooms in garlic
sauce to crab salad, Peking duck or chicken
in cider. For those in a conservative mood,
there are also more familiar items like
burgers and fry-ups. Delicious desserts,
too. The terraced garden has lovely views.

Calderbridge (B & B)
Stanley Arms

Near Egremont · *Cumbria* · Map 3 B2
Beckermet (094 684) 235

Brewery Younger
Landlord Mr I. W. Robinson·

BEDROOMS 9 Grade 2 £C
🍺 Younger's XXPS Scotch, Bitter, Lager;
Taunton cider. *Real ale*

This modernised 18th-century roadside pub stands in extensive grounds reaching to the river Calder, on which it has fishing rights. The garden is a popular spot in summer, while in cooler weather the spacious panelled bar comes into its own. Decently furnished bedrooms offer simple comforts for an overnight stay, and there's a modest little TV room. **Family pub**

Callington (B & B)
Coachmakers Arms

Newport Square · *Cornwall* · Map 8 B4
Liskeard (0579) 82567

Free House
Landlords Ken & Sheila Hadfield

BEDROOMS 4 Grade 1 £B (No dogs)
🍺 Bass; Stones Bitter; Worthington Best Bitter, 'E'; Tennents Pilsner; Carling Black Lager; Taunton cider. *Real ale*

Friendly landlords and staff make visitors very welcome at this characterful old pub in a part of the world once closely linked with coachmaking. Oak beams and horse brasses provide period atmosphere in the bar, while the bedrooms are smartly contemporary. All have private facilities and one boasts its own sun terrace. No under-eights overnight. Accommodation closed 2 weeks Christmas.

Calstock (B & B)
Boot Inn

Fore Street · *Cornwall* · Map 8 B4
Tavistock (0822) 832331

Free House
Landlords Mr & Mrs Bob Slack

BEDROOMS 2 Grade 2 £C (No dogs)
🍺 Flowers Original, IPA; Whitbread Best Bitter, Best Mild; Poacher Bitter; Guinness; Stella Artois; Taunton cider. *Real ale*

Hobnail boots as a decorative theme recall the name of this charming village inn perched on a hillside above the river Tamar. Liz and Bob Slack are very welcoming hosts, and traditional pub games add to the friendly atmosphere in the stone-walled bar. The two bedrooms, each with a shower cubicle, are prettily furnished and have tea-makers. Patio.

Carey (Food, B & B)
Cottage of Content

Hereford & Worcester · Map 7 D2
Carey (043 270) 242

Free House
Landlord Peter Nash
BEDROOMS 3 Grade 2 £C
Rabbit casserole £4.25 Lamb curry £4.25 (Last order 10pm)
🍺 Hook Norton Best Bitter, Old Hookey; Worthington Best Bitter; Flower's Original; Guinness; cider. *Real ale*

Landlord Peter Nash is celebrating the 500th birthday of this delightfully rustic little inn by providing private facilities for all three bedrooms, which are centrally heated and have sturdy furniture, good carpets and tea-makers. The bar menu changes frequently, offering tasty home-cooked dishes like ham and eggs, chilli con carne and rabbit casserole. Soup and sandwiches, too, plus a summer cold table and nice sweets. Garden. **Family pub**

Cartmel Fell   *(Food)*

Mason's Arms

Strawberry Bank, Near Grange-over-Sands
Cumbria · Map 3 B2
Crosthwaite (044 88) 486

Free House
Landlord Mrs Helen Stevenson
Coachman's casserole with vegetables £3.50
Lasagne £2.50 (Last order 9pm)
🍺 Thwaites Mild, Bitter; Guinness;
McEwans Export; Beck's Bier; Kronenbourg;
cider.

There are splendid views from this fine old converted farmhouse, and Helen Stevenson's sustaining bar food makes the trip doubly worthwhile. Sandwiches and ploughman's are made to order, and weightier dishes include home-cooked pies and casseroles. In summer, the blackboard menu might offer a Morecambe crab or shrimp salad. Lovely desserts, too. Terrace.
Family pub

Casterton   *(Food, B & B)*

Pheasant Inn

Near Kirkby Lonsdale · *Cumbria* · Map 3 B2
Kirkby Lonsdale (0468) 71230

Free House
Landlord Mr D. Hesmondhalgh
BEDROOMS 16   Grade 1   £B
Pork pie with mushy peas 75p Battered
haddock £2.25 (Last order 9.30pm)
🍺 Younger's Scotch Bitter; Tetley's Bitter,
Mild; Kronenbourg; Oranjeboom; cider.
Real ale

Food and accommodation are both excellent at this immaculate white-painted inn. Bedrooms are attractively decorated and comfortably furnished; TVs are standard, and most rooms have private facilities. The lounges are cosy and chintzy and there's a homely beamed bar, where the long menu of tasty snacks ranges from pâté and plated salads to steak and kidney pie and roast chicken. Terrace.
Family pub

Castle Combe   *(B & B)*

Castle Hotel

Near Chippenham · *Wiltshire* · Map 7 D2
Castle Combe (0249) 782461

Free House
Landlords Mr & Mrs D. Packer &
Mrs A. J. Randle

BEDROOMS 9   Grade 1   £A
🍺 Whitbread Best Bitter; Wadworth's 6X;
Flower's Original; Guinness; Heineken;
Tuborg; cider. *Real ale*

Right in the centre of a picture postcard village, this fine 14th-century hostelry is rich in period atmosphere. Exposed timbers, steep staircases and low ceilings are all part of the charm, and there are even secret passages and a tunnel leading to the village church. First-class bedrooms of various sizes have freestanding furniture, TVs, radio-alarms and good modern bathrooms. Garden.
Family pub

Castleton   *(Food, B & B)*

Castle Hotel

Castle Street · *Derbyshire* · Map 4 C3
Hope Valley (0433) 20578

Brewery Bass
Landlords Mr & Mrs G. Walker

BEDROOMS 5   Grade 1   £B   (No dogs)
Steak & kidney pie £2.50 Sweets 85p
(Last order 10.15pm)
🍺 Stones Bitter; Worthington 'E'; Guinness;
Carling Black Label; Hemeling; cider. *Real ale*

Close to Peveril Castle, this fine old pub makes an excellent haven in the heart of the Peak District. Tasty snacks served in the cosy beamed bars range from soup and sandwiches to lasagne, grilled fish and a daily roast. Luxuriously furnished bedrooms (including two with four-posters) all have fitted carpets, TVs, tea-makers and up-to-date bath or shower rooms.

Castleton (B & B) — Ye Olde Cheshire Cheese

How Lane · *Derbyshire* · Map 4 C3
Hope Valley (0433) 20330

Free House
Landlords Mr & Mrs J. A. Nuttall

BEDROOMS 6 Grade 1 £C
 Webster's Yorkshire Bitter, Pennine, Mild; Guinness; Foster's; Carlsberg; cider. *Real ale*

Hikers, holiday-makers and locals are all made to feel at home in the Nuttalls' friendly pub in the heart of the Peak District National Park. There are two pleasant bars, both fitted out in traditional rustic style. Compact bedrooms with pretty wallpaper and attractive modern whitewood units are equipped with duvets and tea-making facilities; all have neatly designed shower rooms.

Castleton (Food, B & B) — Ye Olde Nag's Head

Cross Street · *Derbyshire* · Map 4 C3
Hope Valley (0433) 20248

Free House
Landlords Mr & Mrs G. Walker

BEDROOMS 8 Grade 2 £C
Taramasalata £1.95 Prawns on rye £2.50 (Last order 10.15)
 Stones Bitter, Mild; Tennent's Lager; Carling Black Label; Taunton cider. *Real ale*

Dazzling flower displays are a feature throughout this well-kept former coaching inn, where the beamed bar has bags of charm and atmosphere. A good variety of snacks is available, from soup and sandwiches to salads, lasagne and steak and kidney pie. Cheerfully decorated bedrooms have whitewood furniture and tea-makers and, like the bathrooms, are spotlessly clean. There's a cosy residents' lounge.

Castleton (Food, B & B) — Moorlands Hotel

Near Whitby · *North Yorkshire* · Map 4 D2
Castleton (0287) 60206

Free House
Landlords Mr & Mrs J. E. Aubertin

BEDROOMS 10 Grade 1 £B
Paella £3 Home-baked ham & salad £3.20 (Last order 9.30pm)
 Tetley's Bitter, Imperial, Falstaff; Skol.

Fresh flowers and plants are a charming feature in this pleasant moorland pub, where ten smartly kept bedrooms with pretty floral curtains and fitted furniture provide homely overnight accommodation. There's also a comfortable residents' lounge and a separate TV room. Bar snacks include home-baked ham, tasty steak and kidney pie, spaghetti, curries and lots of moreish sweets. Closed end October–Easter.

Cavendish (Food, B & B) — Bull

High Street, Near Sudbury · *Suffolk* · Map 5 C2
Glemsford (0787) 280245

Brewery Adnams
Landlords Laura & Michael Sansome

BEDROOMS 3 Grade 2 £C (No dogs)
Chicken casserole £2 Cheesecake 65p
(Last order 9pm. No bar food Sun–Thurs eves)
 Adnams Bitter, Old (winter only); Carling Black Label; cider. *Real ale*

Visitors are greeted like old friends at this convivial red-brick pub, where Mrs Sansome prepares super snacks from fresh local produce. A savoury pie, quiche and roast may be among the tempting offerings, along with salads, evening grills and some delicious sweets. Comfortably furnished bedrooms share two spotless bathrooms, and residents can watch TV in the Sansomes' lounge. No under-12s overnight. Garden.

England

Cavendish (B & B)   *George*

The Green, Near Sudbury · *Suffolk* · Map 5 C2
Glemsford (0787) 280248

Brewery Truman
Landlords Mr & Mrs M. Vincent

BEDROOMS 3   Grade 2   £C   (No dogs)
🍺 Truman's Bitter, Special, Prizebrew, Ben
Truman; Carlsberg; Foster's; cider. *Real ale*

Mr and Mrs Vincent are welcoming landlords at this white-painted pub on the
village green and the cosy, friendly bars are
perfect for a relaxing pint. Bedrooms are
neatly furnished and all have TVs; one has
its own shower cabinet, the rest share a
spotless bathroom. No children under five
overnight.   **Family pub**

Cerne Abbas (B & B)   *New Inn*

14 Long Street · *Dorset* · Map 8 D3
Cerne Abbas (03003) 274

Brewery Eldridge Pope
Landlords Mr & Mrs M. W. Austin

BEDROOMS 4   Grade 2   £C
🍺 Eldridge Pope Royal Oak, Dorchester
Bitter, Dorset IPA; Guinness; Faust; Taunton
cider. *Real ale*

This fine stone-roofed pub in a showpiece
Dorset village has an interesting history
that traces back to the 16th century. Public
rooms include a cheerful bar (note the
collection of horse tackle and farm
implements), a children's room and a large
garden. Bedrooms, all with TVs and tea-
makers, are neat and simple; they share
two public bathrooms. Good breakfasts.
                                    Family pub

Chaddesley Corbett   (Food)   *Talbot Inn*

Near Kidderminster · *Hereford & Worcester*
Map 7 D1
Chaddesley Corbett (056 283) 388

Brewery Wolverhampton & Dudley
Landlord Mr P. B. Cartwright

Steak & mushroom pie £2 Cold buffet £2 (Last
order 9.30pm. No bar food Sun & Mon eves)
🍺 Banks's Best Bitter, Mild; Kronenbourg.
Real ale

The cold table offers an extensive choice
and good value for money at this fine old
part-timbered inn. The salads are fresh and
colourful, ideal accompaniments for
succulent cooked meats, savoury pies and
quiches. A blackboard lists daily specials
like plaice, liver and bacon, casseroles and
hot pots, plus a few home-made sweets.
Table service in the attractive bar is friendly
and efficient. Patio.   **Family pub**

Chaddleworth   (Food)   *Ibex*

Near Newbury · *Berkshire* · Map 6 A3
Chaddleworth (048 82) 311

Brewery Courage
Landlord Sheila Cunningham
Steak, kidney & mushroom pie with
vegetables £2.95 Prawns in garlic butter with
crusty bread £2.60 (Last order 9.30pm. No bar
food Sun eve)
🍺 Courage Best Bitter; Guinness;
Hofmeister; cider. *Real ale*

Set among the Newbury Downs, this cosy
litle pub is very popular with the racing
fraternity, who are happy to put their
money on the highly commendable bar
snacks. As well as salads and sandwiches
made with lovely crusty bread, the wide-
ranging menu features items like country
pâté, Cumberland sausage, pizza and
tender steak and kidney pie, plus spicy
specials such as South African bobotie and
Mexican goulash.   **Family pub**

Chagford (B & B)   Globe Hotel

High Street · *Devon* · Map 8 C3
Chagford (064 73) 3485

Free House
Landlord Mrs B. Abson

BEDROOMS 5   Grade 1   £C
🍺 Bass; Harvest; Whitbread Trophy, Best;
Ansells Mild; Guinness; Harp; Carlsberg.
Real ale

Pleasant staff and excellent housekeeping
contribute to the delights of a stay at this
18th-century coaching house in the heart of
Dartmoor. Locally made pine units are
fitted in the spacious bedrooms, which are
all supplied with fridges and tea-makers.
Public rooms include a residents' lounge,
lounge bar and a splendid public bar with
authentic Victorian decor. Good breakfasts.
Family pub

Chale (B & B)   Clarendon Hotel

Newport Road · *Isle of Wight* · Map 6 A4
Niton (0983) 730431

Free House
Landlords John & Jean Bradshaw

BEDROOMS 13   Grade 1   £A
🍺 Burt's Bitter; Whitbread Strong Country
Bitter, Best Bitter, Trophy; Flowers Original;
Guinness; Stella Artois; cider. *Real ale*

Lovely views out over the sea towards the
Needles make this 17th-century coaching
inn a delightful place to stay. Charming,
individually decorated bedrooms (several
are family-size) have duvets, and bathrooms are well equipped. There's a homely
TV lounge, and the hotel's own pub – the
characterful Wight Mouse Inn – is a popular
meeting place with a collection of some 150
malt whiskies. Pleasant garden for fine
weather. **Family pub**

Chappel (Food)   Swan Inn

The Street, Nr Colchester · *Essex* · Map 5 C2
Earls Colne (078 75) 2353

Free House
Landlords Terence & Frances Martin

Jumbo peeled scampi £4.75 Grilled fresh
sardines £1.95 (Last order 10.30pm)
🍺 Greene King IPA, Abbot Ale, Mild XX;
Guinness; Harp; Dörtmunder; Kronenbourg;
Taunton cider. *Real ale*

The garden of this 500-year-old pub runs
right down to the river Colne, and the
heavily beamed lounge bar is very
welcoming in cooler weather. Terence
Martin makes weekly shopping trips to
London for the ingredients of his excellent
bar snacks, which range from home-made
soups and succulent grills to a variety of
seafood dishes including a delicious
assortment of crisply battered fish. Sandwiches and salads cater for light appetites

Charlbury (Food, B & B)   Bell at Charlbury

Church Street · *Oxfordshire* · Map 5 A2
Charlbury (0608) 810278

Free House
Landlords Carlos & Dorothy da Cruz

BEDROOMS 13   Grade 1   £A
Guinness & steak pie & vegetables £2.25
Lasagne £1.95 (No bar food eves or Sun)
🍺 Wadworth's 6X, IPA; Whitbread Trophy;
Guinness; Heineken; Grünhalle. *Real ale*

Tasty lunchtime fare adds to the popularity
of this handsome 18th-century Cotswold
inn. The blackboard menu might offer
onion soup to start, followed by tempting
main courses such as chilli con carne, hot
smoked mackerel with Biscay sauce, and
roast stuffed venison. Elegant bedrooms
combine antique furniture with modern
comforts like TVs and telephones.
Family pub

Charlton Village *(Food)*   *Harrow*

142 Charlton Road, Shepperton · *Middlesex* ·
Map 6 B3
Sunbury (76) 83122
Brewery Watney
Landlord Ralph John
Shepherd's pie £1.85 Roast beef, Yorkshire
pudding & vegetables £3 (No bar food Sun
or eves)
🍺 Watney's Stag Bitter; Ben Truman;
Wilson Great Northern Bitter; Guinness;
Foster's; Carlsberg. *Real ale*

Generous portions of tasty home-cooked
fare are served at lunchtime in this attractive thatched cottage, reputedly the oldest
inhabited building in Middlesex. In the two
low-beamed bars you can make your
choice from the blackboard menu – perhaps a jacket potato with savoury mince,
stuffed pancakes, roast lamb or ham and
eggs with bubble and squeak. Also sandwiches (the only Saturday choice),
ploughman's and simple puds. Garden.

Cheddington *(Food)*   *Rosebery Arms*

Station Road, Near Leighton Buzzard, Beds
Buckinghamshire · Map 5 B2
Cheddington (0296) 668222

Brewery Wells
Landlord Mr Len Large

Steak & game pie 65p Treacle tart with ice
cream 50p (Last order 10pm)
🍺 Wells Bitter, Noggin; Guinness;
Kellerbräu.

Len Large's efforts in the kitchen are well
rewarded at this friendly, red-brick pub.
Home-cooked savoury pies – perhaps
chicken and mushroom or steak and game
– are a speciality and go nicely with a crisp
side salad. You can also enjoy flavoursome
soups, salmon mousse and an excellent
pork and parsley brawn. Don't miss the
gooey treacle tart. Cheese and sandwiches
in the evening and on Sunday. **Family pub**

Chedworth *(Food)*   *Seven Tuns*

Near Cheltenham · *Gloucestershire* · Map 5 A2
Fossebridge (028 572) 242

Brewery Courage
Landlords Brian & Barbara Eacott

Ploughman's £1.50 Chilli con carne £1.50 (Last
order 9pm)
🍺 Courage Best Bitter, Directors Bitter, JC;
Guinness; Hofmeister; Taunton cider. *Real ale*

Barbara Eacott's simple, wholesome
snacks are among the attractions of this
cosy old stone pub, which also boasts a
children's games room and an upstairs
skittle alley. There's a good choice of pâtés
and ploughman's, as well as tasty, home-
cooked ham. More elaborate items include
a delicious turkey loaf or perhaps chilli con
carne, and cinnamon-flavoured apple pie
makes an excellent finish. **Family pub**

Chelsfield *(Food)*   *Bo-Peep*

Hewitts Road · *Kent* · Map 6 C3
Knockholt (0959) 34457

Brewery Courage
Landlord Mr & Mrs A. Peel

Devilled kidneys & vegetables £1.65 Treacle
sponge 65p (No bar food eves or Sun)
🍺 Courage Directors Bitter, Best Bitter, JC;
Guinness; Hofmeister; Kronenbourg. *Real ale*

Check directions, or you could go astray
while heading for this fine old country pub,
where crowds flock to enjoy hearty, well-
prepared bar fare. Smoked mackerel fillet
and chicken liver pâté make tasty snacks or
starters, and main courses – the menu
changes frequently – could include chicken
Kiev, chilli beef or devilled kidneys. Before
leaving the fold try a nice fruit pie or
steamed pudding. Garden.

Chelsworth   *(Food, B & B)*   *Peacock Inn*

The Street, Near Ipswich · *Suffolk* · Map 5 D2
Bildeston (0449) 740758

Free House
Landlords Anthony & Lorna Marsh
BEDROOMS 5   Grade 1   £B   (No dogs)
Game pie £3.25 Quiche £2.50
(Last order 10.30pm)
🍺 Adnams Bitter; Greene King IPA, Abbot
Ale; Mauldon's Bitter, Porter (winter only);
Guinness; cider. *Real ale*

Visitors will find wholesome food and comfortable accommodation at this friendly old village pub. Besides sandwiches and quiches, tasty bar snacks include local game, plus a cold buffet in summer and spit-roast rib of beef for lunch on Sundays in winter. The five bedrooms are solidly furnished and share a neat modern bathroom. Good breakfasts. No children under five overnight. Garden.

Chenies   *(Food)*   ★   *Bedford Arms Thistle Hotel*

Near Rickmansworth · *Hertfordshire* · Map 6 B3
Chorleywood (092 78) 3301

Owners Thistle Hotels
Landlord Mr C. Freybourger

Baked avocado with mushrooms £3.90
Salmon trout £4.90 (Last order 10pm)
🍺 Younger's No. 3 Ale, Scotch Bitter, Tartan;
McEwan's Export; Guinness; Kestrel;
McEwan's Lager. *Real ale*

The bar snacks served at this handsome hotel are a delight to both eye and palate. A long and varied lunchtime menu offers sandwiches, superb country pâté, bangers and mash, ravioli, plated salads... and, widening the choice still further, daily specials like soft herring roes and perfectly prepared calf's sweetbreads. Scrumptious sweets, too. Sandwiches only evenings and Sunday. *For accommodation see Egon Ronay's Lucas Hotel & Restaurant Guide 1985.* **Family pub**

Cherington   *(Food)*   *The Cherrington*

Near Tetbury · *Gloucestershire* · Map 7 D2
Rodmarton (028 584) 255

Free House
Landlord Mr B. Nunn
Italian hamburger £1.95 Chicken
Caribbean £3.45 (Last order 10pm)
🍺 Wadworth's 6X; Flowers Original;
Whitbread Best Bitter; Hook Norton;
Guinness; Heineken; Hofmeister; cider.
Real ale

A narrow winding lane leads to this welcoming pub, where you will find a splendid choice of well-prepared food which ranges from French onion soup and lasagne to chicken casserole and an excellent beef burgundy. There's also a tempting cold buffet featuring honey-roast ham and various quiches, and delicious puddings and ice creams round things off nicely. Garden.   **Family pub**

Chester   *(B & B)*   *Ye Olde King's Head*

48 Lower Bridge Street · *Cheshire* · Map 3 B4
Chester (0244) 24855

Brewery Greenall Whitley
Landlords Mr & Mrs R. Musker

BEDROOMS 11   Grade 2   £B
🍺 Greenall Whitley Local Bitter, Festival;
Grünhalle. *Real ale*

Dating back to the 16th century, this splendid old half-timbered inn is a great favourite with foreign visitors. Oak-beamed bedrooms offer comfortable accommodation, with solid furnishings and modern amenities like radios. Bath and shower rooms are well kept. Guests can relax in the TV lounge, or admire the relief map of Civil War battles in the open-plan bar.

Chichester   *(Food, B & B)*   *The Nags*

3 St Pancras · *West Sussex* · Map 6 B4
Chichester (0243) 785823

Brewery Whitbread
Landlords Brian & June Kirby & son
BEDROOMS 10   Grade 1 & 2   £B   (No dogs)
Carvery meal £5.50 Toasted sandwich £1.20
(Last order 9.15)
🍺 Flower's Original, Strong Country Bitter;
Whitbread Bitter; Guinness; Heineken; Stella
Artois; cider. *Real ale*

Food is a strong point at this handsome
town pub, where each weekday lunchtime
there's a good buffet selection that includes
cold meats, salads and tasty specials like
shepherd's pie. A hot carvery takes over in
the evening (Sunday lunchtime too), and
sandwiches are always available. Ten bedrooms with washbasins and colour TVs are
in period style and offer traditional
comforts (no children overnight). Patio and
garden.

Chickerell   *(B & B)*   *Turks Head Inn*

6 East Street, Near Weymouth · *Dorset*
Map 8 D4
Weymouth (0305) 783093

Brewery Devenish
Landlords Williams family

BEDROOMS 4   Grade 1   £C
🍺 Devenish Bitter, Wessex Bitter,
Weymouth Bitter, Mild; Guinness; Heineken;
Grünhalle; cider. *Real ale*

A delightful, stone-built pub in a peaceful
location. Overnight guests (no under-
threes) will find plenty of space and comfort in the well-furnished bedrooms, which
all have TVs, tea-makers and spotless
modern bathrooms. Good breakfasts, too.
There's a large, cheerful public bar, and the
skittle alley is a popular attraction. Accommodation closed 1 week Christmas. Patio.
Family pub

Chiddingfold   *(B & B)*   *Crown Inn*

The Green · *Surrey* · Map 6 B3
Wormley (042 879) 2255

Free House
Landlord Mr K. Playter

BEDROOMS 5   Grade 1   £A+   (No dogs)
🍺 Gales HSB; Badgers Best Bitter; Young's
Special; Charrington IPA; Guinness; cider.
Real ale

The handsome half-timbered facade testi-
fies to the great age of this splendid village
inn, originally a stopping place for pilgrim
monks and a hostelry for 600 years. Solid
oak beams, a great inglenook fireplace and
fine linenfold panelling characterise the
lounge bar, and there's a wealth of period
charm in the comfortable bedrooms, which
have TVs, tea-makers and private bathrooms. Courtyard.   **Family pub**

Chiddingfold   *(Food)*   *Swan*

Petworth Road · *Surrey* · Map 6 B3
Wormley (042 879) 2073

Brewery Friary Meux
Landlords Mr & Mrs N. I. G. Bradford

Pigeon breast in port £5.10 Steak & kidney pie
& vegetables £1.85 (Last order 10pm)
🍺 Friary Meux Bitter; Ind Coope Burton
Ale, Mild, John Bull; Guinness; Löwenbräu;
cider. *Real ale*

The landlord of this friendly village pub is
an enthusiastic angler, and fish features
strongly on the menu – whether caught by
himself or bought fresh from the market.
Local trout, prawns in garlic and grilled
sardines are popular choices, and you can
also have a home-made soup or meat pie, a
jacket potato or a crusty French bread
sandwich. Tables are set out in the garden
across the road in summer.

Chilgrove (Food)   *White Horse Inn*

Near Chichester · *West Sussex* · Map 6 B4
East Marden (024 359) 219

Free House
Landlords Barry & Dorothea Phillips

White Horse prawns £3.45 Home-made
dessert 95p (No bar food eves)
🍺 Ben Truman; Antelope Ale; Guinness;
Carlsberg. *Real ale*

Nestling peacefully below the South
Downs, this fine old country pub is a
favourite spot to pause for a lunchtime
snack. The little bar soon fills up with
customers enjoying Adrian Congdon's
excellent fare, which ranges from smoked
salmon sandwiches and a summertime
cold buffet to crab gratin, coq au vin and
delectable puds like gooey treacle tart.
Garden. Closed Monday, all January & last
week October.

Chilham (Food, B & B)   *Woolpack*

High Street · *Kent* · Map 6 D3
Canterbury (0227) 730208

Brewery Shepherd Neame
Landlord Mr John Durcan
BEDROOMS 13 Grade 1 £A
Prawns in oil & garlic £1.85 Grilled lemon
sole £3.45 (Last order 10pm)
🍺 Shepherd Neame Master Brew, Invicta
Bitter; Guinness; Hürlimann. *Real ale*

Once an overnight stop on the London–
Dover coaching route, this handsome
whitewashed pub is equally welcoming to
today's travellers, offering comfortable
accommodation and good, simple fare.
Well-carpeted bedrooms, most with private
facilities, have neat modern furniture, tea-
makers and colour TVs. Snacks served in the
oak-beamed bar include sandwiches and
salads based on cold meats, plus a few hot
dishes like chilli.   **Family pub**

Chipping (Food)   *Dog & Partridge*

Hesketh Lane, Near Preston · *Lancashire*
Map 3 B3
Chipping (099 56) 201

Free House
Landlords John & Mary Barr

Roast duckling £4 Pâté with toast £1.25
(Last order 9.45pm. No bar food Sat eve &
Sun lunch)
🍺 Tetley's Bitter, Mild; Skol.

Stop at this sturdy white-painted inn for a
very friendly welcome and some wholesome, enjoyable snacks. John and Mary
Barr's short menu offers simple treats like a
delicious chicken liver pâté with toast,
home-made vegetable soup, roast chicken
or duckling, scampi and a hearty ploughman's. You can eat in the cosy bar or out on
the cobbled terrace in fine weather.

Chipping Camden (Food)   *King's Arms Hotel*

The Square · *Gloucestershire* · Map 5 A2
Evesham (0386) 840256

Free House
Landlord Mr A. S. Guthrie

Lamb cutlets café de Paris £2.70 Samosa with
apple chutney £2.10 (No bar food eves &
all Sun)
🍺 Hook Norton Bitter; Carlsberg Hof.
Real ale

New owner Mr Guthrie has retained the
excellent team that runs this fine old market-
square inn. Lunchtime bar snacks put
the emphasis on seafood, with moules
marinière, baked smelts and tasty salmon
pancakes among the favourites. Also available are soup, garlicky chicken livers and
savoury pies, with a yummy strawberry
fool to finish. Garden. *For accommodation
see Egon Ronay's Lucas Hotel & Restaurant
Guide 1985.*   **Family pub**

Chipping Norton   *(B & B)*   *Crown & Cushion*

High Street · *Oxfordshire* · Map 5 A2
Chipping Norton (0608) 2533

Free House
Landlord Mr J. M. Fraser

BEDROOMS 14   Grades 1 & 2   £B
🍺 Wadworth's 6X, IPA; Hook Norton Best
Bitter; McEwan's Export; Guinness;
Kronenbourg. *Real ale*

This well-maintained inn opened its doors
in 1497 and has been providing good
hospitality ever since. The past looms large
in the popular beamed bar with its fine old
fireplace shining with brass ornaments;
there's also a cosy TV room and a spacious
residents' lounge. Nicely coordinated
bedrooms are thoroughly up to date with
simple contemporary furniture, TVs, telephones and good modern bathrooms.
Patio.   **Family pub**

Chipping Norton   *(B & B)*   *Fox Hotel*

Market Place · *Oxfordshire* · Map 5 A2
Chipping Norton (0608) 2658

Brewery Hall
Landlord Mr & Mrs J. D. Philp

BEDROOMS 6   Grade 2   £C
🍺 Hall's Harvest Bitter; Tetley's Bitter; Ind
Coope John Bull Bitter, Double Diamond;
Guinness; Löwenbräu; cider. *Real ale*

New managers the Philps make visitors feel
very much at home in this comfortable
hotel facing the town hall. The bedrooms,
all with televisions and tea-makers, are
furnished in a variety of styles and share
two carpeted bathrooms. There are two
bars (the main one quite large, with darkwood panelling and copper ornaments)
and a pleasant little lounge.   **Family pub**

Chiseldon   *(B & B)*   *Patriots Arms*

New Road · *Wiltshire* · Map 6 A3
Swindon (0793) 740331

Brewery Courage
Landlords Mr & Mrs D. Day

BEDROOMS 3   Grade 2   £C   (No dogs)
🍺 Courage Directors Bitter, Best Bitter, Mild;
Simonds Bitter; Guinness; John Smith's
Lager; Taunton cider. *Real ale*

A family room and patio are part of the plans
that have recently been taking shape at this
unpretentious, white-painted pub. Overnight accommodation is modest but comfortable in three centrally heated bedrooms
with simple furnishings and coordinated
fabrics. The bathroom they share is practical, modern and well-maintained. The
lounge and bar areas are also part of the
improvement scheme. Garden. **Family pub**

Christow   *(B & B)*   *Artichoke Inn*

Village Road, Near Exeter · *Devon* · Map 8 C4
Christow (0647) 52387

Brewery Heavitree
Landlords Mr & Mrs M. H. Fox

BEDROOMS 3   Grade 2   £C
🍺 Flower's IPA, Original; Whitbread Trophy;
Poachers; Guinness; Heineken; cider. *Real ale*

Flagstone floors, low beams, horse brasses
and an inglenook fireplace are familiar
features in a traditional English pub, and
you'll find them all in the bar of this ancient
thatched inn not far from Exeter. Steep,
narrow stairs lead to the pretty bedrooms
(one family size, all with TVs and tea-
makers), which share a well-equipped
bathroom. A cosy breakfast room overlooks the garden!   **Family pub**

Church Stretton *(B & B)*

Kings Arms

High Street · *Shropshire* · Map 7 D1
Church Stretton (0694) 722807

Brewery Shrewsbury & Wem
Landlords Ken & Jean MacKechnie

BEDROOMS 2   Grade 2   £C
🍺 Wem Best Bitter, Best Mild; Guinness;
Grünhalle. *Real ale*

Long-serving landlords Ken and Jean
MacKechnie keep everything really spick
and span at their popular late-Tudor pub on
the main street of an ancient market town.
Behind a white pebbledash facade, solid
oak beams give a homely old-world appeal,
and the two little bedrooms provide simple
comforts for an overnight stay. They share
a well-fitted modern bathroom.

Churchstow *(Food)*

Church House Inn

Near Kingsbridge · *Devon* · Map 8 C4
Kingsbridge (0548) 2237

Free House
Landlords Messrs Nicholson & Tucker

Devilled chicken £1.95 Speciality fish pie £1.85
(Last order 9pm)
🍺 Usher's Best Bitter; Founder's Ale; Bass;
Carlsberg; Guinness; cider. *Real ale*

You'll find this cosy, beamed 15th-century
inn right opposite the church. Wholesome,
enjoyable bar snacks range from simple
salads and sandwiches to warming soups
in winter, a tasty fish pie, spicy devilled
chicken and cold meats served with
delicious bubble and squeak. Lemon
meringue pie is a favourite among the
lovely homely sweets. Patio.

Clanfield *(Food, B & B)*

Clanfield Tavern

Near Witney · *Oxfordshire* · Map 6 A3
Clanfield (036 781) 223

Free House
Landlords Mr & Mrs K. Nadin
BEDROOMS 3   Grade 2   £B
Spiced pork pancake £2.95 Steak & mushroom
kebab £3 (Last order 9.45pm)
🍺 Morland's Bitter; Hook Norton Best Bitter;
Arkell's BBB; Greenall Whitley Festival;
Guinness; Carlsberg; cider. *Real ale*

An attractive old stone tavern with thick
walls, heavy beams and well-worn flagstone floors. Mrs Nadin's bar snacks are a
popular feature: try her flavoursome
smoked mackerel pâté, followed perhaps
by a burger, steak or chicken and ham vol-
au-vent. Nice sweets, too. The bedrooms
have good carpets and comfortable beds;
they share an up-to-date bathroom.
Garden.   **Family pub**

Clare *(Food, B & B)*

Bell Hotel

Near Sudbury · *Suffolk* · Map 5 C2
Clare (0787) 277741

Free House
Landlords H. Jones & M. Jones
BEDROOMS 21   Grades 1 & 2   £B
Suffolk sausages £1.95 Fruit pie 95p
(Last order 9.30pm)
🍺 Greene King IPA; Adnams Bitter, Old
(winter only); Mauldon's Bitter; Guinness.
Real ale

This fine old half-timbered inn serves very
good snacks in its rustic bar. Starters like
soup or pâté could be followed by a richly
flavoured steak and onion pie, and there's
plenty of variety among the sandwiches,
salads and homely puds. Courtyard bedrooms have lovely period furnishings,
colour TVs and private bathrooms. Rooms
in the original building are generally
simpler. Garden.   **Family pub**

Clare *(Food)*   *Seafarer Inn*

Nethergate Street · *Suffolk* · Map 5 C2
Clare (0787) 277449

Free House
Landlords John & Celia Blanshard

Seafood bake £4.50 Pork fillet Celia £3.50
(Last order 10pm. No bar food Mon eve)
🍺 Adnams Bitter, Mild, Old Ale; Double
Diamond; Hurlimann; cider. *Real ale*

Fish and shellfish are the speciality of this
aptly named pub that prides itself on good
fresh produce. Try the king prawns, ceviche
or fish soup to start, with perhaps a seafood
bake to follow. Meat lovers are catered for
with dishes like pork fillet or hunter's
chicken. There are salads and sandwiches
for light eaters, and a selection of simple
sweets. Garden.

Clare *(Food)*   *Swan Inn*

4 High Street, Near Sudbury · *Suffolk*
Map 5 C2
Clare (0787) 278030
Brewery Greene King
Landlords Mr & Mrs R. Greybrook
Cheese-topped cottage pie £1.50 Beefsteak,
kidney & mushroom pie £2.40 (Last
order 10pm. No bar food Mon eve)
🍺 Greene King Abbot Ale, IPA, Dark Mild;
Guinness; Harp; Kronenbourg; Taunton cider.
Real ale

An imposing carved swan, reputedly the
oldest inn sign in Europe, stands above the
portal of this ancient hostelry. In the cosy
bars they serve a good variety of fare: hot
potted shrimps, Camembert fritters or
garlicky tsatsiki makes a tasty light snack,
and more hearty main courses might
include saucy porterhouse steak, baked
trout and the ever-popular beefsteak,
kidney and mushroom pie enriched with
ale. Daily specials too. Garden.

Clayton *(B & B)*   *Jack & Jill Inn*

Brighton Road · *West Sussex* · Map 6 C4
Hassocks (079 18) 3595

Brewery Watneys
Landlords Mike & Joan Harman

BEDROOMS 4 Grade 2 £C (No dogs)
🍺 Watneys Stag Bitter; Tamplins Bitter;
Webster's Yorkshire Bitter; Guinness;
Holsten; Foster's; cider. *Real ale*

About seven miles north of Brighton on the
A273, this friendly roadside inn has a playground and special children's room that
make it especially useful for families. The
cosy bar is a relaxing spot for a drink and
the bedrooms are clean and cheerful, with
whitewood furniture, tea-makers and
washbasins. There are two well-fitted
shower rooms.   **Family pub**

Clearwell *(Food, B & B)*   *Wyndham Arms*

Near Coleford · *Gloucestershire* · Map 7 D2
Dean (0594) 33666

Free House
Landlords Mr & Mrs J. Stanford
BEDROOMS 5 Grade 1 £A+
Grilled Portuguese sardines £2.75 Chicken
liver pâté £2.15 (Last order 10pm)
🍺 Flower's Best Bitter, Original, West
Country Pale Ale; Guinness; Heineken; Stella
Artois; cider. *Real ale*

Two new bedrooms have recently
increased the accommodation at this spick
and span 14th-century pub; all rooms have
central heating, TVs, tea-makers and
private bathrooms. The bar menu offers a
good choice of simple, tasty snacks, from
soup and sandwiches to grilled rainbow
trout, prawn curry and chilli con carne.
Snack service may be suspended when the
restaurant is busy. Closed 2 weeks end
October. Garden.

Clifton Hampden   *(Food, B & B)*   *Barley Mow*

Near Abingdon · *Oxfordshire* · Map 6 A3
Clifton Hampden (086 730) 7847

Owners Thames Hosts
Landlords Mr & Mrs Paul Turner
BEDROOMS 4   Grade 2   £C
Beef, lamb & mussel pie £2.60 Beef curry £2.10
(Last order 10pm. No bar food Sun eve)
🍺 Usher's Founder's Ale, Best Bitter, Pale
Ale; Webster's Yorkshire Bitter; Guinness;
Carlsberg. *Real ale*

Tasty bar snacks bring a cheerful clientele
to this delightful old thatched pub, which
enjoys a pleasant setting near the Thames.
Hand-raised pies and home-baked ham
make popular salad platters, and other
choices include roast beef (hot and cold),
spare ribs and turkey drumsticks. Well-kept
bedrooms with TVs and tea-makers share
a modern bathroom. Good breakfasts.
Garden.   **Family pub**

Clun   *(Food, B & B)*   *Sun Inn*

High Street, Near Craven Arms · *Shropshire*
Map 7 C1
Clun (058 84) 559
Free House
Landlords Rodney & Beryl Marsden
BEDROOMS 7   Grade 2   £C   (No dogs)
Vegetable soup 80p Escalope of pork with
apple sauce £3.25 (Last order 9.30pm)
🍺 Wood's Parish Bitter; Mitchells & Butlers
Springfield Bitter; Ansells Mild; Bass;
Guinness; Tennent's Extra; cider. *Real ale*

A 15th-century village pub of cruck construction abounding in rustic charm.
Snacks served in the little beamed bars are
simple and delicious – flavoursome vegetable soup, home-cooked ham for sandwiches or salads, escalope of pork, fresh
plum tart. Bedrooms range from homely
and old-fashioned in the main building to
more modern, with tea-makers and shower
facilities, in the annexe. There are two cosy
lounges, one with TV. Patio.

Clyst Hydon   *(Food)*   *Five Bells*

Cullompton · *Devon* · Map 8 C3
Plymtree (088 47) 288

Free House
Landlords Mr & Mrs J. A. Hayward
Mushroom omelette with chips & salad £1.70
Steak & kidney pie & vegetables £2.50 (Last
order 9.45pm)
🍺 Hall & Woodhouse Badger Best Bitter;
Bass; Worthington Best Bitter; Carlsberg Pils;
Taunton cider. *Real ale*

Tasty snacks are available both at lunchtime and in the evening in the handsome
beamed bar of this secluded farmhouse
inn. Omelettes, served nicely soft with
fillings of ham, cheese or mushroom are a
house speciality, and other favourites
range from fresh-flavoured vegetable soup
to sandwiches, ploughman's platters,
home-made pies and basket meals. Apple
crumble rounds things off nicely. Closed
Mon evenings in winter. Garden.

Cobham   *(Food)*   *Plough*

Plough Lane · *Surrey* · Map 6 B3
Cobham (093 26) 2514

Brewery Courage
Landlords John & Irene Huetson

Ploughman's lunch £1.10 Prawn salad £2.75
(Last order 9.30pm)
🍺 Courage Directors Bitter, Best Bitter;
John Smith's Bitter; Guinness; Hofmeister;
Kronenbourg; cider. *Real ale*

Goats, bantams and a donkey make this
friendly little red-brick pub near Downside
Bridge especially popular with children. A
cold cabinet in the lounge features an
appetising display of succulent beef, fresh
crab, smoked salmon and salads, and you
can also choose hot dishes like a prawn-
filled baked potato, tasty shepherd's pie or
a toasted sandwich.   **Family pub**

111

England

Cockwood   *(Food)*   *Ship Inn*

Starcross, Near Exeter · *Devon* · Map 8 C4
Starcross (0626) 890373

Brewery Courage
Landlord Mr B. Hoyle
Cockwood special £4.95 Moules
marinière £1.75 (Last order 10.15pm)
🍺 Courage Directors Bitter, Best Bitter, JC;
John Smith's Yorkshire; Simmonds Mild;
Guinness; Hofmeister; Kronenbourg;
Taunton cider. *Real ale*

This unassuming old pub stands just a
short walk from Cockwood harbour, so it's
not surprising that seafood is a speciality.
Crab, lobster, mussels and monkfish are
carefully prepared and prettily presented,
and you can push the boat out with a splendid mixed platter. Also sandwiches and
salads, excellent chicken liver pâté and
steaks, plus nice home-made sweets.
Garden.   **Family pub**

Coggeshall   *(Food)*   *White Hart Hotel*

Market End · *Essex* · Map 5 C2
Coggeshall (0376) 61654

Free House
Landlords Mr & Mrs R. Pluck

Scallop & prawn Mornay £2.50 Rack of
lamb £5.25 (No bar food eves & Sun)
🍺 Ansells Best Bitter; Stella Artois. *Real ale*

History abounds at this 500-year-old hostelry, whose public rooms feature some
marvellous timbers. The bar menu ranges
from sandwiches and pâté to steak and
kidney pie, smoked trout and savoury pancakes. There's also a wide selection of
charcoal grills from calf's liver to steaks.
Closed August and 1 week Christmas.
Patio. *For accommodation see Egon
Ronay's Lucas Hotel & Restaurant Guide
1985.*   **Family pub**

Coggeshall   *(Food, B & B)*   *Woolpack Inn*

91 Church Street · *Essex* · Map 5 C2
Coggeshall (0376) 61235
Brewery Ind Coope
Landlords Mr & Mrs W. T. Hutchinson
BEDROOMS 2 Grade 2 £B (No dogs)
Fresh Dover sole £2.95 Game pie £2.50 (Last
order 9.30pm. No bar food Sun–Tues eves)
🍺 Ind Coope Bitter, Friary Meux Bitter;
Benskins Bitter; Taylor Walker Bitter;
Löwenbräu; Skol; cider. *Real ale*

Built for a wool merchant in the 15th
century, this splendid pub still boasts fine
beams, panelling and lattice windows. Mrs
Hutchinson's excellent bar snacks are an
additional attraction, ranging from soup
with garlic bread to smoked mackerel pâté,
fresh fish, game pie or a cold meat salad,
with perhaps a treacle tart to finish.
Bedrooms are homely and comfortable. No
children overnight. Garden.

Colesbourne   *(Food)*   *Colesbourne Inn*

Nr Cheltenham · *Gloucestershire* · Map 5 A2
Coberley (024 287) 376

Brewery Wadworth
Landlords Mr & Mrs M. J. Pringle

Herby beef £2.50 Turkey & ham pie salad £3.50
(Last order 10pm)
🍺 Wadworth's IPA, 6X, Old Timer (winter
only), Northgate Bitter, Löwenbräu; Heineken.
Real ale

Appetising salads featuring home-cooked
meats and locally made pies are a popular
choice at this comfortable roadside pub,
and spare ribs and lamb hot pot are typical
hot specials at lunchtime. You can also get
a sandwich, and there are delicious fruit
pies for dessert. Grills are a staple of the
more extensive evening menu. Garden.

Coleshill *(B & B)*   *Coleshill Hotel*

152 High Street · *Warwickshire* · Map 5 A2
Coleshill (0675) 65527

Free House
Landlord Mr T. J. Lock

BEDROOMS 15 Grade 1 £B
🍺 Mitchells & Butlers Mild, Bitter; Ansells
Bitter; Banks's Mild; Carling Black Label; cider.

Conveniently situated close to junction 4 of
the M6, this comfortably refurbished
hostelry is a welcome stopping place for
tired motorists. Visitors can relax in the
attractive beamed lounge or enjoy a drink
in the pleasant bar. Spotlessly clean
bedrooms (including a bridal suite with a
four-poster) have plenty of wardrobe
space, radios, TVs and tea-makers, plus
prettily tiled bath or shower rooms. Patio.
Family pub

Coleshill *(B & B)*   *Swan Hotel*

High Street · *Warwickshire* · Map 5 A2
Coleshill (0675) 62212

Brewery Ansells
Landlords P. J. Stubbins & G. C. Donovan

BEDROOMS 35 Grade 1 £B
🍺 Ansells Bitter, Mild; Tetley's Bitter;
Guinness; Skol; cider. *Real ale*

Smartly updated behind its 17th-century
façade, this former coaching inn appeals
to modern travellers with its excellent
accommodation and handy position (it's
very near the M6 and National Exhibition
Centre). Bedrooms (all with extras such as
hairdryers) have practical built-in units, TVs
and trouser presses, and the 20 annexe
rooms have shower rooms. There's a
spacious public bar and intimate cocktail
lounge. **Family pub**

Collyweston *(Food, B & B)*   *Cavalier*

Near Stamford · *Northamptonshire* · Map 5 B1
Duddington (078 083) 288
Free House
Landlords A. B., N. A. & E. J. Haigh
BEDROOMS 5 Grade 2 £C
Steak & kidney pie £2.95 Salmon steak
trouvillaise £4.25 (Last order 9.30pm)
🍺 Bateman's XXXB; Greene King IPA;
Webster's Yorkshire Bitter; Ruddle's County;
Younger's Tartan; Guinness; Taunton cider.
Real ale

A varied menu caters for all tastes at this
welcoming village pub just off the A43.
Besides sandwiches and pizzas, there's
garlicky pâté plus a selection of hot dishes
like curry, steak and sweet and sour
chicken. The traditional Sunday roast is a
popular feature. Prettily decorated bedrooms (three with smart modern bathrooms) have TVs and tea-makers.
Family pub

Coln St Aldwyns *(B & B)*   *New Inn*

Near Cirencester · *Gloucestershire* · Map 6 A3
Coln St Aldwyns (028 575) 202

Free House
Landlords Mr & Mrs R. Warren

BEDROOMS 5 Grade 2 £B
🍺 Morland's Bitter; Wadworth's 6X;
Mitchells & Butlers Brew X1; Guinness;
Carling Black Label. *Real ale*

Far from being new, this Cotswold-stone
inn actually dates back to the 16th century!
The public bar is the social centre of village
life, and there's a comfortable lounge bar
with oak beams and an inglenook fireplace.
Homely bedrooms in the main building
share a well-maintained bathroom, while
those in the annexe have their own
facilities. There's a TV lounge for residents.
Terrace. **Family pub**

England

Compton *(Food)* — *Harrow Inn*

Guildford · *Surrey* · Map 6 B3
Guildford (0483) 810379

Brewery Friary Meux
Landlords Roger & Sue Seaman

Seafood special £3.75 Lasagne with
salad £2.50 (Last order 10pm)
🍺 Friary Meux Bitter; Ind Coope Burton
Ale; Guinness, Skol; Löwenbräu; cider.
Real ale

Racing pictures line the walls of this comfortable pub but the lavish cold counter is
the real winner. Seafood lovers can choose
between mussels, prawns, trout and
smoked mackerel, while meat eaters have
juicy roast beef, chicken and ham pie or
lasagne to go with a selection of fresh,
colourful salads. Pizzas and toasted sandwiches too. Garden.

Congleton *(Food, B & B)* — *Lion & Swan Hotel*

West Street · *Cheshire* · Map 4 C4
Congleton (026 02) 3115

Free House
Landlords Messrs T. R. & B. Harrison
BEDROOMS 13 Grade 1 £A (No dogs)
Quiche & salad £1.85 Steak & kidney pie £2.25
(Last order 9.30pm. No bar food Sun eve)
🍺 Marston's Bitter, Pedigree; Burtonwood
Bitter, Mild; Guinness; Tuborg; Löwenbräu;
cider. *Real ale*

Many original features survive in this 16th-
century timbered coaching inn, whose
entrance is flanked by Doric columns and
stone lions. Snacks served in the characterful bars include sandwiches and salads,
well-made quiches and the ever-popular
steak & kidney pie. Smartly refurbished
bedrooms with whitewood furniture, tea-
makers, TVs and direct-dial telephones
provide good comforts. There's a cosy
lounge. **Family pub**

Congresbury *(Food)* — *White Hart & Inwood*

Wrington Road, Near Bristol · *Avon* · Map 8 D3
Yatton (0272) 833303

Free House
Landlords Mellor family

Chicken & almond soup 70p Garlic beef £2.75
(No bar food Sun or eves)
🍺 Wadworth's 6X; Butcombe Bitter;
Flower's Original; Guinness; Heineken; Stella
Artois; Taunton cider. *Real ale*

Lunchtime sees a wide selection of hot and
cold fare in the cosy, characterful bars
of the timbered White Hart and its neighbour just across the car park. Ploughman's
platters and toasted sandwiches are
popular choices for quick snacks, and
other favourites from a daily-changing
selection range from hearty soups and
jacket potatoes to baked ham, quiches,
curries and casseroles. Garden. **Family pub**

Constable Burton *(Food)* — *Wyvill Arms*

Near Leyburn · *North Yorkshire* · Map 4 C2
Bedale (0677) 50581

Free House
Landlord Mr S Dean

Steak & kidney pie £2.50 Madras beef
curry £2.60 (Last order 9.30pm)
🍺 Theakston's Best Bitter; John Smith's
Bitter, Magnet; Hofmeister; Carlsberg Hof;
Taunton cider. *Real ale*

Bar snacks are varied and satisfying at this
handsome converted farmhouse. The
choice ranges from soup or a sandwich for
a quick bite to grilled trout, braised chicken,
beef curry, juicy steaks and huge cold meat
platters. There are also some delicious
sweets and fine English cheeses. Lunch on
Sunday is a traditional roast. Garden.
Family pub

114

Cornhill-on-Tweed (B & B) Collingwood Arms Hotel

Northumberland · Map 2 D4
Coldstream (0890) 2424

Free House
Landlords Mr & Mrs Scott

BEDROOMS 18 Grade 1 £B
🍺 Drybrough's Heavy, Best Scotch; Burns
Special; Guinness; Carlsberg; Foster's.
Real ale

Just a few miles from the Scottish border
this fine old creeper-covered inn on the
A697 is a good place for an overnight stop.
A blazing winter fire provides a welcome in
the entrance hall, and there are two
pleasant bars. Bright, well-kept bedrooms
are furnished mainly in traditional style.
Seven have TVs and nicely decorated bath
or shower rooms. Garden.   **Family pub**

Corsham (B & B) Methuen Arms

High Street · *Wiltshire* · Map 7 D2
Corsham (0249) 714867

Brewery Gibbs Mew
Landlord Mr Tom Stewart

BEDROOMS 23 Grades 1 & 2 £A+
🍺 Gibbs Anchor Best Bitter, SPA; Bass;
Guinness; Harp; cider. *Real ale*

The Georgian façade of this fine old inn
hides a history that goes back to the 15th
century. The aptly named Long Bar in the
oldest part features splendid beams,
exposed stone walls and a popular skittle
alley. Good-sized bedrooms vary from basic
to very comfortable; all have darkwood
furniture, tea-makers and direct-dial telephones and many have televisions. Good
modern bathrooms.   **Family pub**

Corton (Food) Dove

Near Warminster · *Wiltshire* · Map 8 D3
Warminster (0985) 50378

Free House
Landlords Jane & Michael Rowse

Steak, kidney & oyster pie £3 Tipsy cake £1.20
(Last order 9.30pm)
🍺 Usher's Best Bitter, Triple Crown,
Country; Carlsberg. *Real ale*

This charming Victorian pub is well worth a
visit for its excellent snacks. In the cosy,
attractive bar you can enjoy really tasty
home-prepared fare, from gazpacho and
smoked trout to salads, savoury pies and
well-seasoned salmon and sweetcorn
bake. More hot choices in winter, and
always some delectable desserts. Closed
Sunday evening, Monday (except Bank
Holidays) & 2 weeks mid Jan. Garden.

Cottesmore (Food) Sun Inn

Rutland · *Leicestershire* · Map 5 B1
Oakham (0572) 812321

Brewery Everards
Landlord Mr Allan Plummer

Steak & kidney pie with vegetables £2.30
Seafood pie £4.50 (Last order 10.30pm)
🍺 Everards Tiger, Beacon, Old Original,
Mild; Guinness; cider. *Real ale*

Pull in at this attractive, white-painted
village pub to enjoy a sunny welcome from
Allan Plummer and some tasty, wholesome
home cooking by his wife Gillian. The
lunchtime menu changes daily, offering
soup, salads, a very good roast with all the
trimmings and another hot choice like liver
and onions, while evening options might
include steaks, seafood pie and smoked
gammon. Excellent English cheeseboard.
Terrace.   **Family pub**

Cousley Wood   *(Food)*   *Old Vine*

Near Wadhurst · *East Sussex* · Map 6 C3
Wadhurst (089 288) 2271

Brewery Whitbread
Landlords Mr & Mrs A. Peel
Steak, kidney & mushroom pie £1.95 Chicken
breast in cream sauce £2.75 (Last order
9.30pm. No bar food Sun eve)
🍺 Fremlins Tusker; Whitbread Best Bitter;
Guinness; Stella Artois; Heineken; cider.
Real ale

Good food is a major attraction at this
charming and bustling village pub. The
blackboard menu in the low-ceilinged bar
advertises interesting daily specials like
pork chop with mushrooms, chicken in red
wine and lamb provençale. There are
salads, sandwiches and ploughman's, too,
as well as some delicious sweets from the
trolley. Garden.

Coxwold   *(Food, B & B)*   *Fauconberg Arms*

North Yorkshire · Map 4 C2
Coxwold (034 76) 214

Free House
Landlords Mr & Mrs R. Goodall
BEDROOMS 4   Grade 2   £B   (No dogs)
Soup 80p Sandwich 80p (No bar food eves)
🍺 Younger's Scotch Bitter; Tetley's Bitter;
Theakston's Best Bitter; Guinness; Harp;
Carlsberg. *Real ale*

Lunchtime visitors are assured of an excellent snack at this nicely kept 17th-century
stone inn. Home-made soups like cream of
cauliflower or fennel and mushroom make
a most enjoyable prelude to freshly cut
sandwiches such as the Fauconberg
special – filled with cottage cheese, fruit
and nuts. Simple sweets and cheese, too.
Prettily decorated bedrooms include one
with TV and a private bathroom.
                                            Family pub

Cranborne   *(Food, B & B)*   *Fleur de Lys Hotel*

Near Wimborne · *Dorset* · Map 6 A4
Cranborne (072 54) 282
Brewery Hall & Woodhouse
Landlords Mr & Mrs C. T. Hancock
BEDROOMS 4   Grade 2   £C
Steak pie with vegetables £1.95 Smoked
trout £2.85 (Last order 9.45)
🍺 Hall & Woodhouse Badger Best Bitter;
Hector's Bitter, Tanglefoot; Mitchells & Butlers
Mild; Guinness; Stella Artois; Taunton cider.
Real ale

Mrs Hancock is justly proud of the flowers
that provide a splash of colour outside this
historic, centuries-old inn, while in the
beamed bar there's an atmosphere of rustic
charm and character. Here you can enjoy
traditional fare like rich Dorset pâté, home-
made soup, salads and savoury pies, as
well as grills and basket meals. Bedrooms
are sturdily furnished, and the public bathroom is adequate. Accommodation closed
1 week Christmas. Garden.   **Family pub**

Crawley   *(Food)*   *Fox & Hounds*

Near Winchester · *Hampshire* · Map 6 A3
Sparsholt (096 272) 285
Free House
Landlords Mr & Mrs Dodge &
Mr & Mrs Silsbury
Sparsholt smokie £1.20 Bacon & mushroom
open toasted sandwich £1.70 (Last order 9pm.
No bar food Sun eve)
🍺 Whitbread Best Bitter;. Flowers Original
Bitter; McEwan's Export; Wadworth's 6X;
Guinness; Stella Artois; cider. *Real ale*

The cosy bars of this fine old red-brick
village inn are very welcoming, and there's
always an enjoyable snack, whether at
lunchtime or in the evening. Nourishing
soups, pâtés, varied sandwiches and
ploughman's are the staples of the menu,
which also features tempting daily specials
like gammon with sauté potatoes, courgette quiche and tongue and ham mousse.
Patio.

Crazies Hill   *(Food)* — *Horns*

Near Wargrave · *Berkshire* · Map 6 B3
Wargrave (073 522) 3226

Brewery Brakspear
Landlords Mr & Mrs A. Wheeler

Thai noodles £1.40 Lasagne verdi £1.70
🍺 Brakspear's Bitter, XXXX; Heineken.
Real ale

There's always a south-east Asian dish on Mrs Wheeler's daily menu at this pleasant old black and white pub. Chicken satay or Thai noodles might be the day's spicy special, joining more familiar pub fare like flavoursome soup, lasagne and robust lamb hot pot. Curries make a popular appearance on Tuesday evenings and Saturday lunchtime; limited menu Sunday and Monday evenings.

Croscombe   *(Food)* — *Bull Terrier*

Near Wells · *Somerset* · Map 8 D3
Shepton Mallet (0749) 3658

Free House
Landlords Mr & Mrs S. A. Lea & Mrs J. Preston
Turkey, ham & mushroom pie £2.05 Pork in cider £2.30 (Last order 9.30pm, 9pm in winter. No bar food Sun & Mon eves Oct–April)
🍺 Bull Terrier Bitter; Butcombe Bitter; Wadworth's 6X; Guinness; Holsten; Stella Artois; Taunton cider. *Real ale*

A refuge for pilgrims in medieval times, this fine old pub still has plenty of character with its stone-flagged floor, beams and handsome oak furniture. Bar food also holds a lot of interest, with a choice ranging from tasty pâtés, pies and soups to well-prepared dishes like cannelloni or chicken Maryland. Salads, too, and delicious sweets such as chocolate profiteroles.
Family pub

Croyde   *(Food, B & B)* — *Thatched Barn Inn*

Braunton · *Devon* · Map 8 B3
Croyde (0271) 890349

Free House
Landlords Bruce & Pat Jefford
BEDROOMS 4   Grades 1 & 2   £C
Salmon mayonnaise £1.95 Stuffed chicken breast £4.25 (Last order 10pm)
🍺 Flower's Original; Bass; Whitbread Best Bitter; Guinness; Stella Artois; Heineken; Taunton cider. *Real ale*

Charming hosts and friendly, efficient staff make it a real pleasure to visit this attractive thatched inn, skilfully converted from a 16th-century barn. An extensive menu is offered in the characterful bars, including sandwiches, salads, poultry and charcoal-grilled steaks. Overnight accommodation comprises three simple, spotless bedrooms and a splendid suite, the latter with colour TV and a smart modern bathroom. Patio.
Family pub

Croydon   *(B & B)* — *Windsor Castle*

415 Brighton Road · *Surrey* · Map 6 C3
01-680 4559

Brewery Bass
Landlords Mr & Mrs G. R. Wenham

BEDROOMS 30   Grade 1   £A   (No dogs)
🍺 Charrington's IPA, Stones Bitter; Bass; Guinness; Tennent's; Carling Black Label; Taunton cider. *Real ale*

Situated on the A235 Brighton Road, this former coaching inn provides accommodation of hotel standard in a purpose-built modern extension. All bedrooms have good carpets and practical built-in furniture, and TVs, tea-makers and radio-alarms are standard features, along with compact tiled bathrooms. There are three pleasant bars, one for residents only. Staff are young and friendly. Garden.

Cumnor *(Food)*   Bear & Ragged Staff

Appleton Road · *Oxfordshire* · Map 6 A3
Cumnor (0865) 862329

Owners Sun Taverns Ltd
Landlord Mr Howard Hill-Lines

Pork & Calvados casserole £3.25 Fresh Scotch
salmon in pastry parcel with herb sauce £3.75
(Last order 10pm)
🍺 Morrell's Bitter, Varsity; Guinness; Harp;
Kronenbourg; cider. *Real ale*

Enterprising, carefully prepared food is the
trademark of this charming Cotswold-
stone pub. The menu in the rustic bar might
offer dishes like veal escalope with herbs,
casseroled pork with Calvados or duckling
with Dubonnet and orange. Equally
tempting is the cold buffet display of pies,
cold meats and salads, and there are some
delicious sweets and well-kept cheeses.
Family pub

Damerham *(Food, B & B)*   Compasses Inn

Near Fordingbridge · *Hampshire* · Map 6 A4
Rockbourne (072 53) 231

Free House
Landlords Mr & Mrs Reilly
BEDROOMS 4 Grade 2 £C (No dogs)
Damerham trout £4.50 Liver & bacon
casserole £2.50 (Last order 9.30pm)
🍺 Courage Best Bitter, Directors Bitter; John
Smith's Yorkshire Bitter, lager; Guinness;
Hofmeister; Taunton cider. *Real ale*

There's an unspoilt charm about this
friendly old pub, a popular spot with fishermen and a favourite village meeting place.
June Reilly's snacks will delight all lovers of
good, flavoursome cooking: try her homely
soups, superfresh local trout, liver and
bacon casserole, delicious summer pudding. Simple bedrooms with pretty floral
bedspreads and well-polished period furnishings share a spotless old-fashioned
bathroom. **Family pub**

Darrington *(B & B)*   Darrington Hotel

Great North Road, Near Pontefract
West Yorkshire · Map 4 C3
Pontefract (0977) 791458

Brewery Younger
Landlord Mr James Weatherhead
BEDROOMS 30 Grade 1 £A
🍺 Younger's Scotch Bitter; Newcastle Bitter;
Kestrel; Harp; Becks Bier; Taunton cider.
Real ale

Just off the A1 and conveniently near the
M62, this unassuming red-brick pub is a
comfortable, characterful stopping place
for the motorist. The spacious L-shaped bar
has a cosy Victorian atmosphere, with
buttoned velour banquettes, and there's
also a small cocktail bar. Spacious bedrooms, most with shower/bathrooms,
have neat fitted units, telephones and tea-
makers. Guests can bask in the sauna and
solarium. Garden. **Family pub**

Dartington *(Food, B & B)*   Cott Inn

Devon · Map 8 C4
Totnes (0803) 863777
Free House
Landlords Mr & Mrs Yeadon &
Mr & Mrs Shortman
BEDROOMS 6 Grade 2 £A
Suprême of chicken with mushroom
sauce £4.25 Cheese & onion flan £2.95
(Last order 10pm)
🍺 Ansells Bitter, Mild; Worthington 'E';
Bass; Guinness; Carlsberg Export; cider.

Dating back to the 14th century, this rambling thatched inn offers enjoyable, homely
fare in its heavily beamed bar. Most appealing of all is the elaborate cold buffet, with its
flans, pies and treats like salmon coulibiac,
and there are always some hot dishes too.
Leave room for delicious traditional sweets
like Bakewell tart. Six cottage bedrooms
and a comfortable TV lounge cater for overnight guests. Patio.

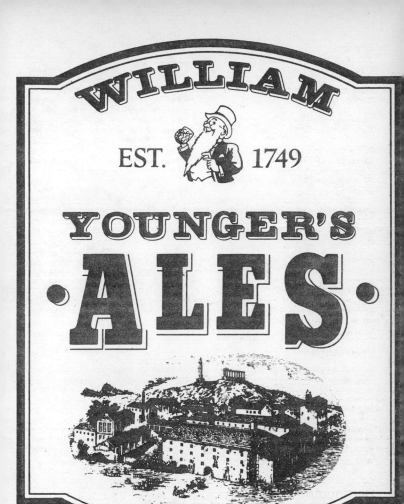

WILLIAM

EST. 1749

YOUNGER'S
·ALES·

Brewers of Fine Ales since 1749.

Dedham   *(Food, B & B)*

Marlborough Head

Mill Lane · *Essex* · Map 5 D2
Colchester (0206) 323124

Brewery Ind Coope
Landlord Mr Brian Wills
BEDROOMS 4   Grade 2   £B   (No dogs)
Marlborough soup 70p Poached halibut £4
(Last order 9.30pm)
🍺 Ind Coope Bitter, John Bull, Double
Diamond, Mild; Skol; Löwenbräu; cider.
Real ale

A fine 15th-century inn, with sturdy beams,
carved wooden fireplaces and few right
angles. Its bar snacks are a popular feature,
ranging extensively from sandwiches
and delicious vegetable soup to cottage
pie, poached halibut and beef curry. Four
traditionally furnished bedrooms with
washbasins and colour TVs make for a
comfortable overnight stay (no children).
Accommodation closed 2 weeks Christmas.
Garden.   **Family pub**

Derry Hill   *(Food)*

Lansdowne Arms

Near Calne · *Wiltshire* · Map 6 A3
Calne (0249) 812422

Brewery Wadworth
Landlord Mrs Evelyn Jones & family

Steak & kidney pie £1.60 Wiltshire
faggots £1.40 (Last order 10pm)
🍺 Wadworth's Old Timer, 6X, Farmer's
Glory; Guinness; Löwenbräu; Heineken;
cider. *Real ale*

Evelyn Jones and her family run this handsome Victorian pub, where good food is
served in pleasant surroundings. Sandwiches, ploughman's and coarse liver pâté
are popular quick snacks, while more substantial items include basket meals and
tasty home-made pies – pheasant, steak
and kidney, chicken with mushrooms. To
finish, try the delicious mint and chocolate
gâteau served with lashings of whipped
cream. Garden.

Dersingham   *(B & B)*

Feathers Hotel

Manor Road · *Norfolk* · Map 5 C1
Dersingham (0485) 40207

Brewery Charrington
Landlord Mr A. P. Martin

BEDROOMS 6   Grade 2   £B
🍺 Springfield Bitter; Adnams Bitter;
Worthington 'E'; Carling Black Label;
Tennent's Export; Taunton cider. *Real ale*

The Prince of Wales' feathers are depicted
on an old stable wall at this welcoming
stone inn, which stands in attractive countryside on the fringe of the Sandringham
Estate. The comfortable bedrooms are
quite simple in style, with modern furniture, colour TVs and washbasins; they
share a large public bathroom. There are
two inviting bars, one of which overlooks
the well-tended gardens.

We have raised our standards
considerably since last year.
The omission of some houses
that appeared in last year's
Guide is no reflection on their
standing.

Devizes   *(Food, B & B)*   *Bear Hotel*

Market Place · *Wiltshire* · Map 6 A3
Devizes (0380) 2444

Brewery Wadworth
Landlords Mr & Mrs W. K. Dickenson
BEDROOMS 26   Grade 2   £B
Wiltshire ham salad £2.95 Devizes pie £3.25
(Last order 10pm)
Wadworth's IPA, 6X, Old Timer (winter only); Guinness; Harp; Heineken; Taunton cider. *Real ale*

This prominent 400-year-old inn is steeped in history, and it still exudes a richly traditional atmosphere. Wholesome bar snacks range from beefsteak butties and the hearty 'Bear Bait' (plump sausages stuffed with cheese and wrapped in bacon) to Devizes pie, a roast and salads, which include slimmer's and vegetarian. Cheerful bedrooms have sturdy furniture, TVs and tea-makers; most also have simple, well-fitted bathrooms. Patio.   **Family pub**

Devizes   *(B & B)*   *Moonrakers*

29 Nursteed Road · *Wiltshire* · Map 6 A3
Devizes (0380) 2909

Brewery Wadworth
Landlords Mr & Mrs V. Gafney

BEDROOMS 5   Grade 2   £C   (No dogs)
Wadworth's IPA, 6X, Northgate Bitter; Guinness; Heineken; Löwenbräu. *Real ale*

Rose and Vic Gafney make guests feel thoroughly welcome at this 50-year-old red-brick pub. Five spacious bedrooms are comfortably furnished, with good carpeting, TVs, tea-makers and their own shower cubicles. There's also a well-kept public bathroom. Relax with a drink in the pleasant lounge bar or join the locals for darts and pool in the public bar. Garden.

Disley   *(Food)*   *Dandy Cock Inn*

Market Street · *Cheshire* · Map 4 C3
Disley (066 32) 3712

Brewery Robinson
Landlord Mr D. A. Booth

Steak & kidney pie £1.95 Pancakes £1.85 (Last order 10pm)
Robinson's Best Bitter, Mild; Einhorn. *Real ale*

Simple, enjoyable snacks are served at neatly laid tables in this cosy little pub. Daily hot specials might include tomato and basil soup, cannelloni, and a flavoursome home-made pie. Savoury pancakes are always popular, and there are freshly prepared sandwiches and salads. You might finish with a fruit crumble or blackcurrant pie.   **Family pub**

Doddiscombsleigh   *(B & B)*   *Nobody Inn*

Near Exeter · *Devon* · Map 8 C3
Christow (0647) 52394

Free House
Landlords Mr P. W. Bolton, Mrs K. J. Bolton & Mr N. F. Borst-Smith

BEDROOMS 4   Grade 2   £C   (No dogs)
Bass; Hall & Woodhouse Badger Bitter; Bates Bitter; Hancock's Ale; Stones Best Bitter; Guinness; Taunton cider. *Real ale*

Travellers long ago, getting no answer from an inhospitable tenant, concluded that there was nobody in. The name stuck, but not the way of dealing with customers, as today's visitors can look forward to a friendly welcome in the beamed bar. Individually styled bedrooms with tea-making facilities are cosy and comfortable; two have shower rooms, the others shower cubicles. Good breakfasts. No under-14s overnight. Patio.

Dorchester *(B & B)*   *Exhibition Hotel*

London Road · *Dorset* · Map 8 D3
Dorchester (0305) 63160

Brewery Eldridge Pope
Landlords Mr & Mrs A. C. Ripley

BEDROOMS 5   Grade 2   £C   (No dogs)
🍺 Eldridge Pope Dorchester Bitter, 1880 Ale,
Dorset IPA; Faust; Taunton cider. *Real ale*

A friendly, down-to-earth pub on Dorchester's busy main street, with a swinging sign depicting Crystal Palace at the time of the Great Exhibition. Darts and bar billiards are popular pastimes in the simple, cheerful bar, a favourite local meeting place. Overnight accommodation comprises five bright, airy bedrooms (all with tea-makers), which share a well-equipped bathroom with shower. Patio.

Dorchester *(B & B)*   *King's Arms*

30 High East Street · *Dorset* · Map 8 D3
Dorchester (0305) 65353

Brewery Devenish
Landlord Mr Robin Charlton

BEDROOMS 27   Grade 1   £A+
🍺 Devenish Wessex Best Bitter, Ordinary
Bitter; John Grove's Weymouth Bitter;
Guinness; Grünhalle. *Real ale*

The old and the new blend happily in this popular high-street inn, where Thomas Hardy set some scenes in *The Mayor of Casterbridge*. The hall and lofty lounge afford elegant glimpses of the past, while the bedrooms (apart from two with four-posters) have practical modern appeal. All have TVs, telephones and tea-makers, the majority spacious private bathrooms. There are two relaxing bars.   **Family pub**

Dorchester-on-Thames *(Food, B & B)*   *George Hotel*

High Street · *Oxfordshire* · Map 6 A3
Oxford (0865) 340404

Free House
Landlord Mr Brian Griffin
BEDROOMS 16   Grade 1   £A
Ploughman's lunch £1.50 Prawn & pineapple
salad £2.25 (Last order 9.45pm)
🍺 Brakspear's Bitter; Morland's Best Bitter;
Wadworth's 6X; Guinness; Heineken; Stella
Artois. *Real ale*

Although now boasting the best of 20th-century comforts, this medieval hostelry has lost none of its original charm. Most bedrooms are in fine traditional style, compact ones in the annexe being more modern. All have tea-makers, TVs, telephones, and most have good bathrooms. Simple, enjoyable bar snacks consist of pâté, salads, sandwiches, plus a daily special like gammon and peach or kidneys Turbigo.   **Family pub**

Dorking *(Food, B & B)*   *Pilgrim*

Station Road · *Surrey* · Map 6 B3
Dorking (0306) 889951

Brewery Friary Meux
Landlord Mr A. Stappard
BEDROOMS 4   Grade 2   £C   (No dogs)
Ham omelette soufflé £1.30 Steak & kidney pie
£2.25 (Last order 9.45pm. No bar food Sun eve)
🍺 Ind Coope Burton Ale; Friary Meux Bitter;
Romford John Bull Bitter; Guinness;
Löwenbräu; Skol; cider. *Real ale*

This handsome old coaching inn on the outskirts of town has two busy bars and a pleasant beer garden. The food is a major feature with dishes like ham omelette soufflé showing real skill and flair. Pies, both savoury and sweet, are popular orders, along with sandwiches (the only Sunday lunchtime choice) and salads. Well-carpeted bedrooms, all with colour TVs and washbasins, share a bathroom. Accommodation closed Christmas–New Year.

Downside   *(Food)*   *Cricketers*

Near Cobham · *Surrey* · Map 6 B3
Cobham (0932) 62105

Brewery Watneys
Landlords Brian & Wendy Luxford

Beef salad £2.90 Calf's liver £2.15 (Last order 10.30pm)
🍺 Watneys Special; Combes Bitter; Webster's Yorkshire Bitter; Guinness; Carlsberg; Foster's. *Real ale*

Sixteenth-century with harmonious later additions, this characterful, white-painted inn stands in a little lane on the edge of the common. The rustic beamed bar is the scene of a popular lunchtime buffet featuring cold meats, seafood and simple salads. Other home-made dishes include sandwiches, ploughman's and specials like pork chops or a good meaty oxtail casserole. Less evening choice. Garden.
Family pub

Dragons Green   *George & Dragon*

Set in peaceful Sussex countryside, this delightful 17th-century pub is small, cosy and full of old-world charm. It's looked after with great pride by landlord John Jenner, and everything gleams in the low-beamed bar. The local beer is excellent, and in summer you can enjoy it in the garden under the shade of the fruit trees.

Near Shipley, Horsham · *West Sussex* · Map 6 B4
Coolham (040 387) 320
Brewery King & Barnes   *Landlord* Mr John Jenner
🍺 King & Barnes Sussex Bitter, Festive, Old Ale; Guinness; Holsten; Carling Black Label. *Real ale*

Driffield   *(Food, B & B)*   *Bell Hotel*

Market Place · *Humberside* · Map 4 D2
Driffield (0377) 46661

Free House
Landlords Mr & Mrs Riggs
BEDROOMS 14   Grade 1   £A   (No dogs)
Beef in beer £1.75 Steak & kidney pie £2.25 (Last order 9.30pm)
🍺 North Country Old Traditional, Mild; Theakston's Old Peculier; Guinness; Harp; cider. *Real ale*

A lovely glass-covered courtyard is a feature of this welcoming old coaching inn which also offers tasty food and comfortable accommodation. Sandwiches and salads are supplemented by farmhouse soup and hot specials like beef in beer, fried haddock and a roast for Sunday lunch. Excellent bedrooms have TVs, trouser presses, hairdryers and carpeted private bathrooms. No under-12s overnight.
Family pub

Dunchurch   *(B & B)*   *Dun Cow Hotel*

The Green · *Warwickshire* · Map 5 A2
Rugby (0788) 810233

Free House
Landlord Bruno Carouche

BEDROOMS 24   Grade 1   £A   (No dogs)
🍺 Bass; Mitchells & Butlers Brew XI; Springfield Bitter; Highgate Mild; Guinness; Carling Black Label; Taunton cider. *Real ale*

Once the haunt of Dick Turpin, this fine old coaching inn boasts many period features, including heavy beams, oak panelling and handsome antiques. The traditionally furnished bedrooms are warm and comfortable, those in the annexe being particularly roomy. All have TVs and radios, and most are provided with private facilities. There are two mellow bars and a pleasant courtyard.
Family pub

Duns Tew   *(Food)*   *White Horse Inn*

Near Oxford · *Oxfordshire* · Map 5 A2
Steeple Aston (0869) 40272

Free House
Landlords Mr & Mrs Peter Smith
Avocado with prawn mayonnaise &
salad £1.95 Whitebait with salad or chips £1.75
(No bar food eves)
🍺 Courage Directors Bitter, Mild; John
Smith's Bitter; Guinness; Hofmeister;
Taunton cider. *Real ale*

Exposed stone walls and sloping floors
give the bar plenty of character at this
quaint old pub in the centre of the village.
Landlord Peter Smith's enjoyable lunchtime snacks range from soup and freshly
cut sandwiches to pâté, quiche lorraine and
grilled trout or steak. Chocolate mousse
and an excellent crème brûlée are among
the delicious sweets. Traditional roast on
Sunday. Closed Monday.   **Family pub**

Durham   *(Food)*   *Traveller's Rest*

72 Claypath · *Co. Durham* · Map 4 C1
Durham (0385) 65370

Free House
Landlord Mr J. Brown

Ham & pease pudding sandwich 50p Beef &
mushroom pie £1.65 (Last order 10pm)
🍺 Joshua Tetley's Bitter, Falstaff Best;
Archibald Arrol's 70/-; Skol; Löwenbräu;
cider. *Real ale*

Honest, wholesome bar snacks are adver-
tised on a blackboard menu at this unpretentious pub in the city centre. Savoury pies
– leek and ham, ever-popular beef and
mushroom – cater admirably for hearty
appetites, and there's a good range of
sandwiches as well as filling soup and a
summer cold buffet. The fruit crumble of
the day is a nice way to round off a meal.
                                       Family pub

Duxford   *(Food)*   *John Barleycorn*

Moorfield Road · *Cambridgeshire* · Map 5 C2
Cambridge (0223) 832699

Brewery Greene King
Landlords Henry & Chris Sewell

Toasted sandwich 86p Grilled sirloin &
salad £5.70 (Last order 10pm)
🍺 Greene King IPA, Abbot Ale, Mild;
Guinness; Kronenbourg; Harp; Taunton
cider. *Real ale*

Rustic bars with heavy beams and ancient
farm implements displayed on exposed
stone walls make a delightful setting for
Christine Sewell's homely fare. You might
start with soup or tasty chicken liver pâté,
and go on to steak and kidney pie, chilli con
carne or spicy Turkish lamb with apricots
and nuts. There are also grills in the
evening except Sunday.

Eartham   *(Food)*   *George Inn*

Near Chichester · *West Sussex* · Map 6 B4
Slindon (024 365) 340

Free House
Landlord Mr R. J. Colman
Loin of pork with prunes & apples £2.95
Leek & ham au gratin £1.95 (Last order 10pm)
🍺 Hall & Woodhouse Badger Best Bitter;
Fuller's ESB; Harvey's Bitter; Gale's HSB;
Guinness; Stella Artois; Heineken; cider.
Real ale

There's no lack of choice on the bar menu of
this popular, lively pub. Filled jacket
potatoes are a perennial favourite. You can
also get home-made soup, sandwiches,
salads, steak, as well as hot dishes like
curry, lasagne and even daily specials –
perhaps chicken provençale or pork in
cider. Finish with a slice of chocolate
gâteau or apple pie. Garden.

East Dean *Tiger Inn*

This delightful whitewashed pub is part of a cluster of little flint cottages set around the green in a pretty village. It has a great deal of old-world charm, with old beams, mellow paintwork and a gleaming copper canopy over the fireplace. Rustic furniture, pastoral prints and an assortment of homely knick-knacks complete the cosy scene.

East Sussex · Map 6 C4
East Dean (032 15) 3209
Brewery Courage   *Landlord* Mr James Conroy
🍺 Courage Directors Bitter, Best Bitter; Guinness; Hofmeister; Kronenbourg. *Real ale*

East Dereham   *(B & B)* *King's Head Hotel*

42 Norwich Street · *Norfolk* · Map 5 D1
Dereham (0362) 3842

Brewery Norwich
Landlords Mr & Mrs R. Black

BEDROOMS 15   Grade 1   £B
🍺 Norwich Bitter; Ben Truman; Guinness; Carlsberg; Holsten; cider. *Real ale*

Maintenance and housekeeping both score high marks at the Blacks' smartly modernised 17th-century pub in the town centre. Overnight accommodation is excellent, rooms in the converted stable block being particularly desirable. Central heating, TVs and radios are standard throughout, and most rooms have up-to-date private facilities. A comfortably furnished bar overlooks the terrace and popular bowling green.

East End   *(Food)* *Plough & Sail*

Paglesham, Near Rochford · *Essex* · Map 6 D3
Canewdon (037 06) 242

Brewery Watney Combe Reid
Landlords Oliver family

Prawn omelette £2.80 Cheesecake 95p (Last order 9pm)
🍺 Watneys IPA, Stag; Webster's Yorkshire Bitter; Guinness; Foster's; Carlsberg; cider. *Real ale*

With fields close by and the river Roach just down the lane, this popular old inn is aptly named. Two beamed bars with masses of gleaming copper and brass are the setting for the very good snacks, which feature local seafood including oysters, mussels and plaice. Steaks and chops for the red-blooded, plus sandwiches, salads, omelettes and delicious sweets. Well-equipped children's play area in the garden.

East Haddon   *(Food, B & B)* *Red Lion*

Near Northampton · *Northamptonshire*
Map 5 B2
Northampton (0604) 770223

Brewery Wells
Landlords Mr & Mrs Kennedy
BEDROOMS 6   Grade 1   £A   (No dogs)
Steak & kidney pie £3 Quiche with salad £2.75 (No bar food eves or Sun)
🍺 Wells Eagle Bitter, Noggin; Red Stripe. *Real ale*

Pretty gardens make this fine old stone pub particularly pleasant in summer, and the bar with its gleaming copper and brass is both elegant and cosy. Enjoyable lunchtime fare includes soup, pâté, salmon fishcakes, home-cooked meats and excellent sweet and savoury pies. Overnight guests have six comfortably furnished bedrooms and a smart TV lounge.

England

East Layton   *(B & B)*   *Fox Hall Inn*

Near Richmond · *North Yorkshire* · Map 4 C2
Darlington (0325) 718262

Free House
Landlord Mr John Jackson

BEDROOMS 14   Grade 2   £C
🍺 Theakston's Best Bitter, Old Peculier;
John Smith's Bitter; Guinness; Carlsberg Hof;
cider.

Standing on the A66 just outside the
village, this old stone inn has been nicely
modernised by landlord John Jackson.
Homely bedrooms feature some fine
Victorian wardrobes, and eight rooms have
their own neat bath or shower rooms. The
bar with its dark panelling and flagstone
floor is a relaxing place for a drink.
Family pub

Eastbourne   *(Food)*   *Beachy Head Hotel*

Beachy Head · *East Sussex* · Map 6 C4
Eastbourne (0323) 28060

Brewery Charrington
Landlords Phyllis & David Coe

Ploughman's £1.40 Carvery £4.95 (No bar food
eves)
🍺 Bass IPA; Carling Black Label; Toby Bitter;
Stones Bitter; Guinness; Tennent's Lager;
cider. *Real ale*

The surroundings are pleasant and the
views spectacular at this large, brick-built
pub on top of Beachy Head. A two-course
meal at the lunchtime carvery offers decent
roast meats (beef, leg of pork, best end of
lamb) with well-cooked vegetables, and a
simple sweet to follow. There's also a cold
buffet in summer, plus sandwiches and
ploughman's for a lighter bite. **Family pub**

Eastergate   *(Food)*   *Wilkes Head*

Near Chichester · *West Sussex* · Map 6 B4
Eastergate (024 368) 3380

Brewery Friary Meux
Landlords Brian & Kathy Goldsmith

Burger £1.90 Moussaka £2 (Last order
10.30pm. No bar food Sun eve)
🍺 Friary Meux Bitter, Mild; Ind Coope Burton
Ale; Guinness; Löwenbräu; Skol; cider.
Real ale

The homely bar of this modest little pub
between the downs and the sea provides a
cosy setting for Kathy Goldsmith's simple,
wholesome fare. Dishes on her blackboard
menu range from country-style pâté and
jumbo sausages to fisherman's pie,
casseroles and splendid moussaka.
Sweets like rum and raisin truffle pudding
or apple and blackberry pie make the
perfect finish. Less choice Sunday lunch.
Garden.

Easthorpe   *House Without a Name*

Without a name it may be, but this cottagy village pub dating from the
16th century is certainly not without a good deal of rustic charm. A
large inglenook fireplace separates the bar areas, two snug rooms
with heavy beams, velvet-covered banquettes and a variety of old
photographs on the walls.   **Family pub**

Near Kelvedon, Colchester · *Essex* · Map 5 C2
Colchester (0206) 210455
Free House   Landlord Mr B. Medcalf
🍺 Mauldon's Bitter; Adnams Bitter; Greene King IPA, Abbot Ale;
Guinness; Foster's; Carlsberg; cider. *Real ale*

England

Eastling *(Food, B & B)*   *Carpenter's Arms*

Near Faversham · *Kent* · Map 6 D3
Eastling (079 589) 234

Brewery Shepherd Neame
Landlord Mrs M. J. Wright
BEDROOMS 2   Grade 2   £C
Carpenter's lunch £1.75 Beef in ale £3.95 (Last
order 10pm)
🍺 Shepherd Neame Bitter, Mild, Stock Ale
(winter only), Abbey; Hurlimann Sternbräu;
Taunton cider. *Real ale*

Winding lanes lead through Kentish
orchards to this charming old village pub, a
delightful spot for a tasty bar meal. Fresh
mushroom or tomato salad makes a simple,
appetising starter, perfect before a hearty
beef casserole, pan-fried trout or a plate of
ham and eggs. Sandwiches for a lighter
snack. Puddings include treacle tart and
a splendid apple flan. Limited Sunday
choice. Two simple bedrooms share a
spacious bathroom.

Easton *(Food)*   *White Horse*

Near Wickham Market · *Suffolk* · Map 5 D2
Wickham Market (0728) 746456

Brewery Tollemache & Cobbold
Landlords David & Sharon Grimwood
Fisherman's pie £2.50 Wild duck
casserole £2.50 (Last order 9pm. No bar food
Sun & Mon eves)
🍺 Tolly Cobbold Bitter, Mild, Old Strong
(winter only); Guinness; Hansa; Taunton
cider. *Real ale*

David Grimwood provides an enterprising
choice of well-prepared food at this charming old village pub. Specials on the blackboard menu might range from mussels in
garlic butter to moussaka, seasonal game
and an excellent fisherman's pie. You could
also choose soup or a French bread sandwich, and perhaps a slice of home-made
gâteau for dessert. Garden.

Edge *(Food)*   *Edgemoor Inn*

Near Stroud · *Gloucestershire* · Map 7 D2
Painswick (0452) 813576

Free House
Landlords Mr & Mrs M. E. H. Smith

Steak & kidney pie £2.75 Sherry trifle 85p (Last
order 10pm. No bar food Sun eve)
🍺 Flowers Original, IPA, Best Bitter; West
Country Pale Ale; Younger's Tartan;
Worthington Best Bitter; Guinness; cider.

There are splendid views from the terrace
of this large roadside inn, and Mrs Smith's
enjoyable food adds to its popularity. If
you're hungry, go for the special lunch,
consisting of a daily special followed by
home-made fruit pie – excellent value at
£2.35. Otherwise, you could choose soup,
pâté, an omelette or a grill. Salads and
sandwiches, too, and simple sweets to
finish.

Eggesford *(Food)*   *Fox & Hounds Hotel*

Near Chulmleigh · *Devon* · Map 8 C3
Chulmleigh (0769) 80345

Free House
Landlord Mr A. Chappell

Rump steak with vegetables £5.20 Fresh local
salmon £6.20 (Last order 9.30pm)
🍺 Usher's Best Bitter, Triple Crown; Ben
Truman; Carlsberg; Holsten; cider. *Real ale*

The bill of fare is long and varied at this
pleasant old fishing pub, whose rustic bar
features prints of the Devon hunts. Tender,
well-flavoured steaks are a speciality, and
other popular choices range from sandwiches and richly flavoured game soup to
savoury pies and sautéed chicken. Nice
sweets too. Closed all Monday and Tuesday lunchtime in winter. Garden.
Family pub

127

Eggleston   *(Food)*

Three Tuns Inn

Near Barnard Castle · *Co. Durham* · Map 4 C2
Teesdale (0833) 50289

Free House
Landlords James & Christine Dykes

Cottage pie £1.75 8oz. sirloin steak £4.75 (Last
order 9.45pm. No bar food Sun eve)
🍺 Whitbread Trophy; Guinness;
Heineken; cider.

James and Christine Dykes are welcoming
landlords at this appealing village pub
where guests are sure of a nourishing, tasty
snack. There's always a home-made soup,
and you can go on to wholesome cottage
pie, duck with orange sauce or a beefburger
and egg. Ploughman's and salads, too, and
tempting sweets like fresh fruit salad or
treacle lick. The large garden is popular in
summer. Closed Monday.   **Family pub**

Elkstone   *(Food)*

Highwayman

Near Cheltenham · *Gloucestershire* · Map 7 D2
Miserden (028 582) 221

Brewery Arkell
Landlords David & Heather Bucher

Steak & mushroom pie (winter only) £2.95
Lasagne £2.50 (Last order 10.15pm)
🍺 Arkell's BBB; BB, Kingsdown Ale;
Guinness; 1843 Premium Lager. *Real ale*

A splendidly restored black and yellow
stagecoach stands in the car park of this
very popular pub, which caters admirably
for all ages. Families are very much in
evidence in the beamed bars, tucking into
snacks that range from bumper toasted
sandwiches and filled potatoes to jumbo
sausages and a spicy chilli con carne.
Sweets include fruit crumbles and treacle
tart. Garden.   **Family pub**

Elslack   *(Food)*

Tempest Arms

Near Skipton · *North Yorkshire* · Map 4 C3
Earby (0282) 842450

Free House
Landlord Francis Pierre Boulongne

Turkey pie & chips £1.20 Fillets of sole in white
wine £2 (Last order 10pm)
🍺 Thwaites Bitter, Mild; Webster's Green
Label; Guinness; Carlsberg Hof; Harp;
Taunton cider. *Real ale*

In a peaceful location near the junction of
the A56 and A59, this comfortable pub is
well worth a visit for its excellent bar fare.
Soup of the day could be game or flavoursome celery and Stilton, and other choices
include potted shrimps, filled baked
potatoes, steak sandwiches and lunchtime
specials like baked ham in Madeira. Also
available at lunchtime is a help-yourself
salad bar. Garden.   **Family pub**

Elsted   *(Food)*

Three Horseshoes

Near Midhurst · *West Sussex* · Map 6 B4
Harting (073 085) 746

Free House
Landlord Benjamin Heath

Peppered chicken £4.25 Courgette & smoked
haddock pie £2.95 (Last order 10pm)
🍺 Fuller's London Pride; Ballard's Wassail;
Everards Tiger; Guinness; Harp; Foster's;
cider. *Real ale*

A fine selection of real ales and enjoyable
bar food add to the appeal of this delightfully beamed and cosy pub. Filled jacket
potatoes and various ploughman's are
popular choices, and for a heartier meal
you could have tasty rabbit in red wine,
peppered chicken, lasagne or moussaka.
Sweets like lemon soufflé or treacle tart are
equally tempting. Garden.

Elsworth *(Food)* — *George & Dragon*

41 Boxworth Rd · *Cambridgeshire* · Map 5 C2
Elsworth (095 47) 236

Brewery Tollemache & Cobbold
Landlords Mr & Mrs M. Brownlie

Steak & kidney pie £2.75 Lasagne & salad £2.45
(Last order 10pm)
🍺 Tolly Cobbold Original Bitter, Bitter, Old
Strong (winter only); Worthington 'E';
Guinness; Hansa; Taunton cider. *Real ale*

Heavy beams, huge fireplaces and gleaming copperware lend a great deal of charm to this old village pub. Home-made soup, open sandwiches, salads and steaks are all featured on the menu, along with varied daily specials like fresh fish, pizza, moussaka and Southern fried chicken. Homely, tempting sweets include a delicious apple pie. **Family pub**

Elterwater *(B & B)* — *Britannia Inn*

Near Ambleside · *Cumbria* · Map 3 B2
Langdale (096 67) 210

Free House
Landlords Margaret & David Fry

BEDROOMS 10 Grade 2 £B
🍺 Tetley's Bitter; Bass; Hartley's Bitter;
Guinness; Carling Black Label; cider. *Real ale*

Adjoining the village green, this welcoming inn with its cosy little beamed bar is as popular with locals as it is with Lakeland walkers. Bedrooms are cheerfully furnished in a mixture of old and new styles, and there's a comfortable lounge in which to browse through the good supply of books. The two bathrooms are well kept. Super breakfasts. Accommodation closed Christmas week. **Family pub**

Eltisley *(B & B)* — *Leeds Arms*

The Green · *Cambridgeshire* · Map 5 C2
Croxton (048 087) 283

Free House
Landlords Mr & Mrs G. W. Cottrell

BEDROOMS 8 Grade 1 £B (No dogs)
🍺 Greene King IPA; Stones Bitter;
Whitbread Best Mild; Paine's St Neots Bitter;
Guinness; Carlsberg; Harp.

Though altered and modernised over the years, this whitewashed 18th-century coaching house retains much period character, with old beams and an inglenook fireplace in the lounge bar. The bedrooms, in contrast, are in modern motel style, with laminated furniture, colour TVs, tea-makers and neat bath or shower rooms. Maintenance and housekeeping are commendable. There's a large garden with a children's play area.

Empingham *(Food, B & B)* — *White Horse*

2 Main Street · *Leicestershire* · Map 5 B1
Empingham (078 086) 221
Brewery John Smith
Landlord Mr Robert Reid
BEDROOMS 3 Grade 2 £B
Baked sugared ham with parsley
sauce £2.45 Steak, kidney & mushroom pie &
vegetables £3.25 (Last order 10pm)
🍺 Courage Best Bitter; John Smith's Bitter;
Guinness; Hofmeister; John Smith's lager;
Taunton cider. *Real ale*

Good bar food and comfortable accommodation make this low-built inn a useful stopping place. A comprehensive menu ranges from sandwiches to lasagne, curries, steak and kidney pie and baked ham with parsley sauce; there's also a cold buffet at lunchtime. Three large double bedrooms all have TVs and share a shower room and bathroom. Garden. **Family pub**

Enfield *(Food)*   *Robin Hood*

Botany Bay, The Ridgeway · *Middlesex*
Map 6 C3
01-363 3781

Brewery McMullen
Landlords John & Pearl Heard

Shepherd's pie £2.50 Ploughman's lunch £1.25
(Last order 10.30pm)
🍺 McMullen's AK Mild, Country Bitter;
Guinness; Steingold.

The lovely garden at the back of this pub just beyond the outer reaches of London is a popular place to enjoy a pint and a tasty bite. Mornings and evenings, there is a wide choice of plain and toasted sandwiches, along with soup, hot pasties and pizzas. At lunchtime (Mon–Sat) there's also a tempting cold buffet of roast joints and plenteously served salads.

Enstone *(Food)*   *Harrow Inn*

Main Road · *Oxfordshire* · Map 5 A2
Enstone (060 872) 366

Brewery Morrell's
Landlord Mr R. E. Parker

Home-made soup 40p Beef casserole £2.50
(Last order 10pm)
🍺 Morrell's Varsity, Bitter, Mild; Guinness;
Kronenbourg; Harp; Taunton cider. *Real ale*

Food's the name of the game at this unpretentious little pub, where the lunchtime focus is an excellent spread of cold meats, robustly flavoured pâté, well-baked quiches and good fresh salads. This buffet is supplemented by hot specials – lasagne, cannelloni, beef casserole – while in the evening the scene shifts to local trout, steaks, salads and the like. The dining area in the stone-walled lounge bar is attractively traditional in style. Beer garden.

Eskdale *(Food, B & B)*   *Bower House Inn*

Near Holmbrook · *Cumbria* · Map 3 B2
Eskdale (094 03) 244

Free House
Landlords Smith family
BEDROOMS 14   Grade 2   £B
Fillet steak £5.50 Gammon, eggs & chips £2.50
(Last order 9pm)
🍺 Hartley's Best Bitter; Younger's Best
Bitter; Guinness; Carlsberg; Slalom; cider.
Real ale

Peacefully situated in beautiful Eskdale, this fine old inn is a pleasant base for tourists. A good range of enjoyable food is served in the beamed bar, from soup and pâté to salads, steaks and seafood risotto. Six simply furnished bedrooms are in the original building, the rest (with private bath and TV) in the modern annexe. All have tea-makers. Garden.

Eton *(B & B)*   *Christopher Hotel*

110 High Street, Near Windsor · *Berkshire* ·
Map 6 B3
Windsor (075 35) 52359

Free House
Landlords Ron & Barbara France

BEDROOMS 21   Grade 1   £B
🍺 Brakspear's Bitter; Younger's Tartan;
John Smith's Bitter; Guinness; Kronenbourg;
Taunton cider. *Real ale*

Well - appointed chalet - style bedrooms provide excellent overnight accommodation at this former coaching inn. Colour televisions, trouser presses and hairdryers are standard equipment, along with small fridges and the ingredients for producing continental breakfast. All have carpeted shower rooms, many with bidets. There are two well-patronised bars, one with a Victorian feel, the other more contemporary in style. Patio.

Etton   *(Food)*   *Golden Pheasant*

Near Peterborough · *Cambridgeshire*
Map 5 B1
Peterborough (0733) 252387
Free House
Landlords Mr & Mrs B. Loasby
Catalan swordfish £3.15 Niw goo
yok £2.65 (Last order 10pm. No bar food
Sun eve)
🍺 Ruddle's County; Greene King IPA;
Adnams Southwold Bitter; Kronenbourg;
Taunton cider. *Real ale*

Smoked salmon mousse, swordfish
Catalan, Lancashire hot pot and chicken in
cider are among the tasty, enterprising
dishes which help to make this converted
Georgian mansion so popular. There's also
an appetising cold buffet for summer
lunches, as well as a large garden in which
to enjoy it all. Good sweets and cheeses,
too. Closed Monday.

Evercreech Junction   *(Food)*   *Natterjack*

Near Shepton Mallet · *Somerset* · Map 8 D3
Ditcheat (074 986) 253

Free House
Landlords Mr & Mrs G. Hickley

Beef in red wine £2.80 Fresh fruit Pavlova 90p
(Last order 10pm)
🍺 Butcombe Bitter; Courage Best Bitter;
Webster's Yorkshire Bitter; Guinness; Skol;
Kronenbourg; Löwenbräu; cider. *Real ale*

Situated on the A371 between Shepton
Mallet and Castle Cary, this stone pub with
colourful window boxes is well worth a
stop. June Hickley serves delicious quiches
and a superb seafood platter, as well as
blackboard specials like beef in red wine or
ham and mushroom pizza. Mouthwatering
sweets might include raspberry cheesecake or a fresh fruit Pavlova. Sandwiches
and salads, too. Garden.

Ewhurst   *(Food)*   *Windmill Inn*

Pitch Hill, Near Cranleigh · *Surrey* · Map 6 B3
Cranleigh (0483) 277566

Free House
Landlords Dutch & Ann Holland

Salmon & prawn kedgeree £2.50 Chicken
casserole £3.75 (Last order 10pm)
🍺 King & Barnes Sussex Bitter; Whitbread
Trophy; Youngs Special; Guinness;
Carlsberg; Löwenbräu; cider. *Real ale*

Take the Shere road out of Ewhurst to find
Dutch and Ann Holland's neat pub, where
in summer you can sit in the garden and
admire the hilltop view. Appetising snacks
range from sandwiches and salads to hot
dishes like chicken casserole or salmon and
prawn kedgeree. Depending on the season,
you might also get delicious fresh crab and
lobster, or perhaps a pheasant casserole.

Ewhurst Green   *(B & B)*   *White Dog Inn*

Near Robertsbridge · *East Sussex* · Map 6 C4
Staplecross (058 083) 264

Free House
Landlord Tim Knowland

BEDROOMS 6   Grade 2   £B (No dogs)
🍺 Harvey's Bitter; Whitbread Best Bitter;
Guinness; Heineken; Stella Artois; cider.
Real ale

Residents will find plenty to amuse them at
this welcoming village pub. There's a
colour TV in the comfortable lounge, while
more active guests can make use of the
swimming pool or the full-size snooker
table. Bedrooms – three with their own
bathrooms – have simple modern furniture
and tea-makers, plus flowers, fresh fruit
and plenty of magazines. No children under
ten overnight.   **Family pub**

Exford *(Food)*   *Crown Hotel*

Near Minehead · *Somerset* · Map 8 C3
Exford (064 383) 554

Brewery Usher
Landlords J. E. & M. E. Millward

Local trout £3.40 Spaghetti bolognese £1.50
(Last order 10pm)
🍺 Usher's Founders Ale, Country Bitter,
Triple Crown; Carlsberg; Taunton cider.
Real ale

Popular with tourists and the hunting
fraternity, this delightful 17th-century
coaching inn stands opposite the village
green. In the rustic pine-panelled bar the
menu offers a selection of tasty home-
produced fare: local trout is a regular
favourite, and other choices include
lasagne, spaghetti bolognese and chilli con
carne. Garden. *For accommodation see
Egon Ronay's Lucas Hotel & Restaurant
Guide 1985.*   **Family pub**

Eyam *(Food, B & B)*   *Miners Arms*

Water Lane · *Derbyshire* · Map 4 C3
Hope Valley (0433) 30853

Free House
Landlords Mr & Mrs P. B. Cooke

BEDROOMS 4 Grade 2 £C (No dogs)
Ocean salad £1.85 Brunch menu of the
day £3.75 (No bar food eves)
🍺 Ward's Sheffield Bitter; Stones Bitter;
Vaux Mild; Carling Black Label. *Real ale*

Run for more than two decades by jovial
Peter Cooke, this agreeable old pub is
known for its tasty lunchtime fare. Snacks
include soup and sandwiches, salads, fresh
fish and good roast beef, and there's a
daily-changing three-course brunch. For
overnight guests (no children) there are
four well-kept bedrooms that share the
family bathroom. Pub closed Monday
lunchtime except Bank Holidays. Patio.

Eyam *(B & B)*   *Rose & Crown*

Main Road, Near Sheffield · *Derbyshire*
Map 4 C3
Hope Valley (0433) 30858

Free House
Landlords Brian & Val Wharton

BEDROOMS 3 Grade 2 £C (No dogs)
🍺 Tetley's Bitter; Stones Bitter; Bass Mild;
Skol; Carling Black Label; cider. *Real ale*

Brian and Val Wharton are the friendly
hosts at this neat little stone pub in a
famous Peak District village. Pleasantly
furnished bedrooms with shower cubicles,
TVs and tea-makers offer homely overnight
accommodation, and guests can look
forward to a hearty English breakfast.
There's a cosy bar with plush red banquettes, an intimate snug and a games
room. Patio.

Fairbourne Heath *(Food)*   *Pepper Box*

Near Ulcombe · *Kent* · Map 6 C3
Maidstone (0622) 842558

Brewery Shepherd Neame
Landlords Betty & Jack Wood

Fish specials £1.95 Bobotie with saffron
rice £1.95 (Last order 10pm)
🍺 Shepherd Neame Masterbrew, Bitter;
Hurlimann Sternbräu. *Real ale*

The speciality of this friendly little pub off
the Ulcombe–Lenham road is superb fresh
fish from Dungeness. Betty Wood's menu
might offer monkfish provençale or plaice
with beautifully crisp chips. Alternative
choices include home-made soup, sandwiches, casseroles and excellent locally
made herb sausages known as Kent
Korkers. In summer, the rose garden is an
additional attraction.   **Family pub**

Fairford *(B & B)* — *Bull Hotel*

Market Place · *Gloucestershire* · Map 6 A3
Cirencester (0285) 712535

Brewery Arkells
Landlord Mrs C. E. Smith ·

BEDROOMS 18   Grade 1   £A
Arkell's BBB, Kingsdown Ale, John Arkell's Bitter, 1843 Lager; Guinness; Carling Black Label. *Real ale*

An attractive stone inn right on the market place. The oldest part (15th century) used to be a monk's chantry, the rest a wool market, and the atmosphere in the beamed bar and well-furnished residents' lounge is warm and traditional. Bedrooms of various shapes and sizes are pleasant and comfortable, with black beams, pretty fabrics, darkwood fitted units and televisions. Most have modern private facilities. Patio.
Family pub

Faringdon *(Food, B & B)* — *Bell Hotel*

Market Place · *Oxfordshire* · Map 6 A3
Faringdon (0367) 20534

Brewery Wadworth
Landlord Mr W. Dreyer

BEDROOMS 11   Grade 1   £B
Lancashire hot pot £2.15 Watercress soup 90p (Last order 9.30pm)
Wadworth's 6X, Farmer's Glory, Old Timer (winter); Guinness; Harp. *Real ale*

Bar snacks are served in delightfully traditional surroundings at this old coaching inn. The daily special – perhaps cottage pie or tasty Lancashire hot pot – is a popular choice, and other goodies range from delicious cream of watercress soup to French bread sandwiches, plated salads and prawn pancakes. Bedrooms are attractively decorated. Seven have TVs and private facilities, and there's a pleasant lounge with TV. **Family pub**

Farnham *(Food)* — *Spotted Cow*

3 Bourne Grove · *Surrey* · Map 6 B3
Farnham (0252) 726541

Brewery Courage
Landlords Mr & Mrs B. R. Soulsby

Game pie salad £2.50 Lasagne & salad £2 (Last order 10pm)
Courage Best Bitter, Directors Bitter, JC; Guinness; Hofmeister; Kronenbourg; Taunton cider. *Real ale*

A large beer garden surrounded by trees and a special children's room make this pub a popular spot with families. Enjoyable snacks served in the bar include salads and ploughman's, as well as grills and other hot dishes like chicken and chips, lasagne and tasty moussaka. The pub lies just south of Farnham off the Tilford road. **Family pub**

Faugh *(Food)* — *String of Horses Inn*

Heads Hook · *Cumbria* · Map 3 B1
Hayton (022870) 297

Free House
Landlords Mr & Mrs Eric Tasker

Mexican chicken £2.95 Cold table £3.75 (Last order 10.15pm)
Theakstone's Best Bitter, Old Peculier; John Smith's Bitter; Younger's Tartan; Guinness; Carlsberg; Holt. *Real ale*

Open fires and handsome oak furniture create a warm, traditional atmosphere in this fine old village inn. The cold table, with excellent cooked meats, salmon and salads, is a lunchtime favourite and hot dishes include Cumberland sausage, chicken curry and grilled lamb cutlets. Very nice chocolate gâteau to finish. Patio. *For accommodation see Egon Ronay's Lucas Hotel & Restaurant Guide 1985.* **Family pub**

Fawley   *(Food)*   ★   *Walnut Tree*

Near Henley-on-Thames, Oxfordshire
Buckinghamshire · Map 6 B3
Turville Heath (049 163) 360

Brewery Brakspear
Landlords Mr & Mrs F. Harding
Chicken suprême Walnut Tree £4.95 Scallops
baked in cream & herbs £5.50 (Last
order 9.55pm)
🍺 Brakspear's Mild, Ordinary, Special Bitter;
Stella Artois; Heineken. *Real ale*

Unusually imaginative and skilfully prepared food brings the crowds flocking to
this modern red-brick pub down a narrow
lane. Regular offerings include deep-fried
squid and superb hamburgers, and there
are also blackboard specials like quails in
white grape sauce or scallops baked in
cream. Try the delicious treacle tart with
whole walnuts for dessert. Garden and
terrace.   **Family pub**

Felixstowe   *(B & B)*   *Fludyer Arms Hotel*

Undercliff Road East · Suffolk · Map 5 D2
Felixstowe (0394) 283279

Brewery Tollemache & Cobbold
Landlord Mr John Nash

BEDROOMS 10   Grade 2   £C
🍺 Tolly Cobbold Bitter, Original; Guinness;
Hansa; cider. *Real ale*

Splendid sea views are a great asset of this
Edwardian pub right on the front. Spacious,
traditionally furnished bedrooms are well
kept and all have TVs and tea-makers. They
share two large, old-fashioned bathrooms.
Guests can relax in the smart modern
lounge or in the public bar with its little
patio area.   **Family pub**

Felixstowe   *(Food, B & B)*   *Ordnance Hotel*

1 Undercliff Road West · Suffolk · Map 5 D2
Felixstowe (0394) 273427

Brewery Tollemache & Cobbold
Landlords Mr & Mrs D. C. Yeo
BEDROOMS 11   Grade 1   £B (No dogs)
Chilli con carne £1.45 Beef bobotie £3.25
(Last order 10.30pm. No bar food Sun eve)
🍺 Tolly Cobbold Original, Bitter, Mild,
Old Strong (winter only); Guinness; Harp;
Hansa. *Real ale*

The Yeo family preside over this comfortable haven offering friendly, efficient
service, excellent overnight accommodation and very enjoyable food. Spacious
bedrooms with period furnishings have
TVs, tea-makers and direct-dial phones.
Lunchtime bar fare is carefully prepared
and nicely presented, from simple vegetable soup or a sandwich to savoury pancakes and a tasty turkey curry. Evening
snacks can be obtained in YoYo's Bistro.

Fen Drayton   *(Food)*   *Three Tuns*

High Street · Cambridgeshire · Map 5 C2
Swavesey (0954) 30242

Brewery Greene King
Landlords Mr & Mrs D. Threadgold

Sweet & sour pork with rice £1.85 Lasagne
with chips & rice £1.85 (Last order 10pm.
No bar food Sun eve)
🍺 Greene King IPA, Abbot Ale, Mild;
Guinness; Kronenbourg; Harp; cider. *Real ale*

Beams, inglenook fireplaces and an old
baker's oven make this 15th-century
thatched pub a delightfully cosy place for a
drink and a snack. Enjoyable home-made
dishes on the menu might include
shepherd's pie, mushroom fritters, sweet
and sour pork and chicken curry. Grills,
salads and sandwiches are other choices,
with perhaps a lemon meringue pie for
dessert. Garden.

Fenay Bridge   *(Food)*   *Star*

1 Penistone Road, Near Huddersfield
West Yorkshire · Map 4 C3
Huddersfield (0484) 602049

Brewery Bass
Landlords Mr & Mrs Robert G. Lee

Businessman's lunch £4.75 Steak & kidney
pie £2.75 (Last order 10pm)
🍺 Bass Extra Light, Dark Mild; Stones
Bitter; Carling Black Label; Hemeling.

Bob Lee's enjoyable lunchtime fare lures
crowds of visitors to this large stone pub by
the side of the road. The choice ranges from
salads and sandwiches to a hearty steak
and kidney pie, grilled gammon and eggs,
sirloin steak and beef curry. Gâteaux and
pies from an impressive sweet trolley make
a fine finish. Traditional set lunch on
Sundays. Sandwiches only in the evening.

Fenny Bentley   *(Food, B & B)*   *Bentley Brook Inn*

Near Ashbourne · *Derbyshire* · Map 4 C4
Thorpe Cloud (033 529) 278

Free House
Landlords David & Jeanne Allingham

BEDROOMS 8   Grade 1 & 2   £B
Derbyshire hot pot £2.25 Beef & vegetable
stew £2.25 (No bar food eves & Sun lunch)
🍺 Marston's Pedigree Bitter, Lager;
Guinness; Carlsberg; cider. *Real ale*

Standing in well-kept grounds north of
Ashbourne, this pleasant, half-timbered
inn has delightful hosts in David and
Jeanne Allingham. Lunchtime bar snacks
include home-made soup, filled baps and
ploughman's, plus robust hot dishes like
liver and onions or Derbyshire lamb hot pot
and a splendid trifle. Characterful bedrooms, three with private bath, have tea-
makers and colour TVs. Garden.
Family pub

Fiddleford   *(B & B)*   *Fiddleford Inn*

Sturminster Newton · *Dorset* · Map 8 D3
Sturminster Newton (0258) 72489

Free House
Landlords Philip, Valerie & Joyce Wilson

BEDROOMS 4   Grade 1   £C
🍺 Fiddleford Ale; Wadworth's 6X; Gale's
HSB; Holsten; Carlsberg; Taunton cider.
Real ale

Philip Wilson keeps a really excellent selection of real ales at this attractive creeper-
clad pub on the Sturminster Newton–
Blandford road. There are two characterful
bars – one with flagstones and exposed
brickwork – and a garden with swings and
boules. Prettily decorated bedrooms with a
patchwork theme are kept in apple-pie
order; one has its own private facilities, the
others share two spotless public bathrooms.
Family pub

Fifield   *(Food, B & B)*   *Merrymouth Inn*

Stow Road · *Oxfordshire* · Map 5 A2
Shipton-under-Wychwood (0993) 830759

Brewery Donnington
Landlord Philip Waller

BEDROOMS 3   Grade 2   £C
Steak & Guinness pie £2.50 Fish hot pot £1.95
(Last order 10pm)
🍺 Donnington Best Bitter, SBA, 3X Mild;
Carlsberg; Löwenbräu; cider. *Real ale*

Blackboard specials combine with the
standard menu to provide a fine selection of
tasty bar food at this ancient roadside inn.
Salads, ploughman's platters and potato-
topped fish hot pot are among the regular
favourites, while dishes of the day could
include anything from snails to roast lamb
with sage and onion stuffing. Three homely
bedrooms share a bright modern bathroom.
Family pub

England

Fingest *(Food)*   ## *Chequers Inn*

Near Henley-on-Thames · *Buckinghamshire*
Map 6 B3
Turville Heath (049 163) 335

Brewery Brakspears
Landlords Bryan & Christine Heasman

Steak & kidney pie £2.95 Paté £1.50 (Last
order 9.30pm)

🍺 Brakspear's Ordinary, Special, Old;
Heineken. *Real ale*

This 12th-century hostelry stands in a large
garden opposite the Norman church in a
sleepy village. There are two bars, one
featuring a buffet laden with succulent cold
meats and well-dressed salads. Other
items, listed on a blackboard, range from
soup and quiche to cool-weather curries
and steak and kidney pie. Vegetables are
especially nice. **Family pub**

Prices given are as at the time

of our research and are

comparative indications rather

than firm quotes.

Fiskerton *(Food)*   ## *Bromley Arms*

Near Southwell · *Nottinghamshire* · Map 5 B1
Newark (0636) 830789

Brewery Hardys & Hansons
Landlords Mr & Mrs H. Taylor

Poacher's pie with chips & peas £2.10
Ploughman's lunch with chips £1.40
(Last order 10pm)
🍺 Hardys & Hansons Bitter, Mild; Guinness;
Heineken; cider. *Real ale*

Boating enthusiasts favour this 200-year-
old inn right beside the river. Harold Taylor
presides over the bars, while his wife Sheila
takes care of tasty lunchtime specials like
poacher's pie, veal à la crème and delicious
fruit pies. Evening and Sunday fare consists mainly of salads and well-filled sandwiches and ploughman's. The terrace is a
delightful spot for summer drinking.

Fittleworth *(B & B)*   ## *Swan*

Lower Street · *West Sussex* · Map 6 B4
Fittleworth (079 882) 429

Owners Gateway Hosts
Landlord Mr C. Rodriguez

BEDROOMS 8 Grade 2 £B
🍺 Tamplins Bitter; Webster's Yorkshire
Bitter; Guinness; Foster's; Carlsberg; cider.
Real ale

A fine collection of truncheons and bottle-
openers adds extra interest to the beamed
lounge bar of this charming old village inn.
Comfortable bedrooms have simple,
cottage furnishings, and all are equipped
with tea-makers. One room has a private
bathroom, the rest shower cubicles, and
there are also three public bathrooms.
Guests have a small TV lounge. Garden.

Family pub

Flamstead   *(Food)*

2 High Street · *Hertfordshire* · Map 5 B2
Luton (0582) 840330

Brewery Watneys
Landlord Mr Mike Byrne

Steak sandwich £1.75 Speciality
sausages £1.40
🍺 Webster's Yorkshire Bitter; Combes
Bitter; Ruddle's County; Hammerton's Porter;
Guinness; cider. *Real ale*

Window boxes and hanging [...]
this red-brick pub not far from junct[...]
the M1 a cheerful sight in summer. Jumbo
sausages in a variety of flavours (herb,
apple, curry) top the bill among bar snacks,
which also include well-filled sandwiches,
ploughman's and tasty charcoal-grilled
hamburgers. In summer, you can take your
pick from the cold table. Garden.
Family pub

Fonthill Bishop   *(B & B)*   *Kings Arms*

Near Salisbury · *Wiltshire* · Map 8 D3
Hindon (074 789) 523

Free House
Landlords D. M. Reynolds & C. J. Nell

BEDROOMS 3   Grade 2   £C
🍺 Wadworth's 6X, IPA, Farmers Glory,
Northgate Bitter; Younger's Newcastle Bitter;
Guinness; Taunton cider. *Real ale*

Built in 1846 as an agricultural building, this
spotless little roadside pub is run with great
charm and efficiency by Mark and Hilary
Reynolds. Spacious bedrooms with pretty
floral wallpapers and matching curtains
have neat white furniture and very comfortable beds, and the two public bathrooms are bright and modern. There's a
cheerfully decorated bar and a tiny TV
lounge. Garden.   **Family pub**

Ford   *(B & B)*   *White Hart*

Near Chippenham · *Wiltshire* · Map 7 D2
Castle Combe (0249) 782213

Free House
Landlords Gardner family

BEDROOMS 8   Grade 1   £A   (No dogs)
🍺 Wadworth's 6X; Archer's Village Bitter;
Hall & Woodhouse Badger Bitter; Ruddles
County; Fuller's ESB, London Pride; Taunton
cider. *Real ale*

A terrace overlooking a trout stream and a
swimming pool are among the attractions
of this fine old country inn where a collection of armour adds extra interest to the
beamed main bar. Bedrooms are most
attractive, with pine furnishings and pretty
fabrics. Six even have four-poster beds,
and all boast tea-makers, TVs and carpeted
private bathrooms. No children under three
overnight.   **Family pub**

Forton   *(B & B)*   *New Holly Hotel*

Near Preston · *Lancashire* · Map 3 B2
Forton (0524) 791568

Brewery Thwaites
Landlords Monica & Eric Turner

BEDROOMS 5   Grade 2   £C
🍺 Thwaites Bitter, Mild; Kronenbourg;
Stein. *Real ale*

The atmosphere is pleasant and welcoming at this pink-washed roadside pub,
which has a terrace where customers can
take the summer sunshine. The bar is
spacious and convivial, and for guests
staying overnight there are five bedrooms
with homely furnishings, tea-makers and
shower cubicles. Morning brings a hearty
traditional English breakfast.   **Family pub**

Forty Green   *Royal Standard of England*

This renowned 11th-century tavern owes its present name to Charles
II, who sheltered here after the Battle of Worcester. The feeling of
history is everywhere – blackened timbers, uneven floors, a fireplace
from the house of Edmund Burke. Note, too, the lovely stained-glass
created from the windows of blitzed London churches.   **Family pub**

Beaconsfield · *Buckinghamshire* · Map 6 B3
Beaconsfield (049 46) 3382
Free House   Landlord Mr Philip Eldridge
🍺 Marston's Pedigree, Owd Rodger; Samuel Smiths Old Brewery
Bitter; Carlsberg; Foster's; cider. *Real ale*

Fossebridge   *(Food, B & B)*   *Fossebridge Inn*

Near Northleach · *Gloucestershire* · Map 5 A2
Fossebridge (028 572) 310
Free House
Landlords Mr & Mrs A. Prior
BEDROOMS 10   Grades 1 & 2   £B
(No dogs)
Steak & kidney pie £4.50 Treacle tart £1 (Last
order 9.30pm)
🍺 Usher's Best Bitter, Founder's Ale;
Eldridge Pope Dorchester Bitter; Carlsberg;
Taunton cider. *Real ale*

Well-tried favourites ranging from soup
and sandwiches to cottage pie and old-
fashioned puddings are served in this fine
old riverside inn. Bedrooms in the main
(early Georgian) house are quite spacious,
with antique furniture and smartly
modernised bathrooms; those in the
annexe are more functional in style.
There's a comfortable TV lounge and a
peaceful garden. No under-tens overnight.
Family pub

Fotheringhay   *(Food)*   *Falcon Inn*

Near Peterborough, Cambridgeshire
Northamptonshire · Map 5 B1
Cotterstock (083 26) 254
Free House
Landlords Alan & Jill Stewart
Moussaka £2.70 Roast duckling with apple &
rosemary stuffing £4 (Last order 9.45pm. No
bar food Mon)
🍺 Greene King IPA, Abbot Ale; Elgood's
Ordinary; Hereward Bitter; Litchborough;
Guinness; Harp; cider. *Real ale*

Best known as the place where Mary Queen
of Scots was last imprisoned, Fotheringhay
is also noteworthy for this charming little
stone pub whose tempting bar menu keeps
it constantly busy (booking advisable).
There's always a delicious home-made
soup, and you could follow with a super
pigeon or turkey pot pie, seasonal game or
roast duckling. Leave room for one of the
lovely sweets. Less choice weekend lunchtimes.   **Family pub**

Fovant   *(B & B)*   *Cross Keys Inn*

Wiltshire · Map 6 A4
Fovant (072 270) 284

Free House
Landlord Mrs P. Story

BEDROOMS 4   Grade 2   £C
🍺 Gibbs Mew Wiltshire Special, Traditional;
Tisbury Local Bitter; Wadworth's 6X,
Northgate; Carlsberg Hof; Heineken. *Real ale*

Travellers on the A30 will find a
warm welcome at this fine old coaching inn
halfway between Salisbury and
Shaftesbury. Four simple, cottagy bedrooms provide good comfort and share a
well-kept public bathroom. The beamed
bar with its grandfather clock and sturdy
leather armchairs is very relaxing, and
there's also a cosy residents' lounge.
Garden.   **Family pub**

Fowlmere   *(Food)*   ★   *Chequers Inn*

Near Royston · *Cambridgeshire* · Map 5 C2
Fowlmere (076 382) 369

Brewery Tollemache & Cobbold
Landlord Mr Norman Rushton

Chicken & marjoram soup £1.60 Terrine of wild
rabbit £2.40 (Last order 10pm)
🍺 Tolly Cobbold Bitter, Original; Guinness;
Hansa; Taunton cider. *Real ale*

Samuel Pepys, a regular former patron,
would not be disappointed if he returned to
this quaint old village pub today. Skilfully
prepared dishes on an adventurous menu
range from chicken and marjoram soup or
superb champagne pâté to Cromer crab
gratin, moules marinière, pork chop with
mustard sauce and tender lamb with
tomato and basil sauce. Some delicious
sweets to follow.   **Family pub**

Fownhope   *(Food, B & B)*   *Green Man Inn*

Near Hereford · *Hereford & Worcester*
Map 7 D2
Fownhope (043 277) 243
Free House
Landlords Mr & Mrs R. F. Williams
BEDROOMS 8   Grade 1   £B
Steak & kidney pie £2.95 Steak sandwich £2.10
(Last order 10.30pm)
🍺 Hook Norton Best Bitter; Wadworth 6X;
Samuel Smith's Old Brewery Bitter; Flower's
Best Bitter; Guinness; cider. *Real ale*

Five centuries of history attach to this fine
old inn, once a coaching house and petty
sessions court. The beamed bar is a cosy
setting for enjoying a variety of well-
prepared snacks – sandwiches, salads and
hot dishes like grilled trout and roast
chicken. Bedrooms are bright and pleasant,
with good carpets and tasteful furnishings.
Planned improvements include additional
bedrooms, along with private bathrooms
and TVs throughout. Garden.   **Family pub**

Framfield   *(Food)*   *Barley Mow*

Eastbourne Road · *East Sussex* · Map 6 C4
Framfield (082 582) 234

Brewery Phoenix
Landlords Derek & Val Gilbert

Stilton ploughman's £1.35 Lasagne £2.50 (Last
order 9.45pm. No bar food Mon eve)
🍺 Watney's Special; Webster's Yorkshire
Bitter, King & Barnes Draught Festive; Usher's
Triple Crown; Guinness; cider. *Real ale*

The Gilberts have built up a large following
at their little whitewashed pub, Derek the
friendliest of hosts and Val a very capable
cook. Everything on the varied menu is
fresh and tasty, from vegetable broth and
succulent home-cooked ham to omelettes,
pies and chilli con carne. Bubble and
squeak is a treat not to miss, and there are
some nice sweets. Garden.   **Family pub**

Framlingham   *(Food)*   *Crown & Anchor*

Church Street · *Suffolk* · Map 5 D2
Framlingham (0728) 723611

Brewery Tollemache & Cobbold
Landlords Mr & Mrs J. M. Benhassoune

Special of the day £1.60 Steak with garlic &
oregano £4.80 (Last order 9.30pm)
🍺 Tolly Cobbold Mild, Bitter, Original;
Hansa. *Real ale*

At lunchtime, the cosy bar of this attractive
high street pub is crowded with customers
seeking simple, tasty snacks like chicken
liver pâté, sausage and onion pie, a
ploughman's or a hot daily special like beef
casserole. The more elaborate evening
menu might offer tournedos Rossini or rich
steak and pigeon pie. Excellent home-
made sweets, too.

Frampton Mansell   *(Food)*   *Crown Inn*

Near Stroud · *Gloucestershire* · Map 7 D2
Frampton Mansell (028 576) 218

Free House
Landlord Mrs. E. Coley

Home-made soup 75p Cold platter with salads
£3.50 (No bar food eves)
🍺 Wadworth's 6X; Worthington 'E'; Ben
Truman; Younger's Tartan; Guinness;
Carlsberg; cider. *Real ale*

The three low-ceilinged, beamed bars of
this old Cotswold-stone inn make a cosy
setting for Elizabeth Coley's simple, tasty
lunchtime snacks. Soup is served with
fresh home-baked bread, and there are
succulent home-cooked joints to go with a
crisp salad. You can have a ploughman's
too, and in winter hot dishes can be
enjoyed by the open fire. The terrace has
splendid views over hills and valleys.
Family pub

Frilford Heath   *(B & B)*   *Dog House Hotel*

Near Abingdon · *Oxfordshire* · Map 6 A3
Frilford Heath (0865) 390830

Brewery Morland
Landlords Mr & Mrs Morgan

BEDROOMS 10   Grade 2   £A
🍺 Morland's Bitter, Best Bitter, Mild, Artist;
Guinness; Heineken; Stella Artois. *Real ale*

Comfortable overnight accommodation is
a feature of this well-kept hostelry, a
modernised 17th-century building with a
tile-hung first storey. All the bedrooms
have central heating and practical modern
furnishings, and colour TVs and tea-makers
are standard equipment. Some rooms have
compact shower cabinets. Drinkers can
choose between the relaxing bar and the
pleasant garden.   **Family pub** (lunchtime)

Friskney   *(B & B)*   *Barley Mow*

Sea Lane, Near Boston · *Lincolnshire*
Map 4 D4
Friskney (075 484) 483

Brewery Bateman
Landlord Mr T. A. Makemson

BEDROOMS 2   Grade 2   £C   (No dogs)
🍺 Bateman's Bitter, XXXB, Mild;
Guinness; Heineken; cider. *Real ale*

Reclamation has pushed the coastline
about a mile from this attractive old pub,
which stands on the A52 between Boston
and Skegness. It's a comfortable place for
an overnight stay, and there are plenty of
homely touches in the prettily decorated
bedrooms. They have practical modern
furniture, portable TVs and share the landlord's well-equipped bathroom. There are
two bars, plus outside drinking in fine
weather.

Frogmore   *(B & B)*   *Globe Inn*

Near Kingsbridge · *Devon* · Map 8 C4
Frogmore (054 853) 351

Free House
Landlord Mrs J. Wilding

BEDROOMS 7   Grade 2   £C
🍺 Usher's Best Bitter, Founders Ale, Country
Ale; Ben Truman; Guinness; Holsten; cider.
Real ale

In the centre of a small village some three
miles south-east of Kingsbridge on the
A379, this friendly pub has a nautically
themed bar that's a pleasant spot to drop
anchor for a while. Non-mariners may
prefer a game of darts in the lively public
bar before retiring to one of the comfortable, simply furnished bedrooms, which
have tea/coffee-making facilities. Bathrooms are up to date.   **Family pub**

Fulking   (Food)   ★   *Shepherd & Dog*

Near Henfield · *West Sussex* · Map 6 C4
Poynings (079 156) 382
Brewery Phoenix
Landlord Mr H. A. Bradley-Hole
Mermaid's lunch £1.75 Scrumpy chicken £3.75
(Last order 9.30pm. No bar food Sun &
Mon eves)
🍺 King & Barnes Festive; Usher's Best
Bitter; Webster's Yorkshire Bitter; Tamplins
Stag; Guinness; Foster's; Carlsberg; cider.
Real ale

Locally smoked salmon is just one of the
many delights that keep this splendid old
village inn packed to the gills. Lunchtime
brings a tempting range of platters –
mermaid's with prawns, farmer's with pork
sausages, ploughman's with farmhouse
Cheddar – plus hot specials like sweet and
sour chicken. More hot dishes in the
evening, including a marvellous beef and
Guinness pie. Also salads and lovely
sweets. Garden.

Fyfield   (Food)   *White Hart*

Near Abingdon · *Oxfordshire* · Map 6 A3
Frilford Heath (0865) 390585

Free House
Landlord Mr E. Howard

Steak & kidney pie £2.65 Lamb kebabs £2.95
(Last order 10pm)
🍺 Morland's Bitter; Wadworth's 6X;
Theakston's Old Peculier; Ruddle's County;
Guinness; Foster's; cider. *Real ale*

There's a wide-ranging menu at this fine
old pub with an impressive 15th-century
gallery in its flagstoned bar. The choice
might include duck or venison and claret
pâté, whole pigeon braised in beer, spicy
lamb kebabs and even frogs' legs or fried
sardines. Chocolate fudge cake and sherry
trifle are among the appealing desserts.
Garden.   **Family pub**

Ganton   (B & B)   *Greyhound*

Near Scarborough · *North Yorkshire*
Map 4 D2
Sherburn (0944) 70242

Brewery Tetley
Landlords Mr & Mrs R. Mackinlay

BEDROOMS 4   Grade 2   £C   (No dogs)
🍺 Tetley's Mild, Bitter; Guinness; Skol;
cider.

Players and spectators at the nearby
championship golf course favour this
modest village inn beside the A64. Four
bedrooms offer sturdy, old-fashioned comfort and share a single public bathroom.
Guests can relax amid the polished brassware in the lounge bar or play dominoes in
the simple public bar. Accommodation
closed December–January. Garden.

Gargrave   (B & B)   *Anchor Inn*

Near Skipton · *North Yorkshire* · Map 4 C2
Gargrave (0756) 78666

Free House
Landlords Mr & Mrs E. R. Feather

BEDROOMS 8   Grade 1   £B
🍺 Theakston's Bitter, Old Peculier;
Younger's Scotch Bitter No. 3; Timothy
Taylors Bitter; Guinness; Carlsberg Pils; cider.
Real ale

A sturdy converted farmhouse, with the
busy A65 at the front and the Leeds–
Liverpool Canal providing a contrasting
serene setting at the rear. Centrally heated
bedrooms are comfortable and well
equipped, with practical modern furniture,
TVs, radio-alarms and tea-makers. Each
has its own bath/shower room. There's a
roomy bar and lounge, plus a children's
play area in the garden.   **Family pub**

Georgeham   *Rock Inn*

This attractive whitewashed inn, built in the 17th century, stands in a narrow street above the village. Old framed photographs are an interesting feature in the beamed bar, which has a terra-cotta tiled floor and ample pew-style seating. There's also a family-cum-games room, and the garden is popular in summer. **Family pub**

Rock Hill · *Devon* · Map 8 B3
Croyde (0271) 890322
Free House   Landlord Mrs Lesley Ashford
🍺 Ushers Best Bitter, Country Bitter; Ben Truman; Guinness; Carlsberg; Foster's; Taunton cider. *Real ale*

Gestingthorpe   *(Food)*   *Pheasant*

Halstead · *Essex* · Map 5 C2
Hedingham (0787) 61196

Free House
Landlords Mr & Mrs Paul Ruth
Smoked trout £1.90 Beef in red wine £4 (Last order 9.30pm)
🍺 Pheasant Bitter; Wethered's Bitter; Greene King IPA, Abbot Ale; Guinness; Kronenbourg; cider. *Real ale*

Seasonal game, including jugged hare, venison and pheasant casserole, is a feature of the menu at this delightful old country pub. Excellent pork and liver pâté, steak and grilled trout are also on offer, along with sandwiches and cheese to accompany a selection of real ales. If you're still hungry, there are also lovely sweets like elderberry and apple tart. **Family pub**

Gibraltar   *(Food)*   *Bottle & Glass*

Near Aylesbury · *Buckinghamshire* · Map 5 B2
Aylesbury (0296) 748488

Brewery Aylesbury
Landlords John & Eileen Gomersall

Smoked mackerel pâté £1.25 Mixed meat salad £3.50 (Last order 10pm)
🍺 ABC Bitter; Tetley's Bitter; Guinness; Skol. *Real ale*

The cold table is a popular feature at this attractive 15th-century thatched inn, which stands on the A418 between Aylesbury and Thame. Beef, ham and pork are carved to order and served with simple fresh salads; there are also home-made pâtés, ploughman's platters, winter soups and a week-day lunchtime hot special. Only sandwiches and pâtés Saturday and Sunday evenings, pâtés Sunday lunchtime. Patio.

Glastonbury   *(Food, B & B)*   *George & Pilgrims Hotel*

1 High Street · *Somerset* · Map 8 D3
Glastonbury (0458) 31146

Free House
Landlords Jack & Elzebie Richardson
BEDROOMS 14 Grade 1 £B
Somerset bacon bake £1.85 Cold steak & kidney pie & salad £1.85 (Last order 9pm)
🍺 Bass, Toby; Worthington Best Bitter; Guinness; Carling Black Label; Tennents Pilsner; Taunton cider. *Real ale*

Food and accommodation live up to the promise of the splendid stone façade of this 500-year-old inn at the centre of the town. Snacks range from well-filled sandwiches, local cheese and soup with home-baked bread to a tempting cold buffet (lunchtime) and a hot dish of the day. Bedrooms are comfortably furnished in traditional style and there is a relaxing residents' TV lounge. **Family pub**

Goldsborough   *(B & B)*   *Bay Horse Inn*

Near Knaresborough · *North Yorkshire*
Map 4 C2
Harrogate (0423) 862212

Brewery Whitbread
Landlord Mrs June Manks

BEDROOMS 5   Grade 2   £C   (No dogs)
🍺 Whitbread Trophy, Castle Eden Ale, Dark
Mild; Guinness; Stella Artois; cider. *Real ale*

In the centre of a peaceful village just off the
A59, this handsome hostelry offers comfortable overnight accommodation in a
rear extension. The five bedrooms are neat
and compact, the single bathroom well
equipped and spotlessly maintained. Darts
are played in the public bar, while in the
beamed lounge bar there's an interesting
collection of more lethal weapons! Garden.

Gomshall   *(B & B)*   *Black Horse*

Station Road · *Surrey* · Map 6 B3
Shere (048 641) 2242

Brewery Young
Landlord Anne & Andrew Brown

BEDROOMS 6   Grade 2   £B   (No dogs)
🍺 Young's Special, Ordinary, London Lager;
Taunton cider. *Real ale*

Dating from 1690, this solidly built pub
stands on the A25 between Dorking and
Guildford. The lounge bar with its oak
panelling and burnished brass has
a comfortable period appeal. Simply
furnished, good-sized bedrooms, all with
tea-makers and washbasins, share two
bathrooms, and there's a large TV room.
Under-12s not accommodated overnight.
Garden.   **Family pub**

Goostrey   *(Food)*   *Olde Red Lion Inn*

Main Road · *Cheshire* · Map 3 B4
Holmes Chapel (0477) 32033

Brewery Tetley
Landlords Mary & Peter Yorke

Deep-fried stuffed mushrooms £1.75 Seafood
open sandwich £2.25 (Last order 10.15pm)
🍺 Tetley's Bitter, Mild; Walker's Bitter;
Falstaff Bitter; Guinness; Löwenbräu; cider.
Real ale

Head for the Jodrell Bank radio telescopes
to find this friendly, rambling pub with its
excellent range of bar snacks. You could
start with home-made vegetable soup or
deep-fried stuffed mushrooms and go on to
a rump steak or cold meat salad. Tasty
sandwiches include a delicious open seafood one, and there are some tempting
sweets to round things off. Garden.
                                     Family pub

Goudhurst   *(B & B)*   *Star & Eagle*

High Street · *Kent* · Map 6 C3
Goudhurst (0580) 211512

Brewery Whitbread
Landlord Mr Christopher J. Satchell

BEDROOMS 11   Grade 1   £A
🍺 Fremlins Bitter; Whitbread Best Bitter;
Stella Artois; Heineken; cider. *Real ale*

The appeal of the beamed, flagstoned bar
and lovely views of the Weald lure visitors
to this one-time monastery built in the 14th
century. Comfortably furnished bedrooms
are in tasteful modern style, except for one
which has antiques and a fine four-poster
bed. All have TVs and tea-makers, and nine
have neat, well-kept private bathrooms.

England

Grantchester   *(Food)*   *Green Man*

High Street · *Cambridgeshire* · Map 5 C2
Cambridge (0223) 841178

Brewery Tollemache & Cobbold
Landlord Mr Norman Adamson

Turkey fricassee £2.75 Fresh salmon
salad £6.95 (Last order 10pm)
🍺 Tolly Cobbold Bitter, Tolly Original, Old
Strong (winter only); Guinness; Hansa;
Taunton cider. *Real ale*

A popular haunt of Cambridge dons and
undergraduates, this welcoming, beamed
village pub offers a good choice of tasty,
well-prepared snacks. Light eaters can
have sandwiches, ploughman's salads and
omelettes, and there is also home-made
soup and a selection of daily specials such
as turkey fricassee, baked trout or braised
oxtail. Patio and garden.   **Family pub**

Grantchester   *(Food)*   *Red Lion*

High Street · *Cambridgeshire* · Map 5 C2
Cambridge (0223) 840121

Brewery Greene King
Landlords Mr & Mrs D. W. Gration

Poacher's pie £2.75 Chocolate mousse £1.10
(Last order 10pm)
🍺 Greene King IPA, Abbot Ale; Guinness;
Harp; Kronenbourg; Taunton cider. *Real ale*

The cold buffet, with its tempting selection
of quiches, pies and salads, is a popular
lunchtime attraction at this well-run pub in
a village immortalised by Rupert Brooke.
There are plenty of hot choices, too, from
robust French onion soup to basket meals,
beef bordelaise, poacher's pie and grilled
trout with almonds. Mousses and gâteaux
to finish. Garden.   **Family pub**

Great Ayton   *(B & B)*   *Royal Oak Hotel*

Middlesbrough, Cleveland · *North Yorkshire*
Map 4 C2
Great Ayton (0642) 722361

Brewery Scottish & Newcastle
Landlords Mr & Mrs D. Monaghan

BEDROOMS 5   Grade 2   £C
🍺 Scottish & Newcastle Exhibition;
Younger's IPA, Tartan; Guinness; Carlsberg
Hof; Cavalier; cider.

Captain Cook attended school close to this
welcoming village pub beside the village
green. It provides a comfortable overnight
stay in five spacious, well-kept bedrooms,
all with TVs and tea-makers. One room has
a private bathroom, while a public one
serves the rest. Guests can relax in either of
the two bars or in the residents' lounge.
Good breakfasts. Accommodation closed
December.   **Family pub**

Great Chishill   *(Food)*   *Pheasant Inn*

Near Royston · *Hertfordshire* · Map 5 C2
Royston (0763) 838535

Free House
Landlord Denis Ryan
Beef casserole £1.95 Scampi provençale £4.45
(Last order 9.30pm. No bar food Sun
lunch & Mon)
🍺 Younger's IPA, Scotch Bitter, Tartan;
Greene King IPA; Tolly Cobbold Original;
McEwans Export; Harp. *Real ale*

Formerly a jockey, landlord Denis Ryan has
made this peaceful village pub a good bet
for tasty, wholesome food. Home-made
soup served in the cosy, antique-furnished
bar is a welcome addition to sandwiches
and salads, and hot dishes range from
omelettes, fish and grills to beef casserole
or scampi provençale. Steaks are an evening speciality. Closed Mon lunchtime.
    Family pub (lunchtime)

Great Oxendon *(Food)*   *George*

Near Market Harborough · *Leicestershire*
Map 5 B2
Market Harborough (0858) 65205

Free House
Landlords George & Dorothy Taylor
Fish chowder £1.50 Game pie £4.95 (Last
order 10.30pm. No bar food Mon eve)
🍺 Hoskins Bitter; Samuel Smith's Old
Brewery Bitter; Shipstone's Bitter; Stella
Artois; cider. *Real ale.*

Wholesome country fare matches the cosy
charm of this meticulously kept inn, where
you can admire a fine collection of old
pewter. Stockpot soup and fish chowder
have a loyal following, and there are also
salads, pâté, prawn-stuffed trout and
delicious game pie served with fresh
vegetables. Chocolate mousse and spicy
apple pie are among the irresistible sweets.
Garden.

Great Ryburgh *(Food, B & B)*   *Boar Inn*

Near Fakenham · *Norfolk* · Map 5 D1
Great Ryburgh (032 878) 212
Free House
Landlords Mr & Mrs J. Corson &
Mr & Mrs I. Lewis
BEDROOMS 4   Grade 2   £B
Lasagne £1.75 Madras beef curry £1.85
(Last order 9.45pm)
🍺 Tolly Cobbold Original, Bitter; Bass
Springfield Bitter; Guinness; Hansa; Carling
Black Label; Taunton cider. *Real ale*

Two ex-RAF men and their wives run this
friendly village inn. The ladies do the cooking, producing excellent fare that ranges
from flavoursome vegetable soup to shepherd's pie, ham salad and a splendid sherry
trifle. Decor and furnishings are mainly
traditional, both in the comfortable bar and
in the modestly equipped bedrooms, which
share a simple shower room. All have
colour TVs.   **Family pub**

Great Shefford *(Food)*   *Swan*

Newbury Road · *Berkshire* · Map 6 A3
Great Shefford (048 839) 271

Brewery Courage
Landlords Mr & Mrs M. Lovett
Summer buffet £2.75 Home-made beefburger
with salad & chips £1.95 (Last order 9.45pm.
No bar food Sun & Mon eves)
🍺 Courage Directors Bitter, Best Bitter;
Guinness; Kronenbourg; Hofmeister;
Taunton cider. *Real ale*

The garden of this pink-washed pub beside
a stream is a delightful place to enjoy your
pick from the appetising summer buffet of
cold meats, fish and colourful salads. In
winter, the cosy bar serves satisfying hot
snacks such as leek and potato soup, lamb
chops in sherry and splendid home-made
beefburgers. Book for the traditional
Sunday lunch.   **Family pub**

Great Stainton *(Food)*   *Kings Arms*

Co. Durham · Map 4 C1
Sedgefield (0740) 30361

Brewery Whitbread
Landlord Gordon Mitchell

Cold meat salad £1.95 Kidneys in red
wine £2.45 (Last order 10pm. No bar food
Sun eve)
🍺 Whitbread Trophy, Castle Eden Ale;
Heineken; Stella Artois; cider. *Real ale*

About 300 years old, this white-painted pub
in a pretty village has cosy, traditional
decor in its beamed bar, where a fire burns
in winter. An extensive blackboard menu
caters for most tastes with substantial
dishes like seafood platter, ham in onion
and mushroom sauce, lamb Reform or a
tender, rich beef casserole. Sweets include
trifle and coffee mousse. Garden.

Great Waltham   *(Food)*   *Windmill*

Essex · Map 5 C2
Chelmsford (0245) 360292

Free House
Landlord Mr Martin Ridgewell

Steak, kidney & mushroom pudding £3.75
Pheasant in red wine £5.50 (Last order 9.30pm.
No bar food Sat lunch & all Sun)
🍺 Adnams Bitter; Carling Black Label.
Real ale

Generous portions of tasty, well-prepared food brings hungry crowds to this comfortable roadside pub. Steak, kidney and mushroom pudding, and pheasant in red wine are typically satisfying choices, and you could also try the home-cured bloaters and spaghetti bolognese. There are sandwiches, too, and splendid puddings like steamed syrup sponge or blackberry and apple fool.   **Family pub**

Great Wolford   *(Food, B & B)*   *Fox & Hounds*

Near Shipston-on-Stour · *Warwickshire*
Map 5 A2
Barton-on-the-Heath (060 874) 220
Free House
Landlords Mr & Mrs C. Olcese
BEDROOMS 4   Grade 1   £B
Steak & kidney pie £2.35 Lasagne £2.50 (Last order 10pm)
🍺 Manns Bitter; Ben Truman; Webster's Yorkshire Bitter; Guinness; Foster's; Carlsberg; cider. *Real ale*

The genial Signor Olcese and his Scottish wife make a fine team at this pleasant old Cotswold-stone inn. His welcome is warm and sunny, her bar snacks simple and delicious, ranging from ploughman's and country broth to spaghetti bolognese, omelettes and a really good chicken curry. Overnight guests are accommodated in four neatly kept bedrooms with TVs and well-appointed modern bathrooms. Garden.   **Family pub**

Greatford   *(Food)*   *Hare & Hounds*

Main Street, Near Stamford · *Lincolnshire*
Map 5 B1
Greatford (077 836) 332

Brewery Manns
Landlords Mr & Mrs P. Wilkins
Turkey & ham pie £2.95 Apple pie 75p (Last order 9pm. No bar food Mon except Bank Hols)
🍺 Manns Bitter, Triple Crown; Webster's Yorkshire Bitter; Ben Truman; Guinness; Holsten; Carlsberg; cider.

The river Glen runs just across the road from this cosy, cottage pub, where Mrs Wilkins produces a good choice of robust, homely fare. Steak and kidney pie, devilled gammon and a mighty mixed grill are meaty main dishes, and grilled lemon sole is a firm favourite with fish-lovers. To finish, perhaps trifle or a delicious apple and blackberry pie. Garden. Closed 2 weeks October.

Greenhalgh   *(Food)*   *Blues*

Fleetwood Road, Near Kirkham · *Lancashire*
Map 3 B3
Weeton (039 136) 283

Brewery Thwaites
Landlord Mr Kevin Ratcliffe

Prawn salad platter £1.50 Seafood casserole £4.25 (Last order 10pm)
🍺 Thwaites Bitter, Best Mild; Guinness; Stein; cider. *Real ale*

Just north of junction 3 of the M55, this pub is worth seeking out for its enjoyable bar food. Start with pâté, deep-fried onion rings or a hearty broth, and go on to seafood casserole, lasagne or a good traditional steak and kidney pie. There are also nice sweets. In summer you can sit out on the terrace or in the garden with its attractive duck pond and children's playground equipment.   **Family pub**

Greta Bridge *(Food, B & B)* — *Morritt Arms Hotel*

Near Barnard Castle · *Co. Durham* · Map 4 C2
Teesdale (0833) 27232

Free House
Landlords Mr & Mrs S. R. Waldron
BEDROOMS 26 Grade 1 £A
Smoked mackerel £1.95 Fresh salmon
salad £4.75 (Last order 10.30pm)
🍺 Theakston's Best Bitter; Newcastle
Exhibition, Scotch Bitter; Harp; Carlsberg;
cider. *Real ale*

Charles Dickens stayed at this roadside inn
while writing *Nicholas Nickleby*, as visitors
are reminded by murals in the welcoming,
beamed bar. Tasty snacks include home-
made soups, gamy venison pâté, sandwiches, cold meats and salads. Overnight
guests have 26 comfortable bedrooms
furnished in a variety of styles, most with
their own bathrooms. There's also a small
TV room. Garden. **Family pub**

Grimsthorpe *(Food, B & B)* — *Black Horse Inn*

Near Bourne · *Lincolnshire* · Map 5 B1
Edenham (077 832) 247

Free House
Landlords Mr & Mrs Fisher

BEDROOMS 4 Grade 1 £A
Mrs Beeton's steak, kidney & mushroom
pie £2.99 Bramley apple tart with cream £1.39
(No bar food eves or Sun)
🍺 Sam Smith's Sovereign

The delightful bar of this Georgian coaching inn has beams and a flagstone floor,
and there's a residents' lounge with TV.
Bedrooms are comfortable and cosy, with
pretty floral decor, private bathrooms and
extras such as hairdryers. Delicious lunchtime snacks have a distinctly English slant:
Lincolnshire rarebit and potatoes, Yorkshire beef pasties, sausage and mash,
treacle tart. Closed 1 week Christmas.
Family pub

Grindleford *(Food, B & B)* — *Maynard Arms Hotel*

Main Road · *Derbyshire* · Map 4 C3
Hope Valley (0433) 30321

Free House
Landlords Bob & Thelma Graham

BEDROOMS 13 Grade 1 £A
Yorkshire meat pudding £2.25 Neptune
salad £3.25 (Last order 9.30pm)
🍺 Stones Traditional Bitter, Keg Bitter;
Carling Lager. *Real ale*

This fine Victorian hotel in the Peak District
National Park retains attractive original
features like wood panelling, stained-glass
windows and a splendid oak staircase.
Modernised bedrooms are very well
appointed, with direct-dial phones, TVs and
trouser presses, and all have private
facilities. Satisfying bar snacks include
ravioli, steak and kidney pie and filled
Yorkshire puddings; there's also a lunchtime cold table (except Sunday). Patio.

Groombridge *(B & B)* — *Crown Inn*

Near Tunbridge Wells · *Kent* · Map 6 C3
Groombridge (089 276) 361

Free House
Landlords Jeffrey & Barbara Chambers

BEDROOMS 4 Grade 2 £C
🍺 Harvey's Best Bitter; Courage Directors
Bitter; Bass; Mitchells & Butlers Springfield
Bitter; Guinness; Hofmeister; cider. *Real ale*

Full of nooks and crannies, the cosy
beamed bars of this handsome 16th-
century pub are perfect for an intimate chat
and a well-kept pint. The attractive garden
adjoining the village green is ideal for
summer drinking. Pretty floral duvets have
brightened the spotlessly clean bedrooms
with their solid traditional furniture, and the
public bathroom is in perfect order. Tasty
breakfasts. **Family pub**

147

Guisborough   *(B & B)*   *Fox Inn*

10 Bow Street · *Cleveland* · Map 4 C2
Guisborough (0287) 32958

Brewery Scottish & Newcastle
Landlords Mr & Mrs Williamson

BEDROOMS 7   Grade 1   £C   (No dogs)
🏠 Scottish & Newcastle Exhibition;
Younger's Scotch Bitter; McEwan's 80/-,
Guinness; Harp; Taunton cider.

This old pub continues to provide a welcoming haven for travellers, the mounting steps at the front recalling its days as a coaching inn. The seven bedrooms are comfortably furnished and all have colour TVs and tea-makers. They share two nicely kept public bathrooms. You can join the locals for a drink in the lively, beamed public bar or relax in the quieter cocktail bar.   **Family pub**

Guisborough   *(B & B)*   *Moorcock Hotel*

West End Road · *Cleveland* · Map 4 C2
Guisborough (0287) 32342

Brewery Whitbread
Landlord Mr Alan Mitchell

BEDROOMS 6   Grade 1   £C
🏠 Whitbread Trophy; Guinness; Heineken;
Stella Artois; cider.

Alan Mitchell offers a warm welcome and excellent accommodation at this modern purpose-built pub. There are two smart bars (one with pine panelling and plush seating), as well as a brightly furnished residents' lounge. Compact, well-maintained bedrooms have fitted furniture, TVs and up-to-date shower cabinets; there's a public bathroom too. Exemplary housekeeping throughout. Garden.

Gunnislake   *(B & B)*   *Cornish Inn*

The Square · *Cornwall* · Map 8 B4
Tavistock (0822) 832475

Free House
Landlords Messrs Lawrence & Chapple

BEDROOMS 9   Grade 2   £C
🏠 St Austell Tinner's Ale; Flower's Best
Bitter; Younger's Tartan; Guinness; Carlsberg
Hof. *Real ale*

A warm and friendly welcome awaits visitors to this white-painted pub in the centre of the village. Locals and tourists mingle in the convivial surroundings of the bar, and residents have a TV lounge with plenty of comfortable armchairs and settees. The homely, traditional style extends to the bright bedrooms, five of which have their own spotlessly maintained bathrooms. Patio.

Hambleden   *(B & B)*   *Stag & Huntsman Inn*

Near Henley-on-Thames, Oxfordshire
Buckinghamshire · Map 6 B3
Hambleden (049 166) 227

Free House
Landlords Mr & Mrs C. Hubbard

BEDROOMS 3   Grade 2   £B
🏠 Brakspear's Pale Ale; Wadworth's 6X;
Chiltern Ale; Eldridge Pope Royal Oak;
Guinness; Stella Artois; cider. *Real ale*

Overnight guests will find a warm welcome at this delightful little village pub. Comfortable bedrooms have neat modern furniture and an excellent breakfast will set you up for the day. The bar with its old beams and panelling has a loyal following of regulars and provides a cosy, friendly setting for a drink. Children not accommodated overnight. Garden.   **Family pub**

Let TWA be your guide to the USA.

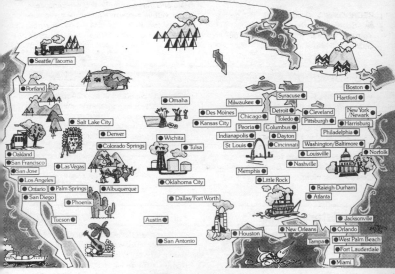

TWA flies to over 60 US cities.

As someone who likes to follow a good guide, you probably get around a bit.

If you're going to America you can do that best with TWA.

TWA flies all over America. Not just to the great cities like New York, Boston, Los Angeles and Chicago,

but some of the more picturesque — like New Orleans or Nashville. To the West, like Albuquerque and Phoenix. Smaller towns like Peoria. Sunny Florida. Spectacular California.

TWA flies to over 60 US cities. If you want a guide to get you around, then TWA's the one.

See your

TWA Main Agent

You're going to like us **TWA**

Handcross   *(Food)*   *Royal Oak*

Horsham Road · *West Sussex* · Map 6 C4
Handcross (0444) 400703

Brewery Phoenix
Landlords Mr & Mrs E. H. R. Field

Guinness, steak & kidney pie £2.55
Cold seafood platter £5.85 (Last order 9.30 pm)
🍺 Tamplins Bitter; Watneys Stag Bitter;
Webster's Yorkshire Bitter; Ben Truman;
Guinness; Holsten. *Real ale*

Just off the A23, this trim little pub formed
out of three adjoining cottages provides
appetising snacks in its cosy bar. Wholesome pies including chicken and mushroom or steak and kidney are popular
choices, and there are also tempting
quiches served with salad, moussaka or
perhaps beef crumble. Additional evening
alternatives are provided by grills and a
seafood platter. Patio.

Harome   *(Food)*   *Star Inn*

Near Helmsley · *North Yorkshire* · Map 4 C2
Helmsley (0439) 70397

Free House
Landlord Mr Tony Bowron

Star special sandwich £1.80 Mushroom soup
60p (No bar food eves)
🍺 Theakston's Best Bitter, Old Peculier;
Cameron's Lion; Vaux Samson Ale; Carlsberg.
Real ale

Carefully prepared soup, sandwiches and
cheese make up the lunchtime bar menu at
this delightful village pub with a thatched
roof and masses of roses. The bar itself is
full of country charm, while the sandwiches
(white or brown bread) come with a score
of fillings like egg and chives, tuna
mayonnaise, home-cooked ham – even
prawn curry. There's a pretty little rear
garden. Closed Bank Holidays. **Family pub**

Harpenden   *(Food)*   *Silver Cup*

West Common, St Albans Road
Hertfordshire · Map 5 B2
Harpenden (058 27) 3095
Brewery Wells
Landlord Mr Roy Mills
Steak pie £1.95 Spaghetti bolognese £1.95 (No
bar food eves or all Sun)
🍺 Wells Bitter, Bombardier, Noggin;
Guinness; Kellerbräu; Red Stripe; cider.
Real ale

This old whitewashed pub – its name a
reminder of the horse races which used to
take place on the nearby common – draws
eager crowds with a tasty, wholesome
selection of lunchtime snacks. Home-made
soups and daily specials such as liver and
bacon or chilli con carne are firm favourites,
along with gammon steak and burgers.
Freshly made sandwiches, pâté and
various ploughman's are also in the
running. Patio.

Harrietsham   *Ringlestone Inn*

Tucked away in the Kentish countryside, this splendid old inn is a
great place to enjoy a pint and soak up the antiquity. Uneven floors,
exposed brickwork, blackened beams and gnarled woodwork
characterise the three small rooms, whose furnishings include sturdy
little oak tables, pews and fine old high-backed chairs.   **Family pub**

Near Maidstone · *Kent* · Map 6 C3
Maidstone (0622) 859207
Free House   *Landlord* Mr M. Millington-Buck
🍺 Boddingtons Bitter, Wadworth's 6X; Gibbs Mew Bishop's Tipple;
Everards Tiger; Heineken; Carlsberg; cider. *Real ale*

England

Harrogate   *(B & B)*   *West Park Hotel*

West Park · *North Yorkshire* · Map 4 C2
Harrogate (0423) 524471

Brewery Tetley
Landlord Mr Charles Gillis

BEDROOMS 18   Grade 1   £A   (No dogs)
🍺 Tetley's Bitter, Dark Mild; Guinness; Skol;
Castlemaine; cider. *Real ale*

Major refurbishment has transformed this
pleasant old inn, which stands in the heart
of the city overlooking verdant West Park
Stray. Well-proportioned bedrooms are
bright, modern and comfortable, with TVs,
tea-makers, trouser presses and fully tiled
shower rooms. The relaxing main bar
features an ornate plaster ceiling, while the
cocktail bar is smartly up to date in pale
grey and pink.   **Family pub**

Hartfield   *(Food)*   *Anchor*

Church Street · *East Sussex* · Map 6 C3
Hartfield (089 277) 424

Free House
Landlords Ken & Janis Thompson

Seafood cassoulet £4.50 Lamb & beef
kebabs £4.75 (Last order 10pm)
🍺 Fremlins Tusker; King & Barnes Sussex
Bitter, Festive; Shepherd Neame Masterbrew;
Guinness; Stella Artois; cider. *Real ale*

A verandah runs along the front of Ken and
Janis Thompson's handsome pub, where a
fine selection of delicious snacks is served
in the bar. Simple sandwiches, ploughman's and burgers are supplemented by
excellent lamb and beef kebabs, steaks and
a range of seafood dishes which includes
moules marinière, seafood cassoulet and
goujons of sole. Garden.   **Family pub**

Hartwell   *(Food)*   *Bugle Horn*

Aylesbury · *Buckinghamshire* · Map 5 B2
Aylesbury (0296) 748209

Brewery Benskins
Landlords Antony & Lady Rose Saint

Beef casserole £2.25 Stuffed baked
potatoes £1.65 (Last order 10pm)
🍺 Benskins Bitter; Ind Coope Burton Ale;
John Bull Bitter; Guinness; Oranjeboom;
Skol; cider. *Real ale*

The lunchtime cold buffet is a popular
feature at this whitewashed 17th-century
pub set in a very attractive garden. Cooked
meats, pâtés and quiches are displayed
temptingly at one end of the bar, and
there's also a large selection of freshly filled
rolls and baps. Hot options include stuffed
baked potatoes and a daily special, perhaps
chicken curry or chunky beef casserole.

Family pub

Haslemere   *(Food)*   *Crown & Cushion*

Weyhill · *Surrey* · Map 6 B3
Haslemere (0428) 3112

Brewery Friary Meux
Landlord Benjamin Heath

Spinach & bacon bake £2.95 Fillet of lamb
with rosemary & redcurrant £4.25
(Last order 10.30pm)
🍺 Friary Meux Bitter; Ind Coope Burton Ale;
Guinness; Löwenbräu; Skol; cider. *Real ale*

Sandwiches, jacket potatoes, quiches and
pâté are just a few of the choices on offer at
this smart pub. Tasty hot dishes range from
soup served with wholemeal bread to
grills, rabbit in mustard sauce, vegetable
curry, lamb with rosemary and spinach and
bacon bake. If you're still hungry, there are
some delicious home-made sweets, too.
Garden.

151

England

Hastingwood Common *Rainbow & Dove*

Not far from the M11, but the surroundings are so peaceful and rural that the age of the motor car seems far removed from this friendly old pub. It's been dispensing hospitality since the 17th century, and the bars, with their low beams, sturdy wooden furniture and warming fires, are delightfully welcoming. There's a pretty garden, too.

Near Harlow · *Essex* · Map 6 C3
Harlow (0279) 415419
Brewery Ind Coope *Landlords* Joyce and Tony Bird
🍺 John Bull Bitter; Double Diamond; Guinness; Löwenbräu; Skol; cider.

Hatherleigh *(Food, B & B)* *George Hotel*

Near Okehampton · *Devon* · Map 8 B3
Okehampton (0837) 810454

Free House
Landlords Mr & Mrs M. E. F. Giles
BEDROOMS 12 Grades 1 & 2 £C
Prawn curry £4.25 Fruit pie £1.10 (Last order 9.30pm)
🍺 Courage Directors Bitter, Best; John Smith's Trophy; Simmonds Bitter; Guinness; Hofmeister; cider. *Real ale*

Originally a monk's retreat and later a coaching inn, this fine old thatched pub continues to provide excellent hospitality. The large beamed bar is the setting for a wide range of tasty fare, from light snacks – ploughman's, toasted sandwiches, delicious tomato soup – to hearty fry-ups, grills and curries. Spick-and-span bedrooms, most with private facilities, have sturdy traditional furnishings. Courtyard.
Family pub

Hawk Green *(Food)* *Crown Inn*

Marple, Near Stockport · *Greater Manchester*
Map 4 C3
061-427 2678

Brewery Robinson
Landlord Mr T. C. Lane

Mushrooms à la grecque £1.65 Pork Normandy £3.45 (Last order 9.45pm)
🍺 Robinson's Best Bitter, Mild; Guinness; Einhorn; Tennent's Lager. *Real ale*

A friendly, popular pub, whose spick-and-span bar is a comfortable setting for enjoying a wide variety of excellent fare. Follow French onion soup or deep-fried whitebait with a succulent steak, tandoori-style chicken or a daily special like delicious beef olives. Also salads and open sandwiches, seafood and tempting sweets. Food is served from noon to closing time on Sunday. Garden.
Family pub (lunchtime)

Hawkhurst *(B & B)* *Royal Oak Hotel*

Highgate · *Kent* · Map 6 C3
Hawkhurst (058 05) 2184

Brewery Courage
Landlord Mr David Jackson

BEDROOMS 15 Grade 2 £B
🍺 Courage Best Bitter, Director's Bitter; Guinness; Hofmeister; Kronenbourg; Taunton cider. *Real ale*

Old-fashioned charm and character abound in this handsome black and white hostelry in the middle of the village. Three homely bars are popular with both tourists and the local community, and there's a tranquil sitting room with comfortable armchairs and sofas. Spacious bedrooms are also traditional in style; one has its own bathroom, two others showers. Garden.
Family pub

Hawkhurst   *(Food, B & B)*   *Tudor Arms Hotel*

Rye Road · *Kent* · Map 6 C3
Hawkhurst (058 05) 2312

Owner Mr Basil Sanderson
Landlord Karen Bradbury

BEDROOMS 13   Grade 1   £A
Lasagne & salad £2.25 Cottage pie £1.80 (Last
order 9pm)
🍺 Fremlins Bitter; Whitbread Best Bitter;
Stella Artois; cider. *Real ale*

Bedrooms are very comfortably furnished
at this handsome brick pub standing in
pleasant grounds beside the A268. All have
fitted carpets and trouser presses, and nine
have TVs and well-fitted private bathrooms. The panelled bar offers an appetising range of snacks like home-made soup,
quiche, cottage pie, lasagne and delicious
blackberry and apple pie.   **Family pub**

Hawkshead   *(Food, B & B)*   *Queen's Head*

Cumbria · Map 3 B2
Hawkshead (096 66) 271

Brewery Hartley
Landlord Mr Allan Whitehead

BEDROOMS 8   Grade 2   £B   (No dogs)
Venison pâté £2.25 Beef & beer casserole £3.25
(Last order 9pm)
🍺 Hartley's Best Bitter, Mild; Guinness;
Heineken; cider. *Real ale*

The panelled bar of this busy village pub
provides a convivial setting for enjoying
some very good snacks. Venison liver pâté
and local smoked trout make tasty light
meals, and more substantial offerings
range from deep-fried scampi to beef and
beer casserole. There are also lunchtime
sandwiches. Simply furnished bedrooms
are well maintained, and there's a plush TV
room. No under-tens overnight. **Family pub**

Haytor Vale   *(Food, B & B)*   *Rock Inn*

Newton Abbot · *Devon* · Map 8 C4
Haytor (036 46) 305

Free House
Landlord Mr C. F. H. H. Graves
BEDROOMS 9   Grades 1 & 2   £B
Stuffed chicken £2.85 Salcombe smokie £1.35
(Last order 10pm)
🍺 Eldridge Pope Royal Oak, Dorset IPA,
Dorchester Bitter; Guinness, Stella Artois;
Faust Export; Taunton cider. *Real ale*

This friendly, welcoming inn stands in a
tiny village below Dartmoor's tallest tors.
Low beams and milk-churn tables give a
rustic feel to the main bar, where snacks
range from soup and sandwiches to pâtés,
smoked mackerel and curries, with nice
home-made sweets to finish. Airy,
spacious bedrooms (all with TV) feature
bright floral patterns and many home
comforts. Five of them have en suite bathrooms. Patio and garden.   **Family pub**

Helford   *(Food)*   *Shipwright's Arms*

Near Helston · *Cornwall* · Map 8 A4
Manaccan (032 623) 235

Brewery Devenish
Landlords Mr & Mrs Flynn
Ploughman's £1.50 Local crab salad £3.95
(Last order 9.15pm. No bar food Mon–Wed
in winter)
🍺 Devenish Cornish Best Bitter, Mild;
Whitbread Tankard; Guinness; Grünhalle;
cider. *Real ale*

You can walk straight down to the sea from
the terrace of this charming little thatched
pub perched above the Helford estuary.
Lunchtime fare consists mainly of
ploughman's and a tempting range of
salads featuring home-cooked ham, beef or
seafood. On winter evenings there are
warming dishes like steak and kidney soup
or scallops Mornay to be enjoyed in the
panelled bar. The covered patio is useful for
children.

England

Helston   *(B & B)*   *Angel Hotel*

Coinage Hall Street · *Cornwall* · Map 8 A4
Helston (032 65) 2701

Free House
Landlords Mr & Mrs S. W. Hudson

BEDROOMS 21   Grade 2   £B
 Devenish Cornish Bitter; Worthington
Bitter; Whitbread Best Bitter; Flowers Bitter;
Guinness; Heineken; Stella Artois. *Real ale*

This welcoming hotel in the town centre
has a history stretching back over 500
years. A well complete with a little water-
wheel is an unusual feature in the foyer-
lounge, and there's a comfortable TV
lounge-cum-writing room as well as two
bars. Bedrooms of various sizes have pretty
floral wallpaper and freestanding furniture.
Accommodation closed 1 week Christmas.
Terrace.   **Family pub**

Henfield   *(Food)*   *White Hart*

High Street · *West Sussex* · Map 6 B4
Henfield (0273) 492006

Brewery Charrington
Landlords Mr John Dean & Mr A. Sephton
Braised lamb's liver £1.95 Carbonnade of
beef £2.45
 Bass; Charrington's Mild; Stones Bitter;
Worthington Best Bitter; Guinness; Carling
Black Label; Tennent's Extra; Taunton cider.
Real ale

Distinctive glass lanterns cast a rosy glow
in the traditionally furnished bar of this
friendly, welcoming pub, where capable
chef Christopher Boyle provides some delicious fare. Nourishing home-made soups
are backed up by tasty main courses such
as chicken Marengo, sole provençale and
grills. There are salads and Danish open
sandwiches too, and simple sweets include
fruit pie and cheesecake. Only light snacks
available Monday and Tuesday evenings.

Henley-on-Thames   *(Food)*   *Argyll*

Market Place · *Oxfordshire* · Map 6 B3
Henley-on-Thames (0491) 573400

Brewery Morland
Landlord Mr R. K. Boswell
Beef stew with dumplings &
vegetables £2.30 Chicken & mushroom pie
with salad £2.20 (No bar food eves)
 Morland's Best Bitter, Bitter, Mild;
Guinness; Heineken; Stella Artois. *Real ale*

Tartan carpets and regimental prints lend a
Scottish flavour to this cosy town-centre
pub, but the emphasis is on traditional
English fare when it comes to bar snacks.
The well-laden hot and cold buffet offers
dishes like stuffed shoulder of lamb or beef
stew with dumplings, as well as tasty
quiche lorraine and crisp, fresh salads.
Don't miss the lovely treacle tart. Less
choice Sunday lunch. Patio.

Henley-on-Thames   *(Food)* ★   *Little Angel*

Remenham Hill · *Oxfordshire* · Map 6 B3
Henley-on-Thames (0491) 574165

Brewery Brakspear
Landlord Mr Paul Southwood

Open seafood sandwich £2.95 Cottage pie £3
(Last order 10pm)
 Brakspear's Bitter, Old Ale; Guinness;
Heineken; cider. *Real ale*

In the bustling beamed bars or out on the
patio you can enjoy food of outstanding
quality at this pretty 16th-century pub. Seafood is something of a speciality (hors
d'oeuvre or open sandwich), and the steak
and pheasant pie is absolutely bursting
with goodness and flavour under its lovely
light puff pastry lid. Other delights include
subtly smooth pâté, French cheeses and
heavenly sweets. Summer cold table.

Henley-on-Thames *(Food, B & B)*   *Victoria*

Market Place · *Oxfordshire* · Map 6 B3
Henley (0491) 575628
Brewery Wethered
Landlord Mr Worsdell
BEDROOMS 4   Grade 2   £C
Steak & kidney pie & vegetables £1.95
Pork in cream & cider £3.75 (Last order
10.30pm)
🍺 Wethered's Bitter, SPA, Winter Royal;
Whitbread Best Bitter, Mild; Heineken; cider.
Real ale

There's a wide variety of tasty home-
cooked fare to keep the customers happy at
this cheerful pub behind the town hall. Beef
and beer stew, casseroled chicken and pork
in cream and cider are hearty main courses,
with sandwiches and Cornish pasties
among the lighter snacks. Nice sweets, too,
and a Sunday lunchtime roast. Recently
refurbished bedrooms share two public
bathrooms. Patio.   **Family pub**

Henton *(Food, B & B)*   *Peacock*

Near Chinnor · *Oxfordshire* · Map 6 B3
Kingston Blount (0844) 53519

Free House
Landlord Mr H. S. Good
BEDROOMS 3   Grade 1   £A   (No dogs)
Salmon trout £4.45 T-bone steak £5.85 (Last
order 10pm)
🍺 Tetley's Bitter; Hall & Woodhouse Badger
Best Bitter; Hook Norton Best Bitter; Adnams
Bitter; Guinness; Carlsberg; cider. *Real ale*

An attractive thatched village pub,
complete with ducks and peacocks in the
garden. Very good snacks are served in the
comfortable bar, including sandwiches and
salads, salmon trout and barbecued lamb
ribs. Roast beef can be enjoyed hot or cold,
and chocolate fudge cake makes a fine
finale. Three spotless bedrooms have
smart freestanding furniture and excellent
modern bathrooms. Accommodation
closed 1 week February.

We neither seek nor accept

hospitality, and we pay for all

food, drinks and accommodation

in full.

Hereford *(Food)*   *Cock of Tupsley*

Ledbury Road, Tupsley · *Hereford & Worcester*
Map 7 D2
Hereford (0432) 274911

Brewery Wolverhampton & Dudley
Landlords Mr & Mrs P. & C. Hancox

Tupsley pie £1.90 Smoked salmon
quiche £1.90 (No bar food eves or Sun)
🍺 Banks's Mild, Bitter; Guinness; Harp;
Kronenbourg; cider.

Food is taken seriously at this friendly
modern pub, and a large part of the bar is
devoted to the enjoyment of tasty, home-
prepared snacks. The appetising cold table
features pâtés, quiches and salads, and
there are also hot daily specials like liver
and bacon. A delicious passion cake makes
an excellent finish. Light snacks only on
Saturday. Garden.   **Family pub**

England

Hetton   *(Food)*   *Angel Inn*

Near Skipton · *North Yorkshire* · Map 4 C2
Cracoe (075 673) 263

Free House
Landlords Denis & Juliet Watkins

Salade niçoise £1.70 Braised oxtail &
vegetables £2.50
🍺 Theakston's Bitter, XB; Taylors Landlord;
Younger's Scotch Bitter; Webster's Light Mild;
Guinness; Carlsberg. *Real ale*

A wide variety of tasty bar food is available
at this trim roadside pub, a cheerful sight
with its climbing plants and window boxes.
In the beamed bars or out on the forecourt
you can enjoy anything from flavoursome
terrine and smoked fish mousse to lasagne
verdi, grills or a generous bowl of salade
niçoise. Also sandwiches, home-cooked
meats and simple sweets.

Hexworthy   *(B & B)*   *Forest Inn*

Near Princetown · *Devon* · Map 8 B4
Poundsgate (036 43) 211

Free House
Landlords Mr A. Wise & Mr A. Oake

BEDROOMS 15   Grade 2   £C
🍺 Bass; Hancocks Bitter; Worthington Best
Bitter; Guinness; Tennent's Extra; Pilsner;
cider. *Real ale*

Set in a landscape of rugged, desolate
beauty, this sturdy Dartmoor inn is a splendid base for tourists and also offers facilities
for fishing and horse-riding. The bedrooms, all centrally heated, provide simple,
practical comforts and nine have private
bathrooms. There are two welcoming bars
and a pleasant covered patio hung with
climbing plants. Good breakfasts, both in
choice and quality.   **Family pub**

High Halden   *(Food, B & B)*   *Chequers Inn*

Near Ashford · *Kent* · Map 6 C3
High Halden (023 385) 218

Brewery Whitbread
Landlords John & Pauline Shaw

BEDROOMS 3   Grade 2   £C
Chicken curry £1.75 Chocolate brandy
cake 85p (Last order 9pm)
🍺 Fremlin's Bitter, Mild; Guinness; Stella
Artois; Heineken; cider. *Real ale*

A friendly and convivial atmosphere pervades this fine old roadside pub in the heart
of the Kentish countryside. The saloon bar
is a suitably homely setting for Pauline
Shaw's simple, tasty snacks, which range
from sandwiches and hearty soups to
curries, grills and basket meals. Sweets like
cheesecake and lemon mousse are a strong
point. Three modest bedrooms share the
family bathroom. Terrace and garden.

High Offley   *(Food)*   *Royal Oak*

Grubb Street · *Staffordshire* · Map 3 B4
Woodseaves (078 574) 579

Free House
Landlords Lynne & Shirley Hartley

Steak & kidney pudding £2 Fish pie £2 (Last
order 10pm. No bar food Sat eve or Sun lunch)
🍺 Younger's Traditional, Tartan, Mild;
Newcastle Bitter; McEwan's Lager. *Real ale*

A sympathetically modernised village pub
run with pride by sisters Lynne and Shirley
Hartley. The bar fare ranges from quick
snacks like sandwiches and ploughman's
platters to deliciously filling vegetable
soup, cottage pie, smoked trout salad and a
hearty helping of tasty veal fricassee. More
limited menu in the evening. Closed Bank
Holidays and last two weeks August.
Garden.

Highclere (B & B)
Yew Tree Inn

Andover Road, Near Newbury · *Berkshire*
Map 6 A3
Newbury (0635) 253360

Free House
Landlords Mr & Mrs A. M. Greenwood

BEDROOMS 4 Grade 1 £B (No dogs)
🍺 Wadworth's 6X; Bourne Valley Andover
Ale, Henchard Bitter; Guinness; Kestrel;
Beck's Bier; Taunton cider. *Real ale*

Everything is kept in apple-pie order at this
comfortably refurbished 17th-century inn,
a warm and friendly spot for an overnight
stop. The bedrooms have very comfortable
beds, ample wardrobe space and modern
bath or shower rooms with big towels. The
spacious open-plan bar boasts two splendid inglenook fireplaces. Patio. **Family pub**

Hildenborough (Food)
Gate Inn

Rings Hill · *Kent* · Map 6 C3
Hildenborough (0732) 832103

Brewery Whitbread Fremlin
Landlord Mr G. R. M. Sankey

Lamb provençale £3 Beef carbonnade £3 (Last
order 10pm. No bar food Sun)
🍺 Wethered's Bitter; Fremlins Bitter; Tusker
Bitter; Guinness; cider. *Real ale*

Seafood is a great attraction at this welcoming inn, with lobster and crayfish at the
top of the list. Our beautifully cooked skate
with black butter was a really super treat,
and there are also meat dishes among the
lunchtime hot specials served in the bar.
Available at both sessions are soup, salads,
prime English cheeses and smashing
home-made sweets. Garden. Bar closed
Bank Holiday Mondays.

Hindon (Food, B & B)
Lamb at Hindon

High Street, Near Salisbury · *Wiltshire*
Map 6 A3
Hindon (074 789) 225
Free House
Landlord Mr C. Nell
BEDROOMS 16 Grades 1 & 2 £A
Lunch dish of the day with vegetables £2.25
Fresh salmon salad £3.50 (Last order 10pm)
🍺 Wadworth's 6X; McEwan's Export;
Usher's Triple Crown; Guinness; Carlsberg
Hof; Kestrel; cider. *Real ale*

The lounge bar of this fine old pub offers a
good choice of light snacks such as pâtés,
pies, ploughman's and tempting salads
featuring local ham or fresh salmon. Curry
served with lots of little side dishes is a
popular choice among more substantial
dishes. Bedrooms are simply furnished –
except for one with a four-poster – and six
have their own well-kept bathrooms.
There's also a small TV lounge. Garden.

Hipperholme (Food)
Hare & Hounds

Denholme Gate Road, Near Halifax
West Yorkshire · Map 4 C3
Halifax (0422) 202661
Owners Viking Taverns
Landlords Mr & Mrs B. Anderson
Roast beef & Yorkshire pudding £1.90
Meat & potato pie £1.70 (Last order 10pm. No
bar food Sat & eves except Tues & Thurs)
🍺 Webster's Yorkshire Light, Bitter;
Guinness; Foster's; Holsten; Carlsberg; cider.
Real ale

Simple, wholesome dishes are well
prepared and attractively presented at this
welcoming beamed pub. Home-made soup
gets things off to a good start, and you
could follow with a roast and trimmings,
meat and potato pie, lasagne or a cold meat
salad. Sweet lovers have plenty to choose
from, with desserts like cheesecake and a
delicious mandarin flan. Terrace.

Holcombe *(Food, B & B)*   *Duke of Cumberland*

Near Bath · *Somerset* · Map 8 D3
Stratton-on-the-Fosse (0761) 232412
Free House
Landlords Mr & Mrs E. G. Pockson
Lasagne & salad £1.70 Tandoori chicken £2.65
(Last order 9.30pm. No bar food Sun lunch &
all Mon)
BEDROOMS 2   Grade 2   £C   (No dogs)
🍺 Wadworth's 6X, IPA; Farmer's Glory;
Tisbury Local Bitter; Worthington 'E';
Carlsberg Export Hof. *Real ale*

Exotic delights like tandoori chicken, lamb
korma and spicy Armenian lamb make for
an enterprising menu at the Pocksons'
friendly pub. Simpler tastes are catered for
by pizzas, lasagne and salads, and you can
always ask for a sandwich. Overnight
guests have two neat, comfortable bedrooms sharing the family bathroom.
Children not accommodated. Terrace.
Closed Monday lunch.

Holmbury St Mary *(Food)*   *Royal Oak*

Near Dorking · *Surrey* · Map 6 B3
Dorking (0306) 730120

Brewery Friary Meux
Landlords Jacques & Irene Lestrade
French steak sandwich £2.25 Pickwick
pie £2.95 (Last order 10.30pm. No bar food Sun
eve)
🍺 Friary Meux Bitter; Ind Coope Burton Ale,
John Bull; Guinness; Skol; Löwenbräu; cider.
Real ale

A Gallic touch to the food adds to the
gastronomic charm of this pretty and
thoroughly English village pub. French
onion soup makes a satisfying start, and to
follow you could have cannelloni, crab
salad, a pork chop or perhaps a delicious
steak sandwich served with locally made
mustard. The restaurant trolley provides a
tempting array of sweets. Garden.
                                      Family pub

Holme *(B & B)*   *Smithy Inn*

Via Milnthorpe · *Cumbria* · Map 3 B2
Burton (0524) 781302

Brewery Yates & Jackson
Landlords Mr & Mrs Barrett

BEDROOMS 2   Grade 1   £C
🍺 Yates & Jackson Bitter, Mild; Guinness;
Heineken; Stella Artois. *Real ale*

The old blacksmith's shop has been
cleverly incorporated into this attractively
modernised coaching house in a peaceful
village. A lot of original stonework survives
in the comfortable bars, and there's a
pleasant courtyard for drinks in summer.
The two bedrooms are very neat and tidy,
with washbasins and good-quality furniture; they share a well-equipped modern
bathroom. Good breakfast.

Holt *(Food, B & B)*   *Old Ham Tree*

Near Trowbridge · *Wiltshire* · Map 8 D3
North Trowbridge (0225) 782581

Free House
Landlords John & Carol Francis
BEDROOMS 3   Grade 2   £C
Cheese, leek & ham pie £1.90 Baked fresh
mackerel £1.95 (Last order 10pm)
🍺 Marston's Pedigree; Eldridge Pope Royal
Oak; Wadworth's 6X; Usher's Country Bitter,
PA; Carlsberg; cider. *Real ale*

Almost opposite the green, this friendly,
cream-painted pub serves a good selection
of simple, appetising fare. Home-made
soup, plaice on the bone and cottage pie
are typical items on the blackboard menu,
and apple and mincemeat crumble is a
delicious way to round things off. Three
neat little bedrooms with modern furniture
share an up-to-date bathroom. Garden.
                                      Family pub

Holton   *Old Inn*

This pleasant little whitewashed pub not far from the A303 is a great place for enjoying a drink and chat with the locals. It's very much in the tradition of village pubs, with beams and rafters, flagstoned floors and a welcoming fire in the hearth. Polished wooden tables and comfortable banquettes complete the homely scene.

Near Wincanton · *Somerset* · Map 8 D3
Wincanton (0963) 32002
Free House   Landlords Colin & Jenny Davey
Wadworth's 6X; Hall & Woodhouse Badger Best Bitter; Guinness; Carlsberg Hof; cider. *Real ale*

Holywell   *(Food)*   *Ye Olde Ferry Boat Inn*

Near St Ives, Huntingdon · *Cambridgeshire*
Map 5 C2
St Ives (0480) 63227

Free House
Landlord Mrs Joyce Edwards
Seafood pancake £2.45 Home-made sorbet & ice cream coupe £1.70 (Last order 10pm)
Greene King IPA, Abbot Ale; Adnams Bitter; Guinness; Carling Black Label; Tennent's Extra; Taunton cider. *Real ale*

With records dating back more than a thousand years, this characterful inn on the banks of the Ouse can claim to be the oldest continuously operating hostelry in the country. It's a popular place for bar meals, offering anything from sustaining vegetable soup and toasted snacks to substantial dishes like flavoursome savoury pancakes, Dover sole and sirloin steak. Sweets include subtly spiced apple pie. Garden.   **Family pub**

Holywell Green   *(B & B)*   *Rock Hotel*

Near Halifax · *West Yorkshire* · Map 4 C3
Halifax (0422) 79721

Free House
Landlord Mr Robert Vinsen

BEDROOMS 18   Grade 1   £B
Younger's IPA, Scotch Bitter; Matthew Brown's John Peel, Lion Bitter; Slalom; Kronenbourg; Taunton cider. *Real ale*

Travellers on the M62 will find unusually comfortable pub accommodation at this modernised 17th-century inn close to junction 24. Smartly furnished bedrooms have fitted carpets, colour TVs, telephones, radios, tea-makers and even drinks trays. All have neat little shower rooms, and some enjoy pleasant country views. The split-level bar is a cosy place for a drink.
                                              Family pub

Hope   *(Food)*   *Poachers Arms*

Castleton Road · *Derbyshire* · Map 4 C3
Hope Valley (0433) 20380

Free House
Landlord Anton & Barbara Singleton

Game casserole £2.85 Crab claws £3.80 (Last order 10.30pm)
Webster's Dark Mild; Wilson's Bitter; Carlsberg; Foster's; cider. *Real ale*

Fresh local produce, including seasonal game, is used for the delicious bar snacks served at this charming little roadside hotel. A mug of vegetable soup makes a good warming starter, preceding garlic mussels, grilled gammon or steak and kidney pie. Try a hot roll filled with minced meat and cheese for a tasty quick snack. Patio. *For accommodation see Egon Ronay's Lucas Hotel & Restaurant Guide 1985.*   **Family pub**

'SCOTCH – It's All A Question Of Taste'

Malt whiskies, as produced in individual distilleries all over Scotland, vary widely in taste and character. Just as wine differs between the variety of grapes, so no two single malt whiskies are exactly the same. Some are forceful and peaty, while others are lighter and gentler. In addition, they all have their own 'nose' or aroma.

What causes this variation is a complex matter involving the location of the distillery, the peat and water, the shape and size of the still, the operation of the still, the air and the climate.

These varied elements contribute to the fact that whiskies produced at, for example, the Lagavulin Distillery on Islay, the Cardhu Distillery in Speyside and the Talisker Distillery on the Isle of Skye all differ in style and character.

There are two distinct types of Scotch whisky – malt and grain. Malt whisky is distilled in a pot-still from malted barley, while the grain spirit is produced in a patent or continuous still from maize mashed with malted barley.

Malts tend to be more expensive than blended whiskies, and are traditionally divided into four geographical regions – Highland, Lowland, Islay and the two remaining distilleries in Campbeltown. Highland malt whiskies are distilled to the north of an imaginary line running from Dundee to Greenock, while the Lowland variety come from the south of Scotland.

Most brands of Scotch sold to the public are blends of malt and grain whiskies. Blending is the art of combining a number of single whiskies so that each makes its particular contribution, though none predominates. The blender's object is to achieve a distinctive whisky of the highest possible quality, consistent in flavour and bouquet from one year to another.

MAPS

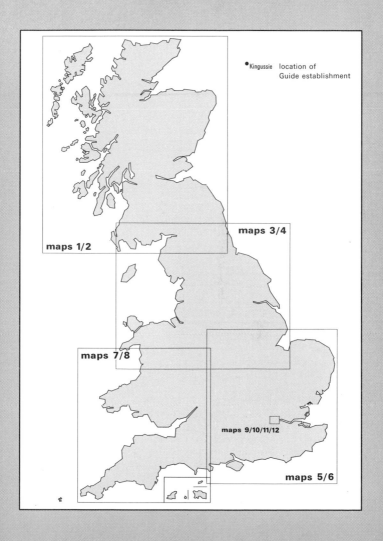

● Kingussie   location of
         Guide establishment

maps 1/2

maps 3/4

maps 7/8

maps 9/10/11/12

maps 5/6

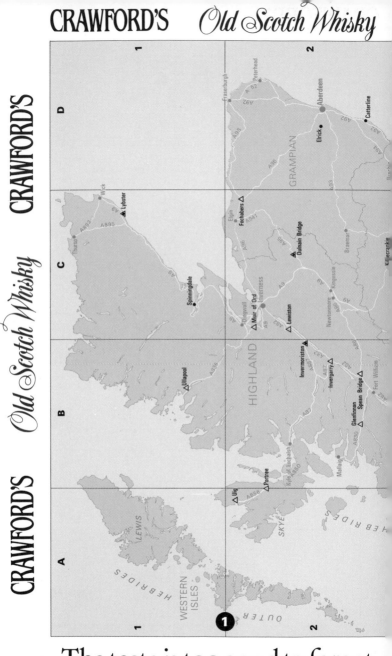

The taste is too good to forget

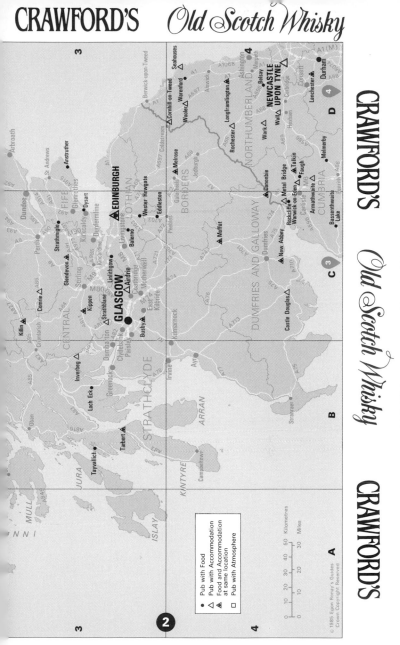

CRAWFORD'S *Old Scotch Whisky*

The taste is too good to forget

Pub with Food
Pub with Accommodation
Food and Accommodation at same location
Pub with Atmosphere

Kilometres
Miles

© 1985 Egon Ronay's Guides
Crown Copyright Reserved

2

Ahead by its nose

Ahead by its nose

Johnnie Walker® Johnnie

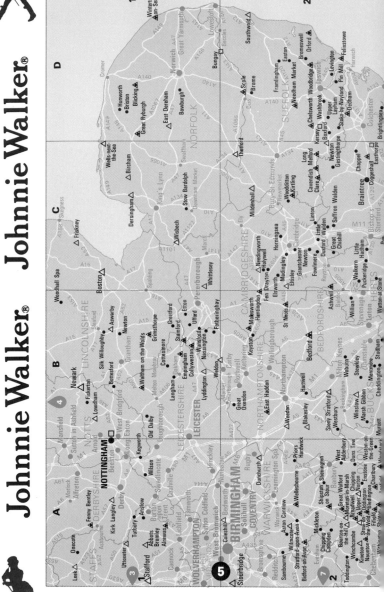

The perfect Scotch at all even

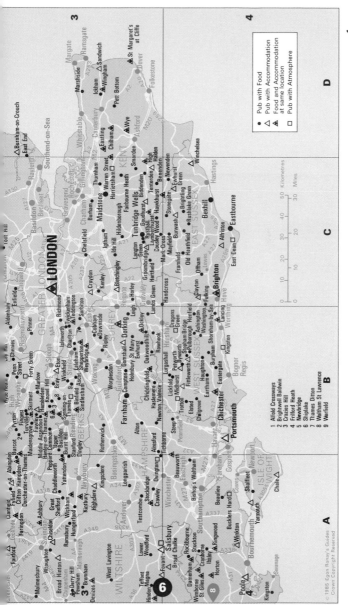

Don't be vague, ask for **HAIG**

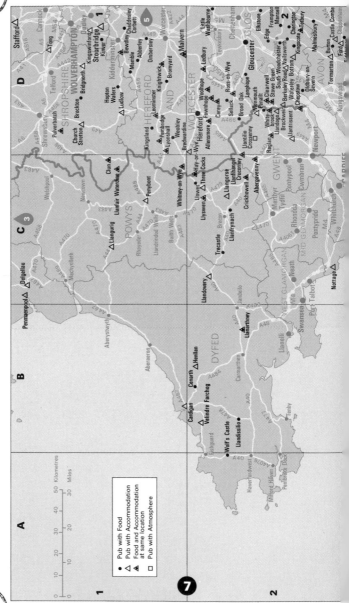

Key:
- ● Pub with Food
- △ Pub with Accommodation
- ▲ Food and Accommodation at same location
- □ Pub with Atmosphere

CHANNEL ISLANDS

ALDERNEY

St Anne

JERSEY

St Helier

St Aubin's Harbour

SARK

St Peter Port

GUERNSEY

Pleinmont

Kilometres

Miles

DORSET

SOMERSET

DEVON

CORNWALL

Westwood
Wolverton
Bratton
Nunney
Longleat Warminster
Cortan
Fonthill
Fovant
Tarrant Monkton
Bishop
Wincanton
Mere
Semley
Shaftesbury
Fiddleford
Blandford
Forum
Winfrith
Newburgh
Austy
Milton Abbas
Dorchester
Holcombe
Leigh on
Mendip
Stapleton
Evercreech Junction
Holton
Long Sutton
Ashcott Glastonbury
North Wootton
Cerne Abbas
Wells
Croscombe
Bishop's Perherton
Stoke St Gregory
Montacute
Powerstock
Nettlecombe
Bridport
West Bexington
Chickerell
Weymouth
Winscombe
Burtle
Kilve
Nether Stowey
Koap
Taunton
Shave Cross
Beer
Branscombe
Williton
Kilve
Bicknoller North
Bishop's Lydeard
Langley Marsh
Staple Fitzpaine
Clyst Hydon
Woodbury Salterton
Cockwood
Brendon Hills
Porlock Weir
Timberscombe
Withypool
Yarde Down
Exford
Alswear
Eggesford
Winkleigh
South Zeal
Chagford
Moretonhampstead
North Bovey
Haytor Vale
Sandygate
Oddiscombeleigh
Christow
Lympstone
Exeter
Torquay
Paignton
Ashburton
Staverton
Dartington
Stokenham
Frogmore
Churchstow
Bantham
Modbury
Ringmore
Plymouth
Lynton
Brendon
Umberleigh
Hatherleigh
Okehampton
Bridestowe
Lydford
Peter Tavy
Gunnislake
Hexworthy
Milton Combe
Lifton
Metherell
Callington
Calstock
St Dominick
Morval
Pelynt
Georgeham
Croyde
Horn's Cross
Bideford
Lawrenceton
Bude
Marhamchurch
Boscastle
Trebarwith
Pendoggett
Port Gaverne
Bodmin
Wadebridge
Lanteglosh
St Austell
Philleigh
St Mawes
Truro
Helford
Manaccan
St Mawgan
Perranarworthal
Wendron
Breage
Helston
Bedruth
Penzance
Sennen Cove

People go to great lengths to eat the best.

People like you, who use Egon Ronay guides, expect the best whenever they eat out.

Which is why you'll expect Uncle Ben's to be served with your favourite rice dish.

Because Uncle Ben's is the best rice in the world.

And whether you eat fluffy Long Grain, Natural Wholegrain or the more exotic Long Grain & Wild, the same high standards of quality apply.

So go to great lengths to eat the best rice. Uncle Ben's is well worth the effort.

Uncle Ben's®
The Best Rice in the World.

Uncle Ben's Rice, Dornay Foods, P.O. Box 15, Hansa Road, King's Lynn, Norfolk

HINE COGNAC

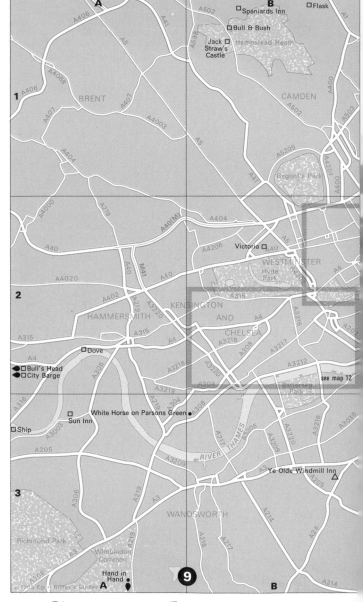

Savour the moment

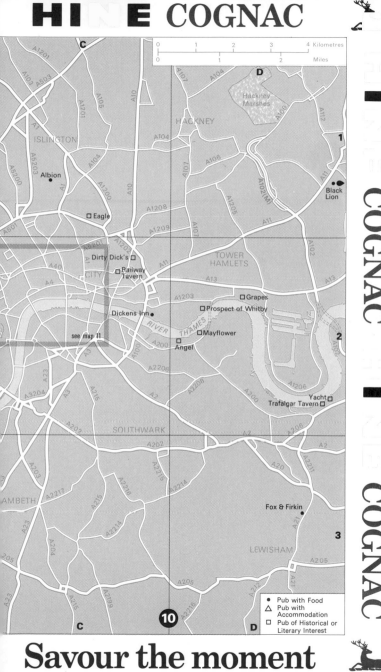

HINE COGNAC

| 0 | 1 | 2 | 3 | 4 Kilometres |
| 0 | | 1 | | 2 Miles |

D

1

Hackney Marshes

HACKNEY

ISLINGTON

Albion

Eagle

Black Lion

TOWER HAMLETS

Dirty Dick's
Railway Tavern
CITY

Dickens Inn

Grapes
Prospect of Whitby

see map 11

RIVER THAMES

Mayflower

Angel

2

SOUTHWARK

Yacht
Trafalgar Tavern

AMBETH

Fox & Firkin

3

LEWISHAM

(10)

C

D

- ● Pub with Food
- △ Pub with Accommodation
- □ Pub of Historical or Literary Interest

Savour the moment

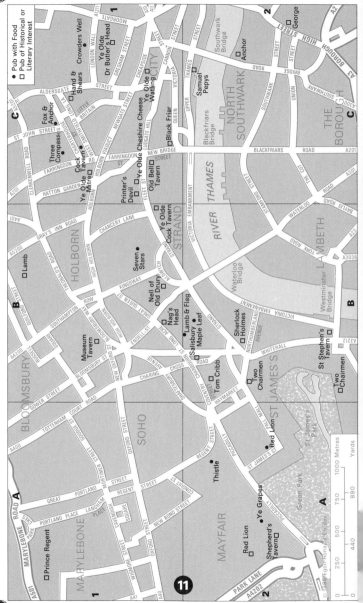

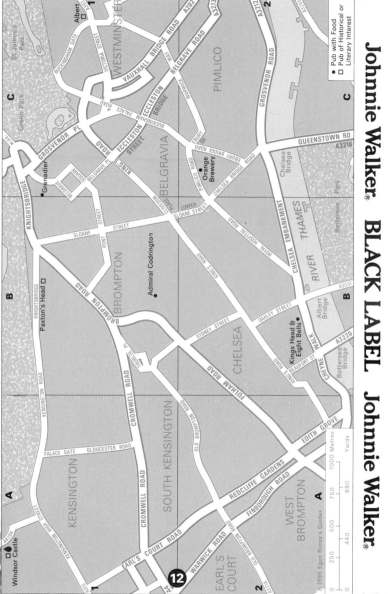

OTHER PLEASURES PALE BESIDE IT

CHEERS FOR ENGLISH CHEESE

IF CHEESE and wine is a comparatively modern pairing – in this country at any rate – cheese and ale has represented the successful marrying of traditional food and drink for longer than anyone can remember.

Both are an integral part of our way of life, and the cheeses of England and Wales form a natural part of every good pub menu.

There are nine traditional English and Welsh cheeses, although new variations are constantly being developed, with additions of herbs, pickles and spices, as well as with the introduction of English soft blue cheeses.

Even today cheese making remains a natural, traditional process. Just as grape juice is fermented into wine and hops into beer, so whole milk is converted into cheese.

The English Cheese Quality Mark signifies that Mark cheese is of a uniformly high standard.

Implemented by established graders with years of experience in selecting cheese, the Mark is awarded only to those cheeses which meet the required standards of quality and consistency set by the English Country Cheese Council.

Cheese naturally complements every drink from local-brewed ciders to real ales. Wines in particular often help bring out the subtlest of flavours – Cheddar, for example, is delicious with a full claret or burgundy, while Lancashire is especially suited to a dry red wine.

Double Gloucester and Cheshire show up particularly well against a light claret or a tawny port, Derby with a ruby port. Stilton and Leicester will be appreciated when eaten with a red burgundy, tawny or vintage port, while the subtlety of Wensleydale and Caerphilly are enhanced by a hock, a fino sherry or a dry white wine.

Chances are you'll find English and Welsh cheese in your local, so enjoy some at lunch today, as a wholesome meal with a pint of cider, ale or milk or as a natural snack with a glass of red or white wine or port.

RED LEICESTER

This russet red cheese is recognisable both by its colour and its clean, buttery flavour. Best when about three months old, it's at its peak when its cutting leaves a smear on the knife.

LANCASHIRE

Lancashire is a creamy white cheese with a crumbly texture and mild, country fresh flavour. It makes mouthwatering melted toppings and sauces.

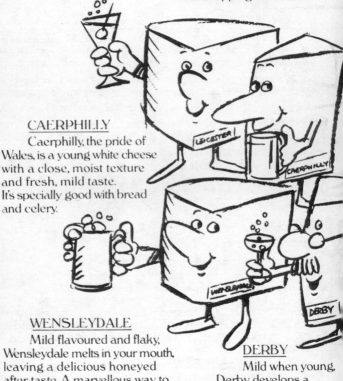

CAERPHILLY

Caerphilly, the pride of Wales, is a young white cheese with a close, moist texture and fresh, mild taste. It's specially good with bread and celery.

WENSLEYDALE

Mild flavoured and flaky, Wensleydale melts in your mouth, leaving a delicious honeyed after-taste. A marvellous way to end a meal, especially with fresh fruit

DERBY

Mild when young, Derby develops a distinct and unique tang as it matures. Sage Derby flavoured with chopped sage leaves, is a Christmas favourite.

CHEDDAR

Cheddar is the most popular cheese in Britain. Quality Selected Mild Cheddar is at least 8 weeks old, while Mature Cheddars are aged for at least 5 months.

Creamy yellow with a full bodied, nutty flavour, Cheddar is ideal for a hearty ploughman's lunch.

CHESHIRE

Cheshire is the oldest English cheese. Red and White Cheshire have a mild, slightly salty flavour and a crumbly texture. Blue Cheshire is mellow and creamy.

STILTON

This King of Cheese is well known for its cream-white colour, royal blue veins and rough, amber crust. The flavour is rich and creamy and blends beautifully with vintage Port.

DOUBLE GLOUCESTER

Golden in colour, Double Gloucester is a smooth, sophisticated cheese with a unique mellow flavour. A marvellous companion to fresh fruit and salads.

English Cheese. Only the best is up to the Mark.

English Country Cheese Council, 5-7 John Princes Street, London W1M 0AP.

Hopton Wafers   *(Food)*   *Crown Inn*

Near Cleobury Mortimer · *Shropshire*
Map 7 D1
Cleobury Mortimer (0299) 270372

Free House
Landlord Mrs L. V. G. Harrison
Hot crab pâté £1.80 Filled pancakes &
salad £2.10   (Last order 10pm)
🍺 Marston's Pedigree; Younger's Tartan;
Guinness; Carlsberg; Stella Artois; Taunton
cider. *Real ale*

You'll find a varied assortment of tasty
dishes at this pleasant, creeper-clad pub.
Hot saffron prawns and savoury stuffed
pancakes are firm favourites, and you can
also get things like steak, lasagne and
salads. To finish there's a super selection of
sweets – from meringue gâteau and syrup
sponge to ice creams and sorbets.
Children's menu too. Closed Monday
except Bank Holidays.   **Family pub**

Horley   *(Food)*   *Ye Olde Six Bells*

Church Road · *Surrey* · Map 6 C3
Horley (029 34) 2209

Brewery Vintage Inns
Landlords Geoffrey & Rish Noble
Home-cooked cold meats with salads from £3
Hot pot £4 (Last order 9.30pm. No bar food Sun
lunch)
🍺 Charrington's IPA; Bass; Toby; Tennent's
Extra; Carling Black Label; Guinness; Taunton
cider. *Real ale*

The Nobles take great pride in running this
fascinating old pub, whose history can be
traced back more than a thousand years.
Under an extraordinary beamed roof (mind
your head) you'll find some very good bar
snacks, from succulent cold meats and
crisp salads to hot dishes such as cottage
pie and evening specials like Somerset
pork. Free hot herb bread at Sunday lunchtime. The large rear garden borders the
river Mole.

Horningsea   *(Food)*   *Plough & Fleece*

High Street · *Cambridgeshire* · Map 5 C2
Cambridge (0223) 860795

Brewery Greene King
Landlords Mr & Mrs K. Grimes

Suffolk ham hot pot £2.40 Welsh fish pie £3.25
(Last order 9.30pm. No bar food Sun & Mon
eves)
🍺 Greene King Abbot Ale, IPA, Mild;
Guinness; Harp; Kronenbourg; cider. *Real ale*

Imaginative, tasty bar fare complements
the charms of this pretty village pub. Mr
and Mrs Grimes' tempting menu features
dishes like hot garlic cockles, Suffolk ham
hot pot and casseroled pigeon. There are
salads, too, and some marvellous desserts
like cherry cobbler and treacle tart. Sandwiches are an additional option at lunchtime. Ploughman's only for Sunday lunch.
Garden.

Horn's Cross   *(Food, B & B)*   *Hoops Inn*

Near Bideford · *Devon* · Map 8 B3
Horn's Cross (023 75) 222

Free House
Landlords June & Jimmy Malcolm
BEDROOMS 14   Grade 1   £B
Cheesy hammy eggy £1.35 Home-made
sweets 90p (Last order 10pm)
🍺 Whitbread Best Bitter, Flower's Best
Bitter, IPA; Guinness; Heineken; Stella Artois;
cider. *Real ale*

A steaming bowl of home-made soup in
front of a log fire provides an inviting introduction to this cosy old thatched pub. Other
simple bar snacks include the popular ham,
egg and grilled cheese on toast and
tempting puds, and June Malcolm also does
a good breakfast. Delightful traditional
bedrooms in the main building are sur-
passed by modern ones in the converted
coach house, which boast TVs, drinks,
fridges and luxurious bathrooms.

Horton *(Food, B & B)* — *Horton Inn*

Cranborne, Near Wimbourne · *Dorset*
Map 6 A4
Witchampton (0258) 840252
Free House
Landlords Mr & Mrs P. J. Purtill
BEDROOMS 5 Grade 1 £C (No dogs)
Steak & kidney pie £3.25 Crevettes in garlic
butter £2.95 (Last order 10pm)
🍺 Wadworth's 6X; Burton's Bitter; Poole's
Bitter; Guinness; Löwenbräu; Oranjeboom;
cider. *Real ale*

New owners have many plans for this handsome 18th-century inn standing outside the village on the B3078. The five immaculate bedrooms are spacious, airy and very comfortable, and two have large private bathrooms. Excellent snacks served in the bar include pâté en croûte, garlic prawns and flavour-packed steak and kidney pie, with home-made ice creams and splendidly rich chocolate mousse to finish. Garden.

Horton in Ribblesdale *(B & B)* — *Crown Hotel*

Near Settle · *North Yorkshire* · Map 3 B2
Horton in Ribblesdale (072 96) 209

Brewery Matthew Brown
Landlord Mr Richard Hargreaves

BEDROOMS 10 Grade 2 £C
🍺 Matthew Brown's John Peel, Bitter, Mild;
Guinness; Slalom; cider. *Real ale*

Grouse-shooting parties and hikers alike favour this old whitewashed inn standing right on the Pennine Way just off the A65. Comfortable bedrooms are warm and attractively decorated and share two neat bathrooms. Guests can relax in the homely TV lounges or in the welcoming beamed bars with French windows opening on to the beer garden. **Family pub**

Houghton *(Food)* — *George & Dragon Inn*

Near Arundel · *West Sussex* · Map 6 B4
Bury (079 881) 559

Free House
Landlord Mr Tyler

Roast beef salad £3.75 Trout £4.25 (Last order 10pm)
🍺 Young's Special; Fuller's London Pride;
King & Barnes Bitter; Guinness; Carlsberg;
Holsten; cider. *Real ale*

Charles II is said to have stopped at this fine old flint inn while fleeing after the battle of Worcester. It's best, however, not to rush over the well-prepared bar snacks, which range from egg mayonnaise or pâté to devilled whitebait, cold meat salads, fresh trout and daily specials like king prawns or lamb cutlets. There are some tempting sweets, too, plus grills in the evening. Garden.

Hovingham *(Food, B & B)* — *Worsley Arms Hotel*

North Yorkshire · Map 4 C2
Hovingham (065 382) 234

Free House
Landlord Mr B. Precious
BEDROOMS 14 Grade 1 £A+
Home-made quiche £1.65 Cold meats &
salad £2 (No bar food eves)
🍺 Theakston's Best Bitter, Old Peculier;
Younger's Tartan; Double Diamond;
Guinness; Carlsberg; cider. *Real ale*

Good food and comfortable accommodation are to be found at this handsome Georgian stone inn. Lunchtime snacks in the bar include tasty soups and pâtés, plus salads, flans and fresh fish, with delicious sweets to finish. Overnight guests have 14 prettily decorated bedrooms, all with their own bathrooms, and can relax in the cosy lounge or TV room. Garden. **Family pub**

Howden   *(B & B)*   *Bowmans Hotel*

Bridgegate · *Humberside* · Map 4 D3
Howden (0430) 30805

Brewery North Country Breweries
Landlord Mr Tomas Munoz

BEDROOMS 13   Grade 1   £A
🍺 North Country Old Traditional, Ridings
Bitter, Mild; Guinness; Stella Artois; cider.
Real ale

Horse brasses and old prints recall coaching inn days in the bars of this welcoming hostelry. It's a very good place for an overnight stop, being in the centre of town and just a short drive from the M62. Centrally heated bedrooms are neat and comfortable, with smart white fitted furniture, floral print duvets, TVs and telephones. All but two have compact tiled bathrooms. Patio.
Family pub

Hubberholme   *(Food, B & B)*   *George Inn*

Kirk Gill, Near Skipton · *North Yorkshire*
Map 4 C2
Kettlewell (075 676) 223

Free House
Landlord John Frederick
BEDROOMS 4   Grade 2   £C
Steak & kidney pudding £2.35 Chicken & ham
pie £2.35 (Last order 9.30)
🍺 Younger's IPA, Scotch Bitter; Harp;
Taunton cider. *Real ale*

A walk in the fells is just the thing to work up an appetite for the tasty, robust fare served at this welcoming village pub by the river. Thick soups, pies, casseroles and home-cooked ham are all featured on the menu, along with a splendid apple pie. Four prettily decorated bedrooms cater for overnight guests who can enjoy a hearty breakfast in the morning. Children under eight not accommodated. Patio. **Family pub**

Hungerford   *(Food)*   *Bear at Hungerford*

Charnham Street · *Berkshire* · Map 6 A3
Hungerford (0488) 82512

Owners Fine Inns
Landlords Mrs J. Dickson & Mr D. Evans

Spinach flan £1.85 Rare beef open sandwich
£2.15 (Last order 9.30pm)
🍺 Arkell's BB, BBB; Morland's Pale Ale;
Guinness; Carlsberg Hof; Arkell's 1843 Lager;
cider. *Real ale*

An ancient and historic inn, where snacks are served in two characterful bars boasting splendid fishing trophies. Soup, spinach flan and devilled whitebait are popular for starters or light meals, while main courses include eggs and bacon, roast turkey salad and cooked-to-order steak and kidney pie. Also sandwiches at lunchtime. Patio. *For accommodation see Egon Ronay's Lucas Hotel & Restaurant Guide 1985.* **Family pub**

Huntingdon   *(Food, B & B)*   *George*

George Street · *Cambridgeshire* · Map 5 B2
Huntingdon (0480) 51947

Free House
Landlord R. L. Gardiner

BEDROOMS 25   Grade 1   £A
Ploughman's platter £1.60 Lasagne verdi £2.95
(Last order 9.30pm)
🍺 Greene King IPA, Abbot Ale; Younger's
Tartan; Stones Bitter; Carlsberg. *Real ale*

A fine galleried courtyard is just one of the many charming period features of this old posting house. Tasty snacks served in the comfortable, popular bar include sandwiches, quiches, salads from the cold buffet and hot dishes like lasagne or braised liver (less choice evenings and Sunday lunch). Bedrooms are spacious and nicely furnished; and all have TVs and most have private bathrooms. **Family pub**

Huntingdon *(Food)* ★ *Old Bridge Hotel*

1 High Street · *Cambridgeshire* · Map 5 B2
Huntingdon (0480) 52681

Free House
Landlord Mr R. Waters

Tortellini carbonara £3.25 Gruyère cheese
fritters £2.65 (Last order 10.30pm)
🍺 Ruddle's County; Paine's St Neots Bitter;
Tolly Cobbold Best Bitter; Adnams Southwold
Bitter; Kestrel. *Real ale*

This smart, ivy-clad Georgian house by the
Great Ouse offers high-quality bar snacks
in comfortable, civilised surroundings.
Gruyère fritters and richly flavoured
chicken liver pâté are splendid starters,
which you might follow with tortellini
carbonara or delicious seafood pancakes.
There's also a popular cold buffet and some
lovely sweets. Garden. *For accommodation see Egon Ronay's Lucas Hotel &
Restaurant Guide 1985.* **Family pub**

Hunworth *(Food)* *Bell Inn*

The Green, Near Holt · *Norfolk* · Map 5 D1
Holt (026 371) 2300

Free House
Landlords Brian & Dolores Bunting
Gammon with salad & chips £3.20 Home-
cooked ham £2.20 (Last order 8.30pm)
🍺 Adnams Bitter; Whitbread Mild; Sam
Smith's Sovereign; Woodforde's Bitter;
Guinness; Hansa; Löwenbräu; Taunton cider.
Real ale

Bar snacks are simple and satisfying at
this welcoming, 17th-century village pub.
Soups, pâtés and ploughman's are supplemented by steaks and daily specials like
spaghetti bolognese, game pie, home-
cooked ham and delicious pork and vegetable hot pot. Barbecues are a popular
feature in summer, and there are always
salads and sandwiches, too. Garden.
Family pub

Hyde Heath *(Food)* *Plough*

Near Amersham · *Buckinghamshire* · Map 6 B3
Chesham (0494) 783163

Brewery Benskins
Landlord Mrs S. Willcocks
Prawn & asparagus au gratin £2.25 Beef
carbonnade £2 (Last order 10pm. No bar
food Sun eve)
🍺 Benskins Bitter, Pale; Ind Coope John
Bull Bitter; Guinness; Skol; Löwenbräu;
cider. *Real ale*

Sandra Willcocks provides an imaginative,
flavoursome range of bar snacks at this
cosy little village pub. Hot garlic mushrooms, prawn and asparagus au gratin,
paprika pork casserole and beef
carbonnade are some of the tempting
items on her menu, and there are also
splendid salads like lettuce with walnuts
and cucumber. Fish or sausage and chips
caters for simpler tastes. Garden.

Ibsley *(Food)* *Old Beams Inn*

Near Ringwood · *Hampshire* · Map 6 A4
Ringwood (042 54) 3387

Free House
Landlords Major family
Steak pie £3.50 Grilled steak from £5.70 (Last
order 10.15pm)
🍺 Ringwood Best Bitter; Wadworth's 6X,
Old Timer; Gibbs Mew Bishop's Tipple;
Eldridge Pope Royal Oak; Guinness; Harp;
cider. *Real ale*

A huge display of a score of eye-catching
salads is a feature of the bar at this delightful old pub made up of two thatched
cottages. There's also a wide choice of hot
dishes such as vegetable soup, steak pie,
braised oxtail and excellent roast lamb. If
you're still hungry, finish with sherry trifle
or a home-made fresh fruit pie. Garden.
Family pub

Ickham   *(Food)*   *Duke William*

The Street · *Kent* · Map 6 D3
Canterbury (0227) 721308

Free House
Landlord Mr A. R. McNeill
Braised rabbit & veg £2.95 Steaks from £4.50
(Last order 10pm)
🍺 Young's Bitter, Special; Fuller's London
Pride; Shepherd Neame Masterbrew;
Guinness; Tennent's Extra; Hurliman's Lager;
cider. *Real ale*

Festooned with hops, the bar of this pretty
high-street inn is a cosy place to enjoy a
pint and a tasty snack from Mr McNeill's
wide-ranging menu. Salt beef, poached
haddock, braised rabbit, steak and quiche
are all featured on the menu, along with
simpler items like sandwiches, salads and
soup. Nice sweets, too, such as blackberry
and apple pie. Garden and patio.
Family pub

Ide Hill   *(Food)*   *Cock Inn*

Near Sevenoaks · *Kent* · Map 6 C3
Ide Hill (073 275) 310

Brewery Friary Meux
Landlord Mr Arnett

Plate of fresh prawns £2.50 Gammon, egg &
chips £3
(Last order 8.30pm. No bar food Sun eve)
🍺 Friary Meux Bitter; Ind Coope Mild, Burton
Ale; Guinness; Löwenbräu; cider. *Real ale*

Facing the village green, this 15th-century
inn is popular with locals who like to gather
round the inglenook fireplace in the
beamed bar. Mr Arnett's wholesome
snacks range from herb sausages and
pâté and cheese to burgers served with
crisp chips, cold meat and seafood salads
and toasted sandwiches. Steak and kidney
pie is a tasty winter special. Sandwiches
only Sunday lunchtime. Terrace.

Ightham   *(Food)*   *George & Dragon*

The Street, Near Sevenoaks · *Kent* · Map 6 C3
Borough Green (0732) 882440

Brewery Whitbread
Landlord Mr T. K. Peters
Steak & kidney pie £2.50 Chicken curry £2.40
(Last order 10pm. No bar food Sun &
Mon eves)
🍺 Whitbread Best Mild, Bitter; Wethered's
Bitter; Guinness; Heineken; Stella Artois;
cider. *Real ale*

Parts of this handsome pub date back to the
16th century, and it still has a splendid
timbered façade. Inside you will find a
welcoming atmosphere and appetising
snacks such as delicious home-made
soups, rich, tender steak and kidney pie,
chicken curry and ham carved off the bone.
For a lighter snack there's a wide choice of
sandwiches. The large garden is an
additional asset.

Isleworth   *(Food)*   *London Apprentice*

62 Church Street · *Middlesex* · Map 6 B3
01-560 6136

Brewery Watneys
Landlord A. Cain

Ploughman's £1.05 Beef salad £2.25
(Last order 9.30pm)
🍺 Watneys Stag Bitter, Special, Coombe
Bitter; Ben Truman; Guinness; Foster's; cider.
Real ale

Royal patrons at this famous 500-year-old
pub are said to have included Henry VIII,
Charles II and Lady Jane Grey. Nowadays,
there's a cheerful welcome in the long bar,
and next door is a fine display of cold meats
and fresh salads. At lunchtime, there are
also a few hot dishes such as steak and
kidney pie (except Sunday). Patio.
Family pub

Kegworth   (Food)   *White House*

London Road, Near Derby · *Leicestershire*
Map 4 C4
Kegworth (050 97) 2245

Brewery Bass
Landlord John Batchelor
Cold mixed seafood £4.75 Nigerian peppered
chicken £4.75 (Last order 10pm)
🍺 Bass; Worthington 'E'; Mitchells & Butlers
Mild; Guinness; Carling Black Label; Taunton
cider. *Real ale*

The patio of this cheerful pub on the outskirts of town overlooks the river Soar.
Enjoyable food served in the bar includes a
cold buffet featuring seafood, home-
cooked joints and a variety of colourful
salads. There are basket meals and grills,
too, and a few hot specials such as the
unusual Nigerian peppered chicken.
Lunchtime specials like cottage pie provide
further choice.   **Family pub** (lunchtime)

Kenley   (Food)   *Wattenden Arms*

Old Lodge Lane · *Surrey* · Map 6 C3
01-660 8638

Brewery Charrington
Landlords Joan & Ron Coulston

Steak pie £2 Curried chicken Madras £2
(Last order 9pm)
🍺 Charrington's IPA; Bass; Mitchells &
Butlers Mild; Stones Bitter; Guinness; Carling
Black Label; Taunton cider. *Real ale*

Former airline steward Ron Coulston now
looks after his customers on terra firma,
and has built up a reputation for cheery
hospitality and fine food. In the cosy
panelled bar of his village pub you can
choose from a tempting display of mouthwatering cold joints, fresh crab and smooth
garlicky pâté, or go for one of the hot dishes
like curry, steak and kidney pie or a
mammoth plateful of ham, egg and chips.
Sandwiches only on Sundays. Garden.

Kersey   *Bell Inn*

Attractive flower baskets festoon the timbered facade of this fine old
inn in a village once renowned for its cloth industry, now known for its
main-street watersplash and picture postcard prettiness. Open fires
keep winter at bay in the brass-bedecked bars, while in summer the
large garden comes into its own.

The Street, Near Ipswich · *Suffolk* · Map 5 D2
Hadleigh (0473) 823229
Free House   Landlords Mr & Mrs G. Slater
🍺 Adnams Bitter; Mauldon's Bitter; Greene King Abbot Ale;
Guinness; Skol; Carlsberg Hof; cider. *Real ale*

Keswick   (B & B)   *Pheasant Inn*

Crossthwaite Road · *Cumbria* · Map 3 B2
Keswick (0596) 72219

Brewery Jennings
Landlords Mr & Mrs Wright

BEDROOMS 3   Grade 2   £C
🍺 Jennings Traditional, Bitter, Mild; Stones
Bitter; Guinness; Ayinger Bräu; Taunton cider.
Real ale

A popular spot with the locals, this homely
little pub stands just off the A66 about a
mile from the centre of town. Cartoons of
hunting scenes lend interest to the panelled
bar, and there's a patio for fair-weather sipping. The three modestly furnished bedrooms (two of them of a suitable size for
families) share a modern bathroom.

Kettlewell *(B & B)*   *Bluebell Hotel*

Near Skipton · *North Yorkshire* · Map 4 C2
Kettlewell (075 676) 230

Free House
Landlord Mr J. A. F. Croft

BEDROOMS 8 Grade 2 £B
🍺 Theakston's Best Bitter, Old Peculier;
Tetley's Bitter, Mild; Guinness; Foster's;
Carlsberg Hof; cider. *Real ale*

Popular with trout fishermen and walkers
on the Yorkshire Dales, this whitewashed
pub with a pleasant beer garden at the rear
stands near the river Wharfe. The bar is a
welcoming place for a hard-earned drink,
and the TV lounge is well provided with
deep armchairs. Comfortable bedrooms,
furnished in a variety of styles, are warm
and neatly kept.   **Family pub**

Kettlewell *(Food, B & B)*   *Racehorses Hotel*

Near Skipton · *North Yorkshire* · Map 4 C2
Kettlewell (075 676) 233

Free House
Landlords Mr & Mrs Rowbottom

BEDROOMS 16 Grade 1 £B
Steak pie £2.50 Lasagne £1.50 (Last order 9pm)
🍺 Younger's Scotch Bitter; Webster's
Yorkshire Bitter; Tetleys Bitter; Taunton cider.
Real ale

Enjoyable bar snacks and comfortable
accommodation make this friendly old pub
beside the river Wharfe a good base for
exploring the Dales. Delicious local trout is
a popular choice on the menu, which also
offers soup, lasagne, cold meat salads and
steak and kidney pie. Overnight guests
have 16 bright, practical bedrooms, five
with well-fitted private bathrooms. TV
lounge.   **Family pub**

We have raised our standards
considerably since last year.
The omission of some houses
that appeared in last year's
Guide is no reflection on their
standing.

Keyston *(Food)*   *Pheasant Inn*

Near Huntingdon · *Cambridgeshire* · Map 5 B2
Bythorn (080 14) 241

Free House
Landlord Mr Steve Klamer

Paris mushrooms £2.85 Swordfish in
raspberries £4.25 (Last order 10.30pm)
🍺 Tolly Cobbold Bitter; Ruddle's County;
Younger's Tartan; Stella Artois. *Real ale*

Once the village bakehouse, this smart
thatched pub offers a combination of
familiar favourites and more unusual items
on its chalked-up snack menu. Start perhaps with soup, pâté or deep-fried squid
and go on the flavoursome turkey and
mushroom pie, sweet and sour chicken or
maybe something really different like
swordfish marinated with raspberries. Cold
buffet in summer. Patio.   **Family pub**

Kilve *(B & B)* — *Hood Arms*

Near Bridgwater · *Somerset* · Map 8 C3
Holford (027 874) 210

Free House
Landlords Mr C. R. Rutt & Mr N. A. White

BEDROOMS 6 Grade 1 £B
🍺 Flowers Original, IPA; Whitbread Bitter,
Trophy; Guinness; Heineken; Taunton cider.
Real ale

Named after Admiral Hood, this smoothly
run village pub provides very satisfactory
accommodation. Neatly furnished bedrooms have pretty floral fabrics and are
equipped with tea-makers; iced water and
pot plants are thoughtful touches. Residents can watch TV in a charming little
lounge or drink in either of the two convivial bars. There's also a skittle alley. No
under-sevens overnight.

Kineton *(B & B)* — *Halfway House*

Near Guiting Power, Cheltenham
Gloucestershire · Map 5 A2
Guiting Power (045 15) 344

Brewery Donnington
Landlords Mr & Mrs D. Marshall

BEDROOMS 3 Grade 2 £C (No dogs)
🍺 Donnington's Special, Best Bitter;
Carlsberg; cider. *Real ale*

Hospitality comes naturally to the
Marshalls, who run this popular village pub
in the heart of rural Gloucestershire. Corn
dollies and farm implements adorn the
spacious bar, where you can relax with a
drink or join the locals in a game of darts.
Three simple, spotless bedrooms share a
neat bathroom. No under-sevens overnight. Accommodation closed ten days
Christmas. Garden. **Family pub** (lunchtime)

Kingsclere *(Food)* — *Crown*

Near Newbury · *Berkshire* · Map 6 A3
Kingsclere (0635) 298956

Brewery Courage
Landlords Mr & Mrs G. Worrall

Trawlerman's pie £2.50 Treacle tart & cream £1
(Last order 9.45pm. No bar food Sun eve)
🍺 Courage Directors Bitter, Best Bitter,
Mild; Hofmeister; Kronenbourg; Taunton
cider. *Real ale*

The daily-changing blackboard menu at
this welcoming old pub on the high street
offers unusual delights like steak kebab,
Thai chicken with brown rice or bratwurst,
as well as lasagne, steak and kidney pie and
quiche. There are also toasted sandwiches,
plus a few more elaborate dishes in the
evening. Less choice Sunday lunchtime.
Children's room for family eating at lunchtime (weekends only in winter). Patio.

Kingscote *(Food)* — *Hunter's Hall Inn*

Near Tetbury · *Gloucestershire* · Map 7 D2
Dursley (0453) 860393

Free House
Landlords Mr & Mrs David Barnett-Roberts
Seafood pancakes £2.50 Sauté of kidneys with
watercress sauce £2.50 (Last order 9.45pm)
🍺 Bass; Fussell's Best Bitter; Guinness;
Carling Black Label; Tennent's Extra;
Taunton cider. *Real ale*

More than 500 years old, this welcoming
inn on the A4135 has four cosy, panelled
bars with cheerful log fires to ward off the
cold. A tempting buffet features pâtés,
meats and colourful salads, and there are
also tasty hot dishes like seafood pancakes,
chicken curry and cottage pie. Don't miss
out on the deliciously rich chocolate
mousse. Garden.   **Family pub**

Kingsland   *(Food)*   *Angel Inn*

Near Leominster · *Hereford & Worcester*
Map 7 D1
Kingsland (056 881) 355

Free House
Landlords Mr & Mrs M. W. Thompson

Steak & kidney pie £2.50 Pheasant
casserole £3.50 (Last order 9.45pm)
🍺 Marston's Pedigree, Best Bitter;
Guinness; Carlsberg; cider. *Real ale*

Mr and Mrs Thompson's bar menu caters
for all tastes at this fine old half-timbered
inn. There are staple items such as pâté,
salads, scampi in the basket and steak and
kidney pie, as well as more unusual things
like delicious cauliflower soup and an
excellent pastry-topped venison and
pheasant casserole. Toasted sandwiches,
too.   **Family pub**

Kingston   *(Food)*   *Scott Arms*

Near Corfe Castle · *Dorset* · Map 6 A4
Corfe Castle (0929) 480270

Brewery Devenish
Landlord Gerald Lomax
Steak & kidney pudding & vegetables £2.20
Dorset apple cake 65p (Last order 9.15pm.
No bar food Sun eve)
🍺 John Devenish Bitter, Wessex Bitter,
John Groves; Guinness; Taunton cider.
Real ale

Pretty flower displays make the two cosy
bars especially welcoming at this creeper-
clad pub. Tasty light snacks include crab
pâté, pizzas, ploughman's and a selection
of home-cooked meats, while steak and
kidney pudding caters for hearty appetites.
Leave room for sweets such as Dorset
apple cake or rich treacle tart. Garden.
                                          Family pub

Kingston   *Juggs*

Nestling under the South Downs, this pretty, tile-hung pub dating
from the 15th century is one of the most picturesque drinking places
in the area. Its bars are full of character, with low ceilings, beams and a
brass-hooded open fireplace. As well as the family room, there are
two gardens and a children's play area.   **Family pub**

Near Lewes · *West Sussex* · Map 6 B4
Brighton (0273) 472523
Free House   *Landlord* Mr F. A. Browne
🍺 Harveys Best Bitter; King & Barnes Festive Bitter; Guinness;
Tennent's Extra; Carling Black Label; Taunton cider. *Real ale*

Kingswinford   *(B & B)*   *Summerhill House Hotel*

Swindon Road · *West Midlands* · Map 7 D1
Kingswinford (0384) 295254

Brewery Allied
Landlord Mr R. H. Beatty

BEDROOMS 10   Grade 2   £C (No dogs)
🍺 Ansells Bitter, Mild, Castlemain XXXX;
Harp; Skol; Löwenbräu. *Real ale*

Fine gardens and trees surround this
extended Regency house, which stands on
top of a hill to the west of the town centre.
The spacious bar is in plush Edwardian
style, while good-sized bedrooms have a
more contemporary appeal, with practical
freestanding furniture, tea-makers and
telephones. Bathrooms (two private, three
public) are well fitted and smartly maintained. There's a pleasant TV lounge.
                                          Family pub

Kintbury *(Food, B & B)*   *Dundas Arms*

Berkshire · Map 6 A3
Kintbury (0488) 58263

Free House
Landlords David & Wendy Dalzell-Piper
BEDROOMS 6   Grade 1   £A (No dogs)
Smoked salmon pâté £1.60 Cornish pasty with
chips & peas £1.70 (No bar food eves or Sun)
🍺 Morland's Bitter; Usher's Best Bitter;
John Smith's Bitter; Guinness; Carlsberg Hof;
Anchor Export; Taunton cider. *Real ale*

The patio of this large pub beside the canal
is a pleasant place to enjoy a pint in
summer. A fine display of china plates is a
feature of the bar, which offers enjoyable
snacks like smoked salmon pâté, ploughman's and tempting daily specials such as
crab au gratin. Smartly furnished bedrooms, including one in a separate chalet,
all have neat private bathrooms. Accommodation closed Christmas–New Year.

Kinver *(Food)*   *Whittington Inn*

Near Stourbridge, West Midlands
Staffordshire · Map 7 D1
Kinver (038 483) 2496

Owners Messrs Hickman & Mucklow
Landlord Miss Julie Pike
Cold meat salad £2.75 Chilli £2 (Last
order 10.15pm)
🍺 Courage Directors Bitter; Bass;
Marston's Pedigree, Owd Rodger (winter
only); Guinness; Stella Artois; cider. *Real ale*

Excellent snacks served in the upstairs
wine bar-cum-bistro are a popular feature
of this fine timber-framed pub which
stands just outside the village on the A449.
Julie Pike's menu ranges from delicious
home-made soup, fresh-cut sandwiches
and a tempting buffet of cold meats and
salads to hot specials like cannelloni, chilli
con carne and a hearty beef stew. Good
English cheeses, too. Garden.

Kirk Langley *(B & B)*   *Meynell Arms Hotel*

Ashbourne Road · *Derbyshire* · Map 4 C4
Kirk Langley (033 124) 515

Brewery Bass
Landlords Mr & Mrs J. R. Richards

BEDROOMS 10   Grades 1 & 2   £B
🍺 Bass; Worthington Bitter; Stones Bitter;
Mitchells & Butlers Mild; Tennent's Lager.
Real ale

Converted from a handsome Georgian
farmhouse, this well-maintained three-
storey hotel stands alongside the A52
between Derby and Ashbourne. Ten bedrooms – five with their own up-to-date
bathrooms – provide comfortable overnight accommodation; all have central
heating, TVs and thoughtful extras like
information folders. The bars are simply
furnished. Garden.   **Family pub**

Kirkby Stephen *(Food, B & B)* ★   *King's Arms Hotel*

Cumbria · Map 3 B2
Kirkby Stephen (0930) 71378

Brewery Whitbread
Landlords Mr K. Simpson & Mrs J. Reed

BEDROOMS 9   Grade 2   £B
Toasted steak sandwich £2.10 Curry £1.75
(Last order 8.45pm)
🍺 Castle Eden Ale; Whitbread Trophy;
Heineken; cider. *Real ale*

The bar food is of very high quality at this
attractive old town-centre posting inn.
Succulent home-baked ham is delicious in
sandwiches and salads or with eggs
scrambled or fried, and other choices
include soup, curries, beautifully cooked
steaks and mouthwatering sweets. Smaller
evening choice (served in the restaurant).
Colourful, well-furnished bedrooms offer
plenty of modern comfort, and there's a
pleasant lounge with TV. Garden.

England

Kirkbymoorside *(Food, B & B)* — George & Dragon

Market Place · *North Yorkshire* · Map 4 C2
Kirkbymoorside (0751) 31637
Free House
Landlords Mr & Mrs Curtis & Mr & Mrs Austin
BEDROOMS 23 Grade 1 £A (No dogs)
Steak & kidney pie £2.25 Roast beef &
Yorkshire pudding £2.25 (No bar food eves or
Sun)
🍺 Theakston's Best Bitter; Younger's Scotch
Bitter; Guinness; Carlsberg; Taunton cider.
Real ale

Lunchtime crowds appreciate the tasty home-made fare served in the beamed bar of this welcoming old coaching inn. Soup, steak and kidney pie and roast beef are among the hot dishes, and there are also salads, sandwiches and a delicious sherry trifle. Neat modern bedrooms in converted granaries across the courtyard provide comfortable accommodation. No children under five overnight.

Kirtling *(Food, B & B)* — Queen's Head

Near Newmarket · *Cambridgeshire* · Map 5 C2
Newmarket (0638) 730253

Brewery Tolly Cobbold
Landlord Ann Bailey

BEDROOMS 3 Grade 2 £C
Fidget pie £2.50 Chocolate rum log £1.20
(Last order 9.30pm. No bar food Thurs eve)
🍺 Tolly Cobbold Original, Ordinary, Best
Bitter, Mild; Guinness; Hansa; cider. *Real ale*

Built during the reign of Elizabeth I, this attractive inn is run with energy and charm by horse-loving Ann Bailey. Snacks served in the cosy bars range from ploughman's platters and spicy crab pâté to omelettes, fried plaice and flavour-packed savoury pies. Overnight guests climb a winding staircase to reach the simply fitted bedrooms, which share a spotless bathroom. Garden.

Knapp *(Food)* — Rising Sun

North Curry, Near Taunton · *Somerset*
Map 8 C3
Taunton (0823) 490436
Free House
Landlords Derek & Gena Geneen
Grilled lamb steak £3.95 Baked cheesecake 90p
(Last order 10pm. No bar food Mon lunch
except Bank Holidays)
🍺 Flower's Original, IPA; Carne's Falmouth
Bitter; Whitbread Trophy; Guinness;
Heineken. *Real ale*

Antiques add to the rustic charm of this splendid former cider house, down a narrow country lane off the beaten track but well worth the search for its very enjoyable bar snacks. A blackboard announces the day's choice, which ranges from sandwiches and ploughman's to super smoked mackerel pâté, cauliflower cheese and beef Stroganoff. Leave room for the delicious speciality cheesecake baked to a German recipe. Garden. **Family pub**

Knightwick *(Food, B & B)* — Talbot Hotel

Near Worcester · *Hereford & Worcester*
Map 7 D1
Knightwick (0886) 21235
Free House
Landlords Mr D. Hales & Mrs J. Clift
BEDROOMS 10 Grade 1 £C
Chicken & prawn pie £2.75 Venison pie £2.75
(Last order 10pm)
🍺 Whitbread IPA; Wethered's Bitter;
Banks's Bitter; Bass; Guinness; Heineken;
cider. *Real ale*

Regular supplies of market-fresh fish and meat make for excellent eating at this popular riverside pub. Trout with bacon, prawns and garlic bread, lamb curry and venison pie are typical treats on a nicely varied menu, and syrupy steamed pudding is a good, old-fashioned sweet. Well-carpeted bedrooms have practical modern furnishings and most have their own up-to-date bathrooms. Garden. **Family pub**

Knowl Hill   *(Food)*   *Bird in Hand*

Near Maidenhead · *Berkshire* · Map 6 B3
Littlewick Green (062 882) 2781

Free House
Landlords Jack & Moira Shone

Chicken in garlic & honey £3.50 Steak & kidney
pudding £3.50 (Last order 10.15pm)
🍺 Brakspear's Pale Ale, Old Ale; Young's
Special; Courage Directors Bitter; Guinness;
Carlsberg Hof; cider. *Real ale*

Mrs Shone's well-laden lunchtime cold
table is a popular attraction at this old red-
brick pub beside the A4. Fresh salmon,
roast beef, gammon, turkey and sausages
compete for attention amidst a host of
imaginative salads. For something hot
there's always soup served with lovely
home-baked bread, as well as a daily
special like steak and kidney pudding or
chicken casserole. Less choice in the
evening.

Knutsford   *(Food, B & B)*   *Angel Hotel*

King Street · *Cheshire* · Map 3 B3
Knutsford (0565) 52627

Brewery Greenall Whitley
Landlords Mr & Mrs A. Nardi

BEDROOMS 12   Grade 2   £B   (No dogs)
Beef stew £1.80 Plaice, chips & peas £1.90 (No
bar food eves)
🍺 Greenall Whitley Bitter, Best Mild;
Guinness; Grünhalle.

The bar of this old coaching inn is very cosy
with its beams and various little snugs, and
it provides an enjoyable range of lunchtime
snacks, from soup, salads and vol au vents
to fish and chips, roast chicken and beef
stewed in ale. Bright, well-kept bedrooms
are comfortably furnished and all have TVs
and shower cubicles.   **Family pub**

Lacock   *(Food, B & B)*   *Red Lion*

Near Chippenham · *Wiltshire* · Map 7 D2
Lacock (024 973) 456

Brewery Wadworth
Landlord Mr J. Levis
BEDROOMS 3   Grades 1 & 2   £B
Fresh Cornish shrimps & garlic
mayonnaise £1.75 Lacock beef pie £3.20 (Last
order 9pm. No bar food Sun eve)
🍺 Wadworth's 6X, IPA, Farmers Glory,
Northgate Bitter; Guinness; Heineken. *Real ale*

Home cooking is a strong point at this fine
old coaching inn, where a large courtyard is
a popular summer alternative to the cosy,
rustic bars. Start with the day's soup and
proceed to delicious baked sole, special
sausages or beef pie, finishing with lovely
home-made ice cream. Three spacious
bedrooms with traditional furnishings
include one with its own modern
bathroom.

Laleham   *(Food)*   *Three Horseshoes*

Shepperton Road · *Surrey* · Map 6 B3
Staines (0784) 52617

Brewery Watneys
Landlords Roland & Frances Thanisch
Egg & prawn sandwich 95p Roast pork
salad £3.20 (Last order 9.45pm. No bar food
Sun & Bank Holidays)
🍺 Watneys Stag Bitter, London Bitter;
Webster's Yorkshire Bitter; Ruddle's County;
Guinness; Carlsberg. *Real ale*

A huge variety of sandwiches caters for all
tastes at this charming little roadside pub;
generous, interesting fillings might be
Camembert and onion or prawn and
asparagus. As an alternative, there are also
fresh, colourful salads to go with fish, cold
meats and the unusual fidget pie, plus
several pâtés including the tasty duck and
brandy. Homely sweets to finish. Garden.

Lamberhurst *(Food, B & B)* — *Chequers Inn*

The Broadway · *Kent* · Map 6 C3
Lamberhurst (0892) 890260

Brewery Whitbread
Landlord Mr K. C. Smith
BEDROOMS 4 Grade 2 £C
Home-made soup from 60p Veal escalope à la
crème £5.30 (Last order 9.30pm)
Fremlins Bitter; Whitbread Best Bitter,
Mild; Guinness; Heineken; Stella Artois; cider.
Real ale

Standing in the heart of the village by the little river Teise, this friendly old coaching inn provides good food and comfortable accommodation. Snacks served in the beamed bars include soup and sandwiches, lasagne and cauliflower cheese, with more substantial evening choices such as garlicky chicken Kiev. Cheerful, good-sized bedrooms (three with TV) have solid furniture and private bathrooms. Garden.

Lamberhurst *(B & B)* — *George & Dragon Inn*

High Street · *Kent* · Map 6 C3
Lamberhurst (0892) 890277

Free House
Landlords Reg & Pat Godward

BEDROOMS 8 Grade 1 £C
Harvey's Bitter; Charrington's IPA; Toby
Bitter; Carling Black Label; Tennent's;
Taunton cider. *Real ale*

The landlord's welcome is warm and friendly at this whitewashed roadside inn with flower boxes at the front and a neat garden running down to the river Teise at the back. Bright, cheerful bedrooms – some quite small, others almost palatial – have modern furniture and tea-makers. Breakfast is a positive feast! The convivial bar is a popular local meeting place.

Lambs Green *(Food)* — *Lamb Inn*

Near Rusper · *West Sussex* · Map 6 B3
Rusper (029 384) 336

Free House
Landlords John & Kathy Thompson
Salmon trout £4.50 Half pheasant £4.25
(Last order 10pm)
Badger Best Bitter; Courage Directors
Bitter; Young's Bitter; Sussex County Ale;
Guinness; Tennent's Extra; Holsten; Taunton
cider. *Real ale*

Landlord John Thompson is a welcoming host at this village pub, and his wife Kathy helps to keep customers happy with excellent, nourishing bar snacks. Try her rich meat and vegetable soup or a helping of home-made meat pie with especially delicious gravy. You can also get fresh fish, game in season and curry. If you're not too hungry, go for a ploughman's or a toasted sandwich. Patio.

Lanchester *(Food, B & B)* — *Kings Head*

Station Road · *Co. Durham* · Map 4 C1
Lanchester (0207) 520054

Brewery Scottish & Newcastle
Landlord Mr H. Bainbridge

BEDROOMS 5 Grade 2 £C
Roast of the day £1.95 Steak & kidney pie £1.65
(No bar food eves & all Sun)
Scottish & Newcastle Exhibition;
McEwan's Scotch; Harp; Taunton cider.

A short lunchtime menu of enjoyable cooked dishes is a popular feature of this stone pub at a crossroads. Besides the daily roast, you might find liver and bacon, steak and kidney pie or grilled lamb cutlets. There are also salads, sandwiches and sweets like blackberry sponge. Bedrooms have neat modern furniture, TVs and tea-makers. Accommodation closed 21 December–1 Jan.

Lancing   *(Food, B & B)*   *Sussex Pad*

Old Shoreham Road · *West Sussex* · Map 6 B4
Shoreham-by-Sea (079 17) 4647

Free House
Landlord Mr Wally Pack
BEDROOMS 6   Grade 1   £A
Double-decker sandwich £1.35 Local crab
salad £4.75 (Last order 10pm. No bar food
Sat eve)
 Tetley's Bitter; Ind Coope John Bull;
Guinness; Skol; Löwenbräu; cider.

Just opposite Shoreham airport, this modernised pub offers good accommodation
and tasty bar fare. Spacious bedrooms with
practical fitted units have TVs, telephones,
tea-makers and smart modern bathrooms.
Head for the plush Edwardian Bar to find
freshly cut sandwiches, a splendid steak
and kidney pie, plus a lunchtime buffet
featuring salads, cold meats and delicious
local crab.   **Family pub**

Langdale   *(Food)*   *Pillar Hotel, Hobson's Pub*

Near Ambleside · *Cumbria* · Map 3 B2
Langdale (096 67) 302

Free House
Landlord Mr Jim Craig

Beef in Guinness casserole £3.25 Baked lemon
sole £3.25 (Last order 9.30pm)
 Hartleys Best Bitter, Mild; Tetley's Bitter;
Skol; cider. *Real ale*

Check directions when heading for this
rustically styled modern pub, a self-
contained element in an impressive hotel-
cum-country club complex. Bar snacks are
quite a feature and include sandwiches,
salads, Barnsley chops and the popular
Cumberland sausage. The spacious terrace
is a pleasant summer alternative to the
stone-floored bar. *For accommodation see
Egon Ronay's Lucas Hotel & Restaurant
Guide 1985.*

Langham   *(Food)*   *Noel Arms*

Near Oakham · *Leicestershire* · Map 5 B1
Oakham (0572) 2931

Free House
Landlord Alan Eacott

Steak & kidney pie £2.30 Roast meat
salad £4.20 (Last order 10pm)
 Ruddle's County, Rutland Bitter;
Whitbread Trophy; Guinness; Stella Artois;
Taunton cider. *Real ale*

A selection from the eye-catching cold
buffet is your best bet in the nicely furnished bar of this fine old converted farmhouse. Ham, turkey and sirloin, roasted on
the premises, are carved to order and
accompanied by a serve-yourself selection
of freshly prepared salads. Ploughman's is
a popular choice for a quick snack. Patio.
                                   Family pub

Langley Marsh   *(Food)*   ★   *Three Horseshoes*

Near Wiveliscombe · *Somerset* · Map 8 C3
Wiveliscombe (0984) 23763

Free House
Landlords Mr & Mrs J. Marsden

Trout pâté £1.40 Pineapple & lentil curry £1.30
(Last order 10.30pm)
 Golden Hill Exmoor Ale; Cotleigh Tawny
Bitter; Hall & Woodhouse Badger Best Bitter;
Palmer's IPA, Tally Ho; cider. *Real ale*

Jill Marsden's adventurous cooking is the
crowning glory of this charming village
pub, and she is always coming up with new
ideas to tempt the customers. Super soups
and traditional specialities such as roast
beef salad and stargazey pasty are first
class, and there's always a vegetarian dish
like our subtle vegetable curry accompanied by hot granary bread and butter.
You can finish on a high note with sublime
souffléed orange. Less choice Thurs eve.

Langton Green   *(Food)*   *Greyhound*

Near Tunbridge Wells · *Kent* · Map 6 C3
Langton (089 286) 2028

Brewery Courage
Landlords Mr & Mrs Keith Parker

Ham, leek & mushroom pie £1.50 Bacon &
onion roll £1.50 (Last order 10pm)
🍺 Courage Best Bitter, Directors Bitter, JC,
Dark Mild; Guinness; Kronenbourg; cider.
Real ale

On the edge of the village green, this attractive red-brick and timbered pub is a popular place for bar snacks. Wholesome home-cooked dishes like ham, leek and mushroom pie or bacon and onion roll are great favourites, perhaps followed by some excellent apple and mince pie. Sandwiches, ploughman's and salads make lighter bites. A traditional roast is an extra feature for Sunday lunch.

Lanreath   *(B & B)*   *Punch Bowl Inn*

Near Looe · *Cornwall* · Map 8 B4
Lanreath (0503) 20218

Free House
Landlords Mr & Mrs T. C. Mansfield

BEDROOMS 18   Grade 1   £B
🍺 Bass; Tinner's Ale; Worthing Best Bitter,
Dark; Guinness; Carling Black Label; cider.
Real ale

First licensed in 1620, this fine old hostelry has been at various times a court house, coaching inn and smugglers' distribution house. The beamed bars, agleam with copper and brass ornaments, are cosy, welcoming spots, and there's a lounge with a pool table. Bedrooms vary from traditionally furnished (two have four-posters) to more modern extension rooms with smart fitted units. Most have TVs. Garden.
Family pub

Leafield   *(Food)*   *Old George Inn*

Near Witney · *Oxfordshire* · Map 5 A2
Asthall Leigh (099 387) 288

Free House
Landlords Bob & Valerie Taylor

10oz sirloin steak £4.95 Ploughman's lunch £1
(Last order 10.30pm)
🍺 Wadworth's 6X; Hook Norton Best Bitter;
Glenny's Witney Bitter; Guinness; Tennent's;
Carling Black Label; Taunton cider. *Real ale*

People come from a wide area to tuck into the tasty, tender steaks that are the speciality of this well-kept inn. Valerie Taylor's menus offer plenty of other choice, too, from quick lunchtime snacks like sandwiches and ploughman's platters to basket meals, baked trout and lightly cooked veal escalope. Tables are well spaced in the comfortable bar. Garden.

Ledbury   *(B & B)*   *Feathers Hotel*

High Street · *Hereford & Worcester* · Map 7 D2
Ledbury (0531) 2600

Brewery Mitchells & Butlers
Landlord Mr Michael Hester

BEDROOMS 11   Grade 1   £A+
🍺 Mitchells & Butlers Brew XI, Springfield
Best Bitter; Bass; Guinness; Carling Black
Label; cider. *Real ale*

The interior of this handsome half-timbered building at the centre of town is suitably rich in heavy oak beams and fine old furniture. The large, old-fashioned bedrooms provide modern conveniences like TVs, radio-alarms and tea-makers and all have well-fitted private bathrooms. The public bar is a convivial place for a drink; you can also relax in the spacious foyer-lounge with its cheerful winter fire.
Family pub

Ledbury *(Food, B & B)* — *Verzons Country Hotel*

Trumpet · *Hereford & Worcester* · Map 7 D2
Trumpet (053 183) 381
Free House
Landlords Phillip & Mary Stanley
BEDROOMS 6   Grade 1   £B
Deep-fried potato skins with garlic
mayonnaise 65p Pork chop in cider & cheese
sauce £2.25 (Last order 10pm)
Marston's Pedigree; Ind Coope Burton
Bitter; Guinness; Stella Artois: Marston's
Pilsner; cider. *Real ale*

A quiet rural setting alongside the A438 is
enjoyed by this splendid Georgian house,
where the welcoming Bistro Bar serves a
good selection of tasty fare. Deep-fried
potato skins with garlic mayonnaise make a
scrumptious snack, and other choices
include quiches, savoury pies and navarin
of lamb. Bedrooms (all with TV) are divided
between compact singles and comfortable
doubles with modern bath or shower
rooms. Garden.

Ledbury *(B & B)* — *Ye Olde Talbot Hotel*

New Street · *Hereford & Worcester* · Map 7 D2
Ledbury (0531) 2963

Brewery Ansells
Landlords Mr & Mrs E. Harrison

BEDROOMS 6   Grade 2   £C   (No dogs)
Gibbs Mew Bitter; Tetley's Bitter;
Ansells Bitter; Guinness; Löwenbräu; Skol;
cider. *Real ale*

The panelled dining room of this lovely
half-timbered pub was once the scene of a
bloody Civil War struggle, and evidence of
the fray can still be seen. It's more peaceful
now, although a mischievous poltergeist
apparently makes his presence felt from
time to time! You can relax in one of the
beamed bars or watch TV in the cosy little
upstairs lounge, and you'll rest easy in the
neat, sturdily furnished bedrooms (two
with bathrooms).   **Family pub**

Ledsham *(Food)* — *Tudor Rose*

Two Mills, South Wirral · *Cheshire* · Map 5 B2
051-339 2399

Brewery Higsons
Landlord Mr F. Fairclough

Chicken Kiev £2 Grilled trout £2
(Last order 9.45pm)
Higsons Best Bitter, Mild; Bass;
Guinness; Carling Black Label; cider.
Real ale

Copper and brassware, plates and jugs
adorn the bar of this smart modern pub at
the junction of the A540 and A550. Lunchtime and evening bar snacks provide plenty
of choice, with hot dishes like soup, grills,
home-made pie and tasty omelettes. You
can also get cold meat salads, filled baps
and some fine English cheeses. Garden.

Ledston — *White Horse*

Graham Bedford is the affable landlord at this busy village pub,
modernised but still retaining much of its original appeal. Stuffed
birds and animals, horse brasses and harnesses are decorative
features in the long bar, with beams, copper-topped tables and
cheerful fires all contributing to the warm, welcoming atmosphere.
                                                Family pub

Main Street, Near Castleford · *West Yorkshire* · Map 4 C3
Castleford (0977) 553069
Brewery Whitbread   *Landlord* Mr Graham Bedford
Whitbread Castle Eden Ale, Trophy, BYB; Guinness; Stella
Artois; Heineken; cider. *Real ale*

England

Leek   *(B & B)*   Three Horseshoes Inn

Blackshaw Moor · *Staffordshire* · Map 4 C4
Blackshaw (053 834) 296

Free House
Landlords Bill & Jill Kirk

BEDROOMS 7   Grade 1   £C
🍺 McEwan's Scotch, 80/-, 70/-, Export,
Lager; Guinness; Kestrel; Taunton cider.
Real ale

Dating back some 300 years, this well-kept
former farmhouse enjoys a superb setting
north of Leek on the A53. The views are
lovely from the cottage-style bedrooms,
which feature pine furniture and colour
TVs. Six have shower cabinets, and there
are two carpeted bathrooms. The public
bar is cheerful and lively, the beamed
lounge bar more intimate. Accommodation
closed 1 week Christmas. Garden.

Family pub

Leigh   *(Food)*   Plough Inn

Church Road, Near Reigate · *Surrey* · Map 6 B3
Dawes Green (030 678) 348

Brewery King & Barnes
Landlords Mr J. Browning & Mr M. Morrell

Steak & kidney pie with vegetables £1.95
Pâté £1.40 (Last order 9pm. No bar food Sun)
🍺 King & Barnes Festive, Sussex Bitter, Old
Ale (winter only); Guinness; Carling Black
Label; Heineken; cider. *Real ale*

The oldest part of this well-kept village pub
is the low ceilinged lounge bar with original
16th-century beams. Generous portions of
tasty, home-prepared dishes are served in
this characterful setting, including pâté and
ploughman's, jumbo sausages and
scampi. The day's special could be chicken
pie or chilli con carne, and the lunchtime
sandwiches are replaced in the evening by
simple grills. Garden.

Leigh   *(Food)*   Seven Stars

Bunce Common Road, Near Reigate · *Surrey*
Map 6 B3
Dawes Green (030 678) 254

Brewery Ind Coope
Landlord Mr Tom Doyle
Moussaka £2.25 Home-cooked ham & salad
£2.75 (Last order 10pm)
🍺 Friary Meux Bitter; Ind Coope Burton Ale,
Double Diamond; Guinness; Löwenbräu;
cider. *Real ale*

A warm welcome from landlord Tom Doyle
and enjoyable bar fare keep the customers
flocking to this charming old country pub.
You can sit by the fire and enjoy winter
specials like savoury pies and curries, while
in summer there are appetising salads to
go with quiche and home-cooked joints.
Ploughman's, mixed grills and fry-ups are
available all year, along with sweets like
delicious apple pie. Garden.

Leigh on Mendip   *(Food)*   Bell Inn

Near Bath · *Somerset* · Map 8 D3
Mells (0373) 812316
Free House
Landlords Dick Erith & Ian Holdsworth
Seafood Thermidor £4.50 Fried chicken breast
stuffed with prawns & crab £5.20
(Last order 9.30pm)
🍺 Wadworth's 6X; Devenish Bitter;
Worthington Best Bitter; Carling Black Label;
Youngers; Guinness; Löwenbräu; Taunton
cider. *Real ale*

This whitewashed 17th-century inn in a
quiet village provides some excellent bar
fare. The regular menu features interesting
dishes like duck and port pâté, pizza and
curries – served complete with poppadums
and chutney – and there are also tempting
blackboard specials such as pepper
chicken, seafood Thermidor and Norfolk
venison. Garden. Closed Monday lunchtime except Bank Holidays.   **Family pub**

Leominster   *(Food, B & B)*   *Royal Oak Hotel*

South Street · *Hereford & Worcester* · Map 7 D1
Leominster (0568) 2610

Free House
Landlord Mr John Pallant
BEDROOMS 16   Grade 1   £B
Beef sandwiches £1.50 Mushroom
omelette £3.45 (Last order 9pm)
🍺 Wood's Parish Bitter; Hook Norton Best
Bitter; Younger's Dark Mild; Guinness;
Carlsberg Hof; cider. *Real ale*

Sandwiches generously filled with rare
roast beef are one of the favourite snacks at
this welcoming Georgian inn with two comfortable bars. There's also home-made
soup and pâté, omelettes, steaks and tasty
lunchtime specials such as chicken
espagnole. Overnight accommodation is in
16 well-maintained bedrooms, all equipped
with TVs, tea-makers and spacious modern
bathrooms. There's a smart lounge, and
staff are helpful. Patio   **Family pub**

Levens   *(Food)*   *Hare & Hounds Inn*

Near Kendal · *Cumbria* · Map 3 B2
Sedgwick (0448) 60408

Brewery Vaux
Landlords Myra & Jim Stephenson
Cumberland sausage with chips £2.05
Ploughman's £1.30 (Last order 9pm. No bar
food Mon eve)
🍺 Vaux Sunderland Bitter, Mild, Samson;
Guinness; Tuborg; Taunton cider.
Real ale

A turning off the A590 leads to this friendly
village pub with its relaxing lounge bar
where you can enjoy Myra Stephenson's
splendid home-cooked fare. Start with
soup or pâté, and go on to Cumberland
sausage, scampi or chicken served with a
baked potato, chips or salad. Home-cooked
ham and beef make delicious toppings for
open sandwiches, and there are steaks in
the evening. Patio.
                        Family pub (lunchtime)

Levington   *(Food)*   *Ship*

Gun Hill, Ipswich · *Suffolk* · Map 5 D2
Nacton (047 388) 573

Brewery Tollemache & Cobbold
Landlords Mr & Mrs L. Wenham

Mariner's tart £2.50 Bread pudding &
cream 70p (No bar food eves)
🍺 Tolly Cobbold Bitter, Original; Guinness;
Hansa. *Real ale*

The location, atmosphere and cooking are
all delightful at this 14th-century smuggler's
inn overlooking the Orwell estuary. Nautical
knick-knacks deck the cosy beamed bar, and
a tame parrot aids a piratical touch. Lunchtime snacks include home-smoked ham,
hearty savoury pies, ploughman's and
quiches; crab is a summer favourite, and
there are some lovely old-fashioned puddings. Ploughman's and prawns only on
Sunday. Terrace.

Ley Hill   *(Food)*   *Swan Inn*

Chesham · *Buckinghamshire* · Map 6 B3
Chesham (0494) 783025

Brewery Benskins
Landlords Mr & Mrs Brian Williams

Cottage pie £1.50 Fruit crumble 85p (Last
order 9pm. No bar food Sun eve)
🍺 Benskins Bitter; Ind Coope Burton Ale;
John Bull Bitter; Guinness; Skol; Löwenbräu;
cider. *Real ale*

This cosy, intimate and inviting inn
opposite the village green was originally a
hunting lodge and dates back to the 16th
century. It's a fine place for snacks – country
vegetable soup with granary bread,
smoked mackerel and trout, cider-baked
gammon, daily specials like tuna bake or
chilli con carne. Puddings feature seasonal
fruits. Soup and ploughman's only Sunday
lunchtime. Garden.

Lickfold *(Food)* — *Lickfold Inn*

Near Petworth · *West Sussex* · Map 6 B4
Lodsworth (079 85) 285

Free House
Landlord Mr C. Tyler
Lasagne £2.50 Steak & kidney pie with vegetables £2.95 (Last order 10pm)
Fuller's London Pride, ESB; Hall & Woodhouse Badger Best Bitter, Tanglefoot; Marston's Pedigree; Eldridge Pope Royal Oak; Guinness; cider. *Real ale*

This 500-year-old pub with a handsome timber-framed façade serves enjoyable fare in its comfortable, beamed bars. The wide choice ranges from salads and sandwiches to grills, pies, omelettes and fresh fish. Lasagne, moussaka and spare ribs are other options, with more elaborate specialities like chicken cordon bleu in the evening. Leave room for sweets such as the delicious rum crunch. **Family pub**

Lifton *(Food)* — *Arundell Arms*

Devon · Map 8 B3
Lifton (0566) 84666

Free House
Landlord Anne Voss-Bark

Cold buffet £4 Arundell Arms pâté with French bread £1.85 (No bar food eves)
Usher's Country Bitter; Carlsberg. *Real ale*

Anne Voss-Bark's attractive creeper-clad hotel is a super place for a lunchtime bar snack. The cold buffet, with succulent cooked meats, crisp, light quiches and colourful fresh salads, is the chief attraction, supported by creamy vegetable soup and the occasional hot dish. Sweets include treacle tart and a nice light lemon soufflé. **Family pub**

Lincoln *(Food)* — *Wig & Mitre*

29 Steep Hill · *Lincolnshire* · Map 4 D4
Lincoln (0522) 35190

Brewery Samuel Smith
Landlord Mr Michael Hope

Waldorf salad £1.50 Chicken cordon bleu £4.25 (Last order 10.30pm)
Samuel Smith's Old Brewery Bitter; Pils; Alpine. *Real ale*

A wide range of imaginative fare is served all day in this charming pub-cum-wine bar, where breakfast starts the day at 8 o'clock. Then come sandwiches, pâtés and tempting blackboard specials like delicious spinach and mushroom soup, ham and sweetcorn cheesecake and rich, beery harvest casserole, as well as plenty of vegetarian specialities. Superb puddings include a marvellous banana Pavlova. Garden. **Family pub**

Linton *(Food)* — *Crown*

11 High Street · *Cambridgeshire* · Map 5 C2
Cambridge (0223) 891759

Free House
Landlords Luis & Doreen Sanz
Deep-fried stuffed mushrooms £3.35 Fresh grilled salmon £3.95 (Last order 9.30pm. No bar food Sun eve)
Adnam's Bitter; Greene King IPA; Younger's Tartan; Guinness; Carlsberg. *Real ale*

Fresh seafood is a feature of the varied menu at this whitewashed village pub. Delicious and unusual soups like carrot and curry are served with lovely granary bread, and other favourites include deep-fried mushrooms stuffed with cream cheese, liver pâté, quiche lorraine and cannelloni. Cold meat salads, too. Garden.

Linton · *Windmill Inn*

Standing at the heart of a pleasant little village, this 200-year-old converted farmhouse retains a great deal of rustic charm and character. Winter fires warm the two bars, whose stone walls are hung with a variety of highly polished brassware. A popular, convivial place with delightful staff and good beer. **Family pub**

Near Wetherby · *West Yorkshire* · Map 4 C3
Wetherby (0937) 62938
Brewery Younger's   *Landlord* Mrs J. Oxley
Younger's No. 3 Ale, Scotch Bitter; McEwan's Lager. *Real ale*

Little Bollington   *(Food)* · *Ye Olde No. 3*

Lymm Road, Near Altrincham · *Greater Manchester* · Map 3 B3
Lymm (092 575) 6115

Brewery John Smith
Landlords Bill & Thelma Bentley
Steak & kidney pie, chips & vegetables £1.30
Omelette with chips or salad £1.30
(Last order 10pm. No bar food Sun eve)
John Smith's Bitter, Mild; Guinness; Hofmeister; cider.

Once the third posting house on the Liverpool to London coach route, this friendliest of pubs is kept in absolutely sparkling condition by delightful Bill and Thelma Bentley. Satisfying bar snacks are simple: sandwiches and salads or such hot dishes as omelettes, fish and a superb steak and kidney pie. Roast for Sunday lunch. Less choice evenings. Garden.

Little Hadham   *(Food)* · *Nag's Head*

The Ford, Near Ware · *Hertfordshire* Map 5 C2
Albury (027 974) 555
Brewery Rayment
Landlord Mr M. Robinson
Prawns Thermidor £2.95 Veal steak with rice £4.20 (Last order 9pm. No bar food Sun eve)
Rayment's Bitter; Greene King Abbot Ale; Guinness; Kronenbourg; cider. *Real ale*

Local ladies provide the superb cakes and sweets which are the undoubted winners at this friendly, 16th-century village pub. We finished our meal with a sublime Austrian coffee cake that was simply out of this world. The rest of the menu is full of variety, and you can get anything from salads and freshly cut sandwiches to liver and bacon, prawns Thermidor, steaks and nicely cooked veal. There are tables outside on the patio.

Little Langdale   *(B & B)* · *Three Shires Inn*

Near Ambleside · *Cumbria* · Map 3 B2
Langdale (096 67) 215

Free House
Landlords Neil & Sheila Stephenson

BEDROOMS 8   Grade 1   £B   (No dogs)
Wilsons Bitter, Mild; Guinness; Carlsberg; Foster's; cider

The beer garden beside the beck running through the garden is the perfect place to appreciate the idyllic setting of this immaculate pub. It's also pleasant inside, whether in the walkers' bar or the slate-walled cocktail bar. Bedrooms are first-rate with modern furniture, pretty fabrics and dainty prints – not to mention the glorious views from the windows. Bathrooms are spotlessly clean.

England

Little Walden *(Food)* ★ *Crown Inn*

Saffron Walden · *Essex* · Map 5 C2
Saffron Walden (0799) 27175

Free House
Landlord Mr Chris Oliver

Apple pie with cream 95p   Local trout £4.50
(Last order 9.30. No bar food Sun)
🍺 Ruddle's County, Bitter; Courage Bitter,
Directors; Ben Truman; Kronenbourg;
Taunton cider. *Real ale*

An enticing selection of superb seafood is
the jewel in the crown of this lovely old
village pub, where all the bar snacks are
freshly prepared with great skill and care.
Crab, Dover sole and stuffed rainbow trout
are among the fishy favourites, and
samphire makes an unusual and delicious
starter. Also sandwiches, hearty winter
pies and an exquisitely spiced apple pie.
Garden.

Little Washbourne *(Food)* *Hobnails Inn*

Near Tewkesbury · *Gloucestershire*
Map 7 D2
Alderton (024 262) 237

Brewery Whitbread
Landlord Mr S. Farbrother
Gammon & pineapple bap £1 Steak &
mushroom bap £1.50 (Last order 10.30pm)
🍺 Whitbread West Country Pale Ale;
Flowers Original, Best Bitter; Guinness;
Heineken; Stella Artois; cider. *Real ale*

Speciality baps and gorgeous sweets bring
customers from far and wide to this small
roadside pub. The choice of fillings for
delicious fresh, farmhouse-style baps
ranges from gammon and pineapple to
liver and onions or steak, egg and mushrooms. Mouthwatering gâteaux, flans and
ice creams make a splendid finish to the
meal. Patio.   **Family pub**

Liverpool *Philharmonic Dining Rooms*

Built in 1898 by Walter Thomas, the Philharmonic is a marvellous
example of late-Victorian extravagance. Rich rosewood panelling,
polished mahogany and glittering chandeliers combine in a dazzling
symphony of style, and even the fittings in the gents are made of pink
marble! Definitely one of the sights of Liverpool.   **Family pub**

36 Hope Street · *Merseyside* · Map 3 B3
(051) 709 1163
Brewery Tetley Walker   *Landlord* Mr Stroud
🍺 Tetley's Bitter, Mild; Guinness; Skol; cider. *Real ale*

Llanfair Waterdine *(Food, B & B)* *Red Lion*

Near Knighton, Powys · *Shropshire* · Map 7 C1
Knighton (0547) 528214

Free House
Landlords Mr & Mrs S. J. Rhodes

BEDROOMS 3 **Grade** 2 **£B** (No dogs)
Cheese & bacon flan £1.50 Lemon gâteau 75p
(Last order 10pm)
🍺 Ansells Pale Ale, Dark Mild; John Smith's
Bitter; Wrexham Lager; cider. *Real ale*

Once frequented by drovers, this appealing
stone-built pub stands on the banks of the
river Teme (watch for the sign on the
B4355). Sturdily furnished bedrooms in
traditional style are quite comfortable. In
the two homely bars you'll find simple
snacks like smooth pâté, as well as quiches
and pizzas. No children under 15 overnight;
sometimes closed at lunchtime in winter.
Garden.

Long Hanborough *(Food)* — *Bell*

Near Oxford · *Oxfordshire* · Map 5 A2
Freeland (0993) 881324

Brewery Morrell's
Landlord Mr Graham Laer

Chicken & turkey pie 95p Beef & venison
casserole in port 95p (No bar food eves)
🍺 Morrell's Varsity; Guinness; Harp;
Kronenbourg; cider. *Real ale*

Good food at old-fashioned prices is the
trademark of this traditional, welcoming
village pub, where the lunchtime snacks –
prepared by a gifted local lady – consist of
simple, homely dishes like a bowl of
Berkshire broth, hot pot luck and an
Oxfordshire pâté. Dressed crab with
mayonnaise sandwiches and ploughman's
too, and a hot treacle pudding not to be
missed. Less choice weekends. Patio.

Long Melford *(Food, B & B)* — *Crown Inn Hotel*

Near Sudbury · *Suffolk* · Map 5 C2
Sudbury (0787) 77666

Free House
Landlords Mr & Mrs B. Sell

BEDROOMS 14 Grades 1 & 2 £B
Pâté & toast £1.20 Steak & kidney pie £2.15
(Last order 9pm)
🍺 Adnams Bitter; Mauldon's Bitter; Greene
King IPA; Carlsberg Hof. *Real ale*

Cheerful awnings and window boxes adorn
the front of this old village inn, and the
interior retains its beams and antique furniture. Simple snacks in the bar include
tasty herb pâté, pies, scampi and chips and
nice sweets like treacle tart. Bedrooms in
the main building are traditional in style,
those in the annexe neat and modern, with
TVs, tea-makers and small private bathrooms. Garden. **Family pub**

Long Sutton *(B & B)* — *Devonshire Arms*

Near Langport · *Somerset* · Map 8 D3
Long Sutton (045 824) 271

Free House
Landlords John & Maureen Hodder

BEDROOMS 4 Grade 2 £B (No dogs)
🍺 Wadworth's 6X; Hancock's HB; Toby;
Worthington Best Bitter; Guinness; Carling
Black Label; Taunton cider. *Real ale*

Good standards of maintenance and
housekeeping prevail at this ivy-clad 18th-
century inn, built by the Duke of Devonshire
as a private shooting lodge. Spacious bedrooms have sturdy traditional furniture,
tea-makers and colour TVs and share two
well-equipped bathrooms. There's a smart
lounge area and a delightful, immaculately
kept walled garden. **Family pub**

Longframlington *(Food, B & B)* — *Granby Inn*

Northumberland · Map 2 D4
Longframlington (066 570) 228

Brewery Bass
Landlord Mr G. Hall

BEDROOMS 6 Grade 1 £B (No dogs)
Steak & kidney pie £2.65 Fresh cod &
chips £2.55 (Last order 9.30pm)
🍺 Piper Best Scotch Bitter; Stones Bitter;
Guinness; Carling Black Label; Taunton cider.

The Halls extend a friendly welcome at this
roadside coaching inn, where visitors flock
to enjoy reliably prepared bar snacks like
smooth chicken liver pâté, sandwiches,
salads, grills and the ever-popular steak
and kidney pie (lunch only). Attractive bedrooms (including three compact chalet
rooms) with colour TVs and tea-makers
provide first-rate comfort. No under-
tens overnight. No accommodation 23
December–2 January. Patio.

Longhope   (Food)   *Nags Head*

Ross Road · *Gloucestershire* · Map 7 D2
Gloucester (0452) 830284

Free House
Landlord Roger & Roslyn Salter

Steak & kidney pie £1.50 Moussaka £1.50
(Last order 10pm)
🍺 Brain's SA; Smiles Best Bitter;
Wadworth's Northgate Bitter; Tetley's Bitter;
Carlsberg Hof; cider. *Real ale*

This welcoming pub on the A40 is a spruce
little black and white building with tables
on its tiny front lawn. In Oscar's Wine Bar
(there's another bar as well) you can enjoy
straightforward, home-prepared fare like
spaghetti bolognese, chilli con carne and
trout with almonds. Simple starters, ice
creams to finish. For Sunday lunchtime,
only a traditional roast is served.
Family pub

Longleat   (Food, B & B)   *Bath Arms*

Near Warminster · *Wiltshire* · Map 8 D3
Maiden Bradley (098 53) 308

Free House
Landlords Beryl & Joseph Lovatt
BEDROOMS 7   Grade 1   £B
Turkey & mushroom pie £2.95 Brixham pot pie
£2.95 (Last order 10pm)
🍺 Eldridge Pope Dorchester Bitter; Bass;
Wadworth's 6X; Guinness; Holsten;
Carlsberg; cider. *Real ale*

Right in the middle of the Longleat Estate,
this well-managed hostelry is the place for
good food and excellent accommodation.
Fresh fish and seasonal game are highlights of the enterprising bar menu, which
also offers quiches and casseroles, curries
and a cold buffet in summer. Attractively
furnished bedrooms (six with private bathrooms) have tea-makers and TVs. There are
three splendidly rustic bars and a cosy
residents' lounge.   **Family pub**

Longparish   (Food)   *Plough Inn*

Near Andover · *Hampshire* · Map 6 A3
Longparish (026 472) 358

Brewery Whitbread
Landlord Mr Trevor Colgate
Home-made pâté & toast £1.40 Venison
sausages, tomato & egg £2.95 (Last order
10.30pm. No bar food Mon eve)
🍺 Whitbread Poacher Bitter, Best Bitter,
Strong Country Bitter; Devenish Wessex Best
Bitter; Guinness; cider. *Real ale*

Very much food-orientated, this popular,
brick and tile pub and its pretty garden
stand about a mile from the A303 in a
picturesque little village. Among the dried
hops in the thatched bar you can kick off
with a superb chicken liver pâté and go on
to a grill, venison sausages or a tasty daily
special like squab pie. Also toasted snacks,
ploughman's and nice home-made puds.

Lowdham   (B & B)   *Springfield Inn*

Old Epperstone Road · *Nottinghamshire*
Map 5 B1
Nottingham (0602) 663387

Free House
Landlords Gordon & Mavis Ferriman
BEDROOMS 11   Grade 1   £B
🍺 Mansfield Bitter, Mild; Mitchells & Butlers
Springfield Bitter; Marston's Pedigree; Home
Brewery Bitter; Guinness; Foster's; cider.
Real ale

You're staying with an aircraft enthusiast at
this gabled inn, converted and extended
from a private house. The extensive lawned
grounds are in fact a licensed helipad and
parachute drop zone, and some of the pro-
pellers decorating the walls of the spacious
bars come from planes owned by welcoming landlord Gordon Ferriman. Bedrooms
furnished in simple contemporary style
have tea-makers, colour TVs and either
showers or bathrooms.

Lower Peover *(Food)*

Bells of Peover

Near Knutsford · *Cheshire* · Map 3 B4
Lower Peover (056 581) 2269

Brewery Greenall Whitley
Landlord Mr J. R. Fisher

Beef sandwich 70p Prawn sandwich £1.40
(Last order 10pm)
🍺 Greenall Whitley Local Bitter, Mild;
Guinness; Grünhalle; cider. *Real ale*

Keep your eyes peeled for the narrow cobbled lane that leads from the B5081 to this captivating whitewashed inn. The tiny snug bar features a fascinating collection of Toby jugs, and in the comfortable lounge bar there are some fine antiques, including a splendid Welsh dresser. Bar snacks consist of freshly cut sandwiches with generous fillings of beef, prawns, turkey or cheese. Patio.

Lower Woodford *(Food)*

Wheatsheaf

Near Salisbury · *Wiltshire* · Map 6 A3
Middle Woodford (072 273) 203

Brewery Hall & Woodhouse
Landlord Mr Peter Charlton
Smoked mackerel pâté with toast £1.40
Steak & kidney pie with vegetables £2.25
(Last order 10pm)
🍺 Hall & Woodhouse Badger Best Bitter,
Tanglefoot; Guinness; Brock; Stella Artois;
Taunton cider. *Real ale*

Relax in the garden or enjoy the darts and other games inside this charming village pub. A bridge over a fish pond makes a novel entrance to the dining area, where you can tuck into freshly prepared soup or tasty pâté with toast, followed perhaps by steak, chicken Kiev or rainbow trout. Home-made fruit pie makes an excellent finish. Special children's menus – even cold milk on draught! **Family pub**

Loweswater *(Food, B & B)*

Kirkstile Inn

Near Cockermouth · *Cumbria* · Map 3 B2
Lorton (090 085) 219

Free House
Landlord Mr Joe Habens
BEDROOMS 10 Grade 1 £C
Ham, egg & chips £3.50 Pasties 90p (Last
order 9pm)
🍺 Jennings Best Bitter; Younger's Scotch
Bitter, Tartan; Guinness; Ayingerbräu; cider.
Real ale

Stunning views of lakes and fells are a feature of this friendly old inn next to the village church. The characterful beamed bars are the setting for some enjoyable and satisfying snacks, from nice meaty pasties to baked potatoes, omelettes and sirloin steak. Comfortable bedrooms – most with modern private bathrooms – have good carpets and practical fitted furniture. Break-fasts are excellent. **Family pub**

Lowick *(Food, B & B)*

Farmers Arms

Near Ulverston · *Cumbria* · Map 3 B2
Greenodd (022 986) 376

Brewery Scottish & Newcastle
Landlords Philip & Dorothy Broadley
BEDROOMS 13 Grade 2 £B
Steak & kidney pie £2 Stilton & walnut
pâté £1.50 (Last order 10pm)
🍺 Younger's Scotch Bitter, No. 3; McEwan's
80/-, Export; Guinness; Harp; Taunton cider.
Real ale

Tasty bar snacks can be enjoyed in the flag-stoned bars or out on the patio of this agreeable old inn, once a farmhouse that brewed its own beer. Chicken liver pâté, steak and kidney pie and haddock with chips are typical fare, and at lunchtime there are also sandwiches. Bedrooms are furnished in simple, traditional style and there's a comfortable TV room.
Family pub (lunchtime)

England

Ludlow   *(B & B)*   *Angel Hotel*

Broad Street · *Shropshire* · Map 7 D1
Ludlow (0584) 2581

Free House
Landlords Colin & Joan Espley

BEDROOMS 16   Grades 1 & 2   £B   (No dogs)
🍺 Flowers Bitter; Whitbread Bitter; Stella
Artois; Heineken; cider. *Real ale*

Back in 1802, this fine half-timbered coaching inn played host to Lord Nelson on a trip
to the Forest of Dean to inspect oak trees
felled for the building of the fleet. Today's
visitors sleep soundly in the unassuming,
traditionally furnished bedrooms (the four
large ones with neat modern bathrooms
are the most appealing). There's also a
comfortable, relaxing bar and a large first-
floor TV lounge with deep armchairs and
settees.

Lurgashall   *(Food)*   *Noah's Ark*

The Green, Near Petworth · *West Sussex*
Map 6 B4
Northchapel (042 878) 346
Brewery Friary Meux
Landlord Mr Ted Swannell
Moussaka £2.10 Fish pie £2.25 (Last
order 10pm. No bar food Sun)
🍺 Friary Meux Bitter; Ind Coope Burton Ale,
Mild, John Bull; Löwenbräu; Guinness; cider.
Real ale

Standing on the edge of a delightful village,
this old beamed pub is full of charm
There's a daily blackboard menu of enjoyable snacks ranging from rich game soup to
tasty moussaka, chilli con carne or
gammon and chips. You can also have
salad with crab, prawns, beef, turkey or
tongue, as well as a wide variety of plain
and toasted sandwiches. Nice sweets like
apple pie or sherry trifle. Garden.
Family pub

Lyddington   *(B & B)*   *Marquess of Exeter*

Main Street, Near Uppingham · *Leicestershire*
Map 5 B1
Uppingham (0572) 822477

Free House
Landlord Mr B. W. B. Cousins

BEDROOMS 15   Grade 1   £A (No dogs)
🍺 Ruddle's Bitter, County; Bateman's Bitter;
Adnams Southwold Bitter; Greene King Bitter;
Guinness; Stella Artois; cider. *Real ale*

On the main village street, this handsome
16th-century pub is full of period charm,
with flagstone floors and low-beamed
ceilings. Hunting prints and horse-racing
photographs abound, and the splendidly
comfortable bedrooms in a quiet annexe are
named after local hunts. All have excellent
carpeted bathrooms and are very well
equipped, with double glazing, colour TVs
and direct-dial telephones. No under-fives
overnight. Patio.

Lydford   *(B & B)*   *Castle Inn*

Near Okehampton · *Devon* · Map 8 B4
Lydford (082 282) 242

Free House
Landlords Mr & Mrs S. B. Reed

BEDROOMS 7   Grade 2   £C
🍺 Bass; St Austell Tinner's Ale; Ben
Truman; Guinness; Carlsberg; cider. *Real ale*

This charming old village pub enjoys a
delightful setting next to the ancient castle
and just a short walk from the dramatic
Lydford Gorge. The low-beamed bars are
full of old-world appeal, with open fires, oil
lamps, Victorian pictures and a fine collection of old plates. Comfortably furnished
bedrooms, all with washbasins, share two
well-equipped bathrooms. No under-tens
overnight. Garden.   **Family pub**

Lympstone   (Food)
Globe Inn

Near Exmouth · Devon · Map 8 C4
Exmouth (0395) 263166

Brewery Heavitree
Landlords Mr & Mrs Smith

Mixed seafood salad £3.95 Fresh salmon
sandwich £1 (Last order 10.15pm)
🍺 Flowers Original; Bass; Whitbread Best
Bitter; Worthington 'E'; Guinness; Taunton
cider. *Real ale*

Fishing nets on the walls and a tempting
display of incomparably fresh seafood set
the tone in this popular harbourside pub.
Superb fresh salmon, lobster, succulent
king prawns and excellent dressed crab are
used for salads and sandwiches, while
meat-lovers can tuck into cold joints, pies
and pasties. There are also hot dishes in
winter, and gorgeous sweets like fruity
apple tart and butterscotch crunch come
topped with rich clotted cream.

Lynton   (B & B)
Crown Hotel

Sinai Hill · Devon · Map 8 C3
Lynton (059 85) 2253

Free House
Landlords Alan & Thelma Westgarth

BEDROOMS 16   Grade 1   £A
🍺 Bass; Whitbread Best Bitter, Trophy;
Flowers IPA; Carling Black Label; Foster's;
cider. *Real ale*

Housekeeping and maintenance are both
first-class at this 200-year-old former
coaching inn, whose lofty situation affords
lovely views of both sea and countryside.
First-class bedrooms are comfortable and
well equipped, with sturdy traditional furnishings, TVs, radio-alarms, tea-makers
and carpeted bathrooms. Five boast fully
draped four-posters, and there are three
family suites. Residents' lounge. Accommodation closed January.   **Family pub**

Lyonshall   (Food, B & B)
Royal George Inn

Near Kington · Hereford & Worcester · Map 7 D1
Lyonshall (054 48) 210

Brewery Whitbread
Landlord Mr John Allen

BEDROOMS 3   Grade 2   £C   (No dogs)
Lamb goulash £3.75 Cypriot curry £2.75 (Last
order 10pm)
🍺 Flower's Original, IPA; Guinness;
Heineken; Stella Artois; cider. *Real ale*

Landlord John Allen bids visitors a warm
welcome to this pleasant old whitewashed
inn, where good food and homely accommodation are the order of the day. The bar
snacks are tasty and satisfying, from vegetable soup and king-size sausages to
gammon steak and really splendid
moussaka. Three neatly kept bedrooms with
TVs and tea-makers share a modern shower
room. Garden.

Madingley   (Food)
Three Horseshoes

Cambridge · Cambridgeshire · Map 5 C2
Madingley (0954) 210221

Brewery Tollemache & Cobbold
Landlord Mr Iain Twinn

Turkey & mushroom pie £3.75 Chocolate
mousse £1.25 (Last order 10pm)
🍺 Tolly Cobbold Original, Bitter; Hansa
Lager; Taunton cider.

Food is a major attraction at this splendidly
run thatched pub, where a blackboard lists
the day's offerings in the smart beamed
bar. Salad cocktails served in large glass
bowls are a very popular feature, and hot
items include tasty soups, savoury pies and
grilled steaks. Avocado and fresh mint
cheesecake is one of several deliciously
different sweets. Garden.   **Family pub**

England

Maidensgrove (Food) ★ *Five Horseshoes*

Near Henley · *Oxfordshire* · Map 6 B3
Nettlebed (0491) 641282

Brewery Brakspear
Landlords Colin & Hazel Funnell
Beef fillet in green peppercorn sauce £3.90
Chicken Kiev £3.90 (Last order 10pm. No bar
food Sun eve in winter)
🍺 Brakspear's Ordinary Bitter, Special
Bitter; Guinness; Heineken; cider. *Real ale*

As the name suggests, your luck is really in
when you visit this cosy red-built pub,
where Colin Funnell is the genial host, his
wife Hazel the talented chef. Her repertoire
ranges from soups and pâtés to chicken
Kiev, nutty pork casserole and tender slices
of beef in a creamy green peppercorn
sauce. Ploughman's and jacket potatoes for
quick snacks, home-made ice cream to
finish. Garden.

Malham (B & B) *Buck Inn*

Near Skipton · *North Yorkshire* · Map 4 C2
Airton (072 93) 317

Free House
Landlord Ruth Robinson

BEDROOMS 10 Grade 2 £B
🍺 Theakston's Bitter, XB, Old Peculier;
Younger's Bitter; Guinness; Kestrel; Harp;
Taunton cider. *Real ale*

Popular with walkers and motorists alike,
this sturdy old stone-built inn enjoys a setting of great beauty among the lovely
Yorkshire Dales. The two bars are both
characterful and convivial, and residents
have a cosy little TV room. There are some
fine old furnishings in the bedrooms, four
of which are family size. Two rooms have
good showers.   **Family pub**

Malmesbury (Food) *Suffolk Arms*

Tetbury Hill · *Wiltshire* · Map 7 D2
Malmesbury (066 62) 2771

Free House
Landlords Mr & Mrs C. Johnson
Steak, kidney & mushroom pie with vegetables
£2.50 Cottage pie with vegetables £1.70 (Last
order 9.45pm. No bar food Sun eve)
🍺 Wadworth's 6X, IPA; Archer's Village
Bitter; Ben Truman; Guinness; Carlsberg
Pilsner. *Real ale*

The rustic lounge bar of this handsome ivy-
clad inn on the Tetbury road is a popular
spot for a drink and a simple, tasty bar
snack. The choice includes soup, pâté,
sandwiches, local sausages with jacket
potatoes, plus a few daily specials like steak
and kidney pie, venison pie or seafood
pancakes. Mousses and flans are typical
delicious sweets.   **Family pub**

Malton (Food) *Green Man Hotel*

Market Street · *North Yorkshire* · Map 4 D2
Malton (0653) 2662

Free House
Landlord Mrs J. Tate-Smith

Hot carvery & vegetables £3.05 Steak & kidney
pie £2.15 (Last order 10pm)
🍺 Tetley's Bitter; Younger's Scotch Bitter;
Cameron's Lion Bitter; Guinness; Skol;
Carlsberg Hof; cider. *Real ale*

Several generations of Tate-Smiths have
run this agreeable white-shuttered pub
near the market square. Bar snacks are a
popular feature, and the lunchtime cold
buffet with appetising quiches and cooked
joints is much in demand. There's also
plenty of hot choice, from Yorkshire pudding with onion gravy to a daily roast.
Pleasant sweets, too. Grills, sandwiches
and things like lasagne in the evening.
                              Family pub

Bring out the Branston.
Bring out the best.

Branston,* the original sweet pickle, has been Britain's favourite since it was first produced over 60 years ago – and is still made with the same care and in the same traditional manner. There are those who try to imitate it – but there is only one **Branston** Pickle.

So ask for it by name when you next have a pub lunch.

<u>You</u> and Crosse & Blackwell make tastier meals.

Branston is a registered trade mark.

BEJAM BM 603 MICROWAVE COOKER

DISCOVER THE 4 MINUTE MEAL.

Discover the speed and efficiency of today's microwaves at Bejam.

Discover how perfectly a microwave complements your freezer.

Bejam have one of the best selections anywhere.

And some of the best prices.

With all the specialist help and advice you need to make the right choice.

DISCOVER

Bejam

THE WORLD OF FROZEN FOOD

Malvern *(Food)* — *Foley Arms Hotel*

Worcester Road · *Hereford & Worcester*
Map 7 D1
Malvern (068 45) 3397

Free House
Landlords Mr N. Ivanzo

Foley special £1.95 Self-service buffet £2.40
(Last order 8.30pm. No bar food Sun)
 Bass; Marston's Pedigree; Guinness;
Carlsberg; Tennent's Extra. *Real ale*

Excellent snacks are served in the bar of
this handsome coaching inn, which enjoys
splendid views of the Severn Valley. The
Foley special – a steak sandwich served
with salad or chips – is a great favourite,
and other choices include soup, casseroles
and local salmon. The self-service buffet is
popular at lunchtime. Terrace. *For accommodation see Egon Ronay's Lucas Hotel &
Restaurant Guide 1985.* **Family pub**

Malvern *(Food, B & B)* — *Mount Pleasant Hotel*

Bellevue Terrace · *Hereford & Worcester*
Map 7 D1
Malvern (068 45) 61837
Free House
Landlord Mr & Mrs R. J. Downing
BEDROOMS 8 Grade 1 £A (No dogs)
Rabbit & gooseberry pie £3.20 Vegetable
macaroni & cheese £1.65 (Last order 9pm)
 Marston Pedigree; Albion Bitter; Burton
Bitter; Hook Norton Bitter; Guinness;
Stella Artois; cider. *Real ale*

Wholesome, well-prepared bar snacks are
appreciated by locals and tourists alike at
this friendly hotel overlooking the priory.
The choice is wide, from flavoursome
chicken liver pâté to scampi, beef curry and
a spirited chocolate and rum mousse.
Antiques abound in the bar, lounges and
very comfortable bedrooms, which have
TVs and well-appointed bathrooms. No
children under 10 overnight. Closed 1 week
Christmas. Patio.

Prices given are as at the time

of our research and are

comparative indications rather

than firm quotes.

Mamble *(Food)* — *Sun & Slipper*

Near Kidderminster · *Hereford & Worcester*
Map 7 D1
Bewdley (0299) 22307

Free House
Landlord Mr P. Fort
Stuffed mushrooms £1.40 Whole plaice £2.35
(Last order 10pm)
 Banks's Bitter; Mitchells & Butlers Bitter;
Holdens; Wadworth's Old Original; Guinness;
Tuborg; cider. *Real ale*

French landlord Philippe Fort offers a
tempting choice of well-prepared bar fare
at his tall, white-painted Victorian pub.
Everything is home-made, from deliciously
rich beef and vegetable soup and well-
seasoned meat pâté to sausages, stuffed
aubergines and a particularly good
lasagne. Other choices range from filled
rolls to trout, sirloin steak and chilli con
carne. Garden. **Family pub**

Manaccan *(Food)*   *New Inn*

Near Helston · *Cornwall* · Map 8 A4
Manaccan (032 623) 323

Free House
Landlord Mr Patrick Cullinan

Steak & kidney pie £3.50 Fresh local
salmon £5.50 (Last order 9.30pm. No bar food
Tues eve)
🍺 Devenish Cornish Bitter, John Devenish
Bitter; Guinness; Grünhalle. *Real ale*

Set in one of the loveliest parts of Cornwall,
this fine old country pub serves excellent
food in civilised, convivial surroundings.
Everything is home-cooked, from soup
with a real taste of the stock pot to fish
quenelles, first-rate steak and kidney pie
and lamb cutlets in a mint and orange
sauce. Sandwiches and salads for lighter
snacks, and a terrific treacle tart to finish.
Garden.   **Family pub**

Manchester *(Food)*   *Sinclairs*

Shambles Square · *Greater Manchester*
Map 3 B3
061-834 0430

Brewery Samuel Smith
Landlords Peter & Jean Wild

Seafood platter £2 Beef & oyster pie £2.50
(No bar food eves)
🍺 Sam Smith's Old Brewery Bitter, 4X Mild;
Ayinger Bräu; cider. *Real ale*

Oysters are a popular feature of the lunchtime snacks at this fine old half-timbered
inn, served either fresh on the half shell
or gently cooked in the excellent beef and
oyster pie. There's also a tempting display
of other seafood, cold meats and salads,
along with a regularly changing selection
of hot specials. Upstairs is a soup and
sandwich bar. Sandwiches are the only
snacks available on Sundays. Patio.

Marhamchurch *(B & B)*   *Bullers Arms*

Near Bude · *Cornwall* · Map 8 B3
Widemouth Bay (028 885) 277

Free House
Landlords Mr & Mrs Kneebone

BEDROOMS 7 Grade 1 £C
🍺 St Austell Tinner's Ale, Hick's Special
Draught; Whitbread Best Bitter; Worthington
Best Bitter; Guinness; Carlsberg; cider.
Real ale

Bill Kneebone offers very comfortable
accommodation for tourists and travellers
in this peacefully situated village pub.
Spacious bedrooms, which are furnished in
simple modern style, have TVs and spotlessly clean bathrooms. Five suites have
kitchen/dining/lounge areas. Most drinkers
choose to relax in the popular beamed
Hunter's Bar; the other bar is smaller and
more intimate. Garden.   **Family pub**

Mark Cross *(Food)*   *Mark Cross Inn*

East Sussex · Map 6 C3
Rotherfield (089 285) 2423

Brewery Whitbread
Landlord Mr Martin Roberts

Plate of prawns £1.20 Beef & mushroom
casserole £1.90 (Last order 10pm)
🍺 Fremlins Bitter, Tusker; Whitbread Best
Bitter; Guinness; Stella Artois; Heineken;
cider. *Real ale*

Meals are served from the smart tiled
counter of the comfortable bar at this large
pub with a garden. You can choose from
eight sorts of ploughman's and there's
also an ample selection of cold meat and
seafood salads. Hot dishes include rich,
satisfying farmhouse soup, beef and mushroom casserole, tasty turkey pie – even a
vegetarian dish of the day.   **Family pub**

Market Drayton   *(B & B)*   *Corbet Arms Hotel*

High Street · *Shropshire* · Map 3 B4
Market Drayton (0630) 2037

Free House
Landlords Mr & Mrs John Beckett

BEDROOMS 10   Grade 1   £B
🍺 Mitchells & Butlers Springfield Bitter,
Mild; Stones Bitter; Guinness; Carling Black
Label; Tennent's Pilsner; Taunton cider.
Real ale

Much of Market Drayton's social life is
centred on this creeper-clad coaching inn,
whose attractions include a splendid bowling green. Open-plan bars offer abundant
space for exercising elbows, and there's a
restful residents' lounge. Bedrooms, too,
are large and comfortable, with practical
modern furnishings, colour TVs and well-
appointed bathrooms. Bachelors speak
warmly of the amorous lady ghost that
haunts room 7. Good breakfasts. **Family pub**

Market Weighton   *(B & B)*   *Londesborough Arms*

High Street · *Humberside* · Map 4 D3
Market Weighton (0696) 72219

Brewery North Country Breweries
Landlords Mr & Mrs Cuckston

BEDROOMS 14   Grade 1   £B
🍺 North Country Riding Bitter, Old Tradition,
Mild; Hopfenperle; Stella Artois. *Real ale*

Located in the town centre, this handsome
Georgian hotel has a classical red-brick
facade and a white-painted portico. There
are two comfortable bars, one of them
named after a celebrated 18th-century
giant, William Bradley (you can still see his
chair). Potted plants add a homely touch to
the spacious bedrooms, which have
modern built-in units, colur TVs and neat,
compact bathrooms.   **Family pub**

Marlow   *(Food)*   *Hare & Hounds*

Henley Road · *Buckinghamshire* · Map 6 B3
Marlow (062 84) 3343

Brewery Whitbread
Landlords Mr & Mrs Gladman

Seafood crumble £1.85 Beef & duck pie £1.95
(No bar food eves or Sun lunch)
🍺 Wethered's Bitter, SPA; Guinness; Stella
Artois; Heineken; cider. *Real ale*

This delightful creeper-clad pub is as pretty
as a picture, and inside there are two cosy
beamed bars where you can enjoy a delicious snack in convivial surroundings. The
menu is full of interesting and tempting
fare, ranging from creamy chilled summer
soup and a 'breakfast' sandwich to terrine
with apricot relish, moussaka and chicken
curry. You can also get a straightforward
ploughman's.

Marsh Gibbon   *(Food)*   *Greyhound Inn*

Near Bicester · *Oxfordshire* · Map 5 B2
Stratton Audley (086 97) 365

Free House
Landlords Sylvia & Henry Phillips

Venison pie £2.25 Steak & kidney pie £2
(Last order 9pm. No bar food Sat eve)
🍺 Phillips Heritage, Allric's Old Ale;
Newcastle Bitter; Kestrel; cider. *Real ale*

Marvellous atmosphere and real ale
brewed on the premises are just two of the
many good things about this fine, spotlessly kept pub. Excellent bar food is
another, including home-roasted meats,
beautifully baked pies, full-flavoured pâtés
and splendid seasonal game. Fresh herbs
feature in many dishes, and you can finish
your meal with some prime English
cheeses. Closed Monday lunchtime. Patio.
                                                Family pub

Marshside *(Food)*   *Gate Inn*

Near Canterbury · *Kent* · Map 6 D3
Chislet (022 786) 498

Brewery Shepherd Neame
Landlord Christopher John Smith

Gateburger in wholemeal bread 75p Black
pudding ploughman's £1.10 (Last order
10.15pm. No bar food Sun lunch)
🍺 Shepherd Neame Best Bitter, Masterbrew,
Mild, Stock Ale; Taunton cider. *Real ale*

Nothing could be simpler or more delightful than this super village pub with its
enthusiastic landlord, lovely rose garden,
fine locally brewed beer and no-nonsense
food. In the beamed bar you can tuck into
an excellent home-made hamburger
(served in a bap or delicious wholemeal
bread) or choose a hearty sandwich of
bacon, sausage, cheese or black pudding.
And in winter you can enjoy a bowl of soup
before the roaring fire.   **Family pub**

Mayfield *(Food)*   *Rose & Crown*

Fletching Street · *East Sussex* · Map 6 C4
Mayfield (0435) 872200

Free House
Landlords Richard & Claudette Leet
Seafood pancake £1.55 Chicken curry
mayonnaise £1.65 (Last order 9.45pm.
No bar food Mon eve & all Sun)
🍺 Everards Old Original, Tiger; Adnams
Best Bitter; Guinness; Tennent's Extra; cider.
Real ale

Low beamed ceilings, log fires and sturdy
old furniture create an atmosphere of
mellow charm at this long, white-painted
pub that was once a brewhouse. A blackboard announces the day's bar snacks,
which range from soup to sirloin steak by
way of savoury cheese slice, whitebait and
smoked chicken with orange. There are
salads in summer, when you can enjoy
them outside in the garden.

Mellor *(B & B)*   *Millstone Hotel*

Church Lane, Near Blackburn · *Lancashire*
Map 3 B3
Mellor (0254 81) 3333

Brewery Shire Inns
Landlord Mr A. Simmons

BEDROOMS 16   Grade 1   £A+
🍺 Thwaites Bitter, Mild; Guinness; Stein
Lager. *Real ale*

Just a short drive from junction 31 of the
M6, this pleasantly modernised hotel is
popular with both businessmen and
holiday-makers. Light oak is much in
evidence in the open-plan lounge and bar
and the dining room, where splendid
breakfasts are served. Compact, well-
furnished bedrooms are equipped with tea-
makers, trouser presses and direct-dial
telephones. Patio.   **Family pub**

Melmerby *(Food)*   *Shepherds Inn*

Near Penrith · *Cumbria* · Map 3 B1
Langwathby (076 881) 217

Brewery Marston
Landlords Martin & Christine Baucutt

Fillet of pork Thai style £3.20 Cumberland
sausage hot pot £2.70 (Last order 9.45pm)
🍺 Marston's Pedigree; Ind Coope Burton
Bitter; Mercian Mild; Marston's Pilsner; cider.
Real ale

Home-prepared bar meals attract a loyal
following at this pleasant village inn, where
Martin Baucutt also keeps a good selection
of real ales. Standard fare like ploughman's,
scampi and steak are supplemented by
specialities such as baked rainbow trout and
flavoursome pork and mushrooms Thai
style. Delicious sweets, too, including
apricot and almond gâteau. A roast joint is
the main Sunday lunchtime offering. Patio.

Mentmore *(Food)* — *Stag Inn*

Near Leighton Buzzard, Bedfordshire
Buckinghamshire · Map 5 B2
Cheddington (0296) 668 423

Brewery Wells
Landlords Michel & Helen Rigal
Steak pie £2.25 Scampi with chips £2.50
(Last order 10pm. No bar food Sun lunch or
Sat eve)
🍺 Wells Bitter, Noggin; Guinness; Red
Stripe; Kellerbräu; cider. *Real ale*

Whether it's a sandwich or a generous
helping of roast lamb, you can be sure that
your chosen dish will be carefully prepared
from good fresh ingredients at this friendly
hilltop pub. The French onion soup is the
real McCoy – dark, rich and full of flavour –
and there's also quiche, cold meats, salads
and simple sweets. Garden.

Mere *(B & B)* — *Old Ship Hotel*

Castle Street · *Wiltshire* · Map 8 D3
Mere (0747) 860258

Brewery Hall & Woodhouse
Landlord Mr Philip Johnson

BEDROOMS 24   Grades 1 & 2   £A
🍺 Hall & Woodhouse Badger Best Bitter,
Malthouse; Worthington Dark; Guinness;
Brock; Stella Artois; Taunton cider. *Real ale*

Period charm and up-to-date comfort
combine happily at this sturdy 17th-century
coaching inn. The oak-panelled hotel bar is
cosy and intimate, and the lounge bar, with
its stone walls and splendid open fireplace,
has a pleasantly rustic character. Bedrooms in the main building are also traditional in style, while annexe rooms with
private bathrooms are smartly modern; all
have tea-makers and TVs. Enjoyable
breakfasts. **Family pub**

Metal Bridge *(B & B)* — *Metal Bridge Inn*

Near Gretna · *Cumbria* · Map 3 B1
Rockcliffe (022 874) 206

Brewery Younger
Landlord Mr D. O'Brien

BEDROOMS 5   Grade 1   £C
🍺 Younger's IPA, Tartan, Scotch Bitter;
McEwan's Export, Lager; Kestrel. *Real ale*

Motorists travelling between England and
Scotland can pull in at this white-painted
pub just off the A74 for a pleasant overnight
stay. Spacious, spotlessly clean bedrooms
with smart fitted units, TVs and tea-makers
are double-glazed to keep out the winds
and the traffic noise. Public bathrooms are
functional. Visitors can enjoy a drink in the
bar decorated with fishing prints or enjoy
the views of the river Esk from the patio or
the attractive conservatory. **Family pub**

Metherell *(B & B)* — *Carpenters Arms*

Near Callington · *Cornwall* · Map 8 B4
St Dominick (0579) 50242

Free House
Landlords Douglas & Jill Brace

BEDROOMS 3   Grade 2   £C
🍺 Bass; Flower's Original; Guinness;
Tennent's Pilsner; Heineken; cider. *Real ale*

The 15th and 20th centuries come together
at this delightful old inn, which is tucked
away just south of the A390 Gunnislake–
Liskeard road. Flagstone floors, rough-
hewn walls and black beams create a
splendid old-world atmosphere in the bars,
while the three bedrooms have a simple
modern appeal. Neat and tidy, they have
tea-makers and share a spacious shower
room. Terrace. **Family pub**

Mickleton   *(Food)*   *Butchers Arms*

Near Chipping Camden · *Gloucestershire*
Map 5 A2
Mickleton (038 677) 285

Brewery Whitbread
Landlords Alan & Judy Strong
Ploughman's £1.65 Cotswold chicken
casserole £2.70 (Last order 9.45pm. No bar
food Sun eve)
🍺 Flowers IPA, Original Bitter, Best Bitter;
Heineken; Stella Artois; cider. *Real ale*

Alan and Judy Strong take good care of this
cosy little pub with its collection of antique
weapons and military prints. Relax in the
bar and enjoy some hearty, wholesome
dishes like tasty chicken casserole in cider,
beef pie or ragout of venison. Light eaters
have a choice of sandwiches, salads and
ploughman's, and you can finish with
homely apple pie and whipped cream.
Patio.

Middle Assendon   *(Food)*   *Rainbow Inn*

Near Henley-on-Thames · *Oxfordshire*
Map 6 B3
Henley-on-Thames (0491) 574879

Brewery Brakspear
Landlords Nick & Mary Carter

Herby beef casserole £2.60 Spicy lamb hot
pot £2.30
🍺 Brakspear's Bitter, Special, Mild, Old Ale
(winter only); Guinness; Heineken. *Real ale*

There's a thriving darts team at this friendly
country pub, where Nick Carter is the jovial
landlord and his wife Mary the capable
chef. She hits the target every time with her
simple, satisfying and flavoursome bar
food, from salads and sandwiches to
quiches, curries, hot pots and roasts – and
her excellent fruit pies provide a splendid
finish. Sandwiches only in the evening &
restricted choice Sunday lunch. Garden.

Middleham   *(B & B)*   *Black Swan Hotel*

Market Place · *North Yorkshire* · Map 4 C2
Wensleydale (0969) 22221

Free House
Landlords Mr & Mrs K. B. Burton

BEDROOMS 3   Grade 2   £C
🍺 Theakston's Best Bitter, Old Peculier;
John Smith's Best Bitter, Magnet; Carlsberg;
Guinness; Taunton cider. *Real ale*

This delightful old inn makes an ideal base
from which to explore the beauty of the
Yorkshire Dales. You can while away the
hours in the beamed bar while enjoying a
pint and listening to the local tales. There's
also a beer garden. Very pretty, tastefully
decorated bedrooms are furnished in
modest style and equipped with TVs and
washbasins; one room at the top of the pub
has its own spacious bathroom. Superb
breakfasts.   **Family pub**

Midhurst   *(B & B)*   *Angel Hotel*

North Street · *West Sussex* · Map 6 B4
Midhurst (073 081) 2421

Brewery Gale
Landlord Mr N. Gibson

BEDROOMS 18   Grade 2   £B
🍺 Gale's HSB, BBB; Guinness; Carlsberg.
Real ale

The Pilgrim Fathers reputedly stayed at this
handsome old inn, and today's visitors will
find a wealth of period charm, with ships'
timbers and fine panelling much in evidence. Bedrooms, all with TVs and tea-
makers, are a mixture of old and modern,
and there are two bars and a large, comfortable residents' lounge – once the local court
room. Pretty rose garden.   **Family pub**

Mildenhall *(B & B)*   *Bell Hotel*

High Street · *Suffolk* · Map 5 C2
Mildenhall (0638) 712134

Free House
Landlords Carolyn & John Child

BEDROOMS 18   Grades 1 & 2   £A
🍺 Younger's IPA; Newcastle Bitter;
McEwan's IPA; Adnams Bitter; Guinness;
Carlsberg; Taunton cider. *Real ale*

There's a warm, friendly feel about this fine
old inn opposite the church. A beamed
foyer-lounge greets visitors, and the large
bar area, warmed by open fires, is well
filled with comfortable armchairs. Spotlessly maintained bedrooms have good
modern furnishings, tea-makers and colour
televisions; most of them have bath or
shower rooms with plentiful supplies of
towels. Patio.   **Family pub**

Millthorpe   *(Food)*   *Royal Oak*

Holmsfield, Near Sheffield · *Derbyshire*
Map 4 C3
Sheffield (0742) 890870

Free House
Landlords Mr & Mrs Wills
Lasagne £1.50 Brie ploughman's £1.80 (Last
order 9pm. No bar food Thurs–Sun eves)
🍺 Ward's Sheffield Bitter; Darley's Thorne
Bitter; Guinness; Carlsberg; Norseman;
Taunton cider. *Real ale*

The locals who crowd the main panelled
bar of this attractive stone-built pub will
testify to the excellence of the ploughman's
lunches – great wedges of English cheese
with a generous salad garnish. Equally
tasty are the sandwiches – perhaps fresh
crab – fluffy omelettes and winter-warmers
like cottage or fisherman's pie. Apple and
raisin pie is popular too. Sandwiches only
Sunday lunch. Steak and baked potatoes
provide further evening choice.

Milton Abbas   *(Food, B & B)*   *Hambro Arms*

Near Blandford Forum · *Dorset* · Map 8 D3
Milton Abbas (0258) 880233

Brewery Devenish
Landlords John & Judy Dance
BEDROOMS 2   Grade 1   £C
Venison in red wine sauce £3.75 Goulash &
wild rice £2.65 (Last order 9.30pm)
🍺 Devenish Wessex Best Bitter, Ordinary
Bitter, John Groves Bitter; Guinness;
Heineken; Grünhalle; cider. *Real ale*

A friendly atmosphere prevails in this rustic
thatched pub, where Judy Dance delights
customers with her varied choice of delicious food. In summer the main attraction
is a hot and cold lunchtime buffet, while at
other times you can have classic stews, hot
pots and pies, as well as things like creamy
mushroom soup, haddock and cheese pancakes and curries. Comfortable bedrooms
have pretty fabrics, tea-makers and shower
cubicles.   **Family pub**

Milton Combe   *(Food)*   *Who'd Have Thought It*

Yelverton · *Devon* · Map 8 B4
Yelverton (0822) 853313

Free House
Landlords Gary Rager & Keith Yeo

Beef pasty 90p Roast beef salad £2.60
(Last order 9.45pm)
🍺 Usher's Best Bitter; Wadworth's 6X;
Golden Hill Exmoor Ale; Palmer's IPA;
Guinness; Heineken; cider. *Real ale*

Nestling at the bottom of a valley in the
heart of Dartmoor, this 16th-century village
pub is a friendly place to enjoy some homely
food in pleasant surroundings. As well as
monster ploughman's and salad platters,
you can feast on nourishing vegetable soup
or – if you're lucky – one of the famous
home-made pasties. There are also daily hot
dishes like tasty cottage pie or chicken and
bacon pie. Less choice Sunday lunch.
Garden.

199

Minster Lovell *(Food, B & B)*　　　　　*Old Swan Hotel*

Near Witney · *Oxfordshire* · Map 5 A2
Minster Lovell (0993) 75614

Brewery Halls
Landlords Mr & Mrs Tim Turner

BEDROOMS 10 Grade 1 £A+ (No dogs)
Cotswold ploughman's £1.60 Chicken pie £2
(No bar food eves or Sun)
🍺 Halls Harvest Bitter; Ind Coope Burton
Ale; Löwenbräu. *Real ale*

Take the Old Minster turning off the B4070
Witney to Burford road to find this marvellous 600-year old inn. Warmed by log fires
in the flagstone-floored bar you can enjoy
tasty lunchtime snacks ranging from
sandwiches and pâté to salads and specials
like chicken and mushroom pie. Comfortable, well-equipped bedrooms have TVs
and excellent private bathrooms. No
children overnight. **Family pub**

Modbury *(Food, B & B)*　　　　　　　*Exeter Inn*

Church Street · *Devon* · Map 8 C4
Modbury (0548) 830239
Brewery Usher
Landlord Mr James Mogg
BEDROOMS 2 Grade 1 £C (No dogs)
Scallops & bacon in mushroom & cream
sauce £2.95 Spanish chicken £5.50 (Last
order 9.45pm)
🍺 Usher's Best Bitter, Founder's Ale, Triple
Crown; Ben Truman; Guinness; Holsten
Export; Carlsberg; cider. *Real ale*

Present-day travellers are well cared for at
this fine old coaching inn. Friendly, hardworking landlord James Mogg offers an
excellent choice of imaginative food in the
large beamed bar – from stuffed baked
mushrooms to steak and Guinness
casserole or succulent scallop and prawn
kebabs. There are two comfortable bedrooms, the one boasting a four-poster and
huge bathroom with gold-plated fittings
being quite luxurious. **Family pub**

Molesworth *(Food, B & B)*　　　　　　*Cross Keys*

Huntingdon · *Cambridgeshire* · Map 5 B2
Bythorn (080 14) 283

Free House
Landlord Mrs Frances Bettsworth
BEDROOMS 4 Grade 2 £C
Moussaka £2.25 Rhubarb crumble 75p (Last
order 10.45pm)
🍺 Adnams Bitter; Stones Bitter; Younger's
Tartan; McEwan's Export; Guinness;
Carlsberg; cider. *Real ale*

Good breakfasts are a bonus of a stay at this
friendly, unpretentious pub, which offers
simple overnight accommodation. The
cosy bar is the setting for a local version of
skittles and for some homely cooking. Pride
of place on a menu of sandwiches, grills
and salads goes to a real old-fashioned
steak and kidney pie served with wholesome vegetables. Save room for some
rhubarb crumble or a wedge of lemon
meringue pie. **Family pub**

Monksilver *(Food, B & B)*　　　　　　*Notley Arms*

Near Taunton · *Somerset* · Map 8 C3
Stogumber (098 46) 217

Brewery Usher
Landlords Mike & Jill Robinson
BEDROOMS 3 Grade 2 £C
Hot roast beef in French bread £1.95 Beef
casserole £3.45 (Last order 9.30pm)
🍺 Usher's Best Bitter, Triple Crown; Country
Bitter; Guinness; Carlsberg; Taunton cider.
Real ale

A barbecue in the lovely garden is a summertime attraction of this welcoming pub:
Jill Robinson supplies diners with meat and
jacket potatoes, after which it's DIY. Her
lunchtime cold buffet is equally tempting,
and other treats include onion soup, hot
dishes like our steak and kidney pie,
floaters (French bread with grilled topping)
and delicious sweets. Neat little bedrooms
are traditionally furnished and beautifully
kept. No under-sevens overnight.

Montacute   *(Food, B & B)*   *Kings Arms Inn*

Bishopston · *Somerset* · Map 8 D3
Martock (0935) 822513

Free House
Landlords Mr & Mrs T. D. Hague
BEDROOMS 10   Grade 1   £A   (No dogs)
Pâté & salad £2.50 Curry & rice £2.30 (Last
order 10pm. No bar food Sun eve)
🍺 Bass, Toby, Worthington Best Bitter;
Ben Truman; Guinness; Carlsberg; Taunton
cider. *Real ale*

The Hagues extend a cordial welcome to
guests at their plushly converted 16th-
century inn, which offers excellent
accommodation. Attractively decorated
bedrooms have good fitted units. TVs, tea-
makers and carpeted modern bathrooms.
In the comfortable lounge bar the main
attraction at lunchtime is a cold buffet,
while at suppertime you can get things like
tasty soup, mildly spiced curry and pizza
with salad. Super sweets.   **Family pub**

Moreton-in-Marsh   *(B & B)*   *Redesdale Arms Hotel*

High Street · *Gloucestershire* · Map 5 A2
Moreton-in-Marsh (0608) 50308

Free House
Landlord Mr G. R. Jewell

BEDROOMS 14   Grades 1 & 2   £A
🍺 Bass; Worthington Best Bitter; Guinness;
Tennent's Extra; Carling Black Label; Taunton
cider. *Real ale*

This is an attractive 18th-century inn of
mellow sandstone. The cottage, panelled
bar is a pleasant place for a drink, and
there's a patio for nice weather. Comfortable, well-maintained bedrooms (including
some in the annexe) have good-quality
furniture and carpeting, colour TVs and
trouser presses; bathrooms are modern
and fully tiled. Friendly staff add to the
pleasure of a stay here.   **Family pub**

Moretonhampstead   *(B & B)*   *White Hart Hotel*

The Square · *Devon* · Map 8 C3
Moretonhampstead (0647) 40406

Free House
Landlord Mr Peter Morgan

BEDROOMS 16   Grades 1 & 2   £B
🍺 Bass; Ansells Bitter; Tetley's Bitter;
Whitbread Trophy; Guinness; Skol; Carlsberg
Export; cider. *Real ale*

Once a posting house on the Plymouth–
London mail route, this pleasant, well-kept
Georgian inn retains much period charm.
The beamed public bar is a cosy, friendly
meeting place, and there's a relaxing
lounge bar. Centrally heated bedrooms (all
with TVs, tea-makers and extras like hairdryers) vary in size and style; most have
good modern bathrooms. No under-tens
overnight. Patio.   **Family pub**

Morval   *(B & B)*   *Snooty Fox Hotel*

Near Looe · *Cornwall* · Map 8 B4
Widegates (050 34) 233

Free House
Landlord Mr D. S. Mutton

BEDROOMS 10   Grade 1   £A
🍺 Flower's Original; Whitbread Best Bitter;
McEwan's Export; Guinness; Stella Artois;
Heineken; cider. *Real ale*

Views of the lovely Cornish countryside are
a feature of this pleasant hotel, a popular
base for tourists. Bedrooms are of a
uniformly high standard, with good fitted
carpets, modern furnishings, tea-makers
and TVs. All have spotless, well-appointed
bathrooms. Public rooms have plenty to
offer: comfort in the spacious lounge bar,
conviviality in the games room, peace and
quiet in the cosy reading room. Garden.

England

Moulton *(Food)* ★ *Black Bull Inn*

Near Richmond · *North Yorkshire* · Map 4 C2
Barton (032 577) 289

Free House
Landlords Mr & Mrs Pagendam

Welsh rarebit £1.50 Cottage cheese, prawns &
salad £2.50 (No bar food eves or Sun)
🍺 Theakston's Best Bitter, Old Peculier;
Black Bull Bitter; Carlsberg. *Real ale*

At lunchtime visitors from far and wide are
drawn to this simple roadside pub by the
excellent snacks served in the charming bar.
You might tuck into tasty French onion
soup, a first-rate rough terrine finely
flavoured with herbs or a sandwich with a
mouthwatering filling like smoked salmon.
A few luscious sweets – the huge brandy
snaps bursting with cream are famous – and
superb cheeses, including local Swaledale.
Closed 1 week Christmas.

Murcott *(Food)* *Nut Tree Inn*

Near Islip · *Oxfordshire* · Map 5 B2
Charlton-on-Otmoor (086 733) 253

Free House
Landlords Gordon & Diane Evans
Fish with potatoes & salad £3.50 Rump steak
with chips & salad £6.50 (Last order 9pm.
No bar food Sun)
🍺 Wadworth's 6X; Ind Coope Burton Ale;
Hall's Harvest Bitter; Guinness; Skol;
Löwenbräu; cider. *Real ale*

Gordon Evans runs a particularly friendly
ship at this delightful old thatched inn,
circulating among his customers in the
cosy beamed bar. His wife Diane, who
looks after culinary matters, produces a
good range of tasty bar snacks – from cold
meats, salads and sandwiches to basket
meals, local trout and game and a first-rate
beef curry. To finish, nice home-made
sweets and a varied cheeseboard. Garden.

Nailsworth *(Food)* *Tipputs Inn*

Bath Road · *Gloucestershire* · Map 7 D2
Nailsworth (045 383) 2466

Free House
Landlords Mr & Mrs S. Whitebread

Roast gammon £3.75 Beef curry £2.75
(Last order 10.15pm)
🍺 Hook Norton Best Bitter; Robinson's Best
Bitter; Ruddles County; Newcastle Bitter;
Guinness; Carlsberg; Taunton cider. *Real ale*

This attractive stone pub south of town has
a plush, nicely furnished bar as well as both
patio and garden for alfresco snacks. The
bar menu is varied: ploughman's with your
choice from six cheeses, smooth chicken
liver pâté, open baps, hot snacks such as
Tipputs Brunch (2 jumbo sausages, fried
egg and chips, served with salad) or substantial dishes like curry, chicken pie, baked
trout and roast gammon.   **Family pub**

Nantwich *(Food, B & B)* *Lamb*

Hospital Street · *Cheshire* · Map 3 B4
Nantwich (0270) 625286

Brewery Greenall Whitley
Landlords Mr & Mrs R. Jones

BEDROOMS 16 Grades 1 & 2 £B
Ravioli pinocchio £1.95 Chicken
casserole £1.95 (Last order 10pm)
🍺 Greenall Whitley Bitter, Mild; Guinness;
Grünhalle Lager; cider. *Real ale*

Bar snacks served at this comfortable old
coaching inn range from plain and toasted
sandwiches to full-flavoured chicken liver
pâté, shepherd's pie and ravioli with a
peppy sauce made with fresh tomatoes.
There are also puddings at lunchtime; only
sandwiches on Sunday. Spacious bedrooms have mostly sturdy freestanding
furniture; eight have private facilities.
Courtyard.

Nassington   *(Food)*
Black Horse Inn

Near Peterborough, Cambridgeshire
Northamptonshire · Map 5 B1
Stamford (0780) 782324
Free House
Landlord Mr Tom Guy
Seafood pancake £3.35 Stir-fried chicken with
shrimps & mushrooms £5.65
(Last order 10.15pm)
🍺 Greene King IPA; John Smith's Bitter;
Guinness; Harp; Kronenbourg; Taunton cider.
Real ale

Hungry travellers need make only a short
diversion from the Great North Road to
enjoy the excellent bar fare served at this
attractive old stone pub. The regular menu
offers anything from pâté and pasta to
game pie and pepper steak, while a blackboard proclaims fresh fish dishes and other
specials like our beautifully tasty beef in
beer. Super sweets, too. Summer cold
table. Garden. **Family pub**

Naunton   *(Food, B & B)*
Black Horse

Near Cheltenham · *Gloucestershire*
Map 5 A2
Guiting Power (045 15) 378

Brewery Donnington
Landlords Adrian & Jennie Bowen-Jones
BEDROOMS 3   Grade 2   £C   (No dogs)
Mixed meat ploughman's £1.50 Pork in cider
with chips £2.50 (Last order 9.30pm)
🍺 Donnington's SBA, BB; Carlsberg; cider.
Real ale

Adrian and Jennie Bowen-Jones – he
behind the bar, she in the kitchen – take
excellent care of visitors to their friendly
village pub. In the lounge bar you can enjoy
anything from a light snack such as egg
mayonnaise or rarebit to filling lasagne or a
juicy sirloin steak, and you should always
leave room for the super chocolate roulade.
For overnight guests (no children) there are
three homely bedrooms sharing a simple
modern bathroom. Patio.

Needham Market   *(Food, B & B)*
Limes Hotel

High Street · *Suffolk* · Map 5 D2
Needham Market (0449) 720305

Free House
Landlords Terry & Stephanie Watts
BEDROOMS 11   Grade 1   £A+
Steak pie & vegetables £2.50 Spare ribs with
sweet & sour sauce £2 (Last order 10pm)
🍺 Adnams Bitter; Tolly Cobbold Bitter;
Younger's Tartan; Guinness; Kestrel; Skol;
Taunton cider. *Real ale*

Spacious, well-equipped bedrooms (tea-
makers, TVs, telephones, spotless modern
bathrooms) provide first-rate comfort at
this pleasant Georgian-fronted inn.
Carefully prepared snacks on offer in the
smartly rustic Bugs Bar include sandwiches, ploughman's and chicken liver
pâté. There are also tasty daily hot dishes
such as braised liver and onions and
cottage pie, and a cold buffet brings further
weekday lunchtime choice. **Family pub**

Needingworth   *(B & B)*
Pike & Eel

Overcote Lane · *Cambridgeshire* · Map 5 C2
St Ives (0480) 63336

Free House
Landlord J. M. Stafferton

BEDROOMS 9   Grade 2   £B   (No dogs)
🍺 Greene King IPA, Abbot Ale; Adnams
Bitter; Bass; Guinness; Carling Black Label;
Harp; Kronenbourg; Taunton cider. *Real ale*

River-borne visitors can tie up at private
moorings outside this attractive old inn on
the Ouse. It's very popular with anglers as
well as boaters, and mounted fish form part
of the decor in the comfortable lounge bar.
Centrally heated bedrooms with practical
modern furniture and colour TVs provide
excellent overnight accommodation, and
there's a cosy lounge and writing room.
Garden. **Family pub**

England

Nettlecombe   (Food, B & B)   Marquis of Lorne

Near Bridport · *Dorset* · Map 8 D3
Powerstock (030 885) 236

Brewery Palmer
Landlords Bob & Philippa Bone

BEDROOMS 8   Grade 2   £B (No dogs)
Steak & kidney pie £2.25 Chocolate mousse
95p (Last order 10pm)
🍺 Palmer's IPA, Bridport Bitter; Guinness;
Shilthorn. *Real ale*

Ramblers and holiday-makers are drawn to
this friendly, stone-built pub. The menu in
the snug bar offers something for all tastes,
from sandwiches and salads (home-cooked
ham, juicy prawns) to basket meals and
delicious daily specials like rabbit, chicken
and corn pie or whole lobster salad. Lovely
puds, too. Simple, cheerful accommodation
includes four family rooms. There's a
residents' TV lounge, as well as a children's
playground in the garden.   **Family pub**

Newark   (B & B)   Robin Hood Hotel

Lombard Street · *Nottinghamshire* · Map 4 D4
Newark (0636) 703858

Owners Anchor Hotels Ltd
Landlord Diana Wildbur

BEDROOMS 20   Grade 1   £A+
🍺 John Courage Bitter; John Smith's Best
Bitter, Lager; Guinness.

Within striking distance of Sherwood
Forest and nearby industrial centres, this
17th-century coaching inn is a popular base
for tourists and business people. Spacious,
simply furnished bedrooms have fitted
units, tea-makers and colour TVs, plus
adequate private bathrooms. Downstairs
there are two bars – the plush Sheriff's,
which is medieval in style, and the Friar
Tuck, where children are welcome.
Family pub

Newbridge   (Food)   Maybush

Near Witney · *Oxfordshire* · Map 6 A3
Standlake (086 731) 624

Brewery Morland
Landlords Mr & Mrs J. Phillips
Seafood Thermidor £1.35 Toasted beef &
horseradish sandwich 80p (Last order 10pm.
No bar food Mon eve Oct–Feb)
🍺 Morland's Best Bitter, Bitter, Mild;
Whitbread Tankard; Guinness; Heineken;
cider. *Real ale*

A terrace and garden overlooking the
Thames are great summer attractions at
this well-kept pub. There or in the low-
ceilinged bar you can enjoy Mrs Phillips'
dependable home cooking. Favourite daily
specials like spaghetti bolognese or curry
(lunchtime only) are backed up by
omelettes, toasted sandwiches and
scampi, and her tempting sweets include
the popular apple turnover and banana
split.

Newcastle upon Tyne   (B & B)   Corner House

Heaton Road, Heaton · *Tyne & Wear*
Map 4 C1
Newcastle upon Tyne (0632) 659602

Brewery Scottish & Newcastle
Landlords Roland & Brenda Barnes

BEDROOMS 7   Grade 1   £C (No dogs)
🍺 McEwans 80/-; Younger's Scotch Bitter;
Scottish & Newcastle Exhibition, Newcastle
Bitter; Guinness; Taunton cider. *Real ale*

Situated by a busy roundabout on the
eastern outskirts of the city, this cheerful
pub provides good accommodation for the
traveller. Quiet bedrooms (all at the rear of
the building) have well-designed fitted
furniture, tea-makers and colour TVs. The
two public bathrooms are large and nicely
maintained. Downstairs, visitors will find
three spacious bars: a panelled snug bar, a
modernised lounge bar and a public bar
with games. Garden.

Newenden *(Food)*   White Hart

Kent · Map 6 C4
Northiam (079 74) 2166

Brewery Courage
Landlord Mr A. E. Faulkner

Shepherd's pie £1.50 Fishcakes & chips £1.25
(Last order 10pm)
🍺 Courage Best Bitter, Directors Bitter;
Guinness; Harp; Taunton cider. *Real ale*

Mrs Faulkner's excellent bar snacks draw
the crowds to this rustic weatherboarded
pub close by the Rother River. At lunchtime
the attraction is superb crab pâté, shepherd's pie, fishcakes and sweets such as
blackberry and apple pie, while in the evening there are more adventurous dishes
like delicious poached salmon with light,
lemony hollandaise, Rye scallops and
hefty, good-quality steaks. Sandwiches
and salads too. Garden.   **Family pub**

Newton *(Food)*   Queen's Head

Near Cambridge · *Cambridgeshire* · Map 5 C2
Cambridge (0223) 870436

Free House
Landlord D. M. V. Short

Soup 75p Sandwiches from 60p (Last
order 10.30pm)
🍺 Adnams Bitter, Old Ale (winter only);
Guinness; Tuborg Gold; cider. *Real ale*

Run by the Short family for over 20 years,
this ancient village pub oozes old-world
charm. A huge inglenook fireplace warms
the saloon bar, and fine old furniture is a
feature throughout. The snack menu
couldn't be simpler – mugs of nourishing
soup, baked potatoes (lunchtime only) and
super wholemeal bread with generous
fillings of cheese, smoked salmon and
excellent cooked meats.   **Family pub**

Newton *(Food)*   Red Lion Inn

Near Sleaford · *Lincolnshire* · Map 4 D4
Folkingham (052 97) 256
Free House
Landlords Mr & Mrs J. W. Power
Lincolnshire stuffed chine & salads £4
Coffee gâteau 80p (Last order 10pm. No bar
food Sun eve & all Mon, except Bank
Holidays)
🍺 Bateman's Bitter; Manns Triple Crown;
Whitbread Tankard; Guinness; Heineken;
Stella Artois; cider. *Real ale*

Arrive early, as the fame of the marvellous
cold buffet brings the crowds flocking to
the bar of this friendly stone-built pub near
the A52. Sugar-baked gammon, rare roast
beef, turkey, pâté and the outstanding
herb-stuffed chine of pork are served with a
selection of crisp, super-fresh salads. There
are also sandwiches, winter soups and a
delectable lemon meringue pie. Patio.
                                      Family pub

Newton *(B & B)*   Saracen's Head

Near Sudbury · *Suffolk* · Map 5 C2
Sudbury (0787) 79036

Brewery Tollemache & Cobbold
Landlords Mr & Mrs J. Eglin

BEDROOMS 3   Grade 2   £C (No dogs)
🍺 Tolly Cobbold Original, Bitter;
Guinness; Hansa. *Real ale*

The cordial Eglins put out the welcome mat
at their roadside public house. The bars
with their old oak beams and winter fires
are cosy and inviting, the public bar being a
popular local meeting place. Cheerfully
decorated bedrooms, all with tea-makers,
radios and plenty of wardrobe space, share
a well-maintained bathroom. Accommodation closed 1 week Christmas.
Garden.   **Family pub**

England

Newton-in-Bowland   *(Food, B & B)*   **Parkers Arms Hotel**

Near Clitheroe · *Lancashire* · Map 3 B3
Slaidburn (020 06) 236

Brewery Whitbread
Landlord Mr H. Rhodes

BEDROOMS 3   Grade 2   £C   (No dogs)
Steak & kidney pie £1.95 Salmon salad £3
(Last order 10.30pm)
🍺 Whitbread Trophy, Best Mild; Guinness;
Heineken.

In the heart of the beautiful Hodder Valley,
this former deer-keepers cottage offers
peaceful accommodation in its simple,
well-kept bedrooms. Residents also have a
cosy lounge with colour TV. Bar snacks are
nicely varied, with fresh fish dishes like
our lovely salmon salad a regular and
popular feature. Home-made soup, pâtés,
pies and sandwiches round off the
choice. Accommodation closed 2 weeks
Christmas.   **Family pub**

Newton Valence   *(Food)*   **Horse & Groom**

Near Alton · *Hampshire* · Map 6 B3
Tisted (042 058) 220

Brewery Watneys
Landlord Mr A. Gill
Prawns on toast with tomato sauce &
cheese £1.95 Grilled gammon steak £3 (Last
order 9pm)
🍺 Watneys Stag Bitter; Usher's Best Bitter;
Webster's Yorkshire Bitter; Gale's HSB;
Guinness; Holsten; cider. *Real ale*

Visitors to this imposing roadside pub are
assured of a friendly welcome from Mr Gill,
as well as some really tasty bar food. For a
quick snack there are sandwiches and
tempting savouries like prawns with
tomato sauce and cheese. And if you're
looking for something more substantial,
the menu offers cold meats with help-
yourself salads, various grills and a daily
special like ham risotto or cottage pie. The
glazed patio is useful for children.

North Bovey   *(Food, B & B)*   **Ring of Bells**

Near Moretonhampstead · *Devon* · Map 8 C4
Moretonhampstead (0647) 40375

Free House
Landlords George & Cora Batcock

BEDROOMS 6   Grades 1 & 2   £A   (No dogs)
Devonshire hot pot £1.65 Sirloin steak £6.50
(Last order 9.30pm. No bar food Sun lunch)
🍺 Wadworth's 6X; Flowers Traditional;
Whitbread Trophy; Heineken; cider. *Real ale*

This sturdy old thatched inn lies at the heart
of one of Devon's prettiest villages. George
and Cora Batcock are delightful hosts and
the bar fare is tasty and well prepared:
ploughman's, baked potatoes and cottage
pie for lunch, anything from local trout to
roast pheasant in the evening. Charming
bedrooms (two with four-posters) have
their own neat bathrooms. Accommodation closed January. Garden.   **Family pub**

North Cerney   *(Food, B & B)*   **Bathurst Arms**

Near Cirencester · *Gloucestershire* · Map 6 A3
North Cerney (028 583) 281

Free House
Landlords Mrs V. N. Judd & Mr C. R. Kite
BEDROOMS 4   Grade 1   £B   (No dogs)
Steak & kidney pie £1.95 Ploughman's £1.40
(Last order 10pm)
🍺 Flowers Original Bitter; Archer's Best
Bitter; McEwan's Export; Heineken; Stella
Artois; cider. *Real ale*

Attractive, well-furnished bedrooms with
splendid modern bathrooms provide excellent overnight accommodation at this
converted farmhouse with a pretty riverside garden. There are three bars, including
the beamed lounge bar with its own dining
area and table service. Snacks range from
salads and ploughman's to lasagne, steaks
and daily specials like our lovely fresh
grilled sole.   **Family pub** (lunchtime)

North Petherton *(B & B)*
Walnut Tree Inn

Fore Street, Near Bridgwater · *Somerset*
Map 8 C3
North Petherton (0278) 662255

Free House
Landlords Mr & Mrs Goulden

BEDROOMS 11   Grade 1   £A
🍺 Wadworth's 6X Bitter; Whitbread Trophy;
Exmoor Ale; Younger's Tartan Bitter. *Real ale*

There's a comfortable, homely feel about this spotlessly maintained coaching inn, which stands in the middle of the village opposite a 13th-century church. Bedrooms (some in a motel-style block at the rear) are prettily decorated and sturdily furnished; all have tea-makers, TVs and carpeted bathrooms with colourful modern suites. The bars are warm and welcoming, too.
Family pub

North Wootton *(B & B)*
Crossways Inn

Near Shepton Mallet · *Somerset* · Map 8 D3
Pilton (074 989) 237

Free House
Landlords John & Cynthia Kirkham

BEDROOMS 7   Grade 2   £C (No dogs)
🍺 Wadworths 6X; Bass; Usher's Triple Crown; John Smith's Yorkshire Bitter; Tetley's Bitter; Guinness; Hofmeister; cider. *Real ale*

The rural setting makes for a peaceful stay at this rambling inn. The traditionally furnished bedrooms offer simple comforts, and two have their own compact shower rooms. Stone walls and sturdy oak furniture give a rustic feel to the spacious bar, and there's a cosy residents' lounge with TV. Plans include more bedrooms and improvements to the little patio. No children under two overnight. **Family pub**

Nottingham *(Food)*
Lord Nelson Inn

11 Thurgarton Street, Sneinton
Nottinghamshire · Map 4 C4
Nottingham (0602) 54801

Brewery Hardys & Hansons
Landlord Mr Chris Smith

Home-made steak & potato pie £2 Roast beef salad £2.50 (No bar food eves or Sun)
🍺 Hardy's and Hansons Bitter; Guinness; Heineken; cider. *Real ale*

Two converted farmhouses make up this cosy pub on the outskirts of the city. There are four little beamed bars, in one of which you will find a tempting lunchtime display of cold meats, pies and wedges of English cheese to go with fresh, crisp salads. Chris Smith also offers jacket potatoes and hot daily specials like cottage pie. Finish with gâteau or delicious apple pie. Sandwiches only for Saturday lunch. Terrace.

Nottingham
Ye Olde Trip To Jerusalem Inn

A public house since 1189 (reputedly the oldest in the land), this unique inn has a 16th-century façade that hides a maze of cellars, rooms and passages carved out of the rock on which Nottingham Castle stands. Each room has its own appeal: note especially the snug, with its ancient weapons and extraordinary cavernous ceiling.

Brewhouse Yard, Castle Road · *Nottinghamshire* · Map 4 C4 .
Nottingham (0602) 473171
Free House   *Landlords* Mr & Mrs E. Marshall
🍺 Samuel Smith's Old Brewery Bitter; Marston's Pedigree; Everards Old Original; Heineken; Taunton cider. *Real ale*

England

Nunney   *(Food, B & B)*   *George Inn*

11 Church Street · *Somerset* · Map 8 D3
Nunney (037 384) 458

Free House
Landlord Mr J. Lewis
BEDROOMS 12   Grade 1   £B
Somerset beef & Guinness casserole £2.75
Apple charlotte £1 (Last order 10pm)
🍺 Bass; Butcombe Bitter; Double Diamond;
Younger's Tartan; Guinness; Carling Black
Label; Löwenbräu; Taunton cider. *Real ale*

Food and accommodation are both excellent at this charming 14th-century inn in the shadow of the castle. Home-made soups and sandwiches make tasty light snacks, or you could opt for something more substantial like mushroom and turkey pie, beef curry, rabbit casserole – even seasonal game. Comfortable bedrooms decorated in a pretty, cottage style include six new ones; some have TVs and private bathrooms. There's a residents' lounge.   **Family pub**

Oakwoodhill   *(Food)*   *Punchbowl Inn*

Near Ockley · *Surrey* · Map 6 B3
Oakwood Hill (030 679) 249

Free House
Landlords Rob & Shirley Chambers
Curried chicken £2.75 Steak & kidney
pudding £3.50 (Last order 10pm)
🍺 King & Barnes Sussex Bitter; Hall &
Woodhouse Badger Bitter; Young's Special
Bitter; Charrington IPA; Guinness; Taunton
cider. *Real ale*

In this ancient country cottage dating back 600 years, locals and visitors now gather to sample excellent local brews and some really tasty food. You can help yourself to a bowl of soup or tuck into something like a sandwich, sausage with French bread or superb home-cooked ham, eggs and chips. There's also a daily special such as a pie, a casserole or a dish of pasta. And to round things off try one of the nice puddings.   **Family pub**

Ockley   *(Food, B & B)*   *King's Arms*

Stane Street · *Surrey* · Map 6 B3
Dorking (0306) 711224

Free House
Landlords Mrs Mary Kates Doyle & family
BEDROOMS 3   Grade 1   £B
Prawn curry £2.30 Chicken & ham pie with
chips £1.95 (Last order 9.45pm)
🍺 King & Barnes Sussex Bitter; Fuller's ESB;
Hall & Woodhouse Badger Bitter; Guinness;
Carlsberg; Foster's; cider. *Real ale*

Mary Kates Doyle is admirably assisted by her daughters and grandchildren in this immaculate, tile-hung pub, and you couldn't wish for a more friendly welcome. The bar food is good and wholesome, with a choice ranging from salads, sandwiches and ploughman's to smooth chicken liver pâté and tasty steak and kidney pie. For overnight visitors there are three traditionally furnished bedrooms which share an attractive little bathroom. Garden.   **Family pub**

Offham   *(Food)*   *Blacksmith's Arms*

Near Lewes · *East Sussex* · Map 6 C4
Lewes (079 16) 2971

Free House
Landlords Peter & Ann Blackburn
Beef salad £3.95 Pie of the day with chips or
salad £2.50 (Last order 9.30pm)
🍺 Young's Special Bitter; Harvey's Best
Bitter; King & Barnes Sussex Bitter; Guinness;
Tennent's Extra, Pilsner; Tuborg; cider.
Real ale

An eye-catching cold buffet is a central feature of this welcoming roadside pub, where Peter and Ann Blackburn offer a good selection of tasty bar snacks. The menu ranges from omelettes and a choice of sandwiches (our roast beef was lovely and rare) to specials like full-flavoured turkey Stroganoff and a generous seafood platter. French apple flan makes a super sweet. Closed Monday.   **Family pub**

Old Dalby *(Food)*   *Crown Inn*

Near Melton Mowbray · *Leicestershire* · Map 5 B1
Melton Mowbray (0664) 823134

Free House
Landlords Lynne Bryan & Salvatore Inguanta
Seafood pancake £2.95 Chicken medley £3.95
(Last order 10.15pm. No bar food Sun &
Mon eves)
🍺 Marston's Pedigree, Owd Rodger, Merrie
Monk, Burton Bitter; Ruddles County; Adnams
Bitter. *Real ale*

Full of character and atmosphere, with friendly
regulars and cheerful staff, this 200-year-old
inn is tucked modestly away so ask directions.
Delicious food is served in the cosy bars, from
flavoursome cream of mushroom soup and
crab-filled baked avocado to lamb kebabs,
seafood pancakes and our excellent chicken
with tomato sauce in a pastry case, served
with crisp fresh vegetables. Garden.
Family pub

Old Heathfield *(Food)*   *Star Inn*

Church Street · *East Sussex* · Map 6 C4
Heathfield (043 52) 3570

Brewery Watneys
Landlord Mr Ron Gilbert
Home-made pâté & toast £1.45 Turkey & ham
pie £2.50 (Last order 9.45pm. No bar food Sun
& Mon eves)
🍺 Tamplins Bitter; Webster's Yorkshire
Bitter; Gale's HSB; Guinness; Foster's;
Carlsberg; cider. *Real ale*

Generous helpings of good, honest fare
keep the customers smiling at this most
convivial and reliable of pubs, run in
admirable fashion by Ron Gilbert and his
family. A varied menu of familiar favourites
includes richly flavoured pâté, savoury pies
and omelettes, and the delicious bubble
and squeak is always in demand. Simple
sweets to finish. There are two cosy bars
and a lovely garden. **Family pub**

Oldbury-on-Severn *(Food)*   *Anchor Inn*

Near Bristol · *Avon* · Map 7 D2
Thornbury (0454) 413331
Free House
Landlord Mr Michael J. Dowdeswell
Steak, kidney & mushroom pie £1.45
Langoustines in garlic butter £2.50
(Last order 9.30pm)
🍺 Theakston's Best Bitter, Old Peculier;
Marston's Pedigree; Robinson's Best Bitter;
Butcombe Best Bitter; Guinness; Taunton
cider. *Real ale*

Food plays an important part in this attractive converted mill house. Expansive host
Michael Dowdeswell offers an appetising
cold selection that includes fresh Severn
salmon, rare beef and smoked spare ribs to
enjoy with tasty salads. Or you might tuck
into one of the daily-changing hot dishes
such as liver and bacon casserole, followed
by an Oldbury tart that's packed with
gooseberries steeped in brown sugar.
Garden.

Ombersley *(Food)*   *Kings Arms*

Hereford & Worcester · Map 7 D1
Worcester (0905) 620315

Brewery Mitchells & Butlers
Landlords Chris & Judy Blundell
Moussaka & salad £2.95 Steak & kidney pie
with chips & peas £2.95 (Last order 9pm.
No bar food Sun)
🍺 Bass; Mitchells & Butlers Brew XI,
Springfield Bitter, Mild; Guinness; Carling
Black Label; Taunton cider. *Real ale*

Stuffed birds, brass kitchen utensils and
other bric-à-brac add to the charm of this
lovingly kept 15th-century pub. Snacks
cater for even the heartiest appetite: there's
steak or a pork chop, rich home-made steak
and kidney pie, salad or a ploughman's,
and daily specials might include treats like
smoked salmon and asparagus quiche,
with gooseberry fool to finish. There are
also well-filled cobs at lunchtime. Patio.
Family pub

Onecote   *(Food)*   *Jervis Arms*

Near Leek · *Staffordshire* · Map 4 C4
Onecote (053 88) 206
Free House
Landlords Mr & Mrs D. Smith
Home-cooked ham £1.75 12oz. sirloin steak £4
(Last order 10pm. No bar food Mon lunch
except Bank Hols, also Tues–Fri lunch in winter)
🍺 Ruddle's County; Marston's Pedigree;
McEwan's P70; Younger's Scotch, IPA;
Guinness; Carlsberg; Taunton cider; Kestrel.
Real ale

The river Hamps flows past this agreeable
old inn, whose cosy beamed bars are a very
busy, convivial setting in which to enjoy
Mrs Smith's popular snacks. The choice is
excellent, and whether you want a simple
ploughman's, a super ham salad or a
flavoursome shepherd's pie, you'll find
good quality matched by good value. To
finish, try the home-made chocolate
gâteau. Garden.   **Family pub**

Orford   *(Food, B & B)*   *King's Head Inn*

Front Street, Near Woodbridge · *Suffolk*
Map 5 D2
Orford (039 45) 271

Brewery Adnams
Landlords Mrs P. Shaw & Mr A. Shaw
BEDROOMS 5   Grade 2   £B   (No dogs)
Home-made pâté with salad £1.85 Hot cockle
salad with cottage loaf £1.85 (No bar
food eves)
🍺 Adnams Bitter; Skol. *Real ale*

Local seafood features prominently on the
menu of this charming pub, parts of which
date back to the 13th-century. You can also
get home-made pâté, delicious hickory-
smoked ham and a range of freshly cut
sandwiches. Bedrooms are comfortable
and homely and a splendid breakfast
awaits guests in the morning. Accommodation closed 5–28 Jan.

Osgodby   *(B & B)*   *Barn*

Near Scarborough · *North Yorkshire* · Map 4 D2
Scarborough (0723) 583536

Brewery Younger
Landlords Paul & Karen Waugh

BEDROOMS 7   Grade 2   £C   (No dogs)
🍺 Younger's No. 3 Ale; Scotch Bitter;
Newcastle Bitter; Kestrel; Harp. *Real ale*

Standing about a mile from the sea on the
site of an ancient manor house, this
welcoming pub is a pleasant place for an
overnight stay. Centrally heated bedrooms
in an adjoining house vary in size; all have
identical modern fittings, tea-makers and
televisions. They share a simple bathroom
and shower room. There are two bars, one
with games machines and a pool table.
                        Family pub (summer)

Oswaldkirk   *(Food, B & B)*   *Malt Shovel Inn*

Near Helmsley · *North Yorkshire* · Map 4 C2
Ampleforth (043 93) 461
Brewery Samuel Smith
Landlords Ian & Carol Pickering
BEDROOMS 3   Grade 2   £C   (No dogs)
Sweetcorn & crab pancake £1.70 Shovel bun
with chicken curry filling £2.65 (Last order
9.30pm. No bar food Mon eve except Bank
Holidays)
🍺 Samuel Smith's Old Brewery Bitter;
Alpine. *Real ale*

An interesting menu really gets the taste
buds tingling at this fine old 17th-century
manor house. Spinach roulade or tuna
mousse with diced cucumber makes a
lovely light snack, while more substantial
offerings include cold meat salads, lamb
cutlets, game pie and the unique Shovel
buns – little cottage loaves filled with
delicious curried chicken. Three homely
bedrooms share a well-maintained bathroom. Garden.   **Family pub**

Ovington   *Bush Inn*

A lovely tree-lined lane leads from the A31 to this delightful rose-covered pub, whose garden runs down to the peaceful river Itchen, famous for its trout fishing. The setting is enchanting, and the bars, with their nooks and crannies and gleaming copperware, are cosy and convivial. The oldest part is 17th century, the rest 19th century.

Family pub

Near Alresford · *Hampshire* · Map 6 A3
Alresford (096 273) 2764
Free House   *Landlords* Mr & Mrs G. M. Draper
🍺 Strong's Country Bitter; Flower's Original; Wadworth's 6X; Wethered's Spa Bitter; Guinness; Stella Artois; cider. *Real ale*

Oxford   *(Food)*   *Perch*

Binsey · *Oxfordshire* · Map 6 A3
Oxford (0865) 240386

Brewery Halls
Landlords Andy & Julie Little

Lasagne £1.85 Apple crumble 40p (Last order 9.30pm. No bar food Sun & Mon eves)
🍺 Halls Harvest Bitter, Mild; Ind Coope Burton Ale, Double Diamond; Guinness; Skol; Löwenbräu; cider. *Real ale*

Check directions when setting out for this attractive old thatched pub linked by a path to the river Thames. The menu in the roomy flagstoned bar sticks mainly to standard pub fare such as soup, ploughman's platters, lasagne and a good meaty steak and kidney pie with plenty of rich gravy. To finish, there's a nice crunchy apple crumble. Garden.

Oxford   *(Food, B & B)*   *Turf Tavern*

5 Bath Place, Holywell Street · *Oxon* · Map 6 A3
Oxford (0865) 243235
Owner Mr Wally Ellse
Landlord Keith Roberts
BEDROOMS 9   Grade 2   £B
Beef, wine & mushroom pie £2.95
Lasagne £2.35 (Last order 10pm)
🍺 Hook Norton Best Bitter, Old Hookey; Theakston's Old Peculier (winter only); Webster's Yorkshire Bitter; Guinness; Harp; cider. *Real ale*

Tucked away in the shadow of New College tower, this historic inn is very much an Oxford institution. Immensely popular even out of term, it offers a fine selection of bar snacks, both hot and cold: tasty flans and pies, fresh, crunchy salads, shepherd's pie, beef casserole, old-fashioned puddings. Cosy bedrooms in adjacent cottages share two neat little bathrooms. TV lounge. Two beer gardens.   **Family pub**

Parkgate   *(Food, B & B)*   *Ship Hotel*

The Parade Wirral · *Cheshire* · Map 3 B3
051 336 3931

Owners Anchor Hotels
Landlord Mr Michel Kaiser

BEDROOMS 26   Grade 1   £A+   (No dogs)
Quiche lorraine £1.90 Parkgate platter £2.20 (No bar food eves or Sun)
🍺 John Smith's Bitter, Mild; Guinness; Harp; Kronenbourg; Taunton cider.

Savoury pies remain firm favourites among the super lunchtime snacks served in this stone-built inn overlooking the Dee estuary. There are also excellent sandwiches and salads and a roast or fish dish as the daily special. Comfortably furnished bedrooms are splendidly appointed, with tea-makers, direct-dial telephones and neat carpeted bathrooms. High standard of maintenance, and excellent breakfasts.
Family pub

Pelynt   (B & B)   *Jubilee Inn*

Near Looe · *Cornwall* · Map 8 B4
Lanreath (0503) 20312

Free House
Landlord Mr F. E. Williams

BEDROOMS 10   Grades 1 & 2   £B
🍺 Whitbread Best Bitter; Flower's Original;
Poachers Bitter; Guinness; Stella Artois;
Heineken; cider. *Real ale*

A cosy, welcoming atmosphere pervades
this pleasant pink-washed inn, which
started life as a farmhouse in the 14th
century. Its present name dates from 1887
(the 50th year of Queen Victoria's reign), and
there's a display of commemorative china in
the beamed main bar. Spacious bedrooms,
six with private bathrooms, range from
traditional to more modern, and there's a
snug lounge. Garden.

Pembridge   (Food, B & B)   *New Inn*

Market Square · *Hereford & Worcester*
Map 7 D1
Pembridge (054 47) 427

Brewery Whitbread
Landlord Jane Melvin
BEDROOMS 7   Grade 2   £C
Lasagne £1.95 Pork & apricot pie £1.95 (Last
order 9.45pm)
🍺 Flower's IPA; Whitbread Dark Mild, Light
Mild; Stella Artois; Heineken; cider. *Real ale*

The food is good and tasty at this ancient
black and white inn, where log fires create a
warm, cosy atmosphere in the bars.
Ploughman's and baked potatoes are
popular quick snacks, while for a full menu
you could follow kipper pâté with chicken
casserole, beefsteak pie or sugar-baked
gammon, with a nice pudding to follow.
Modest bedrooms share a bathroom and
separate shower. Patio.   **Family pub**

Pendoggett   (Food, B & B)   *Cornish Arms*

St Kew · *Cornwall* · Map 8 B4
Port Isaac (020 888) 263

Free House
Landlords Nigel Pickstone & Alan Wainwright

BEDROOMS 7   Grade 1   £B
Salmon pie £1.60 Roast beef salad £1.75 (Last
order 10pm)
🍺 Bass; Flowers Original Bitter;
Guinness; Carlsberg Hof; cider. *Real ale*

The welcome is warm and the atmosphere
convivial at this fine old Cornish inn, where
the lunchtime centre of attraction is a
splendid buffet of cold meats and salads.
Other options include soup, quiches and a
terrific treacle tart. Less evening choice;
sandwiches only at Sunday lunchtime.
Smartly furnished bedrooms (four with
private bathrooms) provide excellent
accommodation. No under-14s overnight.
Garden.

Penn Street   (Food)   *Hit or Miss*

Near Amersham · *Buckinghamshire*
Map 6 B3
High Wycombe (0494) 713109

Free House
Landlord Mr Mel James
Chicken provençale with rice £1.90
Tongue sandwich 90p (Last order 10pm)
🍺 Wethered's SPA; Younger's Tartan;
McEwan's Export; John Smith's Bitter;
Guinness; Heineken; cider. *Real ale*

There's nothing hit or miss about the bar
food in this attractive, wistaria-clad pub
with its own cricket pitch and team. You
might open your innings with potted
shrimps or a salami salad, and follow on
with sausage and chips, a ploughman's or
the day's special, such as chicken fricassee,
beef bourguignon or quiche lorraine. To
finish there are gâteaux, cheesecakes and
ices, plus sweets like bread and butter
pudding. Garden.

212

Peppard Common *(Food)*

Red Lion

Near Henley · *Oxfordshire* · Map 6 B3
Rotherfield Greys (049 17) 329

Brewery Brakspear
Landlords Ian & Pauline Wadhams

Jacket potato with Swiss steak £1.70
Cannelloni £1.95 (Last order 10pm)
🍺 Brakspear's Bitter, Special, Mild;
Guinness; Heineken; cider. *Real ale*

This little white pub on the edge of the common serves a good selection of tasty lunchtime and evening snacks in pleasant, friendly surroundings. Jacket potatoes, filled with anything from cheese and butter to steak and vegetables, are popular house specials, and other choices include sandwiches, pâté and pot meals – cannelloni, seafood au gratin, sweet and sour pork. Garden. **Family pub**

Perranarworthal *(Food)*

Norway Inn

Near Truro · *Cornwall* · Map 8 A4
Truro (0872) 862081

Brewery Devenish
Landlord Mr W. C. Herbert

Steak & kidney pie £3.25 3-course set dinner £6 (Last order 10pm)
🍺 Devenish Cornish Best Bitter; Mild;
Whitbread Tankard; Guinness; Grünhalle;
Taunton cider. *Real ale*

Mahogany panelling, little booths and soft lighting make the bar of this popular roadside inn pleasantly intimate. Go to the room next door for a well-laden lunchtime buffet featuring succulent cold meats, fresh seafood and salads. There's also a barbecue on Saturday and Sunday nights, while weekday evenings and Sunday lunch bring a splendid roast. **Family pub**

We have raised our standards considerably since last year. The omission of some houses that appeared in last year's Guide is no reflection on their standing.

Pett Bottom *(Food)*

Duck Inn

Bridge, Near Canterbury · *Kent* · Map 6 D3
Canterbury (0227) 830354

Free House
Landlords Mr & Mrs L. C. Boothright

Fish pâté £1.35 Steak & kidney pie £2.95
(Last order 9.45pm)
🍺 Shepherd Neame Bitter; Marston's
Pedigree; Gibbs Salisbury; Fuller's London
Pride; Canterbury Ale; cider. *Real ale*

A well-balanced selection of robust snacks is available at this friendly old country pub, where a large garden is a popular summer alternative to the cosy bars. Steak and kidney pie, garlicky fish pâté and fiery chilli are served with lovely hot rye bread, and there's a choice of salads, ploughman's and jacket potatoes. Nice sweets like treacle tart from the restaurant menu. Closed Monday.

Petworth (B & B) Angel

Angel Street · West Sussex · Map 6 B4
Petworth (0798) 42153

Free House
Landlords Mr & Mrs Pope

BEDROOMS 4 Grade 2 £B
🍺 Flowers Bitter; Whitbread Best Bitter;
John Smith's Bitter; Courage Best Bitter;
Guinness; Heineken; cider. *Real ale*

Sloping beamed ceilings and low doorways give a quaint character to the bedrooms in this welcoming town-centre inn.
Each is furnished in a mixture of styles, and
there are some pretty fabrics to add a
splash of colour. Two carpeted public bathrooms have modern suites. On cold winter
days you can snuggle round the log fire that
burns in one part of the attractive old bar.
Garden. **Family pub**

Pewsham (Food, B & B) Lysley Arms

Near Chippenham · Wiltshire · Map 6 A3
Chippenham (0249) 652864

Free House
Landlord Mr Peter Reeves
Steak & kidney pie £2.50 Baked
crab £1.50 (Last order 10pm)
BEDROOMS 4 Grade 2 £C
🍺 Bass; Worthington 'E'; Mitchells & Butlers
Brew XI; Guinness; Tennent's Extra; Taunton
cider. *Real ale*

A distinctive white building on the A4
between Chippenham and Calne. Bar
meals are a popular feature, and a cold
table displays cooked meats and salads.
There are also sandwiches, ploughman's
and hot dishes ranging from baked crab
and omelettes to basket meals, grills and
specials like mussels and tasty braised
oxtail. Nicely furnished bedrooms have
neat modern bath/shower rooms. Garden.
Family pub

Philleigh (Food) Roseland Inn

Truro · Cornwall · Map 8 A4
Portscatho (087 258) 254

Brewery Devenish
Landlords Margaret & Desmond Sinnott
Seafood mornay £1.90 Savoury pancake £1.50
(Last order 9pm. No bar food eves except July
& August)
🍺 John Devenish Bitter; Cornish Best Bitter;
Whitbread Tankard; Guinness; Heineken;
Grünhalle; Taunton cider. *Real ale*

Country lanes wind their way to this
charming 17th-century inn, whose decor
reflects the area's strong links with farming
and the sea. Seafood is a popular choice
among the wholesome bar snacks, which
also include sandwiches, Cornish pasties
and splendid ploughman's platters.
Summer pudding makes a delicious sunshine sweet, while winter brings stockpot
soup and home-made game pie. Patio.
Family pub

Pickhill (B & B) Nags Head

Near Thirsk · North Yorkshire · Map 4 C2
Thirsk (0845) 567391

Free House
Landlords Messrs E. & R. Boynton

BEDROOMS 8 Grade 2 £B
🍺 Theakston's Best Bitter, XB, Old Peculier;
Younger's Scotch Bitter; Tetley's Best Bitter;
Guinness; Carlsberg Export; cider. *Real ale*

Not far from the A1, the Nags Head is a
pleasant brick building with bedrooms in a
modern annexe. The eight spick-and-span
rooms have attractive pine furniture, radio-
alarms, tea-makers and very good bath or
shower rooms. All are equipped with
colour TVs. Features of the lounge and
public bars are respectively a copper-
hooded fireplace and an impressive collection of neckties. Garden. **Family pub**

Piercebridge *(Food)* George

Near Darlington · *Co. Durham* · Map 4 C2
Piercebridge (032 574) 576

Brewery Vaux
Landlord Mr Ray Wade

Panackletie £2.40 Raspberry surprise £1 (No
bar food eves)
🍺 Vaux Samson; Lorimer's Scotch Bitter;
Guinness; Norseman; cider.

Nestling on the banks of the river Tees just off the A67, this traditional coaching inn offers a simple choice of lunchtime bar food. You might start with a crock of home-made soup or smoked salmon pâté and go on to a hamburger, steak and kidney pie or deep-fried local cod; and to finish there are simple sweets like banana split or chocolate nut sundae. Eat in the cosy bar or outside in the garden. **Family pub**

Pin Mill *(Food)* Butt & Oyster

Chelmondiston · *Suffolk* · Map 5 D2
Ipswich (0473) 84224

Brewery Tollemache & Cobbold
Landlords Dick & Brenda Mainwaring

Pork en croûte £2.50 Smoked salmon £1.60
(Last order 10pm)
🍺 Tolly Cobbold Bitter, Original, Mild;
Guinness; Hansa Lager; Taunton cider.
Real ale

Little has changed down the years at this splendid old inn, whose main bar, with its well-worn wooden floor and yellowing walls, is a room of great character. Seafarers and landlubbers alike appreciate the tasty bar snacks, which range from sandwiches and ploughman's to garlic prawns, savoury mince pie and pork en croûte with apricot sauce. Less choice Sunday lunch. The setting right on the river Orwell is especially noteworthy. **Family pub**

Pinner *(Food)* Queens Head

High Street · *Middlesex* · Map 6 B3

Brewery Benskins
Landlord Mr Passey

Steak & kidney pie £2.50 Prawn sandwich 85p
(No bar food Sun lunch)
🍺 Benskins Bitter; Ind Coope Burton Ale;
Guinness; Skol; Löwenbräu; cider. *Real ale*

Right in the middle of Pinner High Street, this attractive black and white inn of timber construction has a sign dated 1705. The comfortable bar, with its beams and dark-wood panelling, is a warm, mellow setting for enjoying a simple range of lunchtime snacks, including salads, cottage pie and a very tasty meat and vegetable pasty. Only sandwiches in the evening and sausages Saturday lunchtime. Garden.

Plumley *(Food)* Smoker Inn

Near Knutsford · *Cheshire* · Map 3 B3
Lower Peover (056 581) 2338

Brewery Robinson
Landlord Mr Jorge Masso

Steak & kidney pie £2 Moussaka £1.75 (Last
order 9.45pm)
🍺 Robinson's Best Bitter, Best Mild, Lager;
Guinness. *Real ale*

A warm welcome and splendid bar snacks are a winning combination at Jorge Masso's appealing thatched inn alongside the A556. The lunchtime menu offers a wide choice, from sandwiches and salads to Cumberland sausage, cottage pie and turkey fricassee, and from the chef's native India comes samosas and kofta curry. There are no puddings. Less evening choice; only sandwiches Saturday evening and Sunday lunch. Garden.

England

Plymouth   *(Food)*   *Unity*

Eastlake Street · *Devon* · Map 8 B4
Plymouth (0752) 262622

Brewery Halls
Landlords Antony & Theresa Irish

Seafood pie £1.40 Stilton sandwich £1.20 (No
bar food eves except Sun)
🍺 Ind Coope Burton Ale; Tetley's Bitter;
Harvest Bitter; Löwenbräu; Skol. *Real ale*

There's a distinctly Edwardian atmosphere
about this popular city-centre pub, with its
padded leather seating and mahogany-
framed mirrors. At lunchtime, crowds pack
in for well-filled French sticks, sandwiches
bursting with juicy roast beef, pork or
prawns and assorted meat salads with
vinaigrette or home-made mayonnaise.
Creamy tuna flan and mixed seafood pie
are other typical choices. No sweets.
Closed Sunday lunch.

Pocklington   *(B & B)*   *Feathers Hotel*

Market Place · *Humberside* · Map 4 D3
Pocklington (075 92) 3155

Brewery Younger
Landlord Mr K. F. Suttle

BEDROOMS 12   Grade 1   £A   (No dogs)
🍺 Younger's Scotch Bitter, No. 3; Guinness;
Kestrel; Cavalier; Taunton cider. *Real ale*

This handsome pebbledash inn really
buzzes with life on market days, when
drinkers crowd into the cheerful main bar to
chat and warm themselves by the open
fires; there's also a cosy smaller bar. Excellent bedrooms in the main building are
solidly furnished in traditional style (the
bridal suite has a tester bed); rooms across
the car park are in chalet style. All have
colour TVs, tea-makers and spotlessly
clean bathrooms. Garden.   **Family pub**

We neither seek nor accept

hospitality, and we pay for all

food, drinks and accommodation

in full.

Poole   *(B & B)*   *Inn in the Park*

26 Pinewood Road, Branksome Park · *Dorset*
Map 6 A4
Bournemouth (0202) 761318

Free House
Landlords Paula & Alan Potter

BEDROOMS 5   Grade 1   £C
🍺 Wadworth Farmer's Glory, 6X; Poole
Dolphin Bitter; Guinness; Löwenbräu;
Carlsberg; Taunton cider. *Real ale*

Half a mile from Branksome Chine and the
sea, this comfortable inn has been converted from a handsome Victorian house. A
log fire keeps winter at bay in the roomy bar,
and there's a patio for fair-weather drinking.
Overnight accommodation consists of five
spacious bedrooms with smart modern
furniture, tea-makers and colour TVs; two
have private bathrooms.   **Family pub**

Pooley Bridge   *(B & B)*   *Crown Hotel*

Near Penrith · *Cumbria* · Map 3 B1
Pooley Bridge (085 36) 217

Brewery Whitbread
Landlords Mr & Mrs J. W. Huddart

BEDROOMS 5   Grade 2   £C   (No dogs)
🍺 Whitbread Trophy, Mild; Guinness;
Heineken; Stella Artois.

The river Eamont flows through the large
garden of this trim, white-painted hotel,
which the Huddart family has looked after
for over three decades. There are two
bright, spacious bars and a homely
residents' lounge with TV. Roomy, well-
carpeted bedrooms are furnished either in
traditional or more contemporary style,
and they share a single modern bathroom.

Porlock Weir   *(B & B)*   *Anchor Hotel & Ship Inn*

Somerset · Map 8 C3
Porlock (0643) 862753

Free House
Landlords D. H. Wade, P. D. Sechiari,
H. F. Jeune

BEDROOMS 24   Grade 1   £A
🍺 Usher's Best Bitter, Triple Crown Bitter;
Bass; Ben Truman; Guinness; Fosters;
Taunton cider. *Real ale*

The 19th-century Anchor Hotel and 16th-
century Ship Inn are harbourside neigh-
bours, whose picturesque settings afford
fine views across the Bristol Channel to the
Welsh coast. Homely beamed bedrooms,
most with private bath, have darkwood
furniture, TVs and tea-makers. Best public
rooms are the relaxing bar and lounge in
the hotel. Patio. Accommodation closed
2 weeks January.   **Family pub**

Port Gaverne   *(B & B)*   *Port Gaverne Hotel*

Near Port Isaac · *Cornwall* · Map 8 A4
Port Isaac (020 888) 244

Free House
Landlords Mr & Mrs F. P. Ross

BEDROOMS 17   Grade 1   £A
🍺 St Austell HSD; Whitbread Bitter;
Flower's Best Bitter; Guinness; Heineken;
Stella Artois; cider. *Real ale*

Half a mile from Port Isaac on the unspoilt
North Cornish coast, this fine old inn
combines a delightful location with high
standards of service and accommodation.
Stylishly modern bedrooms, many with
patios, are well stocked with reading matter
and all have excellent private facilities.
There's an absorbing collection of local
photographs and paintings in the bars.
Closed 12 Jan–23 Feb.   **Family pub**

Portsmouth   *(B & B)*   *Sally Port Hotel*

High Street, Old Portsmouth · *Hampshire*
Map 8 B4
Portsmouth (0705) 821860

Free House
Landlord Mr K. Moore

BEDROOMS 12   Grades 1 & 2   £B   (No dogs)
🍺 Whitbread Strong Country Bitter; Usher's
Best Bitter; Bass; Gale's HSB; Guinness; Stella
Artois; Foster's Taunton cider. *Real ale*

A splendid Georgian spiral staircase,
supported by the mast of an 18th-century
frigate, is a striking feature of this historic
inn named after the gate in the defence wall
through which officers sallied forth to their
ships. Characterful bedrooms with sloping
floors and a wealth of oak timbers have
pretty furnishings, tea-makers and TVs.
Most have shower cubicles. No children
overnight. Accommodation closed two
weeks Christmas.

England

Potten End   *(Food)*   *Red Lion*

The Green, Berkhamsted · *Hertfordshire*
Map 6 B3
Berkhamsted (044 27) 4318

Brewery Benskins
Landlords Mr & Mrs E. Gleeson
Filled potatoes £1.20 Quiches £1 (Last
order 10pm. No bar food Sun)
🍺 Benskins Best Bitter, Pale Ale; Ind Coope
Burton Ale; John Bull Bitter; Guinness;
Löwenbräu; cider. *Real ale*

Standing on the green of an attractive
village, this popular, brick-built pub serves
a good range of straightforward bar snacks
at lunchtime. Baked potatoes filled with
anything from cheese and ham to chilli con
carne are long-standing favourites, along
with sandwiches, sausages, burgers and
rich, tasty cottage pie. Quiches and salads,
too. Sandwiches and hot dishes in the
evenings. Garden.

Powerstock   *(Food, B & B)*   *Three Horseshoes*

Bridport · *Dorset* · Map 8 D3
Powerstock (030 885) 328

Brewery Palmer
Landlords Pat & Diana Ferguson

BEDROOMS 4   Grade 2   £C
Seafood soup with crusty bread £1.10 Pint of
prawns with garlic dip £2.50 (Last order 10pm)
🍺 Palmer's Best Bitter, IPA; Guinness;
Shilthorn; cider. *Real ale*

This stone-built pub with fine views from its
garden has the flavour of a real local. Fresh
seafood is something of a speciality here,
and in the welcoming bar you can tuck into
pan-fried plaice or a shellfish platter, as
well as summer salads, ploughman's and
warming dishes like beef curry, with apple
pie for afters. Bright bedrooms with traditional furnishings and tea-makers are
pleasant for an overnight stop.

Priors Hardwick   *(Food)*   *Butchers Arms*

Near Southam · *Warwickshire* · Map 5 A2
Byfield (0327) 60504

Free House
Landlords Pires family

Beefburger £1.50 Goujonnades of plaice £1.95
(No bar food eves or weekends)
🍺 Mitchells & Butlers Brew XI, Springfield
Bitter; Carling Black Label; Tennent's Extra.

The owners are Portuguese, but the decor,
atmosphere and cooking are distinctly
English at this pleasant village inn. Low oak
beams, log fires and gleaming brassware
give a delightfully rustic appeal to the bar,
where you can order anything from the
restaurant menu – a satisfying bowl of soup
or perhaps grilled sardines, succulent giant
prawns, even roast partridge. Sweets
include a fine crème brûlée.   **Family pub**

Puckeridge   *(Food)*   *White Hart*

High Street, Near Ware · *Hertfordshire*
Map 5 C2
Ware (0920) 821309

Brewery McMullen
Landlord Colin & Rita Boom

Crab & prawn mayonnaise £4.95 Baked plaice
stuffed with prawns £3.95 (Last order 9.45pm)
🍺 McMullen's Country Bitter, AK Mild;
Guinness; Hartsman. *Real ale*

Fresh seafood is the major gastronomic
attraction in this black and white pub. You
can sit round the huge open fireplace in the
plush lounge bar and enjoy anything from
smoked salmon pâté and rollmop herring
stuffed with firm, tasty prawns to dressed
crab and lobster. Meat-lovers are tempted
by steak, cold ham and turkey and mushroom pie, while simple sweets like trifle
satisfy those with a sweet tooth. Garden.
Family pub

Pulborough   *(Food)*

Waters Edge

Station Road · *West Sussex* · Map 6 B4
Pulborough (079 82) 2451

Brewery Friary Meux
Landlord John Salmon
Wholemeal quiche £1.95 Individual steak &
kidney pie cooked in Guinness £3.25 (Last
order 10.30pm)
🍺 Friary Meux Bitter; Ind Coope Burton Ale,
John Bull; Guinness; Skol; Löwenbräu; cider.
Real ale

Food takes high priority at this agreeable
and popular pub, whose long bar has picture windows overlooking the river Arun.
The carvery and salad bar offer an excellent
choice of hot and cold dishes, and you'll
also find soups, pâté, sandwiches (lunchtime only) and daily specials like macaroni
cheese or tasty pork casserole. Nice
sweets, too. Less choice weekends and
Monday. Garden.

Pulverbatch   *(Food, B & B)*

White Horse

Near Shrewsbury · *Shropshire* · Map 7 D1
Dorrington (074 373) 247

Brewery Whitbread
Landlords Margaret & Hamish MacGregor
BEDROOMS 3   Grade 1   £C
Smoked trout pâté £1.25 Salmon
goujons £2.10 (Last order 10pm)
🍺 Flower's Original, Flower's Best Bitter;
Whitbread Best Bitter; Guinness; Stella Artois,
cider. *Real ale*

This thriving old timbered inn, set in rolling
countryside south of Shrewsbury, is very
much geared to the service of food. Everything on the long bar menu is fresh and
flavoursome, from smoked trout pâté or
eggs à la russe to generous toasted sandwiches, burgers and curries. Neat little bedrooms, which share a well-kept bathroom,
have smart white unit furniture and floral
duvets.   **Family pub**

Pye Corner   *(Food)*

Plume of Feathers

Gilston, Near Harlow, Essex · *Hertfordshire*
Map 5 C2
Harlow (0279) 24154
Brewery Courage
Landlord Mr G. R. Ellis
Mushroom omelette £1.85 Roast beef salad
£2.95 (Last order 10pm. No bar food Sun eve)
🍺 Courage Best Bitter, Directors Bitter; John
Smiths Yorkshire Bitter; Guinness;
Hofmeister; Kronenbourg; Taunton cider.
Real ale

Sandwiches are served in splendid variety
at this characterful black and white pub:
choose them plain, club or toasted, or try
one of the popular baps packed with anything from peanut butter to prawn and
coleslaw. There's also pâté, salads and
omelettes, plus specials like stuffed plaice
or steak and kidney pie. Only sandwiches
Sunday lunchtime. Patio and garden.

Pyrton   *(Food)*

Plough Inn

Near Watlington · *Oxfordshire* · Map 6 B3
Watlington (049 161) 2003

Free House
Landlords Jackie & Jeremy Hunt

King prawns in garlic butter with salad £4.25
Beef romana with jacket potato & peas £3.25
(Last order 10pm)
🍺 Adnams Bitter; Hall & Woodhouse Badger
Bitter; Brakspears Bitter; Guinness. *Real ale*

The very model of a traditional country
pub, with thatched roof, low beams, a
roaring fire and charming hosts in Jackie
and Jeremy Hunt. Good, simple home
cooking is another attraction, with bar
snacks ranging from sandwiches and
ploughman's (lunchtime only) to filled
jacket potatoes, pies, roast pheasant and
flavoursome casseroles. You'll also find
tasty soups, pâtés and terrines and some
smashing sweets. Garden.   **Family pub**

England

Ramsbury   *(Food)*   *Bell at Ramsbury*

The Square · *Wiltshire* · Map 6 A3
Marlborough (0672) 20230

Free House
Landlord Mr Michael Benjamin

Marengo pie £1.95 Shellfish & fruit
platter £3.95 (Last order 9.30pm. No bar food
Sat eve)
🍺 Wadworth's IPA, 6X; Younger's Tartan;
Guinness; Carlsberg Hof; cider. *Real ale*

There's plenty of interest on the menu of
this cheerful pebbledash pub with canopies
at its windows. Besides home-made soups
and pâtés, you might find tempting salmon
and dill pie, an eye-catching shellfish
platter or spicy Calcutta lamb. There are
also colourful fresh salads and a selection
of lovely sweets. Garden.   **Family pub**

Richmond   *(Food)*   *Orange Tree*

45 Kew Road · *Surrey* · Map 6 B3
01-940 0944

Brewery Young
Landlord Mr D. J. Murphy

Steak & kidney pie £2.80 Duck in orange sauce
£3.80 (Last order 10pm. No bar food Sun eve)
🍺 Young's Bitter, Special Bitter; Guinness;
John Young's London Lager; cider. *Real ale*

The mood is lively and friendly at this solid
Victorian pub, where the main centre of
eating activity is the smart Cellar Bar with
its quarry-tiled floor, red-brick walls
and plush seating. The eye-catching cold
buffet offers a good choice of cooked meats
and salads, while blackboard-listed hot
specials might include stuffed peppers,
steaks and duck in orange sauce. Patio.

Richmond   *(Food)*   *Castle Tavern*

Market Place · *North Yorkshire* · Map 4 C2
Richmond (0748) 3187

Brewery Vaux
Landlords Mr & Mrs M. Carter

Castle terrine £1.50 Swaledale pie £2
(No bar food eves & all Mon)
🍺 Vaux Sunderland Bitter, Samson;
Guinness; Tuborg. *Real ale*

Cooking has a definite Yorkshire slant at
this welcoming pub, where snacks are
served in the lounge bar at lunchtime.
Dishes like pheasant or pigeon casserole,
fisherman's pie or rabbit stew with Yorkshire pudding are tasty and satisfying, and
there are some nice traditional sweets, too,
such as curd tart or apple pie made with a
layer of Wensleydale cheese.
                                    Family pub

Ringmore   *(Food, B & B)*   *Journey's End Inn*

Near Kingsbridge · *Devon* · Map 8 B4
Bigbury-on-Sea (054 881) 205
Free House
Landlords Mr & Mrs R. T. Hollins
BEDROOMS 4 **Grades 1 & 2   £B** (No dogs)
Sausages & mash with onion sauce £1.95
Open ham sandwich topped with fried
egg £1.50 (Last order 10pm)
🍺 Badger's Best Bitter; Bate's Bitter; Golden
Hill Exmoor Ale; Wadworth's 6X; Guinness;
Harp; Hofmeister; cider. *Real ale*

Winding country lanes lead to this enchanting little inn, where the panelled lounge bar
is especially cosy. Wholesome bar snacks
might include home-made celery soup with
crusty bread, succulent steak and delicious
blackberry and apple pie. Neat modern
bedrooms have TVs, tea-makers and radio-
alarms. There is a games room with video
games. No under-tens overnight. Garden.
                                    Family pub

Ringwood   *(Food, B & B)*   *Original White Hart*

Market Place · *Hampshire* · Map 6 A4
Ringwood (042 54) 2702
Brewery Eldridge Pope
Landlord Mr T. G. Eales
BEDROOMS 8   Grade 2   £B
Steak & kidney pie £2.95 Home-cooked ham
salad £2.95 (Last order 10pm. No bar food
Sun eve)
🍺 Eldridge Pope Dorchester Bitter, IPA,
Royal Oak, 1880; Guinness; Faust; Taunton
cider. *Real ale*

Food plays a major role at this fine old inn,
whose attractive bars contain a wealth of
period detail. Well-prepared snacks are
exemplified by soup, home-baked ham and
the popular steak and kidney pie with
plenty of tender meat and rich, tasty gravy.
There are also sandwiches and a good
apple pie. Bedrooms are simple and
traditional, spacious and spotlessly clean.
Patio.   **Family pub**

Ripley   *(Food)*   *Anchor*

High Street · *Surrey* · Map 6 B3
Guildford (0483) 224120

Brewery Friary Meux
Landlord Mrs Christine Beale

Steak & kidney pie £1.40 Beef curry £1.80
(No bar food eves)
🍺 Friary Meux Bitter; Ind Coope Burton Ale;
Guinness; Skol; Löwenbräu; cider. *Real ale*

This handsome red-brick building is over
700 years old and its low-ceilinged lounge
bar is filled with knick-knacks, brass
ornaments and pretty porcelain. Best of the
bar snacks are the tasty home-baked
savoury pies – the steak and kidney is
always in demand – and daily specials like
beef curry. Filled rolls and ploughman's
platters for lighter bites. Patio.

Ripon   *(B & B)*   *Unicorn Hotel*

Market Place · *North Yorkshire* · Map 4 C2
Ripon (0765) 2202

Free House
Landlords Mr & Mrs D. T. Small

BEDROOMS 27   Grade 1   £A+
🍺 Theakstons Bitter; Smith's Bitter;
Guinness; Carlsberg Hof; Hofmeister;
Taunton cider. *Real ale*

Hospitality has long been a feature of this
handsome old posting house, which
occupies a prominent position on the
historic market square. The beamed public
bar has a cheerful, rustic charm, and there's
a smart cocktail bar and comfortable residents' lounge. Lofty, simply furnished bedrooms offer plenty of space, with TVs, tea-
makers and functional bath or shower
rooms.

Ripponden   *(Food)*   *Old Bridge Inn*

Priest Lane · *West Yorkshire* · Map 4 C3
Halifax (0422) 822595

Free House
Landlord Mr Ian Hargreaves Beaumont
Fisherman's pie £2.50 Goujons of sole £2.25
(Last order 10pm. No bar food Sat eve &
Sun lunch)
🍺 Younger's Scotch Bitter; Webster's
Pennine Bitter; Tetley's Mild; Taylor's Golden
Best; Guinness; Carlsberg Hof; cider. *Real ale*

The nearby river Ryburn adds to the charm
of this ancient whitewashed inn with its
quaint, cottagy beamed bars. At lunchtime
the help-yourself cold buffet of home-made
quiches, tender roast beef, spicy Virginia
ham and crisp salads is deservedly popular, while in the evening there are sandwiches (plain or toasted), along with tasty
hot dishes such as savoury pancakes and
chilli con carne with garlic bread.

England

Risley *(Food)* — *Noggin*

Near Warrington · *Cheshire* · Map 3 B3
Padgate (0925) 812022

Brewery Greenall Whitley
Landlords Tony & Maureen Edwards

Danish open sandwich from 55p Steak &
kidney pie with chips & vegetables £1.85 (Last
order 10pm. No bar food Sun & Mon eves)
🏴 Greenall Whitley's Original Bitter, Local
Bitter, Mild; Grünhalle. *Real ale*

Maureen Edwards takes care of the cooking
at this pleasant roadside pub, where blackboards proclaim an interesting selection of
tasty, well-prepared dishes. Open sandwiches, steaks and fresh haddock are
regular favourites, while daily-changing
specials could include casseroles, curries
and savoury pies. Sunday lunchtime brings
a traditional roast plus several other dishes.
Home-made fruit pies and trifles to finish.
Terrace. **Family pub** (weekend lunchtime)

Risplith *(B & B)* — *Black-a-Moor Inn*

Pateley Bridge Road, Near Ripon
North Yorkshire · Map 4 C2
Sawley (076 586) 214

Free House
Landlords Mr & Mrs Byron Brader

BEDROOMS 3 Grade 2 £C (No dogs)
🏴 Theakston's Best Bitter; Younger's Scotch
Bitter; John Smith's Bitter, Mild; Hofmeister;
Taunton cider. *Real ale*

This solid stone-built pub stands beside the
B6265 about five miles west of Ripon. It's a
cheerful, popular place, where the Braders
are the friendliest of hosts. You can enjoy a
chat with the locals in the spacious bar or
play pool in a separate room. Bedrooms are
unpretentious with washbasins and simple
furnishings. No children overnight. Closed
Monday lunchtime.

Rochester *(B & B)* — *Redesdale Arms*

Near Otterburn · *Northumberland* · Map 2 D4
Otterburn (0830) 20668

Free House
Landlords Alan & Connie Robertson

BEDROOMS 11 Grade 2 £C (No dogs)
🏴 Drybrough Heavy; Stones Bitter;
McEwan's Scotch Bitter; Carling Black Label;
cider.

The Scottish border is only a dozen miles
from this greystone hostelry, which has
been welcoming travellers for the last 600
years. Friendly farmers congregate in the
public bar, leaving visitors to enjoy the fire
in the beamed lounge bar or do a bit of
viewing in the TV lounge. Spotless bedrooms have all the traditional comforts
(two have four-posters), and the three old-
fashioned bathrooms are well maintained.
All rooms have TVs. Garden.

Rockbourne *(Food)* ★ — *Rose & Thistle*

Near Fordingbridge · *Hampshire* · Map 6 A4
Rockbourne (072 53) 236

Brewery Whitbread
Landlords Mr & Mrs P. A. Read

Steak & kidney pie £3.95 Fresh seafood
from £4 (Last order 9.30pm)
🏴 Whitbread Pompey Royal, Strong Country
Bitter, Best Bitter; Guinness; Heineken; Stella
Artois; cider. *Real ale*

Tended by the Reads with loving care, this
delightful thatched pub is a classic village
hostelry offering wonderful bar food. Pride
of place must go to the superb local seafood – lobster, beautifully sweet giant crab
and a daily special like mussels, sole or
bass. And it doesn't stop there, as other
delights include pea and ham soup, home-
cooked Wiltshire ham and a delectable
apple pie flavoured with cloves. Garden.

222

Rockcliffe *(Food)* — *Crown & Thistle*

Near Carlisle · *Cumbria* · Map 3 B1
Rockcliffe (022 874) 378

Brewery Scottish & Newcastle
Landlords Kevin & Joane Dempsey
Roast ham & salad £1.95 Creamy apple
gâteau 75p (Last order 9pm. No bar food
Sun eve)
🍺 Younger's Scotch Bitter, Dark Ale,
Traditional IPA; McEwan's Export; Guinness;
Harp; Taunton cider. *Real ale*

Bar snacks are a popular feature at this pleasant old pub on the outskirts of the village. Among a wide range of offerings look for the succulent ham and tender, pink beef, both prepared on the premises. Sweets are home-made, too: try the lovely light creamy apple gâteau. Service is cheerful. Only soup and sandwiches are available on Mondays. Patio.

Romaldkirk *(Food, B & B)* — *Rose & Crown*

Teesdale · *Co. Durham* · Map 4 C2
Teesdale (0833) 50213

Free House
Landlords Mr & Mrs D. Jackson
BEDROOMS 15   Grade 1   £A
Lasagne £2.35 Local Cotherstone cheese &
biscuits £1.25 (Last order 10pm)
🍺 Theakston's Best Bitter; Tetley's Bitter;
Cameron's Bitter; Carlsberg; Hansa; Taunton
cider. *Real ale*

There's a genuine warmth and friendliness about this fine old coaching house, whose bars provide a characterful setting for some enjoyable home cooking. Garlic mushrooms, robustly flavoured pâté, lemon sole and lasagne are typical items on the varied menu, and the cold buffet is a popular summertime feature. Very comfortable bedrooms range from traditional in the main building to smartly modern in the courtyard block.   **Family pub**

Rosedale Abbey *(B & B)* — *Blacksmiths Arms*

Hartoft End · *North Yorkshire* · Map 4 D2
Lastingham (075 15) 331

Free House
Landlords Mr & Mrs Barrie

BEDROOMS 12   Grade 1   £B
🍺 Younger's Scotch Bitter; John Smith's
Bitter; Newcastle Exhibition; Guinness;
Hofmeister; McEwan's Lager; Taunton cider.
Real ale

Built in the 16th century with stone taken from Rosedale Abbey, this handsome farmhouse is now a comfortable and welcoming hotel. Its lovely, quiet position is a major asset, and the cottage bars and homely residents' lounge with TV are inviting and relaxing. Bedrooms have simple modern furniture and tea-makers; the seven in the wing offer private facilities. Patio.   **Family pub**

Rosedale Abbey *(B & B)* — *White Horse Farm Hotel*

Near Pickering · *North Yorkshire* · Map 4 D2
Lastingham (075 15) 239

Free House
Landlords Mr & Mrs Wilcock

BEDROOMS 15   Grade 1   £A
🍺 Tetley's Bitter, Mild; Cameron's Lion
Bitter; Skol; cider. *Real ale*

Set high up in the heart of the Yorkshire moors, this sturdy stone pub is a popular base for tourists. A cheerful fire wards off winter in the welcoming bar with its fine old church pew seating, and the well-appointed bedrooms are neat, bright and modern. All have colour TVs and tea-makers, plus compact bath or shower rooms. Garden.   **Family pub**

England

Ross-on-Wye *(Food, B & B)*   *Rosswyn Hotel*

High Street· *Hereford & Worcester* · Map 7 D2
Ross-on-Wye (0989) 62733
Free House
Landlord R. Livesey
BEDROOMS 10   Grade 2   £B
Rabbit, mushroom & ham pie £1.40 Ratatouille &
cheese £1.20 (Last order 10pm. No bar food Sun)
🍺 Wadworth's 6X; Sam Smith's Old Brewery
Bitter; Bass; Whitbread Trophy; Mitchells &
Butlers Springfield Bitter; Carling Black Label;
Harp; cider. *Real ale*

A fine Elizabethan fireplace and handsome
antiques set the characterful tone for this
friendly 15th-century hostelry. The snack
menu changes daily, offering simple, enjoyable fare like chicken liver pâté, sandwiches,
salads and savoury pies. Sweets include
chocolate brandy cake and luscious home-
made ice cream. Bedrooms (three with four-
posters) offer good comfort, and five have
private bathrooms. Garden.   **Family pub**

Rotherwick   *(Food)*   *Coach & Horses*

The Street, Near Hook · *Hampshire* · Map 6 B3
Hook (025 672) 2542

Free House
Landlord Mrs T. A. Williams

Steak & kidney pie £2.30 Home-made soup 65p
(Last order 10.30pm)
🍺 Hall & Woodhouse Badger Bitter,
Tanglefoot; Ringwood Old Thumper; Guinness;
Taunton cider. *Real ale*

The hungry and the thirsty are really well
provided for at this convivial village pub,
which offers a good choice of bar food and up
to a dozen real ales. Ploughman's, pâtés, pies
and pasties typify the simple delicious fare
which customers can enjoy in the cheerful
bars or separate eating area. Sweets include a
deliciously crisp, rich Danish chocolate gâteau.
Roasts only on Sunday. Garden.   **Family pub**

Rowhook   *(Food)*   *Chequers Inn*

Near Horsham · *West Sussex* · Map 6 B3
Slinfold (0403) 790480

Brewery Whitbread
Landlord Mr P. A. Barrs

Steak & mushroom pie £2.25 Fillet steak £5.75
(Last order 10pm. No bar food Sun eve)
🍺 Flowers Bitter; Whitbread Pompey Royal,
Strong Country Bitter; Guinness; Stella Artois;
Heineken; cider. *Real ale*

Mrs Barrs' cooking is a major attraction at
this charming old whitewashed inn deep
in rural Sussex. Lunchtime brings light
snacks, quiches, steak and mushroom pie
and the popular home-cooked ham, while
the evening menu extends to the
restaurant-style dishes like chicken
béchamel or Scotch fillet steak. Desserts
include sorbets, chocolate fudge cake and a
traditional English trifle. Garden.

Running Waters   *(B & B)*   *Three Horse Shoes*

Sherburn House, Near Durham · *Co. Durham*
Map 4 C1
Durham (0385) 720286

Brewery Vaux
Landlords Derek & Leslie Crehan

BEDROOMS 3   Grade 1   £C
🍺 Vaux Samson; Lorimer's Scotch;
Guinness; Tuborg. *Real ale*

There's no mistaking the warmth of the
welcome at Derek Crehan's well-
maintained inn perched high up alongside
the A181 between Durham and Hartlepool.
It's a comfortable spot for an overnight
stop, all the pleasant bedrooms having tea-
makers, TVs, washbasins and shower
cabinets. Leslie Crehan's freshly cooked
breakfasts are a further attraction. There
are two bars, the public one being very
popular with locals. Garden.

224

Rushlake Green   *(Food)*   *Horse & Groom*

Near Heathfield · *East Sussex* · Map 6 C4
Rushlake Green (0435) 830320

Brewery Board's of Lewes
Landlords Anton & Elaine Levy

Sussex smokies £1.60 Steak & oyster pie £3.50
(Last order 9.30. No bar food Sun & Mon eves)
🍺 Board's Traditional Sussex Bitter;
Guinness; Carlsberg Hof; Hürlimann; cider.
Real ale

Winding country lanes lead to this friendly
pub, where low ceilings and oak beams
provide a pleasant, cosy ambience for
sampling the tasty bar snacks. Start perhaps with soup or an enjoyably different
cream cheese pâté, and follow up with
lasagne or lovely grilled lemon sole. There
are also substantial salads, a good selection of puds and some well-kept cheeses.
Garden.   **Family pub**

Rusthall   *(Food)*   *Red Lion*

Near Tunbridge Wells · *Kent* · Map 6 C3
Tunbridge Wells (0892) 20086

Brewery Whitbread
Landlords Mr & Mrs B. Cooter

Smoked salmon pâté with toast £1.30 Kidneys
in red wine £1.10 (Last order 11pm)
🍺 Whitbread Bitter; Fremlins Bitter, Tusker;
Guinness; Stella Artois; Heineken; cider.
Real ale

Mrs Cooter's lunchtime bar snacks are a
popular feature at this handsome old pub,
parts of which date from the 15th century.
Chicken liver pâté, soup and salads are
familiar favourites, with more unusual
options being offered by paprika roast
chicken and savoury meatballs served in a
curry sauce. Cheese and sandwiches only
in the evenings and on Sunday. There are
two pleasant bars and a beer garden.

Saffron Walden   *(Food)*   *Eight Bells*

Bridge Street · *Essex* · Map 5 C2
Saffron Walden (0799) 22790

Brewery Benskins
Landlord Mr R. Moore

Fresh wing of skate £3.75 Coffee meringue £1
(Last order 9.30pm)
🍺 Benskins Bitter; Ind Coope Burton Ale;
John Bull; Guinness; Skol; Oranjeboom;
cider. *Real ale*

Spot the eight brass bells on the sign of this
fine old hostelry, whose inviting beamed
bar offers a varied menu of imaginative,
well-prepared snacks. Start perhaps with
pâté or home-made soup and go on to
lasagne, super grilled swordfish or prawn-
stuffed chicken breast with a saffron-
flavoured sauce. There's even a children's
menu, and at lunchtime sandwiches
(except weekends) and a cold buffet widen
the choice.   **Family pub**

Saffron Walden   *(Food)*   ★   *Saffron Hotel*

10 High Street · *Essex* · Map 5 C2
Saffron Walden (0799) 22676
Free House
Landlords Craddock family
French onion soup 85p Steak, kidney &
Guinness pie with vegetables £2.85 (Last order
9.30pm. No bar food Sun)
🍺 Greene King IPA; John Smith's Bitter;
Ruddles County; Younger's Tartan; Guinness;
Carlsberg; Kronenbourg; Taunton cider.
Real ale

Quality and variety are outstanding
features of the bar snacks served in this
friendly Georgian hostelry. French onion
soup and chicken liver pâté are splendid
preludes to main courses that range from
omelettes and seafood to steak, kidney and
Guinness pie. Also pasta and pizzas, as well
as salads, sandwiches and super sweets.
Patio. *For accommodation see Egon
Ronay's Lucas Hotel & Restaurant Guide
1985.*   **Family pub**

England

St Dominick · *Who'd Have Thought It Inn*

Perched high on a hill with distant views of the Tamar Valley and Plymouth, this sturdy stone house has been an inn since 1849. It's a great favourite with locals and tourists, and there's a choice of three bars, all featuring handsome old furnishings, brassware and china. The amazing name has absolutely no relevance to anything!

Near Saltash · *Cornwall* · Map 8 B4
Liskeard (0579) 50214
Free House   Landlord Mr D. Potter
🍺 Bass; Courage Directors Bitter; Worthington Best Bitter; Ben Truman; Guinness; Carling Black Label. *Real ale*

St Margaret's at Cliffe *(Food, B & B)* · *Cliffe Tavern*

High Street · *Kent* · Map 6 D3
Dover (0304) 852749

Free House
Landlords Westby family
BEDROOMS 12   Grade 1   £B
Cliffe Tavern fruits de mer £4.40 Chicken pie £1.55 (Last order 10pm)
🍺 Shepherd Neame Masterbrew; Courage Directors Bitter; Fremlins Bitter; Guinness; Carlsberg; Taunton cider. *Real ale*

The Westby family run this attractive clapboard pub with great warmth and attention to detail. In the cheerful, old-fashioned bar you can tuck into tasty snacks like rich smoked haddock chowder, excellent crab sandwiches and huge seafood platters, as well as good-looking salads and grills. Accommodation is a strong point, too, neat bedrooms with TVs and excellent bathrooms being superbly furnished. Garden.

St Mawes *(B & B)* · *Rising Sun Inn*

Cornwall · Map 8 A4
St Mawes (0326) 270233

Brewery St Austell
Landlord Mrs Campbell Marshall

BEDROOMS 16   Grade 1   £A
🍺 St Austell Best Bitter, Extra; Guinness; Carlsberg Pilsner, Hof; cider. *Real ale*

Mrs Campbell Marshall ensures a warm welcome and high standards of comfort at this charming hotel overlooking the harbour. There are two cosy little bars, a sunny terrace for summer drinking and a peaceful lounge. Bedrooms are tastefully furnished and bathrooms are immaculately kept. Four rooms in a separate cottage have splendid sea views. Good breakfasts. Accommodation closed Christmas–14 January.   **Family pub**

St Mawgan *(B & B)* · *Falcon Inn*

Near Newquay · *Cornwall* · Map 8 A4
St Mawgan (063 74) 860225

Free House
Landlords Mr & Mrs P. Joyce

BEDROOMS 4   Grade 2   £C
🍺 St Austell Best Bitter, Tinners Ale; McEwan's Bitter, Worthington Bitter; Bass; Guinness; cider. *Real ale*

A huge magnolia tree, a wishing well and a well-equipped children's room are all to be found in the garden of this 16th-century country inn, where the Joyces are the friendly hosts. The popular bar is large and convivial, and there's a peaceful residents' lounge with TV. Homely, spick-and-span bedrooms share a pink-tiled public bathroom. No children overnight July and August. Accommodation closed Christmas week.   **Family pub**

226

St Neots *(Food)*   *Chequers Inn*

St Marys Street · *Cambridgeshire* · Map 5 B2
Huntingdon (0480) 72116

Free House
Landlords David & Ann Taylor

Smoked mackerel mousse £1.50 Spiced
minced beef kebab £2.95 (Last order 10pm)
🍺 Paine's St Neots, XXX; Stones Bitter;
Younger's Tartan; Carling Black Label;
Carlsberg. *Real ale*

The appetising smell of the stockpot wafts
from the kitchen of this delightful 17th-
century pub, where the Taylors are the
most engaging of hosts. There's an excellent choice of delicious bar food, from
warming soups and smoked fish pâté to
pasta, stuffed peppers and steak pie. Also
sandwiches, sweets from the trolley and a
summer lunchtime cold buffet. Patio.
Family pub

St Neots *(B & B)*   *Stephenson's Rocket*

Cross Hall Road · *Cambridgeshire* · Map 5 B2
Huntingdon (0480) 72773

Free House
Landlords Mr & Mrs B. Stephenson

BEDROOMS 9 Grade 1 £A (No dogs)
🍺 Adnams Bitter; Paines St Neots Bitter;
Ben Truman; Charles Wells Redstripe Lager.
Real ale

About a mile from St Neots at the junction
of the A1 and A45, this family-run pub
offers excellent motel-style accommodation. Nine bedrooms in a modern red-brick
annexe have practical fitted furniture,
colour TVs and up-to-date telephones, plus
well-appointed tiled bathrooms. In the
main building (once a farmhouse) there's a
comfortable bar with plush banquette
seating. Patio. **Family pub**

Salisbury   *Haunch of Venison*

Right in the city centre overlooking the ancient Poultry Cross, this fine
old half-timbered pub has a history going back to 1320. The little bar,
with its solid pewter counter, abounds in warmth and character.
Another tiny room, known as the House of Lords, was reputedly once
used as a discreet tippling place by local church dignitaries. **Family pub**

1 Minster Street · *Wiltshire* · Map 6 A4
Salisbury (0722) 22024
Brewery Courage   *Landlords* Mr & Mrs Leroy
🍺 Courage Directors Bitter, Best Bitter; Guinness; Hofmeister.
Real ale

Salisbury *(B & B)*   *High Post Hotel*

High Post · *Wiltshire* · Map 6 A4
Middle Woodford (072 273) 293

Free House
Landlords Messrs Reader & Simpson

BEDROOMS 15 Grade 1 £B
🍺 Wadworth's 6X; Hall's Harvest Bitter; Ind
Coope Burton Ale; Courage Director's Bitter;
John Bull Bitter; cider. *Real ale*

Built in 1936 as an airport control tower,
this pleasant tiled pub alongside the A345
offers plenty of space and comfort for
todays land-based travellers. The bedrooms, restfully decorated in creams and
light browns, have smart modern furniture,
tea-makers and radio-alarms. Most also are
equipped with TVs and private facilities.
There are three roomy bars and quiet
residents' lounge. Garden.   **Family pub**

England

Salisbury *(B & B)*   *King's Arms*

9 St John Street · *Wiltshire* · Map 6 A4
Salisbury (0722) 27629

Owners Wessex Hosts
Landlords Mr & Mrs Tim Wright

BEDROOMS 16 Grade 2 £B
🍺 Usher's Best Bitter, Pale Ale, Triple
Crown; John Smith's Yorkshire Bitter;
Carlsberg; cider. *Real ale*

Period charm oozes from every nook and
cranny of this fine old half-timbered inn
near the cathedral. The residents' lounge,
with its dark oak panelling, Tudor fireplace,
maps and tapestries, is particularly delightful, and there are two little beamed bars.
Bedrooms, too, are appealingly old-
fashioned; one boasts a splendid William
and Mary four-poster. All have tea-makers.
Patio.   **Family pub**

Sambourne *(Food)*   *Green Dragon*

Near Redditch · *Warwickshire* · Map 5 A2
Astwood Bank (052 789) 2465

Brewery Bass
Landlords Mr & Mrs Joseph Kimber
Lemon sole £4 Home-cured gammon £2.75
(Last order 10pm. No bar food Mon eve & all
Sun)
🍺 Bass; Mitchells & Butlers Springfield
Bitter, Brew XI; Guinness; Carling Black
Label; Taunton cider. *Real ale*

Overlooking the village green, this whitewashed pub makes a cheerful sight in
summer with its window boxes and hanging baskets. Snacks served in the cosy
beamed bars range from soup and sandwiches to omelettes, steak and kidney pie,
home-cured gammon, fresh fish and curries. There's a good selection of English
cheeses, and nice sweets include fruit pies
and trifle. Patio.   **Family pub**

Sandiway *(Food)*   *Blue Cap*

520 Chester Road, Near Northwich · *Cheshire*
Map 3 B4
Sandiway (0606) 883006

Owners Lanchester Taverns
Landlords Mike & Joan Beaman
Steak pie £2.25 Lasagne £2.25 (Last
order 9.30pm. No bar food Sun–Tues eves)
🍺 Wilson's Great Northern Bitter, Special
Mild; Guinness; Carlsberg; Holsten; Foster's;
cider. *Real ale*

Friendly service brings warmth to the plain
bar and lightwood panelled lounges of this
large pub. Homely food includes soups,
sandwiches and simple hot dishes, grilled
fish, steaks and omelettes. There is also a
selection of cold meats with help-yourself
salads. Finish with trifle or apple pie. ·
Sandwiches only in the evening. Patio.
                                    Family pub

Sandon Bank *(Food)*   *Seven Stars Inn*

Near Stafford · *Staffordshire* · Map 4 C4
Sandon (088 97) 316

Brewery Burtonwood
Landlords Gill & Ron Roestenburg

Chicken chasseur £3 Apple pie 85p (Last
order 10pm)
🍺 Burtonwood Bitter, Dark Mild, Top Hat;
Guinness; Tuborg Gold, Pils; cider. *Real ale*

Ron Roestenburg is the dedicated landlord
and chef at this friendly pub, which stands
on a hilltop alongside the B5066. Regular
favourites among the tasty bar snacks
include rainbow trout and beef curry, with
additional choice provided by popular daily
specials like chicken à la grecque or pork
in cider. Sandwiches, ploughman's and
salads available at lunchtime (except
Sunday). Nice sweets. Garden. **Family pub**

Sandside (B & B)   *Ship Inn*

Near Milnthorpe · *Cumbria* · Map 3 B2
Milnthorpe (044 82) 3113

Brewery William Younger's Inns
Landlord Mr John Nancarrow

BEDROOMS 5   Grade 2   £C   (No dogs)
🍺 Younger's Scotch Bitter, Dark Mild;
Kestrel; Taunton cider. *Real ale*

Standing right on the Kent estuary, this well-patronised inn affords fine views of the sea and the distant Cumbrian hills. The smartly refurbished bar is roomy and comfortable, and in good weather you can sit outside and watch the tide rushing in. Cheerful, traditionally furnished bedrooms share a single modern bathroom. Children not accommodated overnight. **Family pub**

Sandwich (B & B)   *Fleur-de-Lis*

Delf Street · *Kent* · Map 6 D3
Sandwich (0304) 611131

Brewery Whitbread
Landlord Mr R. J. Tillings

BEDROOMS 8   Grades 1 & 2   £C
🍺 Wethered's Bitter, Fremlins Bitter, Tusker;
Guinness; Heineken; Stella Artois; cider.
Real ale

The landlord's love of the sea is reflected in the nautical knick-knacks that adorn one of the bars in this cheerful red-brick pub. There are three bars in all, including one with a pool table and video game machines. Comfortable bedrooms in the main building have a pleasantly traditional appeal, while annexe rooms with shower cabinets are more modern. All have TV.

Sandygate (Food)   *Blue Ball Inn*

Near Exeter · *Devon* · Map 8 C3
Topsham (039 287) 3401

Brewery Whitbread
Landlords Mr & Mrs Courtenay

Beef steak & oyster pie £3.95 Chicken
Marengo £3.50 (Last order 10pm)
🍺 Flowers Best Bitter; Whitbread Best Bitter;
Bass; Heineken; cider. *Real ale*

Scallops with ratatouille, butter-roasted chicken with courgettes and garlicky tomato sauce, sweet and sour lamb on rice – such enterprising daily specials, many with a Middle Eastern accent, draw the crowds to this modest thatched pub situated down a narrow lane near junction 30 of the M5. Fiery chilli con carne with crusty bread remains popular, and you can also get ploughman's, sandwiches and salads. Ice cream to finish.   **Family pub**

Saunderton (Food, B & B)   *Rose & Crown Inn*

Wycombe Road · *Buckinghamshire* · Map 6 B3
Princes Risborough (084 44) 5299

Free House
Landlords R. M. & J. G. Watson
BEDROOMS 15   Grade 1   £A+   (No dogs)
Steak & Guinness pie £2.25 Home-made
soup 95p (Last order 10pm)
🍺 Morrell's Varsity Bitter; Morland's Bitter;
Wethered's Bitter; Whitbread Best Bitter;
Guinness; Heineken; cider. *Real ale*

Five attractive new bedrooms have been added to this roadside inn on the A4041; all rooms are comfortably furnished, with colour TVs and radio-alarms. The bow-fronted bar features a tempting display of cold meats and salads, and there are also hot dishes like home-made soup, chicken in the basket and Welsh rarebit. Fresh local seafood is particularly well represented in summer. No under-eights overnight. Accommodation closed 25 Dec–1 Jan. Garden.

England

Scole *(Food, B & B)*   *Scole Inn*

Near Diss · *Norfolk* · Map 5 D2
Scole (037 978) 481

Free House
Landlord Mr Bob Nylk
BEDROOMS 20   Grade 1   £A
Duck & lamb casserole £2.40 Lymeswold
ploughman's £1.10 (Last order 10pm)
🍺 Adnam's Bitter; Stones Bitter; McEwan's
Export; Guinness; Tennents's Extra; Carling
Black Label; Taunton cider. *Real ale*

This impressive roadside inn, which has
been dispensing hospitality since 1655,
offers a warm welcome. In the cheerful
bars you can enjoy simple, well-prepared
snacks like soup, sandwiches and salads,
plus hot dishes such as tasty liver and
onions or roast lamb. Bedrooms (all with
baskets of fruit and colour TV) range from
traditional ones in the main building to
especially well-equipped modern rooms in
the converted stable block.   **Family pub**

Seahouses *(B & B)*   *Olde Ship Hotel*

Northumberland · Map 2 D4
Seahouses (0665) 720200

Free House
Landlords Alan & Jean Glen

BEDROOMS 9   Grade 2   £B (No dogs)
🍺 Scottish & Newcastle Exhibition,
Newcastle Bitter; McEwan's Best Scotch,
80/-; Guinness; Cavalier; cider.

The lounge and bars of this quaint little inn
above the picturesque harbour are verit-
able museums of naval bric-à-brac. The
pub is popular with the locals, and fishermen radio in their drinks orders while still
out at sea! Shipshape bedrooms, most with
modern tiled bath or shower rooms, have
traditional furniture, colour TVs and tea-
makers. Breakfast is appropriately hearty.
Accommodation closed mid-Oct to Easter.
Family pub

Sedgefield *(Food)*   *Nag's Head Inn*

8 West End · *Co. Durham* · Map 4 C1
Sedgefield (0740) 20234

Brewery Charrington
Landlords Mr & Mrs I. Campbell

Sirloin steak £4.50 Tacos with rice &
salad £2.95 (Last order 10pm)
🍺 Bass; Stones Bitter; Guinness; Carling
Black Label; Taunton cider. *Real ale*

The enterprising Campbells offer plenty of
attractions in this 300-year-old white-
painted pub. There's an interesting choice
of bar snacks including American hamburgers and some Mexican specialities like
spicy tacos and deep-fried ice cream, as
well as pub favourites such as piping-hot
French onion soup, grills and lasagne. A
sandwich bar provides extra variety at
lunchtime, and the pub also has an extensive cocktail list.   **Family pub**

Sedgefield *(B & B)*   *New Dun Cow*

43 Front Street · *Co. Durham* · Map 4 C1
Sedgefield (0740) 20894

Owners Ramside Estates
Landlord Mr Geoff Raynor

BEDROOMS 6   Grade 1   £C
🍺 Scottish & Newcastle Exhibition,
Newcastle Bitter; Younger's Tartan;
McEwan's Best Scotch; Guinness; Harp;
Taunton cider.

Motorists travelling along the A1 will find
this welcoming white-painted pub con-
venient for an overnight stop. You can
unwind with a drink in the intimate cocktail
bar or the comfortable Victorian-style
public bar. After that you can retire to one of
the spotlessly clean bedrooms, which are
attractively furnished in traditional style
and equipped with radios, TVs and telephones. Tasty breakfasts. Terrace.

Seighford *(Food)*   *Hollybush*

Near Stafford · *Staffordshire* · Map 4 C4
Seighford (078 575) 280

Brewery Ansell
Landlord Mr & Mrs J. Fowden

Lasagne £2.45 Lemon syllabub 95p (Last
order 10pm)
🍺 Ansell's Bitter, Mild; Tetley's Traditional
Bitter; Guinness; Skol; Löwenbräu; cider.
Real ale

This fine 17th-century pub is a characterful
venue for a quiet drink and tasty snack.
Richly flavoured mushroom soup, garlic
prawns and hot Brie in breadcrumbs make
excellent starters or light meals, while
more substantial items include chicken
Kiev, chilli and a good meaty steak and
kidney pie. Leave room for a sweet – perhaps cider-baked apple or exquisite lemon
syllabub. Garden.   **Family pub**

Sellack *(Food)*   *Loughpool Inn*

Near Ross-on-Wye · *Hereford & Worcester*
Map 7 D2
Harewood End (098 987) 236
Free House
Landlord Mr P. Whitford
Pork with peach sauce £3.75 Beef Stroganoff
£4.95 (Last order 10pm)
🍺 Bass; Mitchells & Butlers Springfield Bitter;
Wadworth's 6X; Worthington Best Bitter;
Guinness; Carling Black Label; Harp; cider.
Real ale

One look at the blackboard menus will tell you
that this is a pub where they take their food
seriously! In the friendly surroundings of the
beamed bar you might start your meal with
whitebait, deep-fried Brie or stuffed mushrooms with tasty garlic mayonnaise. Main
courses could include moussaka, trout with
prawns and garlic fried chicken, and the cold
buffet is a popular summer feature. Garden.
                              Family pub

Semley *(Food, B & B)*   *Benett Arms*

Near Shaftesbury · *Wiltshire* · Map 8 D3
East Knoyle (074 783) 221

Brewery Gibbs Mew
Landlord Mr Joe Duthie

BEDROOMS 6   Grade 1   £B
Steak & kidney pie £2.50 Chocolate
mousse £1.20 (Last order 9.45pm)
🍺 Gibbs Premium Bitter; Guinness; Tuborg
Gold; cider. *Real ale*

The lively Joe Duthie has established a
loyal following of regulars at this whitewashed village pub. A good selection of
tasty bar snacks ranges from salads, home-
made soup and pâté to satisfying casseroles, game pie and garlic mushrooms.
Dishes from the restaurant menu add further choice. Attractive bedrooms, including
some in a modern annexe, have colour TVs
and tea-makers.   **Family pub**

Sennen Cove *(B & B)*   *Old Success Inn*

Land's End · *Cornwall* · Map 8 A4
Sennen (073 687) 232

Free House
Landlords John & Anne Cutler

BEDROOMS 18   Grade 2   £C (No dogs)
🍺 St Austell Tinner's Ale, Best Bitter; Carne's
Falmouth Bitter; John Smith's Yorkshire Bitter;
Guinness; Carlsberg; cider. *Real ale*

Overnight guests wake to the sound of the
surf at this delightful old inn, which stands
right above a sandy cove near Land's End.
The simply furnished bedrooms – eight with
their own bathrooms – are bright and cheerful, and many enjoy lovely views out to sea.
There are two bars (one a popular spot with
local fishermen) and a comfortable first-
floor residents' lounge with TV. Patio.
                              Family pub

231

England

Shaftesbury *(B & B)*   *Mitre Inn & Sunridge Hotel*

23 High Street · *Dorset* · Map 8 D3
Shaftesbury (0747) 2488

Brewery Eldridge Pope
Landlord Mr W. M. Davis-Sellick

BEDROOMS 18   Grades 1 & 2   £C
🍺 Eldridge Pope Royal Oak, IPA; Guinness;
Faust Pilsner, Export; Taunton cider. *Real ale*

The Mitre is a fine, traditional stone-built
inn with cosy, homely bars and nice views
over Blackmoor Vale. It also has eight comfortable bedrooms, while ten more modern
ones with private bath and showers are in
the nearby Sunridge Hotel, which also
boasts a health and leisure centre. All
rooms have colour TVs.   **Family pub**

Shalfleet *(Food)*   *New Inn*

Yarmouth Road · *Isle of Wight* · Map 6 A4
Calbourne (098 378) 314

Brewery Whitbread
Landlords Nigel & Brenda Simpson

Steak pie £1 Pint of prawns £1.40 (Last
order 10.30pm)
🍺 Whitbreads Best, Pompey Royal, Strong
Country; Flower's Original; Guinness; Stella
Artois; cider. *Real ale*

A pint of prawns, served in the shell with
garlic mayonnaise or shellfish sauce, is
typical of the simple yet delicious bar
snacks served at this popular and characterful old inn. Local crab and lobster, rainbow trout and conger eel are among the
many other fishy favourites, while meat-
eaters can tuck into steak pies, country
sausages and home-cooked joints. Garden.

Shave Cross *(Food)*   *Shave Cross Inn*

Marshwood Vale, Near Bridport · *Dorset*
Map 8 D3
Broadwindsor (0308) 68358
Free House
Landlords Mr & Mrs W. B. Slade
Shave Cross sausages £1.30 Ploughman's
lunch 95p (Last order 9.30pm)
🍺 Hall & Woodhouse Badger Best Bitter;
Devenish Wessex Best Bitter; Eldridge Pope
Royal Oak; Bass; Guinness; Carlsberg; Carling
Black Label; cider. *Real ale*

The medieval charm of this delightful
thatched pub is preserved in flagstone
floors, beamed ceilings and a fine inglenook fireplace. It also has a lovely rose
garden with a wishing well. Bar snacks
include ploughman's platters, herby Dorset
pâté and excellent locally made sausages,
with summer treats like fresh crab and
lobster salads. Difficult to find, so ask
directions. Closed Monday (except Bank
Holidays).   **Family pub**

Shelley *(Food)*   *Three Acres Inn*

Roydhouse · *West Yorkshire* · Map 4 C3
Huddersfield (0484) 602606

Free House
Landlord Mr D. Truelove
Creamed mushrooms in port £1.25 Ham &
asparagus pancake £2.75 (Last order 9.30pm.
No bar food Sun eve)
🍺 Tetley's Bitter, Mild; Stones Bitter;
Theakston's Best Bitter; Guinness; Carlsberg;
cider. *Real ale*

The Trueloves (father and son) know how
to welcome visitors to this stone-built pub
on the moors. In the roomy bar you can tuck
into generous platefuls of home-made
steak, kidney and mushroom pie, a traditional roast or perhaps fresh crab meat.
Sandwiches are available, too, and tasty
starters like egg and prawn mayonnaise,
with homely crumbles to finish. Closed
lunchtime Monday and Saturday.
Family pub

Shenington *(Food)*   *Bell*

Oxfordshire · Map 5 A2
Edge Hill (029 587) 274
Free House
Landlords Mr & Mrs Keith Brewer
Pheasant & venison casserole £4.75 Crispy
Somerset lamb in cider £3.25 (Last order
10.30pm. No bar food Sun eve, also Sun lunch
Nov–April)
🍺 Hook Norton Best Bitter; Wadworth's 6X;
Bass Special; Worthington 'E'; Guinness;
Harp. *Real ale*

You must book if you want to sample
Vanessa Brewer's excellent and enterprising cooking in the pleasant bar of this lovely
old pub. Start with rich, creamy spinach
soup or fish pâté, and go on to delicious
light asparagus quiche or something more
substantial – perhaps liver and bacon hot
pot, fiery pork vindaloo or crispy Somerset
lamb in cider; there's also game in winter.
Finish with fruity peach and almond tart or
apple charlotte with cream.   **Family pub**

Shepperton *(B & B)*   *Anchor Hotel*

Church Square · *Middlesex* · Map 6 B3
Walton-on-Thames (0932) 221618

Free House
Landlord Peter Wilson

BEDROOMS 24 Grade 1 £A
🍺 Ruddle's County; Eldridge Pope Royal
Oak; 1880 Ale; Webster's Yorkshire Bitter;
Guinness; Foster's; Holsten Export; cider.
Real ale

Richly carved oak panelling creates a
solidly traditional atmosphere in the bars of
this handsome white-painted hotel, which
stands in a quiet square close to the
river Thames. Double-glazed bedrooms,
uniformly decorated in a bright, fairly
modern style, have smart fitted units, TVs,
tea-makers and neat, compact bathrooms.
There's a pleasant terrace for alfresco
summer sipping.   **Family pub**

Shepperton *(Food)*   *King's Head*

Church Square · *Middlesex* · Map 6 B3
Walton-on-Thames (0932) 221910

Brewery Courage
Landlord David Longhurst

Shepperton pie £1.45 Treacle tart 85p (Last
order 10.10pm. No bar food Sun)
🍺 Courage Directors Bitter, Best Bitter; John
Smith's Bitter; Guinness; Hofmeister;
Kronenbourg; Taunton cider. *Real ale*

Here's a fine old pub, close by the Thames,
sporting two 'characters': JC, the bull-
terrier, and Maria, the long-serving
Spanish lady whose versatile bar snacks
are definite crowd-pullers of a lunchtime
and evening. Her delicious versions of
Welsh rarebit, cottage pie and hot treacle
tart are distinguished by original touches;
you might also choose soup (in winter),
quiche, home-cooked ham or just a sandwich. Patio.

Shepperton *(Food)*   *Thames Court*

Towpath · *Middlesex* · Map 6 B3
Walton-on-Thames (0932) 221957

Free House
Landlord Mr L. J. Negus
Prawn sandwich £1.15 Stuffed leg of lamb with
potatoes & vegetables £2.20 (Last
order 9.30pm)
🍺 Bass; Charrington's IPA; Stones Bitter;
Tennent's Extra; Guinness; Carling Black
Label; Taunton cider. *Real ale*

An attractive brick building in an idyllic
location overlooking the Thames by
Shepperton weir. At lunchtime in the finely
panelled bar, you can enjoy hearty chicken
soup and take your pick from a selection of
salads to accompany cold meats and raised
pies. There are also sandwiches, pâtés,
good-looking cheeses and hot specials
(October–April only) like veal provençale.
For a finish with a flourish, try the fresh
strawberry flan.   **Family pub**

Shepton Mallet *(B & B)*   *Kings Arms*

Leg Square · *Somerset* · Map 8 D3
Shepton Mallet (0749) 3781

Brewery Hall
Landlords Mr & Mrs Peter Swan

BEDROOMS 3   Grade 2   £C
🍺 Wadworth's 6X; Hall's Harvest Bitter;
Ind Coope Burton Ale; Guinness;
Löwenbräu; Skol; cider. *Real ale*

Visitors to this really appealing 17th-century stone pub can expect a right royal welcome from friendly hosts Mr and Mrs Swan. There are three charming rustic bars (one with a collection of marvellous old photographs), as well as a peaceful residents' lounge. Pretty bedrooms have traditional furniture and floral fabrics, plus tea-makers; the modern public bathroom is spotlessly clean.   **Family pub**

Shiplake *(Food, B & B)*   *Baskerville Arms*

Nr Henley-on-Thames · *Oxfordshire* · Map 6 B3
Wargrave (073 522) 3332
Brewery Whitbread
Landlords Harry & Pat Caffrey
BEDROOMS 3   Grade 2   £A   (No dogs)
Chilli con carne £2.50 Steak & kidney pie £1.20
(Last order 9.30pm. No bar food Sun &
Mon eves)
🍺 Wethered's Bitter, SPA; Flower's Original;
Whitbread Best Bitter; Guinness; Heineken;
Stella Artois; cider. *Real ale*

In the roomy bar of this sturdy, red-brick pub you can get anything from a sandwich to a three-course meal. Blackboard menus spell out the day's offerings, which could include quiche, home-cooked ham, excellent chilli con carne and deliciously light and tangy lemon syllabub. The three comfortable bedrooms all have TVs and share a well-fitted modern bathroom. Very good breakfasts. Garden.   **Family pub**

Shipston on Stour *(Food, B & B)* ★   *White Bear*

High Street · *Warwickshire* · Map 5 A2
Shipston on Stour (0608) 61558
Brewery Bass
Landlords Mr & Mrs Hugh Roberts
BEDROOMS 9   Grade 1   £C
Steak & kidney pie £2.95 Fresh salmon
quiche £3.75 (Last order 9.30pm. No bar food
Sun eve)
🍺 Bass; Mitchells & Butlers Mild, Brew XI;
Worthington 'E'; Guinness; Carling Black
Label; Taunton cider. *Real ale*

The Robertses are the perfect hosts at this handsome pub, which is justly renowned for its marvellous bar food. Blackboards announce the day's specials, such as deliciously herby vegetable soup, grilled sardines, Lancashire hot pot and pork casserole. There are also lots of salads, sandwiches and glorious puddings. Filled baguettes only for Sunday lunch. Super bedrooms (most with private bathrooms) are traditionally furnished.   **Family pub**

Shipton-under-Wychwood *(Food, B & B)*   *Lamb Inn*

High Street · *Oxfordshire* · Map 5 A2
Shipton-under-Wychwood (0993) 830465
Free House
Landlords Hugh & Lynne Wainwright
BEDROOMS 5   Grade 2   £B   (No dogs)
George's Cotswold pie £3.25 Trout & sauté
potatoes £2.95 (Last order 9.30pm. No bar food
Sun lunch)
🍺 Hook Norton Best Bitter; Wadworth's 6X;
Guinness (winter only); Löwenbräu; Grünhalle;
Taunton cider (summer only). *Real ale*

The atmosphere is warm and welcoming, the bar food excellent at the Wainwrights' characterful Cotswold inn. Meat pies and savoury pancakes are popular choices, along with soup, summer salads, flavoursome pâtés and specials such as roast lamb. Up a steep staircase are five well-kept bedrooms with sturdy old furniture and tea-makers; four have private facilities. Good breakfasts. No children overnight. Terrace.

Shipton-under-Wychwood *(Food, B & B)* *Shaven Crown Hotel*

High Street · *Oxfordshire* · Map 5 A2
Shipton-under-Wychwood (0993) 830330

Free House
Landlords Brookes family
BEDROOMS 9 Grade 1 £A (No dogs)
Steak, kidney & mushroom pie with
vegetables £2.95 Mushroom & walnut
pancake with salad £2.15 (Last order 9.30pm)
🍺 Flowers Best Bitter, Original; Heineken;
Tuborg Gold, cider. *Real ale*

Rich in architectural history, this beautifully
kept place – once a monk's hospice – is
built around an attractive courtyard garden. Charming bedrooms with sturdy old
furnishings provide comfortable overnight
accommodation, while tasty bar snacks
satisfy the inner man. The menu offers
standard items like soup, lasagne and chilli
con carne along with the popular grilled
potato skins with bacon and cheese and an
irresistible banana cake.

Shoreham-by-Sea *(Food)* *Red Lion*

Old Shoreham Road · *West Sussex* · Map 6 B4
Shoreham (079 17) 3171

Brewery Phoenix
Landlord Norman Stevens
Prawns creole £2.50 Chilli con carne £1.75
(Last order 9.45pm. No bar food Mon eve &
all Sun)
🍺 Gale's HSB; Usher's Best Bitter; Tamplins
Bitter; Samuel Websters Yorkshire Bitter;
Guinness; Holsten; cider. *Real ale*

There are lovely views of the South Downs
from this low white-painted pub, whose
fascinating history goes back to Saxon
times. The new tenants take great pride in
their bar food, and everything is good and
fresh, from ploughman's with delicious
home-boiled ham and warm cottage rolls
to lasagne, quiche lorraine and kebabs. To
finish, try the excellent spiced apple flan.
Garden.

Silk Willoughby *(Food)* *Horseshoes*

London Road, Sleaford · *Lincolnshire*
Map 5 B1
Sleaford (0529) 303153

Brewery John Smith
Landlords Mr & Mrs Cuñago

Seafood pancake £2.75 Charlotte russe 95p
(Last order 10pm. No bar food Sun eve)
🍺 John Smith's Bitter, Mild, Lager;
Guinness; Hofmeister.

Careful modernisation has enhanced the
appeal of this 19th-century red-brick pub,
which stands in a charmingly named
village on the A15. The blackboard menu
changes daily to present a good variety of
tasty bar fare, from soup and pâté to
halibut, lasagne and a really scrumptious
steak and kidney pie. Nice sweets, too,
including a moreish charlotte russe.
Garden. **Family pub**

Sindlesham *(Food, B & B)* *Walter Arms*

Bearwood Road · *Berkshire* · Map 6 B3
Wokingham (0734) 780260

Brewery Courage
Landlords Mr & Mrs W. M. Cox
BEDROOMS 4 Grade 2 £B (No dogs)
Country pie & vegetables £2 Hungarian
pancakes £1.75 (Last order 10pm)
🍺 Courage Directors Bitter, Best Bitter, John
Courage; Guinness; Kronenbourg;
Hofmeister. *Real ale*

The three cosy, interconnecting bars of this
imposing Victorian pub are busy at meal-
times, when Mrs Cox's tasty bar snacks
attract a crowd. Her soups are flavoursome,
and there's plenty of substantial fare like
beef in burgundy, curry, moussaka and
good home-made fruit pies. Well-cared-
for bedrooms, traditionally furnished and
all with colour TV, provide comfortable
accommodation. No children overnight;
bedrooms closed 23 Dec–1 Jan.

England

Skidby   *(Food)*   Half Moon Inn

16 Main Street · *Humberside* · Map 4 D3
Hull (0482) 843403

Brewery John Smith
Landlord Peter Madeley

Yorkshire pudding sandwich with beef £2.70
Steak & kidney pie with chips & mushy
peas £2.10 (Last order 10pm)
🍺 John Smith's Bitter, Chestnut Mild;
Guinness; Hofmeister; Harp.

Huge man-sized Yorkshire puddings,
served with rich onion gravy, minced beef
and asparagus, chilli con carne or even
roast beef, are the claim to fame of this jolly
white-painted pub just off the A164. At
lunchtime you can also tuck into home-
made soup, hot salt beef sandwiches or
steak and kidney pie, and round things off
with gâteau or apple pie. There's a more
limited choice in the evening. Patio for fine-
weather drinking.   **Family pub**

Skirmett   *(Food, B & B)*   King's Arms

Near Henley-on-Thames, Oxfordshire
Buckinghamshire · Map 6 B3
Turville Heath (049 163) 247
Free House
Landlords Mr & Mrs R. Grahamslaw
BEDROOMS 4   Grade 2   £B
Beefburger with salad £1.20 Sirloin steak with
potatoes £5.45 (Last order 10pm)
🍺 Ruddle's Bitter; Wethered's SPA, Bitter;
Guinness; Stella Artois; Heineken; cider.
Real ale

Charming hosts Mr and Mrs Grahamslaw
really make guests feel welcome at this
friendly village pub. There's afternoon tea
on arrival, and the cosy bedrooms offer
thoughtful touches such as bottled spring
water, books and tissues, plus ample
storage space. Two have TVs and shower
rooms. Downstairs, you'll find two pleasant
bars where enjoyable bar snacks include
soups, pasta, Cumberland sausages and
home-made ice cream.   **Family pub**

We have raised our standards

considerably since last year.

The omission of some houses

that appeared in last year's

Guide is no reflection on their

standing.

Slaidburn   *(B & B)*   Hark to Bounty Inn

Near Clitheroe · *Lancashire* · Map 3 B2
Slaidburn (020 06) 246

Free House
Landlords Mr & Mrs P. Turner

BEDROOMS 8   Grade 1   £A
🍺 Thwaites Bitter, Mild; Theakston's Old
Peculier; Guinness; Stein; Carlsberg; cider.
Real ale

The Turner family are maintaining admirable standards of friendly hospitality in this
13th-century stone pub. Locals gather for a
pint and a chat in the spacious beamed bar,
and there's a relaxing TV lounge for residents. Prettily decorated, simply furnished
bedrooms (including an especially nice one
in the attic) have radios and tea-makers; all
but one also boast fully tiled modern bathrooms. Garden.   **Family pub**

Slaithwaite   *(Food)*   *White House*

Huddersfield · *West Yorkshire* · Map 4 C3
Huddersfield (0484) 842245

Free House
Landlord Mrs Gillian Sykes
Fried mussels with garlic mayonnaise £1.75
Prawn cocktail platter £2.50 (Last order 10pm)
🍺 Tetley's Mild; Younger's IPA, Scotch
Bitter, Chieftain; Guinness; McEwan's Lager.
Real ale

Ask for directions to this charming country
inn set above the village on the B6107
Marsden to Meltham road. Once there
you'll be welcomed by Mrs Sykes and her
loyal helpers and can look forward to a delicious snack in the beamed bar. As well as
plain and toasted sandwiches and soup,
you can get home-made burgers, a really
tasty cottage pie made in the traditional
style, flans, pizzas and specialities such as
fried mussels with garlic mayonnaise.

Sleights   *(B & B)*   *Salmon Leap*

Near Whitby · *North Yorkshire* · Map 4 D2
Whitby (0947) 810233

Brewery Cameron
Landlords Mr & Mrs B. Gibson

BEDROOMS 10   Grade 2   £C
🍺 Cameron's Best Bitter, Strongarm; Lion;
Guinness; Hansa; cider. *Real ale*

Perched high above the Esk valley, this
sturdy stone inn provides comfortable
accommodation in warm, friendly surroundings. Bedrooms in the modern
extension are neat and compact, with well-
designed fitted furniture, while those in the
main building are more old-fashioned in
style and roomy enough for families. Three
bars offer plenty of elbow room for the
thirsty and there's a very pretty garden.
Family pub

Smarden   *(Food, B & B)*   *Bell*

Bell Lane · *Kent* · Map 6 C3
Smarden (023 377) 283
Free House
Landlord Mr Ian Turner
BEDROOMS 4   Grade 1   £C (No dogs)
Clam fries £1.50 Gammon steak £2.95
(Last order 10pm)
🍺 Theakston's Old Peculier, Best Bitter;
Shepherd Neame Masterbrew; Fuller's
London Pride; Murphy's Stout; cider.
Real ale

In the busy bar of this quintessential
weatherboarded Kentish pub you can
sample Ian Turner's fine real ales and delicious food: in addition to superb lasagne
and the very popular rump steak, you can
also get salads, pizzas and sandwiches, plus
some nice old-fashioned puds. An exterior
spiral staircase leads to the comfortable,
tastefully furnished bedrooms, all with TV.
Continental breakfast only. No accommodation Christmas week.   **Family pub**

Smarden   *(Food)*   *Chequers Inn*

Kent · Map 6 C3
Smarden (023 377) 217

Brewery Courage
Landlords Mr & Mrs Frank Stevens

Chilli con carne £1.95 Steak & kidney pie £2.95
(Last order 10pm)
🍺 Courage Directors Bitter, Best Bitter, Dark
Mild; Guinness; Hofmeister; Kronenbourg;
Taunton cider. *Real ale*

Landlord Frank Stevens does most of the
cooking in this friendly weatherboarded
village pub, and he makes a very good job
of it. We enjoyed subtly flavoured cream of
vegetable soup with superb French bread
(the real thing, specially imported), robust
pork pâté and delicious weiner schnitzel;
other tasty offerings include steaks, chilli
con carne and home-made pies. Simple
sweets. Garden.

Snainton   *(B & B)*   *Coachman Inn*

Near Scarborough · *North Yorkshire* · Map 4 D2
Scarborough (0723) 85231

Brewery Cameron
Landlords Mr & Mrs G. C. Senior

BEDROOMS 12   Grade 1   £A
🍺 Cameron's Best Bitter, Strongarm; Hansa;
cider.

Set back from the A170 in pleasant gardens
and paddocks, this rambling Georgian
coaching house is a good base for
exploring the North Yorkshire moors. The
lounge is comfortable and homely, with
fresh flowers and plenty of magazines, and
there are two bars. Spacious bedrooms,
most with their own bath/shower rooms,
are furnished mainly in bright modern
style. Garden.   **Family pub**

Sonning-on-Thames   *(Food, B & B)*   *Bull Inn*

Near Reading · *Berkshire* · Map 6 B3
Reading (0734) 693901

Brewery Wethered
Landlord Mr D. T. Cotton

BEDROOMS 5   Grade 2   £A+   (No dogs)
Selection of cold meats & salads from £3 Cheese
& biscuits 70p (Last order 10pm)
🍺 Wethered's Bitter, SPA, Winter Royal;
Heineken; cider. *Real ale*

As pretty as a picture, with wistaria hugging its
walls, this centuries-old village pub is an excellent place for a lunchtime snack. A bar display
offers cold meats and simple salads, and in
winter there's soup, toasted sandwiches (the
only evening choice) and a hot special. Simply
furnished bedrooms (all with TV) share a
single public bathroom. No children overnight. Accommodation closed 1 week
Christmas. Patio.

South Leigh   *(Food)*   *Mason Arms*

Near Witney · *Oxfordshire* · Map 6 A3
Witney (0993) 2485

Free House
Landlords The Theobald family
Locally cured salt beef, chips & veg £3.50
Savoury fish pancake £1.95 (Last order 10pm.
No bar food Sun eve)
🍺 Glenny's Witney Bitter; Younger's Scotch
Ale; Newcastle Bitter; Guinness; Beck's.
Real ale

Locally cured salt beef is a speciality at this
attractive old thatched pub in a tiny village.
Enjoy it with chips and peas, in salads or
sandwiches, or with vegetables in a good
warming broth. Other treats include home-
cooked gammon, savoury pancakes and
richly flavoured steak and kidney pie. To
finish, there are some nice puddings made
by ladies in the village. Closed Monday.
Garden.   **Family pub**

South Woodchester   *(Food)*   *Ram Inn*

Near Stroud · *Gloucestershire* · Map 7 D2
Amberley (045 387) 3329

Free House
Landlord Mr David Hicks
Whole prawns & garlic dip £1.95 Lamb &
apricot pie £2.05 (Last order 10pm)
🍺 Archer's Village Bitter; Holden's Black
Country Bitter; Hook Norton Old Hookey;
Cirencester Bitter; Boddington's Bitter;
Guinness. *Real ale*

This attractive little pub in a Cotswold
village wins friends with a fine selection of
real ales and some excellent home cooking.
Mrs Hicks prepares tasty, satisfying dishes
like succulent roast beef or lamb and
apricot pie, along with pizza and savoury
pancakes. There are some tempting cold
choices, too, such as juicy whole prawns
with a garlic dip. Nice views from the
terrace.

South Zeal *(B & B)* | *Oxenham Arms*

Near Okehampton · *Devon* · Map 8 C3
Sticklepath (083 784) 244

Free House
Landlords Mr & Mrs J. H. Henry

BEDROOMS 8   Grades 1 & 2   £B
🍺 Everards Tiger Bitter; Flower's Best Bitter; Guinness; Stella Artois; Kronenbourg; cider (summer only). *Real ale*

Believed to have been built by lay monks in the 12th century, this characterful pub stands in a peaceful village near the A30. Crackling fires warm the beamed public rooms, which include a cosy bar and a restful lounge with antiques and inviting armchairs. There are antiques, too, in many of the bedrooms, plus modern features like colour TVs and tea-makers. Six have private facilities. Garden.   **Family pub**

Southwold *(B & B)* | *Crown Hotel*

High Street · *Suffolk* · Map 5 D2
Southwold (0502) 722275

Brewery Sole Bay Hotels Ltd
Landlord Mrs H. Carpenter

BEDROOMS 21   Grades 1 & 2   £A
🍺 Adnam's Bitter; Skol; Stella Artois. *Real ale*

Comfortable overnight accommodation is provided at this pleasantly run Georgian coaching inn. Rooms at the top boast nice old beams and sloping ceilings, while others have a more modern feel. All are neat, well carpeted and equipped with radio-alarms and colour TVs, and most have their own smart bath or shower room. There's a spacious traditional lounge and two bars. Patio.   **Family pub**

Staddle Bridge *(Food, B & B)* ★ | *McCoy's at the Tontine*

Near Northallerton · *North Yorkshire*
Map 4 C2
East Harlsey (060 982) 207

Free House
Landlords McCoy Brothers
BEDROOMS 6   Grade 1   £A+
Seafood crêpe £2.85 Steak with red wine sauce £6.95 (Last order 10.30pm)
🍺 Cameron's Strongarm; Hansa; Guinness. *Real ale*

Snacks of outstanding quality are served in the informal cellar bar of the McCoy brothers' imposing stone house on the A19. Skill and flair shine through in every dish, from superb soups and succulent steaks to home-made pasta, seafood pancakes and fabulous fruit pies. Large, warm and very comfortable bedrooms are traditionally furnished with great charm. Superb breakfasts.   **Family pub**

Stafford *(B & B)* | *Swan Hotel*

Greengate Street · *Staffordshire* · Map 4 C4
Stafford (0785) 58142

Owners Berni Hotels
Landlord Mr J. Fiddler

BEDROOMS 31   Grade 1   £A+   (No dogs)
🍺 Ansells Bitter, SDB, Mild; Double Diamond; Guinness; Skol; Löwenbräu. *Real ale*

High standards of housekeeping are maintained at this rambling old town-centre hotel, whose white façade includes attractive bow windows. Bedrooms are comfortable and well equipped, with smart fitted furniture, colour TVs, radio/alarms and tea-makers. One room features a four-poster, and all have compact bath or shower rooms. There are two traditionally furnished bars. Accommodation closed 2 weeks Christmas. Garden.   **Family pub**

239

Stamford (B & B)   Bull & Swan Inn

St Martin's · *Lincolnshire* · Map 5 B1
Stamford (0780) 63558

Brewery Melbourns
Landlords William & Rosa Morgado
BEDROOMS 6   Grade 2   £B
Lasagne £2 Mixed grill £2.90
(Last order 10.30pm)
🍺 Sam Smith's Old Brewery Bitter, Mild,
Sovereign; Guinness; Diat Pils; Ayinger Bräu;
cider. *Real ale*

A long tradition of hospitality is being continued at this attractive old coaching inn by
the Morgadoes. Hungry visitors will find
some tasty, homely bar fare, including
chicken liver pâté, hearty ploughman's and
steak sandwiches, as well as hot dishes like
lasagne or perhaps trout provençale, with a
selection of sweets to finish. Prettily
decorated bedrooms, all with washbasins
and colour TVs, share two public bath-
rooms.   **Family pub**

Stamford (B & B)   Crown Hotel

All Saints Place · *Lincolnshire* · Map 5 B1
Stamford (0780) 63136

Free House
Landlords Mr & Mrs R. D. McGahon

BEDROOMS 18   Grade 2   £B
🍺 Ruddle's County; Whitbread Trophy;
Ansells Bitter; Guinness; Heineken; Skol;
Stella Artois. *Real ale*

Robert and Eve McGahon extend a warm
welcome at their fine old stone-built hotel,
which stands near the town centre in the
shadow of All Saints Church. Comfortable
overnight accommodation is provided in
18 good-sized bedrooms, attractively
decorated, solidly furnished and all boasting TVs and tea-makers. Ten have their own
bathrooms. The bar is unpretentiously
modern in style, and there's a simple
lounge.   **Family pub**

Stamford (Food)   ★   George of Stamford

St Martins · *Lincolnshire* · Map 5 B1
Stamford (0780) 55171

Free House
Landlord Mr Jolyon Gough

Antipasto £3.95 Braised oxtail £3.95 (Last
order 11pm)
🍺 Ruddle's Bitter, County; Sam Smith's Old
Brewery Bitter; Kestrel.

The comfortable bars, leafy garden lounge
and cobbled courtyard are equally delightful settings for enjoying the truly super
snacks served at this famous old coaching
inn. An extensive cold buffet is available
each lunchtime (summer evenings as well),
and hot choices include soup, lasagne,
delicious seafood pancakes and steak
sandwiches. Lovely sweets, too. *For
accommodation see Egon Ronay's Lucas
Hotel & Restaurant Guide 1985.* **Family pub**

Standish (Food)   Foresters Arms

Shevington Moor, Near Wigan · *Greater
Manchester* · Map 3 B3
Standish (0257) 421337

Brewery Greenall Whitley
Landlords Ronnie & Jean Baxendale

Chicken & mushroom pie £1.20 Apple pie &
cream 45p (Last order 10pm)
🍺 Greenall Whitley Bitter, Mild; Guinness;
Grünhalle Lager; cider. *Real ale*

Good simple bar fare is available seven
days a week at the Baxendales' friendly
little pub, which stands behind a motel near
junction 27 of the M6. Bumper beef or
ham sandwiches make excellent quick
snacks, and other choices range from tasty
pizzas and savoury pies to scampi, roast
chicken and T-bone steaks. To finish,
home-made apple pie or cheesecake, and
good fresh coffee. Garden.

Stanford Dingley *(Food)* ★ *Old Boot Inn*

Near Bradfield · *Berkshire* · Map 6 B3
Bradfield (0734) 744292

Free House
Landlords John & Eliane Pratt

Roast beef & salad £3.50 Moules
marinière £3.85 (Last order 9pm)
 North Country Breweries Riding Bitter;
Arkell's BBB; Fuller's London Pride; Ruddle's
County; Guinness; Stella Artois. *Real ale*

Eliane Pratt's fine cooking makes it well
worth seeking out this delightful 18th-
century pub in deepest Berkshire. Garlic
mushrooms with bacon on toast makes a
tasty, satisfying snack, and other popular
dishes include lasagne, moules marinière
and rare roast beef with salad (hot roast
Sunday lunchtime). Leave room for a
delicious sweet like profiteroles or apple
flan. The large terrace and attractive garden
add to the pleasure in summer.

Stanton Harcourt *(Food, B & B)* ★ *Harcourt Arms*

Near Eynsham · *Oxfordshire* · Map 6 A3
Oxford (0865) 882192

Brewery Morrell's
Landlord Mr George Dailey

BEDROOMS 16 Grade 1 £B (No dogs)
Grilled king prawns £2.50 Moules
marinière £2.50 (Last order 9.30pm)
 Morrell's Best Bitter, Varsity Bitter
(winter); Guinness; Harp; cider. *Real ale*

Grilled king prawns with garlic mayonnaise
are among the many delights that have put
George Dailey's fine Cotswold pub firmly
on the gastronomic map. Besides the
renowned seafood, you'll find winter soups
and pies and an excellent cold table in
summer. Some lovely puddings too. Well-
equipped bedrooms in charming stone
cottages provide excellent comfort; most
have TVs and private bathrooms. Patio and
garden. **Family pub**

Staple Fitzpaine *(Food)* ★ *Greyhound inn*

Near Taunton · *Somerset* · Map 8 C3
Hatch Beauchamp (0823) 480227
Free House
Landlords Martin Tarr & Paul Toogood
Celery & apple soup 85p Chicken &
vegetable kebabs £2.95 (Last order 10pm.
No bar food Sun eve)
 Golden Hill Exmoor Ale; Eldridge Pope
Royal Oak, Dorchester Bitter; Devenish
Wessex Bitter; Guinness; Faust; Taunton
cider. *Real ale*

Winding lanes lead from the A358 to this
charming, creeper-clad pub, where the air
is tranquil, the welcome warm and the
cooking exceptional. The bar menu is full
of lovely things, from sweetly succulent
prawns with garlic mayonnaise to delicious
seafood, pasta, imaginative vegetarian
dishes and daily specials like lamb curry.
Luscious puddings include a splendid
treacle tart served with clotted cream.
Family pub

Stapleton *(Food)* ★ *Bridge Inn*

Near Darlington · *Co. Durham* · Map 4 C2
Darlington (0325) 50106

Brewery Vaux
Landlords Nicholas & Catherine Young
Salmon with hollandaise sauce £5.75 Lamb's
kidneys with mushrooms & Madeira
sauce £3.75 (Last order 10pm. No bar food Sun
& Mon eves)
 Vaux Samson; Guinness; Norseman;
Taunton cider. *Real ale*

Skill, flair and enthusiasm shine through
Nick Young's cooking at this unpretentious
pub three miles from Darlington. Our celery
soup was a delicious way to start a meal,
and the lamb's kidneys with mushroom
and Madeira sauce made a marvellous
main course. Fresh fish is a great favourite,
and toasted sandwiches are excellent quick
snacks. Don't leave before trying one of
Cathy Young's super sweets. Garden.
Family pub

Starbotton   *Fox & Hounds*

Rebuilt in 1834 after a fearsome flood inundated the village, this
delightful little pub is a haven of warmth and hospitality – even the
exterior looks friendly! A splendid open fireplace surrounded by
burnished brassware dominates the tiny bar, which has a flagstoned
floor and rough stone walls hung with paintings by local artists.

Family pub

Near Kettlewell, Upper Wharfedale · *North Yorkshire* · Map 4 C2
Kettlewell (075 676) 269
Free House   Landlord Mrs B. Hartley
Theakston's Old Peculier, Best Bitter, Mild; Younger's Scotch
Bitter; Carlsberg; cider. *Real ale*

Staveley   *(Food)*   *Royal Oak*

Near Knaresborough · *North Yorkshire*
Map 4 C2
Copgrove (090 14) 267

Brewery Younger
Landlords Peter & Elizabeth Gallagher

Game pie £2.50 Seafood open tart with
vegetables £2.20 (No bar food eves)
Younger's Scotch Bitter, IPA; Guinness;
McEwan's Lager. *Real ale*

The ebullient Gallaghers run this attractive
little village pub. Hunting prints line the
walls of the comfortable lounge bar, and
there's an informal public bar where lunchtime snacks are served. Robust country fare
includes soups, tasty quiches and well-
filled French-bread sandwiches; best of all
is the superb game pie, packed with good
things and served with beautifully cooked
vegetables. Garden.   **Family pub**

Staverton   *(B & B)*   *Sea Trout Inn*

Near Totnes · *Devon* · Map 8 C4
Staverton (080 426) 274

Free House
Landlord Mr Bill McNeill

BEDROOMS 6   Grade 2   £B
John Smiths Yorkshire Bitter, Lager;
Double Diamond; Simonds; Bates; Guinness;
Hofmeister; cider. *Real ale*

Displays of stuffed fish and a large collection of salmon and sea trout flies give the
cosy lounge bar of this peaceful village pub
a distinctly piscatorial atmosphere. But for
those who don't have angling aspirations
there's also a little TV lounge. Prettily
decorated bedrooms have modern furniture and are provided with tea-makers;
bathrooms are spotlessly clean and well
maintained. Patio.   **Family pub**

Steep   *(Food)*   *Harrow Inn*

Near Petersfield · *Hampshire* · Map 6 B4
Petersfield (0730) 62685

Brewery Whitbread
Landlord E. C. McCutcheon

Ham salad £3.75 Stuffed Marrow £2.30
(Last order 9.30pm)
Whitbread Strong Country Bitter, Best
Mild; Flowers Original; Guinness; Heineken;
Stella Artois; cider. *Real ale*

Mr and Mrs McCutcheon maintain this pub
in the nicest traditional style, with few con-
cessions to the 20th century. In the charming atmosphere of the rustic public bar or
the cottage smoke room you can enjoy
simple, hearty fare like ploughman's with
home-cooked ham or rare roast beef, along
with nourishing soup and daily hot dishes
such as lasagne or really delicious stuffed
marrow. There's a neat courtyard for fine-
weather drinking.

Stewkley *(Food)* — *Swan*

Near Leighton Buzzard, Bedfordshire
Buckinghamshire · Map 5 B2
Stewkley (052 524) 285
Brewery Courage
Landlords Colin & Carole Anderson
Chicken liver pâté & toast £1.30 Steak
& kidney pudding with vegetables £2.20
(Last order 9.30pm. No bar food Sun)
🍺 Courage Directors Bitter, Best Bitter, JC;
Guinness; Kronenbourg; Hofmeister;
Taunton cider. *Real ale*

Colin and Carole Anderson generate a really friendly atmosphere in this cosy beamed pub, and Carole delights customers with her interesting choice of fare. As well as favourites like ploughman's and fried scampi, there are lunchtime specials such a superb meaty broth or bacon and onion dumpling. Sweets include a delicious sherry trifle. Grills, a pint of prawns or perhaps fish pie in the evening. Garden. Booking advisable. **Family pub**

Stockbridge *(Food, B & B)* — *Vine Inn*

High Street · *Hampshire* · Map 6 A3
Andover (0264) 810652
Brewery Whitbread
Landlord Mr L. A. Wilkins
BEDROOMS 4 Grades 2 £C
Steak & kidney pie £2.35 Haddock bake £3.25
(Last order 9.30pm. No bar food Sat &
Sun eves)
🍺 Flowers Original; Whitbread Strong
Country Bitter, Best Bitter; Hampshire Bitter;
Guinness; cider. *Real ale*

Mr Wilkins' daughter is queen of the kitchen in this homely little pub, and you can feast regally on her tasty bar snacks. There's plenty of choice ranging from crab mousse and filled jacket potatoes (try the cheesy smoked haddock) to sandwiches, salads and stuffed peppers, with excellent creamy trifle to finish. Four traditionally furnished bedrooms (all with colour TV) are kept in good order, and you'll start the day with a superb breakfast. **Family pub**

Stockbridge *(Food, B & B)* — *White Hart Inn*

High Street · *Hampshire* · Map 6 A3
Andover (0264) 810475
Free House
Landlord Peter Curtis
BEDROOMS 11 Grades 1 & 2 £C (No dogs)
Steak & kidney & vegetables £2.25 Fisherman's
lunch £1.75 (Last order 10.15pm)

🍺 Wadworth's 6X; Bass; Hancock's HB;
Gale's HSB; Guinness; Carling Black Label;
Taunton cider. *Real ale*

This inn is now a pleasant mixture of old and new. Bedrooms range from prettily decorated, beamed rooms in the main building to compact modern ones with up-to-date private bathrooms in converted stables; all have TV. In the two rustic bars you can tuck into flavoursome soups, home-made pâté, sandwiches and substantial dishes like curry or nourishing lamb casserole. Sweets, too, such as fruit pie. Three-course Sunday lunch. Terrace.

Stoke-by-Nayland *(Food)* — *Crown*

Near Colchester, Essex
Suffolk · Map 5 D2
Nayland (0206) 262346

Free House
Landlords Keith & Tony Symonds
Cod & prawn lasagne £2.50 Steak & kidney pie
£2.40 (Last order 10pm)
🍺 Tolly Cobbold Bitter, Original;
McEwan's Export; Guinness; Carlsberg Hof;
cider. *Real ale*

Inside, beams and lots of space, outside, a lovely garden with views over the rolling Suffolk countryside. Inside or out, you'll enjoy your meal at this large white-painted pub, whose extensive bar menu includes delicious soups, home-cooked ham, seafood lasagne and even fresh lobster. Steaks and basket meals are also popular, and sandwiches and salads are made to order. Plenty of sweets, too. **Family pub**

Stoke St Gregory *(Food)* — *Rose & Crown*

Woodhill, Near Taunton · *Somerset* · Map 8 D3
North Curry (0823) 490296
Free House
Landlords Mr & Mrs Browning

Soup with granary bread 75p Scrumpy
chicken £2.75 (Last order 10pm)
🍺 Golden Hill Exmoor Ale; Eldridge Pope
Royal Oak, Dorchester Bitter, 1880; Bass Toby
Bitter; Guinness; Faust; Taunton cider.
Real ale

Twisting country lanes lead to this friendly
old inn, whose interesting features include
an illuminated well that's 60 feet deep. The
menu, chalked up in the cosy bar, offers
simple, well-prepared dishes served in
generous portions. The choice ranges
from soup and omelettes to cold meat
salads, grilled gammon and succulent
scrumpy chicken. There's excellent home-
baked granary bread and some tempting
sweets. Patio. **Family pub**

Stokenham *(Food)* — *Tradesman's Arms*

Near Kingsbridge · *Devon* · Map 8 C4
Kingsbridge (0548) 580313

Free House
Landlord Allan Matthew

Avocado cream pâté £1.20 Honey roast,
Madeira-flavoured gammon £2.95
(Last order 10pm)
🍺 Usher's Best Bitter; Carling Black Label;
Worthington 'E'; cider. *Real ale*

An enormous range of malt whiskies and
delicious bar food are among the attractions of this charming village inn. Avocado
cream pâté or French onion soup is an
excellent starter, and you could follow with
Madeira-flavoured gammon or fresh fish
from Plymouth. The Sunday lunchtime
curry is a popular feature. Pub closed Mon–
Thurs eves Dec–March. Patio and garden.
Family pub

Stonegate *(Food)* — *Bridge Inn*

Near Wadhurst · *East Sussex* · Map 6 C4
Burwash (0435) 883243

Free House
Landlord Mr John Blake

Mushroom pot £1.95 Savoury sausage
pie £2.75 (Last order 10pm)
🍺 Young's Ordinary, Special Bitter; Friary
Meux Bitter; John Bull Bitter; Guinness;
Skol; Löwenbräu; cider. *Real ale*

John Blake and his young team provide a
warm welcome at this friendly inn standing
in extensive grounds. Snacks served in the
cosy beamed bar are good and varied:
well-filled sandwiches, garlicky mushroom
pot, savoury pancakes, daily specials like
excellent grilled plaice. Chilli con carne and
curry cater well for spicier palates, and
there's a barbecue on Friday evenings in
summer. Garden.

Stony Stratford *(B & B)* — *Bull Hotel*

64 High Street · *Buckinghamshire* · Map 5 B2
Milton Keynes (0908) 567104

Brewery Aylesbury
Landlords Mr & Mrs H. W. Willis

BEDROOMS 12 Grade 2 £B (No dogs)
🍺 ABC Bitter; Everards Tiger; Bass; Morell's
Bitter; Burton Bitter; Guinness; Taunton cider.
Real ale

Travellers staying at this friendly hotel in
coaching days would swop tales with
guests at the neighbouring Cock Hotel,
allegedly giving rise to the cock and bull
story. The tales are different now, but the
welcome's just as warm, and the Vaults Bar
is a favourite rendezvous for lovers of real
ale. Comfortable, well-kept bedrooms have
handsome pine furniture and TVs. No
under-fives overnight.

Stony Stratford *(B & B)*   *Cock Hotel*

72 High Street · *Buckinghamshire* · Map 5 B2
Milton Keynes (0908) 562109

Free House
Landlords Mr & Mrs D. P. Hoskins

BEDROOMS 19   Grade 2   £A
Hook Norton Best Bitter; Adnams Best
Bitter; Wadworths 6X; Carlsberg Hof. *Real ale*

Four attractively furnished modern bedrooms with smart tiled bathrooms have
recently been added to the accommodation
at this agreeable old coaching inn, near
neighbour of the Bull and existing on this
site for five and a half centuries. Other
rooms are comfortably old-fashioned; all
have televisions. The public bar leads to a
lovely garden with pretty shrubs and flower
boxes.   **Family pub**

Stopham Bridge *(Food)*   *White Hart*

Near Pulborough · *West Sussex* · Map 6 B4
Pulborough (079 82) 3321

Brewery Whitbread
Landlords William & Elizabeth Bryce
Back bacon & mushroom sandwich £1.10
Daily special with fresh vegetables £1.75
(Last order 10pm)
Whitbread Best Bitter, Best Mild, Strong
Country Bitter; Flowers Bitter; Guinness;
Heineken; Stella Artois. *Real ale*

William and Elizabeth Bryce tempt
customers to this attractive old pub on the
river Arun with a simple menu of wholesome bar snacks. As well as sandwiches,
filled jacket potatoes and nourishing dishes
like cannelloni and grilled jumbo sausages,
there is a daily special such as tasty cod pie
topped with parsley-speckled pastry and
served with nicely cooked vegetables.
Garden.   **Family pub**

Stourbridge *(B & B)*   *Talbot Hotel*

High Street · *West Midlands* · Map 7 D1
Stourbridge (0384) 394350

Brewery Wolverhampton & Dudley
Landlord Mr Mark Chatterton

BEDROOMS 23   Grades 1 & 2   £B
Bank's Bitter, Mild; Guinness; Harp;
Kronenbourg; cider. *Real ale*

This 500-year-old coaching inn in the town
centre offers a warm welcome and good
accommodation. Five bars provide plenty
of choice for the thirsty, and in fine weather
the covered courtyard comes into its own.
Most bedrooms are furnished in a neat
modern style, though antiques feature in
two of them; all rooms have TVs and tea-
makers, seven their own bathrooms.
                                            Family pub

Stow Bardolph *(Food)*   *Hare Arms*

Near Downham Market · *Norfolk* · Map 5 C1
Downham Market (0366) 382229

Brewery Greene King
Landlords Mr & Mrs D. P. McManus

Steak & mushroom pie £1.95 Stilton & bacon
soup 80p (No bar food Sun & eves)
Greene King Abbot Ale, IPA, Mild;
Kronenbourg; Guinness; Harp; Taunton
cider. *Real ale*

The lunchtime bar snacks are simple,
wholesome and absolutely delicious at this
homely gabled inn, run in the most friendly
fashion by the McManuses. Generously
filled sandwiches, ploughman's and salads
are excellent cold fare, and the blackboard
proclaims the day's soup – our turkey and
vegetable was packed full of good things –
and hot specials like lamb curry or super
steak and mushroom pie. Lovely sweets,
too. Garden.   **Family pub**

Stow-on-the-Wold   *(B & B)*   *Royalist Hotel*

Digbeth Street · *Gloucestershire* · Map 5 A2
Cotswold (0451) 30670

Free House
Landlords Mr & Mrs E. J. Hardman

BEDROOMS 13   Grades 1 & 2   £A   (No dogs)
🍺 Wadworth's 6X; Worthington Best Bitter;
Flower's Original; Whitbread Trophy;
Heineken; Carlsberg Export; cider. *Real ale*

Behind the 17th-century façade of this cosy
hostelry are a thousand years of history.
Open log fires warm the bars and lounge,
and the bedrooms (most with private
facilities) are centrally heated. Some rooms
are splendidly old-fashioned in character,
while the four in the annexe are functionally
modern; all have tea-makers and TVs. No
under-fives overnight. Garden. **Family pub**

Stowe Green   *(Food, B & B)*   *Travellers Rest Inn*

St Briavels, Near Coleford · *Gloucestershire*
Map 7 D2
Dean (0594) 530424
Free House
Landlord Mr C. Choremi
BEDROOMS 3   Grade 2   £C   (No dogs)
Moussaka £3.30 Seafood salad £2.80 (Last
order 10.30pm)
🍺 Bass; Toby Bitter; Stones Bitter;
Worthington Best Bitter; Carling Black Label;
Tennent's Extra; cider. *Real ale*

Lasagne, moussaka and spicy sausages are
regular favourites at this secluded pub
situated between St Briavels and Coleford,
and there are savoury pies, the occasional
fresh Wye salmon if you're lucky
and a weekend carvery. Also sandwiches
and salads, plus soups in winter. Three
simple, well-kept bedrooms share a nice
bathroom and separate shower. Pub closed
Wednesday, accommodation closed 1
week Christmas. Garden.   **Family pub**

Stratford-upon-Avon   *(Food)*   *Slug & Lettuce*

38 Guild Street · *Warwickshire* · Map 5 A2
Stratford-upon-Avon (0789) 299700

Free House
Landlord Mr Mark Coles

Mushrooms baked with bacon & garlic £2.25
Ragout of beef £3.25 (Last order 10pm)
🍺 Wadworth's 6X, IPA; Arkell's Best Bitter;
Simpkiss Bitter; Guinness; Tuborg; Taunton
cider. *Real ale*

Don't let the name put you off – the food is
excellent at this pleasant, well-run pub. A
blackboard menu in the panelled bar offers
tempting dishes ranging from creamy
soups and hot bacon sandwiches to
barbecued pork casserole and our super
baked chicken breast with avocado and
cream cheese. Delicious sweets include
chocolate mousse and a lovely sticky
treacle tart. Terrace.   **Family pub**

Stuckton   *(Food)*   ★   *Three Lions Inn*

Stuckton Road, near Fordingbridge
Hampshire · Map 6 A4
Fordingbridge (0425) 52489

Brewery Eldridge Pope
Landlord Karl Wadsack
Soufflé beignet Aida £1.85 Avocado seafood
jambalaya £2.90 (Last order 9.15pm. No bar
food Sun eve, Tues lunch & all Mon)
🍺 Eldridge Pope Royal Oak, Dorset IPA
Dorchester Bitter; Faust. *Real ale*

It's best to book a table at this cosy pub to
sample Karl Wadsack's brilliantly eclectic
cooking. He borrows and blends ideas from
all parts of the globe, creating wonderful
dishes like rich game soup, herby Cumberland sausage with pungent sauerkraut and
gingery pork fillet, to name but a few.
Sweets too are out of this world. A la carte
evening menu. Closed Feb, 1 wk Easter, last
wk July, 1st wk Aug, 1 wk Sept–Oct & 1 wk
Christmas.

Studham   *(Food)*   *Bell Inn*

Dunstable Road · *Bedfordshire* · Map 5 B2
Whipsnade (0582) 872460

Brewery Benskins
Landlords Ann & Ronald Harris

King-size sausages & chips £1.65 Steak &
kidney pie £2.50 (Last order 9.45pm)
■ Benskins Bitter; Ind Coope Burton Ale,
John Bull Bitter, Double Diamond; Guinness;
Löwenbräu. *Real ale*

This friendly pub of traditional mien fits in
well with its peaceful village setting. A
straightforward bar menu featuring dishes
like pâté, scampi or chicken in the basket is
enlivened by an unusually varied selection
of sausages – garlic, onion, apple, Cumberland – as well as flavoursome quiche and
fresh, crisp salads. There are plenty of
tables in the garden for fine weather eating
and drinking.

Surbiton   *(Food)*   *Oak*

Maple Road · *Surrey* · Map 6 C3
01-399 1662

Brewery Charringtons
Landlord Mr Andy Christie

Coronation turkey £2.75 Apricot & lamb
pie £2.20 (No bar food eves or Sun)
■ Charrington IPA; Bass; Guinness; Carling
Black Label; Tennent's Extra; Taunton cider.
Real ale

An attractive corner pub with one bar for
drinking and another, a few steps down,
with an eye-catching display of hot and
cold dishes. Almost everything is made on
the premises, and we very much enjoyed
mildly curried coronation turkey and a pork
hot pot with good lean meat and nicely
browned potato topping. Soups and
sweets in winter. Garden.

Sutton   *(Food)*   *Anne Arms*

Suttonfield Road, Near Doncaster
South Yorkshire · Map 4 C3
Doncaster (0302) 700500

Brewery John Smiths
Landlords Mr & Mrs J. R. Simm

Rabbit pie £1.50 Roast pork £1.50 (Last order
10.15pm. No bar food Sun)
■ John Smith's Bitter, Lager; Guinness;
Hofmeister. *Real ale*

Mrs Simm's flavoursome rabbit pie is
typical of the robust fare that brings the
locals flocking to this ivy-clad village pub.
The daily roast is another great favourite,
and there are sandwiches, ploughman's
and salads for smaller appetites. Sweets
include traditional winter treats like treacle
tart and jam roly-poly. The beamed bar is
warm and cosy, and there's a pleasant
garden complete with gnome colony.
Family pub

Sutton Howgrave   *(Food)*   *White Dog Inn*

Near Ripon · *North Yorkshire* · Map 4 C2
Melmerby (076 584) 404

Free House
Landlords Pat & Basil Bagnall

Venison casserole £3.10 Chilli con carne £1.95
(No bar food eves)
■ Webster's Pennine Bitter; Carlsberg Hof.

In a sleepy village just off the B6267, this
cottagy little pub is a charming setting for
some very good lunchtime bar snacks.
French onion soup is a great favourite, and
other choices include prawn and ham
salads, sirloin steak and a really hearty
venison casserole. Sandwiches, too, and
some tempting sweets. Closed Sun eve,
Mon and 1st 2 weeks February. Garden.

Sutton-u-Whitestonecliffe *(Food)*   *Whitestonecliffe Hotel*

Near Thirsk · *North Yorkshire* · Map 4 C2
Thirsk (0845) 597271

Free House
Landlords Mr & Mrs A. Bartle
Pork fillet in cream & cider sauce £2.35
Gammon with egg & pineapple £2.35 (Last order 10pm)
🍺 Webster's Yorkshire Bitter; Younger's Scotch Bitter; Pennine Bitter; Guinness; Foster's; Carlsberg Export; cider. *Real ale*

The Bartles' appealing white-painted pub is building up an enthusiastic local following with its excellent bar snacks. Soups are nourishing and flavoursome, home-cooked ham makes lovely sandwiches and salads, and there are always interesting specials like fresh halibut, roast pheasant or fillet of pork in a creamy cider sauce. The sweets are just as tempting: try the sherry trifle or golden-topped blackberry and apple pie. Closed Monday lunch.

Sutton-upon-Derwent   *(Food)*   *St Vincent Arms*

Near York, North Yorkshire · *Humberside*
Map 4 C3
Elvington (090 485) 349
Free House
Landlords Mr & Mrs R. F. Tyson
Steak, kidney & mushroom pie with vegetables £3.10 Prawn & sweetcorn quiche with salad & chips £1.75 (Last order 10pm)
🍺 Cameron's Best Bitter; Theakston's Best Bitter, Old Peculier; Younger's Scotch Bitter, IPA, Mild; Guinness; Carlsberg Hof. *Real ale*

Hospitality flows freely at Dick and Jean Tyson's handsome old timbered pub, whose cosy panelled bars offer an enterprising menu of well-prepared snacks. The super steak, kidney and mushroom pie is a perennial favourite, while other popular choices range from soup, salads and sandwiches to flavoursome liver and bacon pâté, American-style hamburgers and sirloin steaks. Less choice Sunday lunch. Garden. **Family pub**

Talkin   *(Food, B & B)*   *Hare & Hounds Inn*

Near Brampton · *Cumbria* · Map 3 B1
Brampton (069 77) 3456

Free House
Landlords Les & Joan Stewart

BEDROOMS 5   Grade 1   £C   (No dogs)
Steak £4.45 Gammon £2.45 (Last order 9pm)
🍺 Theakston's Best Bitter, Old Peculier, XB; Younger's Tartan; Drybrough Heavy; Guinness; Carlsberg; cider. *Real ale*

Homely and hospitable, this 200-year-old black and white inn stands in the centre of a quiet Cumbrian village. Bar snacks are a popular attraction, ranging from rolls and burgers to filled jacket potatoes, fish dishes and succulent steaks. Comfortable bedrooms, including two in the cottage annexe, are attractively furnished, and modern bathrooms are well equipped. Garden. **Family pub**

Tarporley   *(B & B)*   *Swan Hotel*

50 High Street · *Cheshire* · Map 3 B4
Tarporley (082 93) 2411

Brewery Greenall Whitley
Landlords June & Bernard McQueen

BEDROOMS 9   Grade 2   £B   (No dogs)
🍺 Greenall Whitley Bitter, Mild; Guinness; Grünhalle. *Real ale*

The facade is early Georgian, but some of the buildings at the back of the McQueens' imposing inn date from Tudor times. The Old Kitchen Bar, with its open fire, flagstone floor and burnished copperware, is a favourite local gathering place, and there's also the cosy Den Bar. Cheerfully decorated bedrooms, all with central heating, fitted carpets, TVs and tea-makers, are kept in apple-pie order.

Tarrant Monkton *(Food)*   *Langton Arms*

Near Blandford Forum · *Dorset* · Map 8 D3
Tarrant Hinton (025 889) 225

Free House
Landlords Chris & Diane Goodinge

Steak & kidney pudding £2 Pancakes filled with
jam 80p (Last order 10.15pm)
🍺 Bass, Toby; Worthington 'E', Best Bitter;
Guinness; Carling Black Label; Taunton cider.
Real ale

The prospect of cocktails, skittles and excellent food lures visitors to this out-of-the-
way thatched pub. Start with a bowl of
home-made soup (perhaps lentil and onion
or mulligatawny), salmon mousse or a hot
steak sandwich, and go on to chicken and
vegetable curry, steak and kidney pudding
or egg and mushroom mornay. There are
also grills in the evening. Creamy gooseberry fool and orange sorbet are typical
sweets. Garden.

Teddington *(Food, B & B)*   *Clarence Hotel*

Park Road · *Middlesex* · Map 6 B3
01-977 8025

Free House
Landlords Mr R. J. Currall & Mrs R. A. Currall
BEDROOMS 15 Grade 2 £B
Steak & kidney pie £2 Turkey fillet with
mushroom sauce £2 (Last order 10.30pm)
🍺 Wadworth's 6X; Ben Truman; Marston's
Pedigree; Boddington's Bitter; Yorkshire
Bitter; Guinness; Foster's; cider. *Real ale*

A cheerful, welcoming place, where the
cooking is homely and portions are
designed for hearty appetites. Tasty hot
choices include succulent lamb chops,
roast chicken and mixed grills, served with
fresh vegetables, with perhaps apple and
blackcurrant pie to finish. There are sandwiches, ploughman's and salads too. Traditional Sunday lunch. Bright bedrooms with
tea-makers offer simple modern furnish-
ings.   **Family pub** (lunchtime)

Teffont Magna *(Food)*   *Black Horse Inn*

Near Salisbury · *Wiltshire* · Map 6 A3
Teffont (072 276) 251

Brewery Ushers
Landlords Colin & Jacqui Carter

Pork Marengo £3 Steamed pudding 90p
(Last order 10pm)
🍺 Bass; Usher's Founder's Ale, Best Bitter,
Triple Crown; Watneys Mild; Ben Truman;
Guinness; cider. *Real ale*

Rustic charm abounds in this friendly old
village inn, where Colin Carter looks after
the bars while his wife Jacqui attends to
culinary matters. Succulent Wiltshire ham
is one of her most popular offerings, with
lasagne, pan-fried trout and steak and
kidney pie high on the list of favourites.
Sandwiches too. Desserts include fruit pies
and delicious home-made ice cream. Patio
and garden.   **Family pub**

Tenterden *(B & B)*   *White Lion Hotel*

High Street · *Kent* · Map 6 C3
Tenterden (058 06) 2921

Free House
Landlord Mr Gordon Wylde

BEDROOMS 12 Grades 1 & 2 £A
🍺 Whitbread Fremlins Bitter; Shepherd
Neame Invicta; Guinness; Hurliman; cider.
Real ale

Right in the heart of town, this handsome
old coaching inn provides overnight
accommodation of a high standard,
including four characterful rooms with
four-posters. All rooms have colour TVs
and tea-makers and all except the simpler
singles at the rear have their own well-
appointed bath or shower room. There's a
mellow beamed bar and a quiet upstairs
residents' lounge.   **Family pub**

Terrington *(B & B)* Bay Horse Inn

Near York · *North Yorkshire* · Map 4 C2
Coneysthorpe (065 384) 255

Free House
Landlord Grace Hoggard

BEDROOMS 3 Grade 2 £C
 John Smith's Bitter; Younger's Scotch
Bitter; Tetley Bitter; Guinness; Hofmeister;
Carlsberg Hof; cider.

Hospitality comes naturally to Grace
Hoggard, who takes good care of visitors to
her lovely little country inn some 16 miles
from York. A well-stoked fire keeps winter
customers warm in the rustic front bar,
while double glazing keeps the chill from
the spotlessly kept modern bedrooms.
These all have TVs and tea-makers and
share a single neat bathroom. Terrific
breakfasts. Garden. Closed Monday lunchtime except Bank Holidays. **Family pub**

Testcombe *(Food)* Mayfly

Near Stockbridge · *Hampshire* · Map 6 A3
Chilbolton (026 474) 283

Brewery Whitbread
Landlord Mrs Tuckett
Quiches £1.75 Chicken tandoori £2.45
(Last order 9.30pm. No bar food Sun & Mon
eves)
Whitbread Strong Country Bitter, Pompey
Royal, Best Bitter; Guinness; Stella Artois;
Taunton cider. *Real ale*

The garden overlooking the river Test
draws plenty of summer visitors to this
charming red-brick pub, and tasty bar food
is an additional attraction. Mrs Tuckett's
imaginative menu offers delicious soups,
quiches and cold meats to go with salads
such as tomatoes with fennel dressing, and
there are a few hot dishes like game pie or
chicken tandoori. Nice traditional sweets,
too, plus good cheeses.

Tetbury *(Food, B & B)* ★ Gentle Gardener

Long Street · *Gloucestershire* · Map 7 D2
Tetbury (0666) 52884

Free House
Landlords Mr & Mrs W. Knock
BEDROOMS 5 Grade 2 £C
Vegetable pie £1.65 Lemon Cotswold 80p (No
bar food eves)
Usher's Founders Ale; Archer's Best
Bitter; Cirencester Bitter; Ben Truman Bitter;
Guinness; Carlsberg; cider. *Real ale*

A handsome old coaching inn, where super
lunchtime snacks can be enjoyed in the
comfortable bar or out in the courtyard.
Filled rolls and ploughman's platters are
popular quick bites, or you could start with
flavour-packed celeriac soup and go on to
duck pancake with cheese and apple or
splendid spinach roulade. Five simple,
spotless bedrooms share a large
bathroom. Garden. **Family pub**

Thames Ditton *(Food)* Crown Inn

Summer Road · *Surrey* · Map 6 B3
01-398 2376
Brewery Watneys
Landlords John, Marion & Bob Wilder
Cheese salad £2.25 Beef & horseradish
casserole & vegetables £2.35 (Last order
9.45pm)
Watneys Stag Bitter; Webster's Yorkshire
Bitter; Hammerton's Porter; Coombes Bitter;
Ruddles County; Guinness; Foster's;
Carlsberg; cider. *Real ale*

Visitors to this convivial pub can look
forward to a warm welcome and some
splendid home cooking. The Wilders make
their own pickles and chutneys to go with
ploughman's and curries. Their menu also
features soup (perhaps chicken and leek),
mammoth portions of chunky steak and
kidney pie served with heaps of fresh vegetables, plus burgers, salads, grills and
sandwiches (plain or toasted). And to finish
there are super fruit pies.

Thetford *(B & B)*   *Historical Thomas Paine Hotel*

White Hart Street · *Norfolk* · Map 5 C2
Thetford (0842) 5631

Free House
Landlords Mr & Mrs T. Muir

BEDROOMS 14 Grade 1 £A
🍺 Adnams Original; Tolly Cobbold Original;
Stones Bitter; Toby Bitter; Guinness;
Carlsberg Hof; Tennent's Extra; Taunton cider.
Real ale

An awning-covered walkway leads from
the car park to the entrance of this attractive
white-painted hotel, reputedly the birth-
place of the political pamphleteer Thomas
Paine in 1737. The spacious Franklin Bar is a
pleasant spot for relaxing, and there's a
cosy little residents' lounge. Comfortable
bedrooms, most with private facilities,
have smart modern furnishings, colour
TVs, radios and tea-makers. Terrace.
Family pub

Thurnham *(Food)*   *Black Horse*

Pilgrims Way · *Kent* · Map 6 C3
Maidstone (0622) 37185

Brewery Whitbread
Landlords Mr & Mrs Les Broughton

Madras lamb curry £2.50 Smoked turkey open
sandwich £1 (Last order 9pm)
🍺 Whitbread Best Bitter; Fremlins Bitter;
Tusker; Guinness; Heineken; Stella Artois;
cider. *Real ale*

Once a hostelry on the old pilgrim's route to
Canterbury, this popular pub attracts
today's travellers with a selection of
simple, well-prepared bar food. Crisp
salads and tastily topped open sandwiches
for quick snacks, with sausage, egg and
chips, lasagne and a good spicy Madras
lamb curry among the more substantial hot
dishes. Soup in winter, sandwiches only at
weekends. There's a pleasant beer garden.

Tichborne *(Food)*   *Tichborne Arms*

Near Alresford · *Hampshire* · Map 6 B4
Alresford (096 273) 3760

Free House
Landlord Mrs J. M. Salter
Smoked mackerel pâté £1.15 Spare ribs with
barbecue sauce £2.25 (Last order 10pm)
🍺 Courage Best Bitter, Directors Bitter;
Wadworth's 6X; Marston's Pedigree;
Guinness; cider. *Real ale*

Standing in a pretty Hampshire village
surrounded by meadows and farmland,
this attractive thatched pub is a most
agreeable spot to pause for a snack. Everything is carefully prepared by Mrs Salter:
salads, sandwiches, jacket potatoes with a
choice of eight fillings, superb smoked
mackerel pâté, along with popular daily
specials like spare ribs or chicken curry.
Nice sweets, too. Garden.

Timberscombe *(B & B)*   *Lion Inn*

Near Dunster · *Somerset* · Map 8 C3
Timberscombe (064 384) 243

Free House
Landlords Mr & Mrs G. P. Christie

BEDROOMS 5 Grade 2 £C (No dogs)
🍺 Usher's Triple Crown, Best Bitter,
Country; Younger's Scotch Bitter; McEwan's
Export; Carlsberg; Taunton cider. *Real ale*

This charming whitewashed village pub
stands in picturesque hunting country on
the edge of Exmoor National Park. The
main bar is a cosy, convivial spot, and next
to it is a games room where children are
welcome. Neatly kept bedrooms have
practical modern furnishings and pretty
floral duvets, and they share an up-to-date
bathroom with shower. Terrace.

England

Timperley   *(Food)*   *Hare & Hounds*

1 Wood Lane, Near Altrincham · *Cheshire*
Map 3 B3
061-980 5299

Brewery Marston, Thompson & Evershed
Landlords Mr & Mrs J. B. W. Cunningham

Navarin of lamb £2 Poached fresh salmon £2
(Last order 10.30pm. No bar food Sun)
🍺 Marston's Pedigree, Mild, Burton Bitter;
Guinness; Heineken; cider. *Real ale*

The French chef's magnificent cold table
draws the lunchtime crowds to this eye-
catching pub. Help yourself to cooked
meats and fish, quiches and delicious
salads like courgette and cauliflower or
avocado and grapefruit, or go for one of the
hot specials such as pork chops in cider. Do
leave room for a sweet (we noted a light
crème caramel) or a choice of fine cheeses.
Sandwiches only evenings. Barbecues are
a popular feature.   **Family pub**

Toddington   *(Food)*   *Pheasant*

Near Cheltenham · *Gloucestershire* · Map 5 A2
Toddington (024 269) 271

Brewery Hall
Landlord Mr David Strathern
Game pie £2.50 Aloo gosht curry £2.50 (Last
order 9pm. No bar food Tues eve in winter)
🍺 Hall's Harvest Bitter; Ind Coope Burton
Ale; Tetley's Bitter; Ruddles County;
Wadworth's 6X; Guinness; Löwenbräu; cider.
Real ale

Only prime fresh ingredients go into the
simple bar snacks that are a feature of this
well-run pub. David Strathern uses high-
quality beef for his excellent burgers, he
grows his own vegetables, he makes his
own soups and he grinds the spices that go
into daily specials like his very popular
curries. And the light, airy puff-pastry on
the apple pie? Home-made of course!
                              Family pub

Tong   *(B & B)*   *Bell Inn*

Newport Road, Near Shifnal · *Shropshire*
Map 7 D1
Weston-under-Lizard (095 276) 210

Brewery Wolverhampton & Dudley
Landlords Mr & Mrs Silvester

BEDROOMS 3   Grade 1   £C
🍺 Banks's Best Bitter, Best Mild;
Kronenbourg; Harp; cider. *Real ale*

Francis and Valerie Silvester keep this red-
brick roadside pub in perfect condition,
both inside and out. Drinkers enjoy the
homely atmosphere in the beamed bar,
while overnight visitors can slumber
soundly in the simple, traditionally furnished bedrooms and look forward to a
hearty breakfast. Children under seven not
accommodated overnight. Large, well-
tended garden. Rooms closed 1 week
Christmas.

Toot Hill   *(Food)*   *Green Man*

Near Ongar · *Essex* · Map 6 C3
North Weald (037 882) 2255

Brewery Watneys
Landlord Mr John Roads
Mexican chicken with vegetables £3.95 Lamb
cutlets with vegetables £3.95 (Last
order 10.15pm)
🍺 Webster's Yorkshire Bitter; Wilsons Great
Northern Bitter; Ben Truman; Coombes Bitter;
Guinness; Carlsberg; cider. *Real ale*

John Roads certainly has green fingers:
both his front patio and the garden at the
back are delightful places to sample his
selection of champagnes, and the flower-
bedecked bar is a charming setting in which
to enjoy a well-prepared snack. Soups are
made with home-grown vegetables, and
main courses range from appetising ham
salad to lamb cutlets, moussaka or beef
Stroganoff. Salads and basket meals, too,
and a roast lunch on Sunday.

Tormarton *(B & B)*   *Compass Inn*

Near Badminton · *Avon* · Map 7 D2
Badminton (045 421) 242

Free House
Landlords Monyard family

BEDROOMS 11   Grades 1 & 2   £B
🍺 Bass; Wadworth's 6X, Old Timer (winter only); Archer's Village Bitter; Younger's Tartan; Carlsberg Hof. *Real ale*

Motorists leaving the M4 at junction 18 can set a course for this efficiently run inn, which offers good, comfortable accommodation. The best bedrooms are the spacious ones in the modern wing, which have spotless up-to-date bathrooms; six rooms in the main building are more compact. All have radios, TVs and tea-makers. There are four traditional Cotswold-stone bars, plus a glass-roofed orangery. Garden.
Family pub (lunchtime)

Towersey *(Food)*   *Three Horseshoes*

Chinnor Road, Near Thame · *Oxfordshire*
Map 6 B3
Thame (084 421) 2322

Brewery Aylesbury
Landlords Mr & Mrs Smith

King prawn salad £4.30 Tandoori chicken £4.30 (Last order 9.30pm)
🍺 ABC Bitter; Everards Tiger; Ind Coope Pale Mild; Guinness; Skol; Carlsberg; cider. *Real ale*

The range and quality of the bar snacks are both admirable at this simple village inn. An eye-catching cold buffet is a popular feature in summer, and hot choices include evergreens like pâté, shepherd's pie and beef curry, plus more unusual items such as haddock cooked with coriander in a garlicky parsley sauce. Also vegetarian dishes and some nice sweets. Garden.   **Family pub**

Trebarwith *(Food, B & B)*   *Mill House Inn*

Near Tintagel · *Cornwall* · Map 8 B4
Camelford (0840) 770200

Free House
Landlords Mr & Mrs H. D. Thomas
BEDROOMS 9   Grade 1   £A
Chicken curry £2.50 Beef Stroganoff £2.50 (Last order 10pm)
🍺 Flower's Original, IPA; Younger's Tartan; Guinness; Heineken; Stella Artois; cider. *Real ale*

The Thomases are friendly, welcoming hosts at this cosy, slate-built inn situated off the B3263. Tasty snacks are served in the bars, from soup and sandwiches to pizza, chicken curry and home-made puddings. Overnight accommodation (no children under ten) comprises nine attractively decorated bedrooms, all with TVs and private facilities. There's a charming residents' lounge with antique furniture. Garden.   **Family pub**

Trotton   *Keepers Arms*

Hanging baskets and flower tubs make a nice splash of colour outside this welcoming roadside pub, which started life about 150 years ago when a blacksmith decided to open an ale house for his customers. There are fine views over the downs, and the bar is smartly traditional. Closed Monday.

Near Petersfield, Hampshire · *West Sussex* · Map 6 B4
Midhurst (073 081) 3724
Free House   Landlord Mr C. S. Machin
🍺 John Smith Yorkshire Bitter; Badger Best Bitter; Huntsman Royal Oak, Dorchester; Ballards Best Bitter; Guinness; cider. *Real ale*

Troutbeck   *(Food, B & B)*   *Mortal Man*

Near Windermere · *Cumbria* · Map 3 B2
Ambleside (0966) 33193

Free House
Landlord C. J. Poulsom
BEDROOMS 15   Grade 1   £A+
Cumberland hot pot £1.50 Potted shrimps
& salad £1.50 (No bar food eves)
🍺 Scottish & Newcastle Chieftain Mild,
Newcastle Bitter; Guinness; Harp; Taunton
cider.

This famous old inn enjoys a position of
great beauty in a magnificent valley that
sweeps down to Lake Windermere. Lunchtime in the cosy beamed bars brings
simple, tasty snacks ranging from sandwiches and pâté to omelettes, cottage pie
and a daily casserole. Ten of the comfortable, traditionally furnished bedrooms
have private bathrooms. No under-fives
overnight. Closed mid Nov–mid Feb.
Garden.

Tunbridge Wells   *(Food)*   *Royal Wells Inn*

Mount Ephraim · *Kent* · Map 6 C3
Tunbridge Wells (0892) 23414

Free House
Landlords Robert & David Sloan

Steak & kidney pie £2 Toad in the hole £1.75
(Last order 10.30pm. No bar food Sun lunch)
🍺 Shepherd Neame Masterbrew; Courage
Directors Bitter; Guinness; Hofmeister;
Kronenbourg; Taunton cider. *Real ale*

Robert Sloan offers a tempting and
imaginative menu in the large, elegant bar
of this popular Regency inn. Dishes like
vegetable terrine or blanquette of lamb
provide tasty alternatives to the more
familiar steak and kidney pie and toad in the
hole. There's also a cold buffet at lunchtime, and a selection of gorgeous sweets
like raspberry Pavlova.
Family pub

Turville   *(Food)*   *Bull & Butcher*

Near Henley-on-Thames, Oxfordshire
Buckinghamshire · Map 6 B3
Turville Heath (049 163) 283

Brewery Brakspear
Landlords Mr & Mrs Cowles

Cold seafood platter £3.50 Treacle tart 90p
(Last order 10pm)
🍺 Brakspear's Bitter, Special, Old; Heineken.
Real ale

Popular with car club enthusiasts (the landlord used to race saloons), this pleasant old
village inn is a good stop for those in search
of a simple, hearty snack. A soup usually
heads the list of starters, followed perhaps
by ploughman's, quiche or jacket potatoes
(a winter favourite). Also daily specials
(moussaka, steak & kidney pie), a summer
cold buffet and nice sweets. Garden.

Tutbury   *(Food)*   *Ye Olde Dog & Partridge*

High Street · *Staffordshire* · Map 4 C4
Tutbury (0283) 813030

Free House
Landlords Mr & Mrs D. J. Martindale

Hot roast beef £4 Game pie £3.50 (Last
order 10pm)
🍺 Worthington 'E'; Marston's Pedigree,
Premium Bitter, Low 'C'; cider. *Real ale*

Succulent hot and cold joints, including
boiled ham and tender sirloin, are the highlight of the bar food served in this fine old
half-timbered coaching inn. There's also
soup, sandwiches and popular daily
specials such as game pie, Cumberland
sausage and faggots with mushy peas.
Patio and garden. *For accommodation see
Egon Ronay's Lucas Hotel & Restaurant
Guide 1985.* **Family pub**

Twickenham *(Food)*   *Prince Albert*

30 Hampton Road · *Middlesex* · Map 6 B3
01-894 3963

Brewery Fuller, Smith & Turner
Landlords Mr & Mrs B. Lunn
Pork with lemon cream sauce & vegetables £2
Chilli con carne £1.90 (Last order 9pm. No bar
food Sun lunch)
🍺 Fuller's London Pride, ESB, Chiswick
Bitter; Tennent's Extra; Guinness; Heineken.
Real ale

Tasty lunchtime fare is the big draw in this
friendly Victorian pub, where a bevy of
ladies produces a wide range of hearty
dishes from ham pâté, quiche and mushrooms bourguignon to appetising finnan
haddock pancakes and liver and bacon.
Nice fresh vegetables accompany, and
there are delicious sweets like strawberry
fool. Sandwiches only in the evening.
Pretty garden with an aviary, rabbit and
ducks.

Twickenham *(Food)*   *White Swan*

Riverside · *Middlesex* · Map 6 B3
01-892 2166

Brewery Watney Combe Reid
Landlord Shirley Sutton

Hot pot £2.40 Pâté maison & salad £2 (No bar
food Sun)
🍺 Watney's London Bitter; Manns IPA;
Webster's Yorkshire Bitter; Guinness;
Foster's; Carlsberg; cider. *Real ale*

Right beside the river, this cheerful pub is
especially busy at lunchtime, when Shirley
Sutton's excellent snacks are on offer.
Delicious home-made soup makes a good
start, and you can go on to dishes like steak
and kidney pudding, chops in cider or a
hearty beef and vegetable hot pot. Rolls
only in the evening. Sunday lunch only by
prior arrangement. Garden.   **Family pub**

Ufford *(Food)*   *Ye Olde White Hart Inn*

Near Stamford · *Lincolnshire* · Map 5 B1
Stamford (0780) 740250

Brewery Home
Landlords Marion & Nigel Adams

Bobotie £2.50 Pork & apricot tiffin £2.95
(Last order 8pm. No bar food Sat eve, all
Sun & Mon eve)
🍺 Home Traditional Bitter; Skol. *Real ale*

Everything is appetising and carefully prepared at this friendly village pub. There's a
colourful cold buffet in the cosy lounge bar,
featuring home-cooked meats, pâtés and
pies. If you want something hot, there are
interesting dishes like spicy bobotie or pork
and apricot tiffin. Soup, fresh local trout
and ploughman's are other choices, with
enjoyable sweets like cherry pie to finish.
Patio and garden.

Umberleigh *(B & B)*   *Rising Sun*

Devon · Map 8 C3
High Bickington (0769) 60447

Owners Wessex Hosts
Landlord Mr M. A. F. Tate

BEDROOMS 8   Grade 1   £A
🍺 Usher's Country Bitter, Triple Crown;
Carlsberg.

Salmon and trout fishing on the river Taw
brings a steady stream of anglers to stay at
this pleasant country inn, whose little bars
are full of fishy mementos and chatter.
Comfortable bedrooms, four with well-
appointed private bathrooms, have pretty
coordinated fabrics, modern units and tea-
makers. Very good breakfasts. No children
under six overnight. Accommodation
closed mid Oct–1 March.

Upper Basildon   *(Food)*   *Beehive Inn*

Near Pangbourne · *Berkshire* · Map 6 B3
Upper Basildon (049 162) 269

Free House
Landlord Mr K. Peachey
Mexican baked potato £2.50 Seafood
salad £2.75 (Last order 10pm. No bar food
Sun eve)
🍺 Morland's Best Bitter, Ordinary; Hall's
Harvest Bitter; Heineken; Stella Artois; cider.
Real ale

Spuds, in some 20 different guises, are the
speciality of this popular yellow-painted
pub facing the village green. From an
intriguing list of names like the Spanish
Armada, Frenchman and Fisherman we
selected the Indian – a huge baked potato
filled with curried diced turkey and mango
chutney, accompanied by a crisp green
salad. Hot prawns in garlic butter make a
tasty alternative. Garden.   **Family pub**

Upper Basildon   *(Food)*   *Red Lion*

Near Pangbourne · *Berkshire* · Map 6 B3
Upper Basildon (049 162) 234

Brewery Courage
Landlord Mr Ken Woodward

Savoury omelette £1.60 Lasagne £1.85 (Last
order 9.30pm. No bar food Sun)
🍺 Courage Best Bitter, Directors Bitter, John
Courage; Guinness; Kronenbourg;
Taunton cider. *Real ale*

The Woodwards do their own cooking at
this welcoming red-brick village pub. In the
neat, homely bar decorated with horse
brasses and china plates, you can enjoy
such tasty offerings as beef bourguignon
served on a bed of rice mixed with mushrooms and baby onions or perhaps
lasagne, gammon with Cumberland sauce
or a fish dish. Freshly cut sandwiches and
basket meals are also available. Garden.

Upper Layham   *(Food)*   *Marquis of Cornwallis*

Near Hadleigh · *Suffolk* · Map 5 D2
Hadleigh (0473) 822051

Brewery Ind Coope
Landlords John & Nicky Moss

Smoked salmon mousse £1.50 Prawn curry £3
(Last order 10pm)
🍺 Ind Coope Bitter, Double Diamond, Mild;
Guinness; Skol; cider. *Real ale*

Crackling fires keep winter at bay in the
oak-beamed bars of this friendly pub,
where Nicky Moss offers a menu of capably
prepared and attractively presented
snacks. Her smoked salmon mousse is a
finely flavoured, light-textured little master-
piece, and other choices range from soups
and sandwiches to salads, steaks and pan-
fried gammon. Nice sweets include old-
fashioned sherry trifle and delicious raspberry parfait. Garden.

Upper Oddington   *(Food, B & B)*   *Horse & Groom Inn*

Near Stow-on-the-Wold · *Gloucestershire*
Map 5 A2
Cotswold (0451) 30584
Free House
Landlords Mr & Mrs G. Wilmot
BEDROOMS 5   Grade 1   £B   (No dogs)
Cold buffet £3.25 Gloucestershire
sausage £1.25 (No bar food eves)
🍺 Wadworth's Devizes Bitter, 6X;
Worthington Best Bitter; Younger's Tartan;
Heineken; Tuborg; cider. *Real ale*

Standing a couple of miles outside Stow-
on-the-Wold, the Wilmots' immaculate
16th-century inn is a good base for a tour of
the Cotswolds. Centrally heated bedrooms
with beams and rustic doors have pretty
fabrics, modern furniture and private
showers (one bath). Lunchtime snacks
served in the delightfully old-world bars
include delicious soup, ploughman's, a
summer cold table and winter hot specials.
Garden.   **Family pub**

Uttoxeter   (B & B)   *White Hart Hotel*

Carter Street · *Staffordshire* · Map 5 A1
Uttoxeter (088 93) 2437

Brewery Allied
Landlord Mrs H. V. Porteous

BEDROOMS 24 Grades 1 & 2 £A
🍺 Ind Coope Bitter, Burton Ale, Double
Diamond; Guinness; Skol; Löwenbräu;
cider. *Real ale*

This town-centre hostelry is noted for its
friendly atmosphere and comfortable
accommodation. The best bedrooms (in
the annexe) have modern darkwood furnishings, thick carpets and TVs; some
rooms in the main building have splendid
panelling and antique furniture, whereas
others are more up to date. Spacious private bathrooms have lovely large baths.
There's a roomy lounge bar and a cosy TV
lounge.   **Family pub**

Walkern   (Food)   *White Lion*

High Street, Near Stevenage · *Hertfordshire*
Map 5 C2
Walkern (043 886) 251
Brewery Greene King
Landlords Mr & Mrs M. J. Windebank
Steak & kidney pie £2.50 Chilli con carne £2.50
(Last order 10pm. No bar food Sun & Mon
eves)
🍺 Greene King IPA, Abbot Ale, Mild;
Guinness; Harp; Kronenbourg; Taunton cider.
Real ale

Mr & Mrs Windebank both take a share of
the cooking in this pleasant, traditionally
styled pub, whose characterful beamed
bars feature an interesting collection of old
clocks. His lamb curry and her delicious
steak and kidney pie have many admirers,
and pâté, pepper steaks, fish and chips
and appetising salads are other popular
choices. Sweets include a splendid sherry
trifle. Garden.

Wall   (B & B)   *Hadrian Inn*

Near Hexham · *Northumberland* · Map 4 C1
Humshaugh (043 481) 232

Brewery Vaux
Landlords Mr & Mrs Mellors

BEDROOMS 9 Grades 1 & 2 £C
🍺 Vaux Samson, Lorimers Scotch,
Sunderland Ale; Guinness; Tuborg; Taunton
cider. *Real ale*

This homely roadside inn stands about four
miles north of Hexham in a village largely
built with stones taken from nearby
Hadrian's Wall. Bedrooms, which command attractive views, are furnished in a
mixture of traditional and more modern
styles; some have TVs and five have their
own bathrooms. (No children under 12
overnight.) The foyer-lounge features
some fine old prints, and the bar is characterful. Garden.   **Family pub**

Waltham on the Wolds   (Food, B & B)   *Royal Horseshoes*

Melton Road, Near Melton Mowbray
Leicestershire · Map 4 D4
Waltham (066 478) 289

Brewery John Smith
Landlords Mr & Mrs Wigglesworth
BEDROOMS 4 Grade 1 £B (No dogs)
Cock-a-leekie 60p Steak & kidney pie £2.40 (Last
order 9pm)
🍺 John Smith's Bitter, Chestnut Mild;
Hofmeister; John Smith's Lager. *Real ale*

A tempting cold table catches the eye in this
friendly village pub, where anything from pâté
and prawns to turkey and tender beef
Wellington can be enjoyed with a selection of
fresh, crisp salads. There is plenty of hot
choice, too, including soup, scampi and a
Sunday roast. Neat, modern bedrooms in a
converted outbuilding have TVs, tea-makers
and carpeted bathrooms. Patio. **Family pub**

Waltham St Lawrence *(Food)*   *Bell*

Berkshire · Map 6 B3

Free House
Landlord Mr R. Bristow

Steak & kidney pie £1.95 Welsh rarebit £1.10
(Last order 10pm. No bar food Sun & Mon
eves)
🍺 Adnams Mild; Bitter; Arkell's Bitter;
Guinness; Carlsberg; cider. *Real ale*

This is truly a village pub, in that since 1608
it has been owned by a trust on behalf of
the village. The atmospheric beamed bars
offer a good variety of tasty snacks, from
warming bowls of soup to steak sandwiches
made with French bread, shepherd's pie
and garlicky mushroom pancakes. There's a
cold table in summer; jacket potatoes are
the only choice Sunday lunchtime. Garden.
Family pub

Waltham St Lawrence *(Food)*   *Plough Inn*

West End · *Berkshire* · Map 6 B3
Twyford (0734) 340015

Brewery Morland
Landlord Mrs Beryl Boulton-Taylor

Calf's liver & bacon £3.50 Treacle tart £1 (Last
order 9.30pm. No bar food Mon)
🍺 Morland's Best Bitter, Bitter, Pale Ale;
Heineken. *Real ale*

Red-clothed tables in the lounge bar of this
delightful old timbered pub make an
inviting setting for Mrs Boulton-Taylor's
superb home cooking. Cold meats include
tender rare roast beef and succulent ham
off the bone, with grills and steaks at lunchtime and fowl and venison dishes at night.
Sweets are a special treat: maybe a treacle
tart topped with almonds, or a fruit pie
bursting with blackberry and apple.
Garden.

Wansford *(Food)*   *Haycock Inn*

Near Peterborough · *Cambridgeshire*
Map 5 B1
Stamford (0780) 782223

Owners Poste Hotels
Landlords Mr Richard Neale
Braised silverside & salads £4.95 Cheese
fondue (for 2) £7 (Last order 10.30pm)
🍺 Ruddle's County, Bitter; Bass; Younger's
Tartan; Stone's Bitter; Kestrel; Stella Artois;
Taunton cider. *Real ale*

A 17th-century coaching inn standing in
pleasant grounds by the river Nene. A
superb cold buffet is a winning feature in
the River lounge, where hot snacks include
home-made soups, baked mussels and
chunky chicken and ham in a creamy
cheese sauce. To finish, try treacle pudding
or scrumptious lemon meringue pie.
Garden. *For accommodation see Egon
Ronay's Lucas Hotel & Restaurant Guide
1985.* **Family pub**

Wanstrow *(Food)*   *King William IV*

Near Shepton Mallet · *Somerset* · Map 8 D3
Upton Noble (074 985) 247

Brewery Usher
Landlords Mr & Mrs J. Geen

Chilli con carne with crusty bread £2 Chicken
curry with chips £2 (Last order 9pm. No bar
food Wed eve)
🍺 Usher's Country Bitter, Best Bitter; Ben
Truman; Guinness; Carlsberg; cider. *Real ale*

Mrs Geen's tasty bar snacks are a popular
draw at this pleasant pub on the Bruton–
Frome road. The menu's not a large one,
concentrating on familiar favourites like
sandwiches, salads, chilli con carne and
chicken curry (served with crisp, golden
chips). To finish, perhaps fruit meringue or
some good Stilton. The bar features an
interesting collection of artefacts from the
farmer's, farrier's and cheesemaker's
trades. Patio.

Warenford   *(Food)*

Near Belford · *Northumberland* · Map 2 D4
Belford (066 83) 453

Free House
Landlords Ray & Marian Matthewman

Cheese & asparagus savoury £1.95 Grilled
trout £2.70 (Last order 9.30pm. No bar food
Mon Nov–Easter)
🍺 Drybrough Heavy, Scotch; Carlsberg,
Carlsberg Hof.

Warenford Lodge

In a little village just off the A1, this warm,
cosy pub is a splendid place to stop for a
sustaining snack. The cooking is both
imaginative and accomplished, and dishes
range from delicious fresh tomato soup to
Normandy-style guinea fowl, deep-fried
lamb's kidneys and fillets of sole in a lovely
light mornay sauce. Nice sweets, too.
Closed Monday lunchtime November–
Easter.

Warfield   *(Food)*

Cricket Lane · *Berkshire* · Map 6 B3
Winkfield Row (0344) 882910
Free House
Landlords Mr & Mrs R. Turner
Beef in old ale with jacket potato & salad £3.10
Minced lamb kebabs in pitta bread with
salad £1.95 (Last order 10pm)
🍺 Brakspear's Ordinary Bitter; Wethered's
Bitter; Pompey Royal; Flower's Original;
Guinness; Stella Artois; Heineken; cider.
Real ale

Cricketers

Once you've found this charming old pub
(ask the way), the sign depicting a well-fed
cricketer will show you what it's all about!
Good, wholesome dishes – soups, pâtés,
game pie, lamb vindaloo, roast beef, tempting sweets – are served in the cosily rustic
bars. The barbecue house offering kebabs,
spare ribs and the like is a major attraction
on weekends May–Oct. Limited choice
Sunday evening.   **Family pub**

Wark   *(B & B)*

Near Hexham · *Northumberland* · Map 4 C1
Bellingham (0660) 30209

Free House
Landlords Robert & Jane Dodd

BEDROOMS 6   Grade 2   £C
🍺 Drybrough Heavy, Scotch; Guinness;
Carlsberg; cider.

Battlesteads Hotel

Jane and Robert Dodd offer a warm welcome to visitors to their homely village pub
near Hadrian's Wall. The spacious residents' lounge offers a lovely view of the
pretty garden and countryside, and a striking carved serving counter dominates the
beamed lounge bar. Well-maintained bedrooms have modern furniture and cheerful
colour schemes, and the two old-fashioned
bathrooms are spotless.   **Family pub**

Warminster   *(Food, B & B)*

Market Place · *Wiltshire* · Map 8 D3
Warminster (0985) 216611

Brewery Wadworth
Landlords Mr & Mrs Howard Astbury

BEDROOMS 16   Grades 1 & 2   £B
Wiltshire special 90p Cherry pie 45p
(Last order 9pm. No bar food eves in winter)
🍺 Bass; Wadworth's 6X, IPA, Northgate
Bitter; Guinness; Harp. *Real ale*

Old Bell Hotel

Bar snacks are a popular feature of this fine
old coaching inn with a distinguished
colonnaded façade. The choice at lunchtime ranges from pâté and succulent roast
beef salad to hot dishes like stuffed aubergines or sausage and mash. There's only
cold food in the evening. Neat bedrooms
have TVs and tea-makers, and ten have
their own bath or shower rooms.
Courtyard.

England

Warren Street   *(Food, B & B)*   *Harrow Inn*

Near Lenham · *Kent* · Map 6 C3
Maidstone (0622) 858727

Free House
Landlord Mark Watson
BEDROOMS 5   Grade 1   £B   (No dogs)
Stilton soup with roll & butter 75p Spiced
chicken with rice £2.95 (Last order 9.45pm)
🍺 Shepherd Neame Masterbrew, Bitter,
Mild; Young's Special Bitter; Guinness;
Hurlimann Sternbräu; Taunton cider. *Real ale*

You'll find a good choice of delicious
bar food in the tastefully modernised surroundings of this village pub. In addition to
sandwiches, pâté and salads, there are daily
dishes such as superb home-made tomato
soup, stuffed peppers and deliciously
refreshing raspberry and redcurrant flan.
Luxurious bedrooms have good furniture
and pretty floral curtains; bathrooms are
impeccable. There's a comfortable residents' lounge with TV. Garden.

Warwick-on-Eden   *(B & B)*   *Queen's Arms Inn & Motel*

Near Carlisle · *Cumbria* · Map 3 B1
Wetheral (0228) 60699

Free House
Landlords David, Lawrence, Jean & Barbara
Keen

BEDROOMS 8   Grade 1   £B
🍺 Tetley's Bitter, Mild; Skol;
Löwenbräu; Guinness; cider. *Real ale*

Handily placed close to Carlisle and the M6,
this country inn is a nice blend of traditional
and up-to-date features. The two bars have
great appeal with their massive open fires
and assorted bric-à-brac. Bedrooms are
spacious and bright, with pretty floral curtains, TVs, tea-makers and radios, plus
compact bath or shower rooms. The owners
generate a very friendly atmosphere.
Garden.   **Family pub**

Wasdale Head   *(Food, B & B)*   *Wasdale Head Inn*

Near Gosforth · *Cumbria* · Map 3 B2
Wasdale (094 06) 229

Free House
Landlord Mr J. R. M. Carr
BEDROOMS 8   Grade 1   £A
Cumberland tattie pot £2.75 Beef ale
casserole £2.75 (Last order 10pm)
🍺 Theakston's Best Bitter, Old Peculier;
Jennings Bitter; Hartley's XB; Guinness;
Carlsberg; Taunton cider. *Real ale*

Pleasant accommodation and tasty bar food
available from 10.30am to 10pm make this
inn popular with walkers and climbers. In
the rustic bar you can enjoy simple, well-
prepared offerings like pâté, quiche,
Cumberland tattie pot with red cabbage and
tender chicken and vegetable pie. Cosy bedrooms have duvets, tea-makers and tiled
bath/shower rooms. No accommodation
early Nov–28 Dec, when bars are open
weekends only.   **Family pub**

Washbrook   *(Food)*   *Brook Inn*

Back Lane, Near Ipswich · *Suffolk* · Map 5 D2
Copdock (047 386) 455

Brewery Tollemache & Cobbold
Landlords Mr & Mrs W. M. Freeth
Brook Special £2.50 Coffee & brandy
gâteau 85p (No bar food eves, Sun
or Bank Holidays)
🍺 Tolly Cobbold Original, Bitter, Best Bitter,
Mild; Guinness; Hansa; Taunton cider.
Real ale

Hungry businessmen make a beeline for
this attractive village pub to enjoy some
tasty lunchtime bar fare. Home-made soup
is always a good bet (try the delicious
tomato), and other enjoyable offerings
might include chilli con carne, pork
Stroganoff and salads with super home-
cooked ham, or smoked fish. And there's
always the Brook Special – soup, a roll and
a mammoth plateful of ham, salami,
superb Stilton and celery. Patio.

Washington   *(Food)*   *Frankland Arms*

Near Storrington · *West Sussex* · Map 6 B4
Ashington (0903) 892220

Brewery Whitbread
Landlord Mr Robert Carey

Lamb & apricot pie £2.45 Sandwiches
from 70p (Last order 10.30pm)
🍺 Whitbread Country Bitter, Pompey Royal,
Best Bitter; Guinness; Stella Artois; cider.
Real ale

New hosts the Careys are maintaining the
tradition of good home cooking at this
attractive, whitewashed inn just off the
A24. Tasty meat pies (lamb and apricot,
steak and onion, chicken with sweetcorn)
are great favourites, along with succulent
home-boiled ham in sandwiches or salads.
Freshly picked berries are used in delicious
fruit puddings (usually available lunchtime
only). Garden.

Waterley Bottom   *(B & B)*   *New Inn*

Near North Nibley, Dursley · *Gloucestershire*
Map 7 D2
Dursley (0453) 3659

Free House
Landlord Ruby Sainty
BEDROOMS 2   Grade 2   £C   (No dogs)
🍺 Greene King Abbot Ale; Smiles Best
Bitter; Cotleigh Tawry Bitter; Theakston's Old
Peculier; New Inn WB; Hofmeister; cider.
Real ale

Don't take the name literally, as this
pleasant country inn is about as traditional
as you can get: they play darts and
dominoes in the public bar, and real ale
comes from an old pewter beer engine. The
two pretty bedrooms have modern units,
duvets, colour TVs and tea-makers, and
they share a good bathroom. Mrs Sainty
gets guests off to a good start with a hearty
breakfast. Nice garden.

Wath-in-Nidderdale   *(Food, B & B)*   *Sportsman's Arms*

Near Pately Bridge · *North Yorkshire* · Map 4 C2
Harrogate (0423) 711306

Free House
Landlords Mr & Mrs J. R. Carter
BEDROOMS 6   Grade 2   £B
Fresh Nidderdale trout & salad £2.45
Ploughman's platter £1.50 (No bar food eves)
🍺 Tetley's Bitter, Mild; Theakston's Bitter;
Younger's Bitter, Export; Guinness; Carlsberg;
cider.

A secluded setting is enjoyed by this mellow
sandstone inn, which stands in attractive
grounds just a stone's throw from the river
Nidd. Six cosy bedrooms sharing two bathrooms offer simple overnight comforts, and
there's a homely TV lounge. Bar luncheons
include flavoursome home-made soup,
wholemeal rolls generously topped with
prawns and mayonnaise, local trout and
sirloin steak. Nice sweets, too. Garden.
Family pub

Watton-at-Stone   *(Food)*   *George & Dragon*

Hertfordshire · Map 5 C2
Ware (0920) 830285

Brewery Greene King
Landlord Mr Kevin Dinnin

Omelette Arnold Bennett £2.50 Avocado with
prawns & Danish caviar £3 (Last order 10pm.
No bar food Sun)
🍺 Greene King IPA, Abbot Ale, Light Mild,
Yeoman; Harp; Kronenbourg. *Real ale*

The bar snacks are a very popular feature at
this friendly old roadside pub, where Kevin
Dinnin looks after his customers with
cheerful expertise. Favourites on the
appealing menu include soups, sandwiches and salads, along with mushrooms
in a gently curried cream sauce, seafood
Thermidor and daily specials like home-
made burgers. There's an excellent trifle
among the puds. Garden.

Weedon   (B & B)   *Crossroads Hotel*

High Street · *Northamptonshire* · Map 5 B2
Weedon (0327) 40354

Free House
Landlord Mr T. Brown

BEDROOMS 28   Grade 1   £A+   (No dogs)
🍺 Bass; Adnams Bitter; Litchborough
Tudor; Younger's IPA; Guinness;
Carlsberg Hof; cider. *Real ale*

This converted tollhouse close to the M1 (at
the junction of the A5 and A45) is especially
popular with motorway travellers. And no
wonder, for the accommodation is superb.
Traditionally furnished bedrooms in the
main building and more modern annexe
ones are all very comfortable and have
colour TVs, radios, tea-makers and ample
writing space. Bathrooms are plush.
Attractive, welcoming bars too, one styled
like a Victorian chemist's shop. **Family pub**

Weldon   (B & B)   *George Hotel*

Stamford Road, Near Corby
Northamptonshire · Map 5 B1
Corby (053 63) 67810

Brewery Melbourns
Landlords Mr & Mrs I. K. Watts

BEDROOMS 4   Grade 2   £C   (No dogs)
🍺 Sam Smith's Old Brewery Bitter, Dark
Mild, Taddy Bitter, Lager; Guinness; cider.
Real ale

A charming stone pub, centuries old and
once a coaching inn. The mellow beamed
front bar is a quiet spot to relax with a drink,
while pool, darts and video games generate a lively atmosphere in the public bar.
Pleasant bedrooms (in the house next
door) have decent freestanding furniture
and good-quality fabrics. There's a
spacious TV lounge. Children not accommodated overnight.   **Family pub**

Wellesbourne   (Food, B & B)   *King's Head*

Warwickshire · Map 5 A2
Stratford-upon-Avon (0789) 840206

Brewery Bass
Landlord Mr Carl Watkins
BEDROOMS 11   Grade 2   £B
Baked fillet of cod Malaysian style £2.75
Lamb Shrewsbury £2.75 (Last order 9.30pm)
🍺 Bass; Mitchells & Butlers Brew XI;
Worthington 'E'; Guinness; Carling Black
Label; Hemeling. *Real ale*

You're bound to find something to tempt
you on the menu of this large, creeper-clad
pub. Taramasalata and Cornish mussel
soup are among the interesting starters,
and you could go on to Malaysian-style
fillet of cod, pizza, steak or lamb curry.
Blackcurrant ice-cream makes a delicious
finish. Spacious, pleasant bedrooms have
modern fittings, and bathrooms are well
kept.   **Family pub**

Wells-next-the-Sea   (B & B)   *Tinkers Hotel*

Polka Road · *Norfolk* · Map 5 C1
Fakenham (0328) 710288

Brewery Norwich
Landlords Mr & Mrs G. Hibbs

BEDROOMS 9   Grade 2   £C
🍺 Webster's Yorkshire Bitter; Norwich Castle
Bitter, Mild; Ben Truman; Carlsberg; cider.
Real ale

New tenants Mr and Mrs Hibbs provide
basic, no-frills accommodation and hearty
breakfasts at this former railway hotel, a tall
building dating from the 17th century. Bedrooms are neat and simple, the roomiest
being those on the top floor; all have washbasins and share a single bathroom. Bars,
too, are unpretentious in style, and there's a
bright, airy breakfast room. Garden.

Wendron *(B & B)*   ### New Inn

Near Helston · *Cornwall* · Map 8 A4
Helston (032 65) 2683

Brewery Devenish
Landlords Bill & Spider Standcumbe

BEDROOMS 2 Grade 2 £C (No dogs)
🍺 Devenish Cornish Best Bitter, John
Devenish Bitter, Falmouth; Guinness;
Heineken Grünhalle; cider. *Real ale*

Friendly landlord Bill Standcumbe rises
with the lark to polish the horse brasses,
harnesses and bridles that adorn the stone-
walled bars of this welcoming country pub.
His wife Spider does an equally impressive
job on the two spotless bedrooms, which
are decorated in simple, homely style and
have colour TVs and washbasins. There's a
modern public bathroom. Children under
ten not accommodated. Excellent breakfasts. Terrace.

Wentworth *(Food)*   ### George & Dragon

Main Street, Near Rotherham
South Yorkshire · Map 4 C3
Barnsley (0226) 742440

Free House
Landlord Margaret Dickinson

Cold table £2.95 Home-made sweets 75p (Last
order 9pm. No bar food Sun)
🍺 Taylor's Bitter, Landlord, Porter; Tetley's
Bitter; Löwenbräu; cider. *Real ale*

Stuffed birds and hunting trophies lend a
Victorian charm to this unpretentious greystone pub famous for Margaret Dickinson's
superb lunchtime buffet laden with home-
cooked meats, black pudding and the most
imaginative salads. There are hot dishes in
winter, and tempting sweets include a
stunning chocolate crunch cake. Chunks of
home-made bread with generous fillings
are the only evening offerings. Patio.

Weobley *(Food)*   ### Red Lion Hotel

Near Hereford · *Hereford & Worcester*
Map 7 D1
Weobley (0544) 318220
Free House
Landlord Mr Townley-Berry

Beef curry £3 Cold table buffet £3.50 (No bar
food eves)
🍺 Flower's Best Bitter, Original; Ansells
Bitter; Usher's Triple Crown; Carlsberg Hof;
Red Stripe; cider. *Real ale*

Lunchtime bar snacks are served in the
restaurant of this delightful 14th-century
timbered inn. The centrepiece is a cold
buffet offering a wide range of cooked
meats and salads. There are also a couple
of hot dishes – beef curry is a favourite –
and a traditional roast on Sunday. Garden.
*For accommodation see Egon Ronay's
Lucas Hotel & Restaurant Guide 1985.*
Family pub

West Adderbury *(Food)*   ### White Hart

Tanners Lane, Near Banbury · *Oxfordshire*
Map 5 A2
Banbury (0295) 810406

Free House
Landlords D. G. Benstead & Jane Purcell

Moussaka £2.50 Casserole of the day £3 (Last
order 10pm)
🍺 Manns Bitter; Marston's Pedigree, Burton
Bitter; Carlsberg. *Real ale*

Every visitor, whether regular or stranger,
can be sure of a warm-hearted welcome at
this attractive pub near the village centre.
Excellent home-cooked fare is served in the
well-furnished bar, from light, tasty salmon
mousse to casseroled lamb cutlets and a
tasty cold lemon soufflé. There's also an
eye-catching cold buffet. Set three-course
meal for Sunday lunch. Garden.

West Bexington (B & B)   *Manor Hotel*

Bridport · *Dorset* · Map 8 D3
Burton Bradstock (0308) 897616

Free House
Landlord Mr Richard Childs

BEDROOMS 11 Grade 1 £B (No dogs)
🍺 Wadworth 6X; Manor Bitter; Eldridge
Pope Royal Oak; Carlsberg; Taunton cider.
Real ale

This ancient stone manor house enjoys a
peaceful setting just a short stroll from the
sea and the dramatic sweep of Chesil Bank.
Fine oak panelling graces the flagstoned
hall, and the original cellar is now a
characterful bar. Light, airy bedrooms, all
with colour TVs, are kept in spotless condition, and bathrooms are excellent. A
comfortably traditional residents' lounge
overlooks the garden.   **Family pub**

West Lavington (Food)   *Churchill*

High Street · *Wiltshire* · Map 6 A3
West Lavington (038 081) 2287

Brewery Bass
Landlords P. A. & S. Y. Smith & B. C. &
M. R. Goram
Steak & kidney pie £2 Grilled gammon £2.50
(Last order 10pm)
🍺 Bass; Worthington Best Bitter; Toby
Bitter; Guinness; Carling Black Label; Taunton
cider. *Real ale*

This attractive red-brick pub draws an
appreciative clientele with its enjoyable bar
snacks. The list limits itself to familiar
favourites, from sandwiches and home-
made soup to grilled gammon, fried fish
and a good tasty steak and kidney pie
cooked in Guinness. Simple sweets include
apple pie. Enjoy it all in the smartly furnished bar or outside in the beer garden.
                              Family pub

West Lavington (B & B)   *Wheatsheaf*

High Street · *Wiltshire* · Map 6 A3
West Lavington (0380 81) 3392

Free House
Landlord Mr T. Emery

BEDROOMS 5 Grade 2 £C
🍺 Wadworth's 6X; Ind Coope Bitter; Tetley's
Bitter; Guinness; Löwenbräu; Skol. *Real ale*

A smart black and white pub at one end of
the village, with two pleasant bars and a
large beer garden. Well-carpeted bedrooms are bright and airy, nicely furnished
with modern freestanding pieces; they all
have central heating and TV and share an
up-to-date bathroom and a shower cabinet.
Additional rooms are planned, all with
private facilities.

West Witton (B & B)   *Wensleydale Heifer*

Near Leyburn · *North Yorkshire* · Map 4 C2
Wensleydale (0969) 22322

Free House
Landlord Nigel Holdsworth

BEDROOMS 17 Grade 1 £B
🍺 Younger's IPA; McEwan's Export, Lager;
Guinness; Taunton cider. *Real ale*

Set in the splendid scenery of Wensleydale,
this delightful 17th-century inn abounds in
warmth and charm. A roaring log fire
banishes winter from the comfortably furnished lounge, and the bar is cosy and
convivial. Good-sized bedrooms (some in
nearby buildings) have practical furnishings, TVs and tea-makers. One room boasts
a four-poster, and nearly all have up-to-
date private facilities.   **Family pub**

Westbury (Food)   Reindeer Inn

Near Brackley · *Buckinghamshire* · Map 5 B2
Brackley (0280) 704934

Brewery Manns
Landlords Mr & Mrs J. Clarke

Westbury country pie £1.60 Hot chocolate
fudge cake 90p (Last order 10pm)
🍺 Usher's Founder's Ale; Webster's
Yorkshire Bitter; Manns Traditional; Guinness;
Holsten; Carlsberg; cider. *Real ale*

The large beer garden is a popular summer
attraction at this cottagy, stone-built pub,
while in cooler months the cosy bar
beckons with its cheerful open fire. Freshly
prepared snacks, available seven days a
week, include flavoursome chicken liver
pâté, pizzas and excellent cottage pie.
Sandwiches and salads, too, along with
good English cheeses and a wickedly rich
hot chocolate fudge cake.   **Family pub**

Weston (Food)   White Lion

Near Crewe · *Cheshire* · Map 3 B4
Crewe (0270) 587011

Free House
Landlords Mr & Mrs G. Davies

Lionheart £1.85 Poached Dee salmon £3.85
(Last order 9.45pm)
🍺 Tetley's Traditional Bitter; Ind Coope
Burton Ale, Bitter, Mild; Guinness; Skol; cider.
Real ale

The food served in the pleasant snack bar is
a major attraction at this rambling black
and white inn proudly dated 1652. There's a
lot of seafood on the menu, with tempting
treats such as brown shrimps in garlic
butter and Cornish crab. Soup, sandwiches, cold meat platters and an excellent
cheeseboard provide further choice, along
with a lunchtime roast or daily special like
chicken provençale. Service is pleasantly
attentive.   **Family pub**

Weston-on-the-Green (Food)   Chequers Inn

Near Bicester · *Oxfordshire* · Map 5 A2
Bletchington (0869) 50319

Brewery Halls
Landlord Patrick Bennett

Burgers from £1.30 Rump steak £3.95 (Last
order 10.30pm)
🍺 Ind Coope Burton Ale, Mild; Halls Harvest
Bitter; Double Diamond; Guinness;
Löwenbräu; cider. *Real ale*

A very good local butcher supplies this
pleasant old thatched inn that was once the
village blacksmith's shop. Our rump steak
was cooked to a turn – succulent, full of
flavour and tender as butter – and the
burgers are of the same high quality. Also
available are soup, lunchtime sandwiches,
ham salad and a dish of the day, sometimes
beef curry. Garden.   **Family pub**

Westwood (Food)   New Inn

Near Bradford-on-Avon · *Wiltshire* · Map 8 D3
Bradford-on-Avon (022 16) 3123

Brewery Usher
Landlord Mr F. McFadden

Beef casserole £1.80 Sherry trifle 80p (Last
order 10pm)
🍺 Usher's Country Bitter; Ben Truman;
Carlsberg; Holsten; cider. *Real ale*

Local ladies take turns with the cooking at
this pleasant village pub, producing anything from a light bite to a three-course
meal that you can enjoy in the comfortable
bar. Burgers, baked potatoes and lasagne
are popular quick snacks, and other items
on a varied menu range from rich, creamy
fish soup and deep-fried clams to sirloin
steak, roast duckling and turkey cordon
bleu. Patio.

Wetherby *(Food)*   *Alpine Inn*

North Yorkshire · Map 4 C3
Wetherby (0937) 62501

Brewery Samuel Smith
Landlord Mr Colin R. Hooton

Mushrooms in garlic butter £1.55 Fillet steak
sandwich £2.25 (Last order 11pm)
🍺 Samuel Smith's Old Brewery Bitter, Dark
Mild; Ayinger Bräu. *Real ale*

This modern, chalet-style pub beside the
southbound carriageway of the A1 is just
the place for hungry motorists and families.
The choice of bar snacks is simple yet
varied, and preparation is careful. If home-
made soup or a ploughman's doesn't strike
your fancy, you might opt for a sizzling fillet
steak sandwich (the house speciality),
fisherman's pie or a filled jacket potato.
Light cream caramel makes a nice sweet.
Patio.   **Family pub**

Weybridge *(Food)*   *Buffers*

Heath Road, Weybridge Station · *Surrey*
Map 6 B3
Weybridge (0932) 55332

Free House
Landlord James Heyward

Chilli & jacket potato £1.20 Steak & kidney
pie £3.95 (No bar food eves or Sun lunch)
🍺 Whitbread Best Bitter, Best Scotch Bitter;
Stella Artois; Heineken.

A cross between a wine bar and a hamburger restaurant in atmosphere, this
popular place is a clever conversion of the
former station booking office. Garlic mushrooms and grilled sardines are tasty ways
of getting a meal under way, and to follow
there are burgers, steaks, seafood and a
good steak and kidney pie. Sweets are
mainly ice cream-based. Live music most
weekday nights.   **Family pub**

Weybridge *(B & B)*   *Kings Manor Hotel*

Oatlands Chase · *Surrey* · Map 6 B3
Walton-on-Thames (0932) 227790

Brewery Charrington
Landlords Mr & Mrs Braybrook

BEDROOMS 16   Grade 2   £A (No dogs)
🍺 Charrington IPA; Stones Bitter; Guinness;
Carling Black Label; Tennent's; Taunton cider.
Real ale

Situated in a smart residential road, this
substantial white-painted pub with a large
garden at the rear has a cheerful, friendly
atmosphere. There's a comfortable, amply
furnished bar, and accommodation ranges
from simple, compact singles to good-
sized twins (four with shower cubicles). All
rooms have TVs, telephones and tea-
makers, and there are three good modern
bathrooms.

Weymouth *(B & B)*   *Golden Lion*

19 St Edmund Street · *Dorset* · Map 8 D4
Weymouth (0305) 786778

Brewery Devenish
Landlord Mr B. I. Guarraci

BEDROOMS 15   Grade 2   £C
🍺 John Devenish Bitter, Wessex Best Bitter;
John Grove's Weymouth Bitter; Guinness;
Grünhalle; Heineken; Stella Atrois; cider.
Real ale

Just a few steps from the harbour and
cross-Channel ferries, this town-centre pub
has been extensively modernised behind
its handsome white and green facade. Bedrooms with neat, practical furnishings and
pretty floral duvets offer good comfort for
an overnight stop, and there are plenty of
well-kept public bathrooms. There are two
bars and a TV lounge. Accommodation
closed end October–Easter.

Whitefield *(Food)* · *Mason's Arms*

Bury New Road · *Greater Manchester*
Map 3 B3
061-766 2713

Brewery Whitbread
Landlords Phil & Carol Spires
Steak & kidney pie £1.60 Ploughman's
lunch £1.30 (No bar food eves)
🍺 Whitbread Castle Eden Ale, Trophy,
Traditional; Chester's Best Mild; Dutton's
Light; Guinness; Heineken; cider. *Real ale*

Lunchtime bar snacks are brought to your table at this friendly red-brick pub. A hot steak sandwich is a popular choice, home-made steak and kidney pie is reliable and daily specials provide additional interest. If you fancy something cold, the display counter offers delicious-looking salad platters. Eye-catching puddings include things like cheesecake and lemon meringue pie.

Whitewell *(Food, B & B)* · *Inn at Whitewell*

Near Clitheroe · *Lancashire* · Map 3 B3
Dunsop Bridge (020 08) 222
Free House
Landlord Mr Richard Bowman
BEDROOMS 11 Grade 1 £B
Chicken pie £2.85 Fresh Scottish salmon
salad £3.85 (Last order 10pm. No bar food
Sat eve)
🍺 Whitbread Trophy, Best Mild;
Moorhouse's Bitter; Guinness; Heineken;
Stella Artois. *Real ale*

This sturdy stone inn stands in the charming Forest of Bowland by the banks of the river Hodder. The large foyer-lounge is a welcoming place, and interesting prints and antiques are a feature throughout. Tasty bar snacks include superb home-made chicken soup and main courses like salads, seafood pancakes and savoury pies. Double-glazed bedrooms offer abundant space and comfort; roomy bathrooms are well fitted. **Family pub**

Whitley *(Food)* · *Woolpack Inn*

Near Dewsbury · *West Yorkshire* · Map 4 C3
Mirfield (0924) 492718

Free House
Landlord Mr David Hall

Soup of the day 70p Uitsmyter £2.25 (Last
order 10pm. No bar food Mon)
🍺 Tetley's Bitter, Mild; Bass; Stones
Bitter; Guinness; Carling Black Label;
cider. *Real ale*

This attractive stone pub on a hillside is a good spot to pause for a snack. The regular menu offers standard fare – soup, steak and kidney pie, hamburgers – and a blackboard lists daily specials such as lamb chops or goujons of halibut. A popular lunchtime treat is Dutch uitsmyter, a scrumptious open ham sandwich topped with three fried eggs. Terrace. **Family pub**

Whitney-on-Wye *(Food, B & B)* ★ · *Rhydspence Inn*

Hereford & Worcester · Map 7 C1
Clifford (049 73) 262
Free House
Landlords David & Flo Wallington
BEDROOMS 3 Grade 1 £B (No dogs)
Landlord's favourite diet portion £1.60 Curry of
the day £4.25 (Last order 9.30pm)
🍺 Hook Norton Bitter; Bass; Robinson's Best
Bitter; Mitchells & Butlers DPA; Bailey's Bitter;
Guinness; Old Tom (winter only); cider
(summer only). *Real ale*

A really marvellous pub, with an idyllic setting, delightful hosts, homely accommodation and superb food. The choice in the beamed bar ranges from stockpot soup and wonderful English cheeses to herby sausages, curries and seafood Thermidor, with delicious sweets to finish. Tastefully furnished bedrooms (no under-tens) are bright and comfortable; all have TVs. Bar closed Mondays and winter Tuesdays; pub closed 2 weeks in winter. Garden.

Whittlesey   *(B & B)*   *Falcon Hotel*

London Street · *Cambridgeshire* · Map 5 C1
Peterborough (0733) 203247

Brewery Tollemache & Cobbold
Landlords Mavis & Brian Ramsden

BEDROOMS 8   Grade 2   £B
🍺 Tolly's Best Bitter, Bitter, Original;
Younger's Tartan; Hansa; Taunton cider.
Real ale

A brick-built building tucked away behind
the town square, this former coaching inn
offers comfortable overnight accommodation in its spacious, well-kept bedrooms. All
rooms have good carpets, colour TVs and
tea-makers, and the elegant suite boasts a
four-poster and its own lounge. There are
two pleasant bars, one with a thatched
serving area, the other with a fine carved
wooden counter. Patio.   **Family pub**

Wickham   *(Food, B & B)*   *Five Bells*

New Newbury · *Berkshire* · Map 6 A3
Boxford (048 838) 242

Brewery Watneys
Landlord Mrs D. A. Channing-Williams
BEDROOMS 4   Grade 1   £C
Steak & kidney pie £3 Ploughman's £1.50
(Last order 10pm)
🍺 Usher's Best Bitter, IPA; Watneys Special
Bitter; Guinness; Carlsberg; cider. *Real ale*

The emphasis is on home cooking at Mrs
Channing-Williams' 450-year old thatched
pub. Winter specials like rabbit casserole
supplement fish, fried chicken and steak
and kidney pie, and there are crisp, fresh
salads with locally baked ham. Home-made
puddings include delicious treacle tart. All
four bright bedrooms have washbasins
and TVs, and the beds are comfortable.
New features in the garden are a barbecue
and swimming pool.   **Family pub**

Willian   *(Food)*   *Three Horseshoes*

Letchworth · *Hertfordshire* · Map 5 B2
Letchworth (046 26) 5713

Brewery Greene King
Landlord Mr P. Jest

Quiche 80p Steak & kidney pie £1.75 (No bar
food eves or Sun)
🍺 Greene King Abbot, IPA; Guinness; Harp;
Kronenbourg; Taunton cider. *Real ale*

There's a loyal local following at this cheerful village pub, where simple lunchtime
snacks are served in warm, friendly surroundings. The beamed bar has plenty of
space for everyone to enjoy their choice
from a short menu of rolls, sandwiches and
ploughman's. Pâté and smoked salmon,
too, plus tasty specials like Stilton and ham
quiche or steak and kidney pie. Sandwiches
and cheese only Saturday.

Williton   *(B & B)*   *Egremont Hotel*

Fore Street · *Somerset* · Map 8 C3
Williton (0984) 32500

Brewery Usher
Landlord Mr M. C. Smith

BEDROOMS 12   Grade 2   £C
🍺 Usher's Best Bitter, Triple Crown; Bass;
Watneys Special; Guinness; Carlsberg
Pilsner; cider. *Real ale*

The Smiths provide a warm welcome and
simple, homely comforts in this solid 16th-
century inn. Visitors can enjoy a drink in the
basic public bar or the comfortable lounge
bar; there's also a sturdily furnished TV
lounge. Roomy bedrooms have a mixture
of traditional and modern furniture; three
have their own bathrooms. The two public
bathrooms are modern and spotlessly
clean. Enjoyable breakfasts. Garden.
          Family pub

Wilmcote *(B & B)*

Swan House Hotel

Near Stratford-upon-Avon · *Warwickshire*
Map 5 A2
Stratford-upon-Avon (0789) 67030

Free House
Landlords Mr & Mrs H. G. Poole

BEDROOMS 11 Grade 2 £B No dogs
🏠 Everards Old Original, Tiger; Tuborg
Pils, Gold; cider. *Real ale*

Popular with both tourists and peace-seeking businessmen, this handsome black and white hotel stands near the house where Shakespeare's mother lived. Eight bedrooms are in the main building, three in the garden chalet; all have modern furniture, TVs and tea-makers. There's a cosy bar and a patio. The landlords are friendly and welcoming, and guests wake up to a splendid cooked breakfast. **Family pub**

Wilson *(Food)*

Bull's Head Inn

Melbourne · *Derbyshire* · Map 4 C4
Melbourne (033 16) 2644

Brewery Allied
Landlord Mr Michael Johnson

Stilton ploughman's £1.20 Roast beef,
Yorkshire pudding & 2 vegetables £3.50 (Last
order 10pm. No bar food Sun & Mon eves)
🏠 Ind Coope Bitter, Mild; Guinness; Skol;
Löwenbräu; cider. *Real ale*

The sight of cheerful window boxes decorating the smart exterior of this friendly pub suggests that somebody cares about the place. And that somebody is Michael Johnson, who also delights visitors with his delicious bar food. The impressive cold spread offers plenty of seafood choice and there are also jacket potatoes and sandwiches. The highlight is perhaps the juicy roast beef, packed into hunks of French bread and served with Yorkshire pudding.

Wimborne St Giles *(Food, B & B)*

Bull Inn

Near Wimborne · *Dorset* · Map 6 A4
Cranborne (072 54) 284

Brewery Hall & Woodhouse
Landlords Tony & Sharon Sharp
BEDROOMS 3 Grade 2 £C (No dogs)
Rump steak £4.80 Home-made soup 85p (Last
order 10pm)
🏠 Hall & Woodhouse Badger Best Bitter,
Badger Export, Brock; Guinness; Carlsberg;
Stella Artois; Taunton cider. *Real ale*

With its tranquil location in deepest rural Dorset, this well-kept inn is a pleasant spot for a snack or an overnight stop. The bar menu offers something to suit most tastes, from pâté and ploughman's to salads, grills, basket meals, vegetarian dishes, and fish fingers for the children. Three cheerful, spotless bedrooms provide simple comforts and nice views. Accommodation closed 2 weeks Christmas. Garden.

Wincanton *(Food)*

Hunter's Lodge

Bourton · *Somerset* · Map 8 D3
Bourton (0747) 840660

Free House
Landlord Mr A. A. Dean

Jumbo local sausages £1.60 Beef & Guinness
casserole £1.95 (Last order 10pm)
🏠 Hall & Woodhouse Badger Best Bitter;
Guinness; Stella Artois; Carlsberg Hof; Brock;
Taunton cider. *Real ale*

Just over the border from Wiltshire, this substantial old pub on the A303 offers a range of bar fare to satisfy even the hungriest hunter. Our turkey and vegetable soup was packed with goodness and flavour, a splendid prelude to a main-course salad, jumbo sausages or steak and Guinness casserole. Simple sweets include 12 ice creams. Breakfasts served Saturdays in the summer. There's a garden with children's play area. **Family pub**

Wincham   *(Food)*   *Black Greyhound Hotel*

Hall Lane, Near Northwich · *Cheshire*
Map 3 B3
Northwich (0606) 3053

Brewery Greenall Whitley
Landlord Mr David Buckley

Steak pie £2.15 Roast meat platter £2.95
(Last order 10pm)
🍺 Greenall Whitley Bitter, Festival;
Guinness; Grünhalle; cider. *Real ale*

Mrs Buckley's hearty snacks bring the
locals flocking to the homely bar of this
large whitewashed pub. Generous portions
of meat pies, sausages, chicken and scampi
are served with superb crunchy chips that
on their own justify a visit here! There are
also generous ploughman's and filled
baps, salads and a pleasing selection of
English cheeses.   **Family pub** (lunchtime)

Winchcombe   *(Food)*   *Corner Cupboard Inn*

Gloucester Street · *Gloucestershire* · Map 5 A2
Winchcombe (0242) 602303

Brewery Whitbread
Landlords Mr & Mrs M. Elliott

Cottage pie £2   Cheese stuffed pasta
shells £2.20 (No bar food eves or Sun in winter)
🍺 Whitbread Best Bitter; Flowers IPA,
Original, Pale Ale, Best Bitter; Guinness;
Heineken; cider. *Real ale*

A friendly old sandstone inn, where
Michael Elliott is the smiling host and his
wife Jane the capable cook. Lunchtime
snacks, which can be enjoyed in the
beamed bar or out in the attractive walled
garden, include toasted sandwiches,
ploughman's and pâté. Salads are popular,
too, with pasta, savoury pies and specials
like moussaka to satisfy larger appetites.
Garden.

Winchelsea   *(B & B)*   *Winchelsea Lodge Motel*

Sandrock, Hastings Road · *East Sussex*
Map 6 C4
Rye (0797) 226211

Free House
Landlords George Cunliffe & George Morgan

BEDROOMS 20   Grade 1   £B
🍺 Usher's Triple Crown; Websters Yorkshire
Bitter; Carlsberg; Holsten; Fosters; cider.
Real ale

A modern adaptation of a classic Sussex
barn, this up-to-date complex west of
Winchelsea on the A259 offers excellent
accommodation. Motel-style bedrooms
have neat contemporary fixtures and fittings, including built-in wardrobes, colour
TVs and tea-makers, plus functional
shower rooms. Exposed brickwork and
a high raftered ceiling give the bar a
pleasantly traditional atmosphere. Beer
garden.   **Family pub**

Winfrith Newburgh   *(B & B)*   *Red Lion*

Dorchester Road · *Dorset* · Map 8 D3
Warmwell (0305) 852814

Brewery Hall & Woodhouse
Landlords Mike & Libby Smeaton

BEDROOMS 4   Grade 2   £C
🍺 Hall & Woodhouse Hector's Bitter, Badger
Best Bitter, Export, Tanglefoot; Guinness;
Brock; Taunton cider. *Real ale*

All is cosy and cheerful in this popular,
friendly pub on the A352, where caring
hosts Mike and Libby Smeaton provide
spotlessly clean accommodation. Bright
bedrooms have pretty floral wallpapers,
modern fitted units and tea-makers; the
single public bathroom is immaculate.
There's a rustic atmosphere about the pine-
panelled bar, and the upstairs lounge is
extremely comfortable. Accommodation
closed 1 week Christmas.   **Family pub**

Wingham   *(Food, B & B)*   *Red Lion Inn*

High Street · *Kent* · Map 6 D3
Canterbury (0227) 720217

Brewery Whitbread
Landlords Mr & Mrs Adam
BEDROOMS 2   Grade 2   £C
Stuffed mushrooms £1.25   Prawn risotto £2
(No bar food eves or Sun)
🍺 Whitbread Best Bitter, Best Mild, Trophy;
Fremlins Bitter; Guinness; Heineken; Stella
Artois. *Real ale*

Previously a canon's residence and
sessions house, this ancient building
assumed its current role of hostelry during
the 17th century. Customers flock to the
oak-beamed bar to enjoy the lunchtime
snacks, all fresh, tasty and satisfying:
ploughman's platters, stuffed mushrooms,
honey-baked ham, super fish and chips.
The traditionally furnished bedrooms
share a spacious, well-kept bathroom.
Excellent breakfasts. Garden.   **Family pub**

Winkfield   *(Food)*   *Olde Hatchet*

Hatchet Lane, Near Windsor · *Berkshire*
Map 6 B3
Bracknell (0344) 882303

Brewery Charrington
Landlord Mr D. F. Davies

Flemish mussels £2.10 Trifle £1 (Last
order 9pm. No bar food Sun eve)
🍺 Charrington's IPA; Bass; Guinness;
Carling Black Label; Taunton cider. *Real ale*

Climbing plants and creepers hug the walls
of this 16th-century roadside pub, which
stands on the fringe of Windsor Great Park.
A blackboard in the long beamed bar offers
a good choice of well-prepared fare, from
filled rolls and nourishing soups to hot
smoked mackerel, mixed grill and outstanding lasagne verdi. Cold buffet only for
Sunday lunch.   **Family pub**

Winkfield   *(Food)*   *White Hart Inn*

Church Road, Near Windsor · *Berkshire*
Map 6 B3
Winkfield Row (0344) 882415

Brewery Courage
Landlord Ronald Edward Haywood
Steak & kidney pie £2.60 Seafood
pancake £2.25 (Last order 9.30pm)
🍺 Courage Best Bitter, Directors Bitter, JC;
Guinness; Kronenbourg; Hofmeister. *Real ale*

A welcoming open fire warms this 16th-
century village pub, where locals and
visitors gather to drink, chat and enjoy
some tasty fare. Pride of place must go to
the wholesome steak and kidney pie, but
the menu also offers daily specials such as
jugged hare and seafood pancakes, along
with salads and grills. Start with a bowl of
flavoursome soup and finish off with a
seasonal fruit pie. Sandwiches only Sun
eve. Garden.

Winkleigh   *(Food)*   *King's Arms*

Devon · Map 8 C3
Winkleigh (083 783) 384

Free House
Landlords Dennis Hawkes & Roy Falkner

Savoury cheese peach £1.25 Roast duck
lunch £2.95 (Last order 10pm)
🍺 Usher's Best Bitter, Triple Crown;
Carlsberg; Löwenbräu; cider. *Real ale*

It's well worth making a detour for the
highly enjoyable snacks served in this
delightful pub in a tiny village. One of the
highlights is the daily roast lunch: our local
duck was delicious and came with a spicy
apple sauce. There's also excellent soup
(perhaps thick vegetable) and a tempting
cold buffet featuring savoury flans, terrines, rare roast beef and pies. Super
sweets. Closed Monday, 2 weeks Feb & 3
weeks Nov.

Winkton (B & B) Fisherman's Haunt

Christchurch · *Dorset* · Map 6 A4
Christchurch (0202) 484071

Free House
Landlords Mr & Mrs J. Bochan

BEDROOMS 17 Grades 1 & 2 £B
Bass; John Smith's Bitter; Ringwood
Best Bitter; Toby Bitter; Mc Ewan's Export;
Guinness; Tennent's Extra; Taunton cider.
Real ale

A mile from Christchurch on the B3347, this wistaria-covered inn overlooking the Avon offers a friendly welcome and homely accommodation. All bedrooms have TV, central heating and tea/coffee-makers. One room in the main house has a four-poster; nicest are the bedrooms in the adjacent cottages with their own little shower rooms. There's a pleasant residents' lounge on the first floor. Patio. **Family pub**

Winscombe (Food, B & B) Woodborough

Near Weston-super-Mare · *Avon* · Map 8 D3
Winscombe (093 484) 2167

Brewery Courage
Landlords Mary & Graham Ashdowne
BEDROOMS 4 Grade 2 £C (No dogs)
Chicken curry £1.50 Fresh salmon £2.50
(Last order 10pm. No bar food Sun eve)
Courage Best Bitter; Yorkshire Bitter;
Guinness; Hofmeister; John Smith's Lager;
Taunton cider. *Real ale*

Mary Ashdowne's tasty cooking is the attraction in this lively 1930s pub. She spends long hours preparing delicately spiced curries, which are served with excellent rice. She also offers sandwiches with a choice of fresh breads, seafood specialities, savoury flans and basket meals, and her apple pie is delicious. Sturdily furnished, old-fashioned bedrooms have TVs and tea-makers. Children not accommodated overnight.

Winsford (Food, B & B) Royal Oak Inn

Near Minehead · *Somerset* · Map 8 C3
Winsford (064 385) 232

Free House
Landlords Mr & Mrs C. Steven

BEDROOMS 11 Grade 1 £A+
Cold buffet £3.50 Seafood open sandwich £1.75
(Last order 9.30pm)
Flowers Original; Whitbread Best Bitter;
Heineken; cider. *Real ale*

This enchanting thatched pub is a pleasant place for an overnight stay. Bedrooms, cottagy or modern, provide accommodation of a very high standard. In the attractive bar you can always enjoy sandwiches, ploughman's and a hot dish such as cottage pie or chunky steak and kidney pie. At lunchtime in summer the major attraction is the impressive buffet with splendid cold pies, home-cooked joints and delicious salads. Patio and garden.

Winslow (B & B) Bell Hotel

1 Sheep Street, Market Square
Buckinghamshire · Map 5 B2
Winslow (029 671) 2741

Free House
Landlords Mr & Mrs William Alston

BEDROOMS 14 Grade 1 £B
Adnams Bitter; Greene King Abbot Ale;
Marston's Pedigree; Webster's Yorkshire
Bitter; Foster's; Carlsberg; cider. *Real ale*

This fine old coaching inn, whose black and white facade dominates the market square, offers comfortable overnight accommodation and a choice of three characterful beamed bars. Bedrooms are of a high standard, with good-quality carpets, well-made reproduction furniture, tea-makers and colour TVs; most have their own smart up-to-date bath or shower room. Courtyard. **Family pub**

272

NOW'S
YOUR CHANCE
TO DRINK
CALIFORNIA
DRY.
PUSH UP HERE
ONE LITRE
Dry White Wine
PAUL MASSON
California Dry White Wine
1 Litre (e)
Paul Masson.
Now in Dry White.

WE CORDIALLY INVITE

establishments not in this Guide

to write to us if they would like to be considered for inclusion next year — provided their standard of food *served in the bar* is exceptionally high, or their bedrooms clean and very pleasant, or both.

Write to **Egon Ronay's Guinness Pub Guide, Greencoat House, Francis Street, London SW1P 1DH**

We do not accept advertising, payment or free hospitality from any of the establishments we recommend.

You'll find fussy Findus in everyone's good books.

SWISS CHEESE CRÊPES WITH HAM.

Our Swiss Cheese Crêpes with Ham are a perfect example of how Findus have become harder to please. Fussy, some might say.

Only fresh Emmental cheese from Switzerland, our chefs insist, will fit the bill. Lean, sweet-cured ham is an absolute must, too. As is a dash of Madeira wine and fresh cream for the filling.

Truth is, we have to be this fussy about our food. After all, aren't you?

Findus

The finest food-frozen

Cater dish – a new thought for food from Simpsons.

Open up new market areas with Cater dish, the all in one way to present food. Just open, heat, and serve from the tray.

- Cater dish has applications in all areas of catering; especially for pubs, hotels and small restaurants. But it's also a great way to serve food at sports and social functions, or simply when entertaining friends.

- A ready meal needing no refrigeration

- Opens with a good can opener

- Reheats in a conventional oven

- Contains 1.5kg/3lb, enough to serve 6-8 people

- Simpsons, as the first users of Cater dish, include Lasagne, Hot Pot, Moussaka, Steak and Kidney Pie and Beef Casserole in their delicious range of dishes.

Simpson Ready Foods Ltd., Urmston, Manchester, M31 1WH, Tel: 061-865 2241.

 ——————**Cater dish**——————
another great idea from Metal Box Food Packaging Division.

Winster *(Food, B & B)* — Brown Horse Inn

Near Bowness-on-Windermere · *Cumbria*
Map 3 B2
Windermere (096 62) 3443
Free House
Landlords Mr & Mrs G. Millar
BEDROOMS 3 Grade 2 £C (No dogs)
Steak & kidney pie £2.50 Lasagne £2.25 (Last order 9pm. No bar food Mon eve in winter)
🍺 Thwaites Bitter; Tetley's Bitter; McEwan's Scotch Bitter; Guinness; Stella Artois; Becks Bier; cider. *Real ale*

The hardworking Millars are your hosts at this exceptionally friendly pub in picturesque Lyth Valley. They offer a good choice of bar food, including thick vegetable soup, local Cumberland sausage, sandwiches, ploughman's platters and a really smashing meat and potato pie. The three centrally heated bedrooms, which share the landlord's bathroom, have smart furniture and TVs. No under-fours overnight. Closed Mon lunch in winter. **Family pub**

Winterton-on-Sea *(Food, B & B)* — Fisherman's Return

The Lane · *Norfolk* · Map 5 D1
Winterton-on-Sea (049 376) 305

Brewery Norwich
Landlords John & Kate Findlay
BEDROOMS 4 Grade 2 £C
Mushrooms in garlic butter £1.25 Fisherman's omelette £2 (Last order 9.30pm)
🍺 Norwich S & P Bitter; Webster's Yorkshire Bitter; Bullard's Mild; Guinness; Carlsberg; Foster's; cider. *Real ale*

Two panelled bars and a family room provide plenty of space at this charming brick and flint pub just behind the dunes. Snacks range from pâtés and ploughman's to burgers, charcoal-grilled steaks and the filling fisherman's omelette with bacon, onions and mushrooms. Four neat, bright bedrooms share a spotless modern bathroom, and there's a little TV area. Tasty, generously served breakfasts. Garden. **Family pub**

Wisbech *(B & B)* — Rose & Crown Hotel

Market Square · *Cambridgeshire* · Map 5 C1
Wisbech (0945) 583187

Brewery Greene King
Landlords William & Sylvia Lloyd

BEDROOMS 20 Grade 1 £B
🍺 Greene King Abbot Ale, IPA; Guinness; Harp; Kronenbourg.

This impressive town-centre hostelry started life as a coaching inn and still provides a warm welcome and friendly hospitality. Bright, cheerful bedrooms are traditionally furnished to a high standard and equipped with TVs and tea-makers; most have spotlessly clean, up-to-date bathrooms. There's a cosy bar, a comfortable residents' lounge (with TV) and a delightful courtyard festooned with wistaria. **Family pub**

Withington *(B & B)* — Mill Inn

Near Cheltenham · *Gloucestershire* · Map 5 A2
Withington (024 289) 204

Free House
Landlords Mr & Mrs D. T. Lawrence

BEDROOMS 3 Grade 2 £B
🍺 Younger's Tartan, IPA; Bass; Fussell's Best Bitter; Guinness; Foster's; Taunton cider. *Real ale*

You'll find bags of atmosphere at this delightful inn, which stands by the river Coln. Beams, sloping floors and rustic oak furniture characterise the charming, immaculately kept bedrooms, which share a similarly spotless bathroom. The bar and adjoining snugs are irresistible, too, with their inglenook fireplaces, comfortable old seats, interesting prints and bric-à-brac. There's an attractive riverside garden. **Family pub**

Withypool   *(Food, B & B)* — Royal Oak Inn

Near Minehead · *Somerset* · Map 8 C3
Exford (064 383) 236

Free House
Landlords Mr & Mrs Bradley & Mr & Mrs Lucas
BEDROOMS 8   Grade 1   £A
Venison & bacon sausage & salad £2.75 Danish
open prawn sandwich £1.80 (Last
order 9.30pm)
🍺 Usher's Best Bitter, Country, Triple Crown;
Guinness; Carlsberg; Taunton cider. *Real ale*

Lovers of the outdoor life appreciate both
the surroundings and the hospitality at this
lovely old Exmoor inn. Hearty fare is served
in the public bar, from ploughman's and
delicious home-cooked ham to daily hot
specials and nice puds. Attractively
decorated bedrooms provide excellent
overnight accommodation (no under-tens);
four have spotless private facilities, six are
equipped with TVs. Terrace.

Witney   *(Food)* — Butchers Arms

104 Corn Street · *Oxfordshire* · Map 6 A3
Witney (0993) 5745

Free House
Landlord Mr Paul Loftus

Prawn salad £1.50 Jumbo sausage &
chips £1.30 (No bar food eves or Sun)
🍺 Usher's Best Bitter; Morland's Bitter;
Kronenbourg; Carlsberg; Foster's. *Real ale*

The atmosphere is bright and cheerful at
this popular old pub, where well-chosen
pop music entertains a predominantly
youthful clientele. At lunchtime in the bar,
with its attractive furnishings and exposed
stone walls, visitors can tuck into a small
selection of simple snacks: soup (served
with good crusty bread), beefburgers,
omelettes and tasty toasted sandwiches.
Patio.   **Family pub**

Witney   *(Food)* — Red Lion

1 Corn Street · *Oxfordshire* · Map 6 A3
Witney (0993) 3149

Brewery Morrell's
Landlord Mr R. Tams

Brunch muffin 85p Mushroom, mince & onion
pie £2.25 (Last order 10pm)
🍺 Morrell's Bitter, Dark Mild, Friar; Harp; cider.
Real ale

A homely town-centre pub, with an interesting
menu of familiar favourites and some out-of-
the-ordinary dishes. A wholemeal muffin filled
with soft cheese, smoked ham and a poached
egg makes an excellent snack, and other
choices include roast beef (hot or cold), vegetable risotto in a sweet-sour sauce and a
variety of savoury pies. Apple pie to finish.
Courtyard.

Woburn   *(Food)* — Black Horse Inn

Bedford Street · *Bedfordshire* · Map 5 B2
Woburn (052 525) 210
Free House
Landlord Mr. T. Aldous
Pot of cottage cheese with jacket potato &
salad £1.30 Hot seafood quiche & vegetables
£1.50 (Last order 10pm)
🍺 Young's Special Bitter; Marston's Burton
Bitter; Tetley's Bitter; John Marstons;
Benskin's Pale; Guinness; Oranjeboom;
Löwenbräu; cider. *Real ale*

This pleasant old inn offers a pretty walled
garden for summer drinks, while the handsome bar hung with hunting scenes makes
a welcoming retreat. Along with steaks at
lunchtime you'll find well-prepared salads,
ploughman's, pâté and Gloucester
sausages, and at lunchtime look out for the
hot dish of the day, which might be an
appetising meat or fish pie served with
vegetables. Sandwiches are also available.

Woodbridge *(Food, B & B)* — *Bull Hotel*

Market Hill · *Suffolk* · Map 5 D2
Woodbridge (039 43) 2089
Free House
Landlords Mr & Mrs Allen
BEDROOMS 26   Grade 2   £B
Baked ham with parsley sauce &
potatoes £2.30 Fisherman's pie with
vegetables £2.30 (Last order 10pm)
🍺 Adnams Bitter; Tolly Cobbold Best Bitter;
Bass; John Bull; Younger's Tartan; Whitbread
Tankard; Taunton cider. *Real ale*

The welcoming Allens are the latest in a line
of proprietors documented back to 1734 at
this friendly town-centre pub. Popular bar
snacks include lavishly filled omelettes,
meaty Bullburgers, home-made cottage
pie and a choice of grills, salads and sandwiches. Bedrooms, some in a courtyard
annexe, vary from traditional to modern.
Some have private bathrooms and TV, and
there's a comfortable TV lounge.
Family pub

Woodbury Salterton *(Food)* — *Digger's Rest*

Near Exeter · *Devon* · Map 8 C3
Woodbury (0395) 32375

Free House
Landlord Sally Jane Pratt
Cold gammon ham with chips £2.25 Roast
chicken sandwich 85p (Last order 10pm)
🍺 Whitbread Best Bitter; Bass; Blackawton
Bitter; Flowers Best Bitter; Younger's Tartan;
Guinness; cider. *Real ale*

Pretty Sally Jane Pratt and her helpers keep
things turning over in this charming
thatched pub with its own skittle alley. The
main attraction in the beamed bars is the
nicely prepared food, which includes local
pâté, home-made soup and sausages, the
best bets undoubtedly being the cold meats
cooked on the premises, which are served
as salads or packed into hefty sandwiches.
Hot dishes in winter. Garden.
Family pub (till 8pm)

Woodditton *(Food)* — *Three Blackbirds*

Ditton Green · *Cambridgeshire* · Map 5 C2
Newmarket (0638) 730811

Brewery Tollemache & Cobbold
Landlords Ted & Joan Spooner

Beef provençale £2.25 Kidneys in red
wine £1.95 (Last order 10.30pm)
🍺 Tolly Cobbold Original, Bitter, Old Strong;
Guinness; Hansa; Taunton cider. *Real ale*

Racing folk and non-turfites alike enjoy the
Spooner brand of hospitality at this white-
painted thatched pub in a village near
Newmarket. They also agree about the bar
food – simple, satisfying fare ranging from
flavoursome soup, pâté and prawns to
gammon, pizzas and winning lunchtime
hot specials like our splendidly robust beef
and vegetable stew with dumplings. Cold
buffet also in summer. Garden.

Woodhall Spa *(Food)* — *Abbey Lodge Inn*

Kirkstead · *Lincolnshire* · Map 4 D4
Woodhall Spa (0526) 52538

Brewery John Smith
Landlords Tom & Eileen Sloan

Steak & kidney pie £1.90 Lasagne & salad £1.90
(Last order 10pm)
🍺 John Smith's Bitter, Lager; Guinness;
Hofmeister; Taunton cider.

This whitewashed brick pub stands beside
the B1192 south of town. In the farmhouse-
style bar, genially presided over by Tom
Sloan and his family, the food is of the
wholesome, robust variety: full-bodied
chicken and vegetable soup, flavoursome
steak and kidney pie, lasagne, chilli con
carne. Round things off in similar style with
one of Eileen's good fruit pies. **Family pub**

England

Woodstock   *(Food)*   *Black Prince*

2 Manor Road · *Oxfordshire* · Map 5 A2
Woodstock (0993) 811530

Free House
Landlords Larry & Gabrielle O'Brien
Beef burrito £2.20 Mexican combination plate
£4.20 (Last order 10pm. No bar food Mon eve)
🍺 Flowers Original; Ringwood Fortyniner;
Adnams Southwold Bitter; Archers Village
Bitter; Guinness; Stella Artois; Kronenbourg.
Real ale

The garden of this old inn runs right down
to the river Glyme, and interesting bar food
is an additional attraction. The menu combines traditional British dishes like thick
vegetable soup, ploughman's and steak
and kidney pie with exotic Mexican specialities such as nachos, tacos, enchiladas and
spicy beef burritos.   **Family pub**

Woodstock   *(B & B)*   *Marlborough Arms*

Oxford Street · *Oxfordshire* · Map 5 A2
Woodstock (0993) 811227

Free House
Landlords McEwen family

BEDROOMS 15   Grades 1 & 2   £A
🍺 Charrington's IPA, Toby Bitter;
Worthington 'E'; Carling Black Label.
Real ale

Kings and dukes once took their rest in this
historic 15th-century inn which still offers
traditional comfort and hospitality. Neatly
maintained bedrooms have mostly old-
fashioned furniture plus modern touches
like TVs and tea-makers; bathrooms have
pretty patterned wallpaper. Guests can
enjoy a drink round the fine old fireplace in
the bar or relax in one of the pleasant
lounges. Patio.   **Family pub**

Woodstock   *(Food, B & B)*   *Punch Bowl Inn*

12 Oxford Street · *Oxfordshire* · Map 5 A2
Woodstock (0993) 811218

Free House
Landlords Mr & Mrs K. O'Malley
BEDROOMS 14   Grade 2   £C (No dogs)
Hot beef sandwich £1.25 Steak & mushroom
pie £2 (Last order 9pm)
🍺 Wadworth's 6X; Flowers Bitter; Greenall
Whitley Festival; Guinness; Stella Artois;
Heineken; cider. *Real ale*

The home-made dish of the day is always
a good bet in the attractive bar of the
O'Malleys' friendly, town-centre inn: leek
and ham in a cheese sauce, steak and
kidney pie and roast lamb are typical tasty
specials. You'll also find soup, sandwiches,
salads and sweets. Bedrooms are neat and
bright, with modern furnishings and TVs.
Patio.   **Family pub**

Wooler   *(B & B)*   *Tankerville Arms*

Cottage Road · *Northumberland* · Map 2 D4
Wooler (0668) 81581

Free House
Landlords Park & Morton families

BEDROOMS 17   Grade 1   £B
🍺 McEwan's 80/-; Drybrough's Heavy;
Younger's Tartan; McEwan's Best Scotch;
Cavalier; Harp; Taunton cider. *Real ale*

Standing alongside the A697 at the foot of
the Cheviot Hills, this solidly built former
coaching inn is run in friendly, welcoming
style by the Park and Morton families.
Guests can choose between the peaceful
lounge bar and the cheerful public bar, and
there's also a comfortable TV lounge.
Spacious bedrooms have simple, warm
colour schemes and mostly traditional
furnishings. All have radios. Garden.
                              Family pub

Let TWA be your guide to the USA.

TWA is the biggest airline across the Atlantic.

When you extend your visiting to America you want to go with the biggest and the best.

That's TWA.

TWA flies regular direct services from London to New York, Boston, Chicago, Philadelphia and Los Angeles.

And TWA flies more passengers across the Atlantic each year than any other airline.

As good guide-consulters you look for reputation and status. TWA has them both. Which is why you should make us your guide.

Woolhope   *(Food, B & B)*   *Butchers Arms*

Near Hereford · *Hereford & Worcester*
Map 7 D2
Fownhope (043 277) 281
Free House
Landlords Mrs M. Bailey & Mr B. Griffiths
BEDROOMS 3   Grade 2   £B (No dogs)
Chilli con carne £1.95   Prawns in
mayonnaise £2.85 (Last order 10pm)
🍺 Hook Norton Best Bitter, Old Hookey;
Marston's Pedigree; Younger's Tartan,
Mild; McEwan's Lager; cider. *Real ale*

A peaceful 14th-century inn offering a
warm welcome, cosy accommodation and
super bar food. Mary Bailey's tempting fare
includes salads and basket meals, curries,
casseroles and a delicious rabbit and bacon
pie full of goodness and flavour. Soup and
sandwiches are lunchtime extras. Beamed
bedrooms with TVs and tea-makers have a
simple, homely appeal, and breakfast is a
hearty feast. Patio. **Family pub** (lunchtime)

Woolverton   *(Food)*   *Red Lion*

Near Frome · *Somerset* · Map 8 D3
Frome (0373) 830350

Brewery Wadworth
Landlords Barry & Penny Lander

Seafood platter £4.60 Traveller's lunch £1.80
(Last order 10pm)
🍺 Wadworth's 6X, IPA; Bass; Guinness;
Harp; McEwan's Lager; Taunton cider. *Real ale*

King-size portions of excellent bar fare
bring the crowds flocking to this hospitable
stone-built pub alongside the A36. Barry
Lander's repertoire is a splendidly varied
one, ranging from deliciously fresh salad
bowls (niçoise and Waldorf, for instance)
and imaginatively filled jacket potatoes
to lasagne, savoury pies, curries and a
flavour-packed beef carbonnade made with
real ale. Ice creams only for dessert.
Garden.   **Family pub**

Worplesdon   *(Food)*   *Jolly Farmer*

Burdenshott Road · *Surrey* · Map 6 B3
Guildford (0483) 234658
Free House
Landlord Mr Derek Rowley
Chicken & mushroom pancake £3.75 Home-
made pâté £1.95 (Last order 10pm. No bar
food Sun eve)
🍺 Fuller's HSB, ESB; Sam Smith's Old
Brewery Bitter; Whitbread Pompey Royal;
Guinness; Stella Artois; Heineken; cider.
Real ale

This pleasant, cream-painted pub near the
station is a popular place for bar snacks.
Everything is home-prepared, from soup
and very good pâté to steak and kidney pie,
gammon and savoury pancakes. Salads,
sandwiches and ploughman's make up the
cold choice, and sweets include sherry trifle
and gâteaux. Barbecues are a popular
feature in the attractive garden in summer,
when home-made ice cream makes a
lovely finish.

Wroughton   *(Food)*   *White Hart*

High Street, Near Swindon · *Wiltshire*
Map 6 A3
Swindon (0793) 812436
Brewery Wadworth
Landlords Mr & Mrs A. Mitchener
Macaroni cheese £2.15 Cottage pie £2.30 (Last
order 9.45pm. No bar food Mon & Tues eves or
all Sun)
🍺 Wadworth's 6X, IPA, Old Timer;
Guinness; Heineken; Löwenbräu; Taunton
cider. *Real ale*

Sit at one of the tables in the lounge bar or
eat in the skittle alley at this popular
thatched pub. If you want a quick snack
there are freshly cut sandwiches (our roast
beef was pink and delicious), ploughman's
and salads, while hearty appetites will be
more than satisfied by a big steak with all
the trimmings or a tasty home-made dish
like cottage pie or chilli con carne. Fruit or
mincemeat pies to finish.

Wye *(Food, B & B)*   *Kings Head Hotel*

Church Street, Near Ashford · *Kent* · Map 6 D3
Wye (0233) 812418

Brewery Whitbread
Landlords Mr & Mrs A. Smith
BEDROOMS 7 Grade 2 £C
Beef roll with gravy £1 Seafood lasagne £2.75
(Last order 9pm)
🍺 Fremlins Bitter; AK Bitter; Whitbread
Mild; Guinness; Stella Artois; Heineken; cider.
Real ale

Visitors will find a good variety of tasty bar snacks to enjoy in this popular old coaching inn on the main street of the village. The range includes soup and pâté, sandwiches and salads, plus savoury pancakes, seafood lasagne and hearty casseroles. For overnight guests there are seven simple, comfortable bedrooms (one with private bath) and a cosy TV lounge. Nice walled garden.   **Family pub**

Wye *(Food, B & B)*   *New Flying Horse Inn*

Upper Bridge Street · *Kent* · Map 6 D3
Wye (0233) 812297

Brewery Shepherd Neame
Landlord Mr Barry Law
BEDROOMS 10 Grades 1 & 2 £B
Steak & kidney pie & vegetables £2.75 Smoked mackerel salad £2.75 (Last order 10pm)
🍺 Shepherd Neame Masterbrew, Abbey, Mild; Stock Ale; Guinness; Taunton cider.
Real ale

Anita and Barry Law are carrying on a long tradition of hospitality at this fine old inn, once a posting house, on the A28. It's particularly popular for its excellent bar snacks, which range from sandwiches and salads to seafood and Sunday roasts. Best bedrooms are the annexe quartet, with neat tiled bathrooms. All rooms have TVs and tea-makers. Patio and garden. **Family pub**

Wykeham *(B & B)*   *Downe Arms*

Near Scarborough · *North Yorkshire* · Map 4 D2
Scarborough (0723) 862471

Free House
Manager Mr Philip Mort

BEDROOMS 7 Grade 1 £B
🍺 Cameron's Best Bitter; Younger's Scotch Bitter; Guinness; Carling Black Label; McEwan's Lager; cider.

Philip Mort keeps everything in exemplary order at this fine stone inn, built as a farmhouse in 1725. An impressive entrance hall leads to the two attractive bars, and there's a children's summer room as well as a residents' TV lounge. Sparklingly clean bedrooms have pretty floral wallpaper and smart white furniture. The two tiled public bathrooms are spacious. Garden.
Family pub

Wytham *(Food)*   *White Hart*

Near Oxford · *Oxfordshire* · Map 6 A3
Oxford (0865) 244372

Brewery Hall
Landlord Mr R. Godden
Stuffed peppers with salad £2.35 Flemish beef £3.55 (Last order 9.45pm. No bar food 1 week Christmas)
🍺 Hall's Harvest Bitter; Ind Coope Burton Ale; Guinness; Skol; Löwenbräu; cider. *Real ale*

A fine village pub, with a low-beamed, flagstone-floored bar and a delightful walled garden. A tempting cold buffet offers cooked meats, savoury pies and colourful salads. There's also a hot dish of the day (except summer lunch) such as tasty chicken and ham casserole. Evening fare is supplemented by steaks, a mixed grill and chicken Kiev. Delicious sweets too.

Yarde Down   *(Food)*   *Poltimore Arms*

Near South Moulton · *Devon* · Map 8 C3
Brayford (059 88) 381

Free House
Landlords Mr & Mrs R. M. E. Wright

Turkey pie £1.20   Treacle roly-poly 50p
(Last order 9.30pm)
 Usher's Best Bitter, Triple Crown, Country
Bitter; Guinness; Carlsberg; Taunton cider.
Real ale

Fresh local produce is put to excellent use
in this remote Exmoor pub, whose
appearance has changed little in its 300-
year history. Among the hunting
mementoes in the cosy bar you can tuck
into thick, flavour-packed vegetable soup,
turkey pie or a mighty fry-up. Sandwiches,
salads and grills provide further choice,
and sweets include treacle roly-poly
pudding. Garden.   **Family pub**

Yarmouth   *(B & B)*   *Bugle Hotel*

The Square · *Isle of Wight* · Map 6 A4
Yarmouth (0983) 760272

Brewery Whitbread
Landlords Mr & Mrs McKillop

BEDROOMS 10   Grade 1   £A
 Whitbread Strong Country Bitter, Best
Bitter, Mild; Guinness; Heineken; Stella
Artois; cider. *Real ale*

There's plenty of atmosphere inside this
300-year-old stone hostelry. The counter of
the Galleon Bar is modelled like the stern of
a sailing ship, while coaching lamps, horse
brasses and wagon wheels evoke land
travel in the other bar; there's also a cosy
TV lounge. Comfortable bedrooms are well
designed and neatly furnished in modern
style; five have up-to-date bath or shower
rooms. Garden.

Yattendon   *(Food, B & B)*   ★   *Royal Oak Hotel*

Near Newbury · *Berkshire* · Map 6 A3
Hermitage (0635) 201325

Free House
Landlords Kate & Richard Smith
BEDROOMS 5   Grade 1   £A+
Cream of spinach soup & roll £1.75 Plaice
& chips £3.50 (Last order 10pm)
 Bass; Charrington's IPA; Guinness;
Carling Black Label; Taunton cider. *Real ale*

Kate & Richard Smith provide a cheerful
welcome and really excellent bar snacks at
this smart brick inn in the centre of the
village. The menu might range from leek
and potato soup and crispy duck salad to
lamburger with green mustard sauce and
calf's liver and bacon, with perhaps
meringues or a home-made ice cream to
finish. Smartly decorated bedrooms are
most comfortable; all have their own bathrooms and TVs. Terrace.   **Family pub**

SCOTLAND

Scotland

Airdrie   (B & B)   *Staging Post*

8 Anderson Street · *Strathclyde* · Map 2 C3
Airdrie (023 64) 675251

Brewery Scottish & Newcastle
Landlord Mr M. Burns

BEDROOMS 8   Grade 1   £A
🍺 McEwan's Tartan, 80/-, Lager; Beck's Bier;
Guinness; Taunton cider. *Real ale*

The name tells you that this long, low hostelry was once a staging post for horse-drawn coaches. Today's travellers still seek it out for its excellent accommodation: there are eight comfortable, well-kept bedrooms with built-in furniture, tea-makers, TVs and good modern bathrooms. The roomy main bar features some handsome horse brasses and harnesses, and there's a quiet cocktail bar. Garden.   **Family pub**

Anstruther   (Food)   *Craw's Nest Hotel*

Bankwell Road · *Fife* · Map 2 D3
Anstruther (0333) 310691

Free House
Landlords Mrs Clarke & family

Deep fried haddock £2.40 Steak pie £2.40 (Last order 10.30pm)
🍺 Younger's Tartan; McEwan's Export;
Guinness; Carlsberg; Taunton cider.

Fresh local haddock and sole are popular choices among the simple snacks served at this modernised Scottish manse. Also available are sandwiches, omelettes and perhaps a curry or lamb dish. Smaller selection in the evening. There are two bars, one small and intimate, the other sunny and spacious. Garden. *For accommodation see Egon Ronay's Lucas Hotel & Restaurant Guide 1985.*   **Family pub**

Balerno   (Food)   *Marchbank Hotel*

Near Edinburgh · *Lothian* · Map 2 C3
031-449 3970

Free House
Landlords Mr & Mrs W. Waddell

Chicken pie & vegetables £1.75 Open sandwiches from 60p (Last order 9.45pm)
🍺 Lorimer's 80/-, 70/-; Younger's Tartan;
Guinness; Carlsberg Deluxe; cider. *Real ale*

Eye-catching open sandwiches steal the show in this sturdy old house, with fillings of anything from prawns with mayonnaise to tasty salami with potato salad and raw onion. There are also plain sandwiches and salads, as well as hot dishes like appetising home-made soup and specials such as wine-flavoured beef stew, chicken fricassee or toad-in-the-hole. Sandwiches and basket meals in the evening. Garden.
Family pub

Busby   (Food, B & B)   *Busby Hotel*

Field Road, Clarkston, Glasgow · *Strathclyde*
Map 2 C3
041-644 2661

Free House
Landlord Mr J. Hebditch
BEDROOMS 14   Grade 1   £A   (No dogs)
Lentil soup 35p Steak pie £2 (Last order 9pm)
🍺 Younger's No. 3 Ale, Tartan; McEwan's
Export; Guinness; Harp; Taunton cider.
Real ale

Excellent staff keep things running smoothly at this purpose-built modern hotel on the A726 a few miles from the centre of Glasgow. Simple, satisfying snacks served in the very busy bar include home-made soup, savoury pies, quiche and curries, plus filled rolls and salad platters. Attractively decorated bedrooms and bath/shower rooms are absolutely spotless and provide good facilities.
Family pub

Canonbie *(Food, B & B)*   *Riverside Inn*

Dumfries & Galloway · Map 2 D4
Canonbie (054 15) 295

Free House
Landlords Robert & Susan Phillips

BEDROOMS 6 Grade 1 £A (No dogs)
Ploughman's lunch £1.50 Angus sirloin
steak £5.95 (Last order 9pm)
🍺 Theakston's Best Bitter; Bass; Guinness;
Tennent's Lager. *Real ale*

It's a real treat to visit this beautifully maintained hostelry with its delightful, homely
atmosphere. Charming bedrooms (including two in a converted cottage) are furnished in traditional style with careful
attention to detail, and all have excellent
bathrooms. Superb ploughman's and
cheese platters top the comfy bar's bill of
fare; other offerings include smooth pâté,
curry, trout and steaks. Closed Sun lunch &
2 weeks Jan.

Castle Douglas *(B & B)*   *King's Arms Hotel*

St Andrews Street · *Dumfries & Galloway*
Map 2 C4
Castle Douglas (0556) 2626

Free House
Landlords Mr & Mrs I. MacDonald

BEDROOMS 15 Grade 1 £B
🍺 Younger's Tartan, 60/-; Guinness
(summer only); Holsten; Taunton cider.

An attractive sheltered patio stands at the
rear of this former coaching house in the
centre of a thriving market town. Tartan
carpets and hunting trophies take the eye in
the cosy bars, and there's a traditionally
styled residents' lounge and modest TV
room. Centrally heated bedrooms are quiet
and comfortable, with practical fitted furniture and coordinated fabrics; six have
their own bath/shower room. **Family pub**

Catterline *(Food)*   *Creel Inn*

By Stonehaven · *Grampian* · Map 1 D2
Catterline (056 95) 254

Free House
Landlords Allan & Margaret Duncan

Catterline crab £3.95 Lentil broth 85p (No bar
food eves or Sept–March)
🍺 McEwan's Export; Tennent's Lager.

Local seafood is a good bet for a lunchtime
bar snack at this agreeable clifftop pub:
tasty fresh Catterline crab can be enjoyed in
soup or salads, or you might push the boat
out with lobster or a mixed seafood platter.
Cold ham or beef salads for carnivores,
with simple sweets like meringues or apple
pie. Terrace. Closed Monday.

Comrie *(B & B)*   *Royal Hotel*

Melville Square · *Tayside* · Map 2 C3
Comrie (0764) 70200

Free House
Landlords Mr & Mrs I. Gordon

BEDROOMS 16 Grade 2 £A
🍺 Younger's Tartan; McEwan's Pale Ale;
Skol; Harp; Taunton cider.

Welcoming travellers since 1765, this L-
shaped hotel was dubbed royal after a visit
by Queen Victoria. There are several golf
courses nearby, so it's not surprising that
the conversation swings towards bunkers
and bogeys in the tartan-clad cocktail bar.
Bedrooms, all with private facilities, have
simple furniture (except one four-poster),
tea-makers and TVs. There's a comfortable
residents' lounge. Garden.
                              Family pub (lunchtime)

Scotland

Dulnain Bridge   (Food, B & B) ★

Near Grantown-on-Spey · *Highland* · Map 1 C2
Dulnain Bridge (047 985) 257

Free House
Landlords Ogilvie & Fone families
BEDROOMS 9   Grade 1 & 2   £B (No dogs)
Sea trout sandwich £2.15 Home-cooked
gammon sandwich £1.15 (No bar food eves)
🍺 Ind Coope Alloa's Archibald Arrol's 70/-,
Diamond Heavy, Export; Skol. *Real ale*

Muckrach Lodge Hotel

The lunchtime bar snacks are simply superb
at this friendly old shooting lodge set back
from the A938. Sandwiches are packed to
overflowing with goodies like gammon,
garlic sausage and poached salmon, and
there are soups, pâtés, winter hot dishes
and some sublime sweets – chocolate pot
to raspberry mousse. Booking advisable
Sundays. Bedrooms are simply furnished in
traditional style, and the bar and lounge
have lovely views.   **Family pub**

Prices given are as at the time

of our research and are

comparative indications rather

than firm quotes.

Dysart   (Food)

By Kirkcaldy · *Fife* · Map 2 C3
Kirkcaldy (0592) 51211

Free House
Landlords Roger & Marianne Worthy

Moussaka £2.10 Creamed kidneys in ginger
£3.40 (Last order 9.30. No bar food Sat eve)
🍺 Ind Coope Diamond Export; Harp; Skol;
cider.

Old Rectory Inn

The delightful walled garden is a popular
summer alternative to the comfortable,
characterful bars at this fine old house on
the A955. Outside or in, there's a good
variety of bar snacks to enjoy, from homely
soups to cold meats and salads, moussaka
and creamed kidneys in ginger. Nice simple
sweets. Closed Sun and Mon eves and 1st
3 weeks January.

Eddleston   (Food)

Borders · Map 2 C3
Peebles (072 13) 225

Free House
Landlord Mr Alan McIntosh-Reid

Bookmaker's sandwich £3.45 Stilton soup 90p
(Last order 10pm)
🍺 Broughton Greenmantle; McEwan's 80/-;
Belhaven 60/-; Younger's Tartan; Guinness;
Carlsberg; cider. *Real ale*

Horse Shoe Inn

The village blacksmith's shop in Victorian
times, this smart, white-painted inn is now
sought out by lovers of good bar food. The
menu is quite extensive: a different soup
each day, fresh haddock, steak and
Guinness casserole, rare roast beef with
salad. The bookmaker's sandwich – rump
steak in French bread – is a sure winner, and
there are a few simple sweets. **Family pub**

Edinburgh *(Food)* — *Beehive Inn*

18 Grassmarket · *Lothian* · Map 2 C3
031-225 7171

Brewery Scottish & Newcastle
Landlord Mr Alan Lawson Noble

Quiche & salad £1.80 Lentil soup 40p
🍺 Theakstons Best Bitter, Old Peculier;
McEwans 70/-, 80/-, Lager; Youngers
No. 3 Ale; Guinness; Taunton cider. *Real ale*

Businessmen and shoppers make a beeline for this comfortable pub to enjoy the tasty lunchtime snacks. The centre of attraction is the cold buffet, which offers a good selection of cooked meats, pies, quiches and interesting salads. There's also a soup of the day, along with hot specials (perhaps spaghetti bolognese or fresh haddock) and some nice home-made sweets. Filled rolls are the only evening choice. Closed Sun lunch.

Edinburgh *(Food)* — *Cramond Inn*

Cramond Glebe Road, Cramond
Lothian · Map 2 C3
031-336 2035

Free House
Landlord Mr S. Proudfoot
Steak & kidney pie £2 Cold salmon salad £2 (No bar food eves)
🍺 Lorimer's 80/-; Tennent's Extra;
Younger's Tartan; Guinness; Carlsberg; cider. *Real ale*

The Firth of Forth is just a short step from this pleasant white-painted inn, where tasty, well-prepared lunchtime snacks are just the thing after a bracing walk. Soup and pâté are popular starters, and main courses include attractive salads, quiche, herby sausage rolls and two unfailing favourites in the shape of cottage and steak and kidney pies. Terrace.

Edinburgh *(B & B)* — *Rutland Hotel*

3 Rutland Street · *Lothian* · Map 2 C3
031-229 3402
Owners Welcome Inns
Landlord Mr G. Skinner

BEDROOMS 18 Grade 1 £A
🍺 Younger's Tartan; McEwan's 80/-, Export, Cavalier; Kestrel; Guinness; Taunton cider. *Real ale*

Pleasant accommodation is on offer at this modernised city-centre hotel on the corner of Princes Street. Spacious bedrooms have modern furnishings and are equipped with tea-makers and colour TV. Compact bathrooms with old-fashioned fittings are clean and adequate. Cheerful staff help to create a homely atmosphere. **Family pub**

Elrick *(Food)* — *Broadstraik Inn*

Near Aberdeen · *Grampian* · Map 1 D2
Skene (033 05) 217

Free House
Landlord Mrs Anne Horn

Sizzle platter steak £4.60 Chilli con carne £2.55 (Last order 9.30pm)
🍺 Maclay's 80/-; Younger's Tartan; Guinness; Carlsberg Pilsner, Hof Export; Taunton cider. *Real ale*

Sizzling spectacularly on their cast-iron platters, tender, juicy steaks are a popular feature at this busy wayside pub. There's also fried fish, gammon and spicy things like chilliburgers or chilli con carne. A special children's menu including sausages and fish fingers is available until 7.30. This is a notably friendly and cheerful place. **Family pub** (till 7.30pm)

285

Fochabers *(B & B)*   *Gordon Arms Hotel*

High Street · *Grampian* · Map 1 C2
Fochabers (0343) 820508

Free House
Landlord Mr C. Pern

BEDROOMS 14   Grades 1 & 2   £B
🍺 Alice Ale; McEwan's Export; Younger's
Tartan, Light; Guinness; Harp; Taunton cider.
Real ale

Rows of antlers adorn the outside of this
smartly painted former coaching house, a
popular local meeting place and a favourite
of fishermen. Bedrooms – the majority in an
extension – are very well equipped, with
TVs, tea-makers, hair dryers and direct-dial
telephones; nine have private facilities. The
comfortable lounge bar stocks a wide selection of malt whiskies. Garden.
Family pub (lunchtime)

Glasgow *(Food)*   *Archie's*

27 Waterloo Street · *Strathclyde* · Map 2 C3
041-221 3210

Owners Beard Hotels
Landlord Mr David Burns

Chicken provençale £1 Prawn salad £2.25
(Last order 10pm)
🍺 McEwan's 80/-; Guinness; Harp; Taunton
cider. *Real ale*

Tasty snacks are available between
12.15pm and 10pm in this atmospheric
modern bar, a series of rooms with mirrors,
plants and bamboo furniture. A self-service
counter displays cold meats, raised pies,
seafood and a selection of good fresh
salads, and a daily-changing hot choice
could include lasagne, macaroni cheese,
chicken provençale and chilli con carne.
Closed Sunday.

Glendevon *(Food, B & B)*   *Tormaukin Hotel*

Near Dollar · *Tayside* · Map 2 C3
Glendevon (025 982) 252

Free House
Landlords Jack & Annie Dracup

BEDROOMS 6   Grade 1   £A
Bacon burger £2.85 Chicken curry £2.65 (Last
order 9.45pm)
🍺 Ind Coope Burton Ale, Double Diamond,
Alloa's Export; Guinness; Skol; cider. *Real ale*

Tasty home-made snacks bring a loyal
following to this smart roadside pub, whose
traditional beamed bars are warm and
welcoming: beefburgers and chicken curry
are great favourites, with soup, colourful
salads and succulent steaks also in constant
demand. Attractive bedrooms, all with TVs
and tea-makers, have smart pine furniture
and neat little panelled bathrooms. Terrace.
Family pub (lunchtime)

Glenfinnan *(B & B)*   *Stage House Inn*

Highland · Map 1 B2
Kinlocheil (039 783) 246

Free House
Landlords Helen & Andrew Brooks

BEDROOMS 9   Grade 2   £B
🍺 Younger's Tartan; Guinness; Tennent's
Lager.

Fishing rights on nearby Loch Shiel lure
anglers to this attractive wayside inn,
which stands in breathtaking countryside
on the road to Mallaig. Simple comforts are
provided in the bedrooms, which all have
private bath or shower rooms. There's a
cheerful bar and two little sun lounges, the
latter taking full advantage of the fabulous
setting. Closed end October–mid March.
Terrace.   **Family pub**

Inverbeg   *(B & B)*   *Inverbeg Inn*

Luss, Loch Lomond · *Strathclyde* · Map 2 B3
Luss (043 686) 678

Free House
Landlord Bill Porter

BEDROOMS 14   Grade 1   £A
🍺 McEwan's Tartan, Lager; Strathalbion
Bitter; Guinness; Harp; Taunton cider.
Real ale

Cattle drovers have given way to tourists at
this attractively modernised inn, which
stands alongside the A82 on the west shore
of Loch Lomond. A log fire burns in the
pleasant lounge bar, which features fine
paintings of Highland scenes; there's also a
quiet residents' lounge. Bright bedrooms
(half with well-kept private bathrooms)
have tea-makers and radios. Most have TV's
and command lovely loch views.
Family pub

Invergarry   *(B & B)*   *Inn on the Garry*

Highland · Map 1 B2
Invergarry (080 93) 206

Free House
Landlords Iain & Fiona Maclean

BEDROOMS 10   Grade 2   £A
🍺 Ind Coope Alloa's Archibald Arrol's 70/-,
Heavy, Light; Burton's; Guinness; Skol; cider.
Real ale

Standing at the junction of the A82 and A87
(the 'Road to the Isles'), this sturdy Victorian
inn is a popular base for anglers. Fishy yarns
are spun in the rustic bar, and the comfortable lounges are good places to unwind.
Best bedrooms are those on the first floor –
simple, spacious and stoutly furnished.
Accommodation closed October–March;
bar closed at lunchtime mid November–
March.   **Family pub**

Invermoriston   *(Food, B & B)*   *Glenmoriston Arms*

Glenmoriston, Near Inverness · *Highland*
Map 1 B2
Glenmoriston (0320) 51206
Free House
Landlords Mr & Mrs R. Shepherd
BEDROOMS 8   Grade 2   £B
Home-made soup 50p Fisherman's prawn salad
with Marie Rose sauce £2 (Last order 8pm)
🍺 Younger's Tartan; McEwan's 80/-,
Export; Guinness; Carlsberg Hof; Harp;
Taunton cider.

A collection of guns and fishing rods under-
lines the sporting associations at this
welcoming inn, which stands at the junction of the A82 and A887. Simple bar snacks
include soup, sandwiches, pâté and a
variety of meat, fish and cheese platters.
Six of the modestly furnished bedrooms
have TVs and shower or bathrooms.
Accommodation closed November–April.
Garden.   **Family pub**

Killiecrankie   *(Food)*   *Killiecrankie Hotel*

By Pitlochry · *Tayside* · Map 1 C2
Pitlochry (0796) 3220

Free House
Landlords Mr & Mrs Hattersley Smith & Emma

Venison steakette £1.95 Tayside trout £3.95
(Last order 10pm)
🍺 Younger's Tartan; Tennent's Extra

Bar food of good variety and quality
attracts a large and loyal custom to this
beautifully situated hotel. Lunchtime offers
sandwiches, salads and tasty snacks like
potted shrimps, pork sausages and an
excellent smoked haddock flan. A shorter
evening menu includes main courses like
grilled trout and Angus steak. Closed mid
Oct–end March. Garden. *For accommodation see Egon Ronay's Lucas Hotel &
Restaurant Guide 1985.*   **Family pub**

Scotland

Killin   *(Food, B & B)*   *Clachaig Hotel*

Central · Map 2 C3
Killin (056 72) 270

Free House
Landlords Colin & Jean Lewis

BEDROOMS 8   Grade 2   £C
Fresh herring £1.90 Haggis, tatties &
neeps £2.40 (Last order 8.30pm)
🍺 Younger's Tartan; McEwan's 80/-; Harp;
Taunton cider. *Real ale*

There's a real flavour of Scotland about
the food served in this cheerful pub on the
river Dochart. Tay salmon is a treat not to
be missed, and other native specialities
include fried herring, haggis, cloutie
dumplings and oaty fruit crumbles. Also
delicious bread and butter pudding. Spotless bedrooms offer simple comforts, and
there's a cosy TV lounge. Accommodation
closed late Nov–mid Jan.   **Family pub**

Killin   *(Food, B & B)*   *Queen's Court Hotel*

Central · Map 2 C3
Killin (056 72) 349

Landlords Mr & Mrs S. Horn

BEDROOMS 8   Grade 2   £C
Scampi & chips £3 Home-made soup 65p
🍺 Tennent's 70/-, 80/-, Lager; Guinness.
Real ale

The welcome couldn't be warmer at this
solid, stone-built house standing on the
outskirts of a pleasant Highland village.
Neat bedrooms provide simple overnight
comforts, and there's a traditionally furnished TV lounge. Snacks served in the
convivial Coach House bar include hearty
home-made soup, sandwiches, sausages
and steaks, with a nice nutmeggy rice pudding to finish.   **Family pub** (till 9pm)

Kippen   *(Food, B & B)*   *Cross Keys*

Main Street, Near Stirling · *Central* · Map 2 C3
Kippen (078 687) 293
Free House
Landlords Richard & Penny Miller
BEDROOMS 3   Grade 2   £C
Baked trout £3.50 Home-made special ice
cream 80p (Last order 9pm. No bar food Mon
eve)
🍺 Younger's No.3 Ale; McEwan's 80/-,
Export, Pale; Guinness; Taunton cider.
Real ale

A warm welcome, good food, comfortable
accommodation, lovely views – this delightful old inn has them all. Filled rolls, sandwiches and pâté with oatcakes make tasty
light snacks, while heartier fare includes
casseroles, steak and kidney pie and
succulent roast chicken, with home-made
ice cream a popular sweet. (Less choice
Mon lunch.) Three bright, tidy bedrooms
(no smoking, please) share a spotless little
bathroom.   **Family pub**

Lewiston   *(B & B)*   *Lewiston Arms*

Near Drumnadrochit · *Highland* · Map 1 C2
Drumnadrochit (045 62) 225

Free House
Landlords Mr & Mrs N. Quinn

BEDROOMS 8   Grade 2   £C
🍺 Younger's Tartan, No. 3; McEwan's
Export, Lager; Taunton cider. *Real ale*

A convivial 200-year-old pub in a tiny
village close to Loch Ness. Thirsty guests
can choose between the popular public bar
and a modern lounge bar that opens on to
the attractive garden. There's also a cosy
lounge as well as a spacious TV room.
Bedrooms (four in a cottage reached
through the garden) offer simple comforts
for an overnight stay.   **Family pub**

Linlithgow *(Food)* — *Champany Inn*

Lothian · Map 2 C3
Philipstoun (050 683) 4532

Free House
Landlords Anne & Clive Davidson

Pickled fish £1.65 Grilled lamb chops £2.75
(Last order 10pm. No bar food Sun eve)
🍺 Belhaven 80/-, 70/-; Skol; cider. *Real ale*

Choices on the bar menu at this welcoming
roadside complex include juicy steaks,
lamb and veal chops, burgers and deep-
dish pizzas with a variety of toppings.
At lunchtime you might have a bowl of
nourishing soup or turn your attention to
the laden cold table, which offers items like
rich potted ham, tasty roast lamb, beef and
duck, plus some very enjoyable salads.
Family pub

Loch Eck *(Food)* — *Coylet Inn*

Dunoon · *Strathclyde* · Map 2 B3
Kilmun (036 984) 322

Free House
Landlord Mr R. Addis

Pâté & oatcakes £1.20 Open prawn
sandwich £2.40 (Last order 10pm)
🍺 Younger's No. 3 Ale; McEwan 80/-; Heriot
80/-; Guinness; Tennant's Extra. *Real ale*

Excellent home-prepared bar snacks are
served at this long, low pub 'twixt loch and
forest. Scotch broth is a good warming
starter, followed perhaps by home-cooked
ham, chicken and chips or a tasty smoked
haddock and egg pie. Traditional cloutie
dumpling is a popular pud. Open fires keep
the bar cosy in winter, while in summer the
terrace comes into its own. **Family pub**

We neither seek nor accept

hospitality, and we pay for all

food, drinks and accommodation

in full.

Lybster *(Food, B & B)* — *Bayview Hotel*

Highland · Map 1 C1
Lybster (059 32) 346

Free House
Landlords Ranald & Norma Hutton

BEDROOMS 3 Grade 1 £C
Finnan haddock £1.50 Roast sirloin £2.50
(Last order 11pm)
🍺 McEwan's Export, Pale Ale; Younger's
Tartan; Harp.

The Huttons' agreeable little haven of
hospitality stands in a side street just a
short stroll from the tiny harbour. Excellent
fresh fish features among the enjoyable bar
snacks, which also include tasty soup,
salads, grills and lovely home-made
sweets. The three neatly furnished bedrooms share a sparkling bathroom, and
there's a cosy residents' lounge and two
summery sun rooms. **Family pub**

Scotland

Melrose *(Food, B & B)*   *Burts Hotel*

Market Square · *Borders* · Map 2 D4
Melrose (089 682) 2285

Free House
Landlords Graham & Annie Henderson

BEDROOMS 22   Grade 1 & 2   £B
Prawns, bacon & mushrooms in garlic £1.50
Beef bourguignon £2.10 (Last order 9.30pm)
🍺 Belhaven 80/-, Export, Heavy, Light;
Younger's Tartan; Taunton cider. *Real ale*

This distinctive black and white hotel in the town centre is a friendly, well-run place. The spacious bar, which features some deadly looking antique swords, offers a good selection of enjoyable snacks, from smoked mackerel pâté to basket meals, excellent ham salad and beef kidneys Turbigo. Attractively decorated bedrooms, some traditional, others more modern in style, have TVs and tea-makers. Garden.
Family pub

Melrose *(B & B)*   *George & Abbotsford*

High Street · *Borders* · Map 2 D4
Melrose (089 682) 2308

Free House
Landlord Mr J. H. Brown

BEDROOMS 36   Grade 1 & 2   £B
🍺 Younger's Tartan; McEwan's Pale Ale;
Greenmantle Ale; Guinness; Carlsberg Hof;
Pilsner; cider. *Real ale*

Standing in the centre of town, this handsome hotel is a good base for exploring Sir Walter Scott country. Spacious, attractively coordinated bedrooms range from traditional to more modern; all have contemporary furniture, radios and tea-makers and most offer private facilities. There's a roomy, relaxing bar that opens on to an attractive rose garden. Upstairs, a modest lounge doubles as a TV room. **Family pub**

Moffat *(Food, B & B)*   *Balmoral Hotel*

High Street · *Dumfries & Galloway* · Map 2 C4
Moffat (0683) 20288

Free House
Landlords Robin & Denise Stewart

BEDROOMS 15   Grade 2   £B
Breaded lamb chops £2.50 Madras curry £2
(Last order 10pm)
🍺 Younger's Tartan; McEwan's 80/-;
Guinness; Carlsberg Hof; Harp; cider. *Real ale*

The bar snacks are homely and satisfying at this smartly painted town-centre hotel. Breaded lamb chops are a favourite choice, along with sandwiches, ploughman's, chicken curry and steak pie, and the cold luncheon buffet is popular in summer. Bedrooms with coordinated floral fabrics and wallpaper have whitewood furniture and tea-makers. There's a residents' lounge with TV. Patio. **Family pub**

Moffat *(Food)*   *Black Bull*

Station Rd · *Dumfries & Galloway* · Map 2 C4
Moffat (0683) 20206

Free House
Landlord Mrs H. Poynton
Haggis £1.65 Shepherd's pie £1.85 (Last order 9pm. No bar food Sun eve & daily Jan–March)
🍺 Younger's No. 3 Ale, Tartan; McEwan's 80/-; Broughton Greenmantle; Guinness; Carlsberg Hof; cider. *Real ale*

There's a warm, friendly feel about this 16th-century inn, where simple, nourishing bar fare is the order of the day. Haggis and shepherd's pie are firm favourites, and other popular choices range from sandwiches and pâté to macaroni, cold meats and curries. Railway buffs should make tracks for the public bar, which is filled with relics from the Caledonian Railway.
Family pub

Muir of Ord (B & B) — Ord Arms Hotel

Great North Road · *Highland* · Map 1 C2
Inverness (0463) 870286

Free House
Landlords John & Shirley Baillie

BEDROOMS 15 Grade 1 £C
🍺 Younger's Tartan; McEwan's Extra Pale Ale; Harp.

Just off the A9 on the northern outskirts of Muir of Ord, the Baillies' welcoming, sand-coloured inn provides excellent overnight accommodation. Bright, cheerful bedrooms, all with tea-makers and TVs, have plenty of cupboard space, good large mirrors and washbasins. Seven offer private facilities, and there are three public bathrooms. The two bars include one featuring pictures of some of the local regulars. Patio. **Family pub**

New Abbey (Food, B & B) — Criffel Inn

Nr Dumfries · *Dumfries & Galloway* · Map 2 C4
New Abbey (038 785) 305
Free House
Landlords Mr & Mrs McCulloch

BEDROOMS 5 Grade 2 £C
Fresh salmon fishcakes £2.40 York ham salad, scones & cakes £3.60 (No bar food Sun lunch)
🍺 Younger's No.3 Ale; McEwan's 60/-, 70/-; Guinness; Tennent's Extra; Taunton cider.
Real ale

A pleasant village pub, made more delightful by Janet McCulloch's homely snacks. Soup, salads, ploughman's and steak pies are popular lunchtime fare, along with York ham and fresh salmon, which also feature in the popular high teas served from 4.30 to 6. Sandwiches only in the evening. Bedrooms (two with shower cabinets) have simple modern furnishings; there's a residents' lounge with TV and a pleasant patio. **Family pub**

Onich (B & B) — Onich Hotel

Near Fort William · *Highland* · Map 1 B2
Onich (085 53) 214

Free House
Landlords Messrs I. & R. Young

BEDROOMS 25 Grade 2 £B
🍺 Ind Coope Diamond Heavy; Alloa Light; Arrol's 70 Shilling; Burton Ale; Guinness; Skol; Taunton cider. *Real ale*

A magnificent setting on the banks of lovely Loch Linnhe is a major feature of this sizeable white-painted inn, a popular base for touring the Highlands. Compact bedrooms offer simple comforts, and, like other areas, are kept in very good order. The spacious main bar offers superb views, and there are two lounges (one with TV) and a games room. Good breakfasts. Garden. **Family pub**

Portree (B & B) — Rosedale Hotel

Isle of Skye · *Highland* · Map 1 B2
Portree (0478) 2531

Free House
Landlord Mr H. M. Andrew

BEDROOMS 21 Grade 1 £B
🍺 McEwan's Export; Younger's Tartan; Cavalier; Tennent's Extra; Taunton cider.

Right on the waterfront at Portree harbour, this agreeable white-painted hotel has been run by members of the Andrew family for more than 30 years. It's a good place for an overnight stop, with friendly service and comfortable, unpretentious accommodation. Bedrooms have simple fitted furniture and most offer private facilities. There are two lounges (one with TV) and a modern bar. **Family pub** (lunchtime)

Spean Bridge *(B & B)*

Letterfinlay Lodge Hotel

Highland · Map 1 B2
Invergloy (039 784) 222

Free House
Landlords Forsyth family

BEDROOMS 15   Grades 1 & 2   £C
🍺 Alloa's Export; Löwenbräu.

Seven miles north of Spean Bridge, this
former shooting lodge has its own jetty on
Loch Lochy. Huge picture windows in the
bar provide breathtaking views of the
mountains, and there is also a homely
lounge. Most bedrooms are in sturdy traditional style and some have bathrooms with
splendid antique fittings. The Forsyth
family make guests feel thoroughly welcome. Closed end October to March.
Garden.   **Family pub**

Spinningdale *(Food)*

Old Mill Inn

Highland · Map 1 C1
Whiteface (086 288) 242

Free House
Landlord Mr John Warner

Cream of salmon soup 60p Venison
casserole £1.85 (Last order 8.45pm. No bar
food Mon eve)
🍺 Younger's Tartan; McEwan's Pale Ale,
Export; Tennent's Export; Taunton cider.

With its dramatic setting on the north side
of Dornoch Firth, this old, whitewashed
coaching inn is a splendid place to pause
for a snack. In the mellow pine-clad bar
there's a good choice of robust fare:
salmon and venison appear in soups and
pâtés as well as main courses, and other
popular items include sandwiches and
salads, burgers and flavoursome
casseroles.   **Family pub**

Strathblane *(B & B)*

Kirkhouse Inn

Near Glasgow · *Central* · Map 2 C3
Blanefield (0360) 70621

Free House
Landlord Mr R. C. Aird

BEDROOMS 19 Grade 1 £B
🍺 McEwan's No. 3, Export, Tartan;
Tennent's Lager; cider. *Real ale*

Follow the A81 north from Glasgow to find
this handsome roadside inn, which has
been much modernised over the years. The
spacious foyer doubles as a comfortable
lounge, and there are two roomy bars.
Well-kept bedrooms are generally quite up
to date in decor and furnishings, and ten
have their own spick-and-span bathrooms.
Patio.   **Family pub**

Strathmiglo *(Food)*

Strathmiglo Inn

High Street · *Fife* · Map 2 C3
Strathmiglo (033 76) 252

Free House
Landlords John & Barbara Winning

Fried fillet of sole £2.20 Steak & kidney
pie £2.65 (Last order 9.30pm. No bar food
Sun eve)
🍺 Tennent's 70/-, Export, Lager; Guinness.

The bar snacks are tasty and satisfying at
this delightful little white-painted pub in the
middle of the village. Start with the soup of
the day – perhaps cream of cauliflower or
deliciously thick bacon and lentil – and
follow with grilled Arbroath smokies,
gammon with steak or chilli con carne.
Lighter bites include salads and sandwiches, and there's a small choice of
sweets.

Scotland

Tarbert *(Food, B & B)*   *West Loch Hotel*

Loch Fyne · *Strathclyde* · Map 2 B3
Tarbert (088 02) 283

Free House
Landlords A. & J. Thom & D. & J. Thom
BEDROOMS 6   Grade 1   £B
Bobotie with rice £3.25 Grilled Loch Fyne
herring with vegetables £2.50 (No bar food
eves)
🍺 McEwan's Export; Younger's Pale;
Guinness; Carlsberg; Taunton cider.

Warm and welcoming, this black and white roadside inn enjoys lovely views of the loch and surrounding countryside. The bar lunches are superb, with grilled herring, kidneys with rice and game pie typical delights on the daily-changing menu. Lovely sweets, too, like trifle, or caramel mousse. Bedrooms are neat and comfortable, and there's a pleasant little TV lounge. Closed November.   **Family pub**

Tayvallich *(Food)*   *New Tayvallich Inn*

Near Lochgilphead · *Strathclyde* · Map 2 B3
Tayvallich (054 67) 282

Free House
Landlords Pat & John Grafton

Loch Scotnish mussels marinière £1.90
Soup 65p (Last order 7pm)
🍺 Ind Coope Alloa Export, Heavy; Guinness;
Skol; Taunton cider.

This cheery little pub stands on the shores of Loch Sweet. The fare on offer in the cosy public bar includes soup of the day, steaks, burgers, salads and popular fish items such as plump mussels and Dublin Bay prawns. Home-made sweets like fruit crumble and a rich chocolate nut slice.   **Family pub**

Uig *(B & B)*   *Ferry Inn*

Isle of Skye · *Highland* · Map 1 A2
Uig (047 042) 242

Free House
Landlords John & Betty Campbell

BEDROOMS 6   Grade 2   £C
🍺 McEwan's Export; Younger's Tartan;
Guinness; Tennent's Export, Lager; Taunton
cider.

A neatly kept, friendly little pub, which enjoys bird's-eye views of the ferry and fishing boats. Local fishermen are regular customers in the simple public bars; there's also a lounge bar and a small TV room. Spacious, plainly furnished bedrooms have tea-makers and central heating; one offers private facilities and there are two public bathrooms. Patio.
                Family pub

Ullapool *(B & B)*   *Argyll Hotel*

Argyle Street · *Highland* · Map 1 B1
Ullapool (0854) 2422

Free House
Landlords Mr & Mrs I. Matheson

BEDROOMS 8   Grade 2   £C
🍺 McEwan's Export, 80/-, Heavy; Guinness;
Carlsberg; Harp; Taunton cider. *Real ale*

Hospitality is a way of life at this white-painted inn near the quayside. The bars are convivial, and the place really buzzes on the nights when there's live entertainment. The TV room is a quieter spot. Overnight guests will find simply furnished, spotlessly kept bedrooms with fine views. They are equipped with tea-makers and electric blankets and there are three public bathrooms. Hearty breakfasts.   **Family pub**

Weem   *(Food, B & B)*   *Ailean Chraggan Hotel*

By Aberfeldy · *Tayside* · Map 2 C3
Aberfeldy (0887) 20346

Free House
Landlords Gillespie family

BEDROOMS 4   Grade 1   £B
Chicken casserole £3.85 Cream
meringue £1.10 (Last order 10pm, 8.30
in winter)
🍺 Younger's Tartan; Tennent's Extra.

A lot of care goes into the running of this
friendly village pub, which has nice
gardens and fine views. The bar snacks are
simple and delicious, ranging from home-
made soup and pasta to omelettes, Tay
salmon and chicken casserole. Spick-and-
span bedrooms, all with TVs and tea-
makers, feature some fine traditional furniture; they share a single public bathroom.
                                    Family pub

Wester Howgate   *(Food)*   ★   *Old Howgate Inn*

Near Penicuik · *Lothian* · Map 2 C3
Penicuik (0968) 74244

Free House
Landlords Mr & Mrs Di Rollo

Smørrebrød small £1.25 large £2.50
(Last order 10pm)
🍺 Belhaven 80/-; McEwan's 80/-; Younger's
Tartan; Guinness; Carlsberg Pilsner, Export.
Real ale

Danish open sandwiches (smørrebrød)
have for many years been the speciality at
this delightful whitewashed pub alongside
the A6094. The base is light or dark rye
bread, and all the toppings are home-
prepared. Forty mouthwatering varieties
include chicken liver pâté, tomato
rémoulade, ham with vegetable salad and
superb sweet pickled herring with egg and
curry mayonnaise. Garden. Closed Sun
eve.   **Family pub**

WALES

THE
COW
AND
COSMOPOLIS

Wales

Aberaeron *(Food)*   *Harbourmaster Hotel*

Quay Parade · *Dyfed* · Map 7 B1
Aberaeron (0545) 570351

Free House
Landlords Mackay Family

Lasagne £1.85 Seafood platter £3.25
(Last order 10pm)
🍺 Whitbread Best Bitter; Welsh Bitter;
Flowers IPA; Guinness; Heineken; cider.
Real ale

The harbour wall and the splendid little
panelled bar are equally delightful settings
for enjoying a drink and a snack at this
handsome 19th-century pub. Seafood is
something of a speciality, the choice ranging from garlic mussels to crab, lobster,
salmon and a mixed platter. Other popular
items include sandwiches, omelettes, tasty
savoury pies and a cold buffet in summer.
Closed Sunday.   **Family pub**

Abergavenny *(Food, B & B)*   *Crowfield Inn*

Ross Road · *Gwent* · Map 7 C2
Abergavenny (0873) 5048

Free House
Landlords George & Sasha Crabb

BEDROOMS 5   Grade 1   £A (No dogs)
Crowfield smokies £1.50 Beef shobdon £4.65
(Last order 9.30pm. No bar food Sun)
🍺 Worthington Best Bitter; Bass; Carling
Black Label. *Real ale*

A pleasant farmhouse inn, where Sasha
Crabb's bar menu combines familiar
favourites with delightful specialities such
as zippy pepperpot beef or seafood in a
mustardy cheese sauce. Spacious smartly
furnished bedrooms (all in an annexe) have
central heating and well-appointed bathrooms. There's a splendidly comfortable
residents' lounge with a piano for guests to
play. No children under 12 overnight;
accommodation closed 1 week Christmas.

Babell *(Food)*   *Black Lion Inn*

Near Holywell · *Clwyd* · Map 3 B3
Caerwys (0352) 720239

Free House
Landlords Mr & Mrs H. G. Foster

Grilled sardines with salad & sautéed
potatoes £2.60 Steak sandwich £2.95 (No bar
food eves & all Sun)
🍺 Stones Bitter; Carling Black Label;
Taunton cider.

Tucked away in the hills and lanes behind
Holywell and the Dee Estuary, the Fosters'
quaint little whitewashed inn serves very
good lunchtime food in homely and hospitable surroundings. Soup, pâté and fresh
sardines are popular starters, while main
courses range from omelettes and steak
sandwiches to flavoursome stews. Also
salads and nice home-made sweets.
Closed lunchtime Monday and Saturday.

Beaumaris *(Food, B & B)*   *Ye Olde Bull's Head*

Castle Street, Anglesey · *Gwynedd* · Map 3 A3
Beaumaris (0248) 810329

Free House
Landlord Mrs D. M. Barnett
BEDROOMS 17   Grades 1 & 2   £B (No dogs)
Florentine pie 90p Fresh local salmon salad £3
(No bar food eves)
🍺 Bass, Mild, 4X; Stones Bitter; Worthington
'E'; Younger's Scotch Bitter; Guinness;
Carlsberg Hof. *Real ale*

This old posting house is steeped in history,
and its beamed bar is a cosy setting for
simple, satisfying lunchtime snacks. Sandwiches come with a variety of fillings –
cheese and onion, roast duckling, even
banana – and there are also salads and hot
pies like sausage or fish. Less choice Sun.
Individually furnished bedrooms offer good
comforts, and there's a delightful residents'
lounge. Rooms closed two weeks autumn.
                                  Family pub

Betwys-yn-Rhos *(Food)*   *Ffarm Hotel*

Clwyd · Map 3 A3
Dolwen (049 260) 287

Free House
Landlords Lomax family

Ffarm liver pâté £1.25 Steak pipérade £4.40
(Last order 10pm)
🍺 Ind Coope Bitter, Dark Mild; Tetley Bitter;
Wrexham Lager. *Real ale*

This crenellated Victorian Gothic building,
owned by the Lomax family for many years,
is an impressive setting in which to enjoy
some excellent bar fare. Simple starters
like soup, egg mayonnaise and smooth,
flavoursome pâté precede splendid main
courses such as trout amandine, chicken
créole or kidneys in a sherry-based sauce.
Other favourites include salads, steaks and
basket meals. Closed Sunday in winter.
Garden.   **Family pub**

Bodfari *(Food)*   *Dinorben Arms Inn*

Near Denbigh · *Clwyd* · Map 3 B4
Bodfari (074 575) 309

Free House
Landlord Mr G. T. Hopwood

Moussaka with vegetables & potatoes £3.50
Soused herrings £1.40 (Last order 10.15)
🍺 Border Bitter; Whitbread Mild; Younger's
Tartan; Guinness; Heineken; Wrexham Lager;
cider. *Real ale*

A splendid place for all the family, this 17th-
century inn offers fine views from its
attractive terraces and gardens. Soup and
sandwiches are the fare in the bar, while in
the dining room at lunchtime there's an
impressive self-service selection of cold
cuts and salads, plus some hot dishes. The
evening choice, which is even wider,
includes daily specials such as chicken
Kiev.   **Family pub**

Brockweir *(B & B)*   *Brockweir Inn*

Chepstow · *Gwent* · Map 7 D2
Tintern (029 18) 548

Free House
Landlords Mavis & Granville Clegg

BEDROOMS 4   Grade 2   £C
🍺 Flower's Original; Hook Norton Best
Bitter; Whitbread Best Bitter; Stella Artois;
cider. *Real ale*

Mavis and Granville Clegg provide a warm
welcome at this convivial little village inn
by the river Wye. The cosy lounge bar is a
splendid place for a drink and a chat, while
pool is a popular pursuit in the public bar.
Simply furnished bedrooms (two rooms
under the eaves) are fine for an overnight
stay, and guests wake up to a well-cooked
breakfast. Garden.   **Family pub**

Cardigan *(B & B)*   *Black Lion Hotel*

High Street · *Dyfed* · Map 7 B2
Cardigan (0239) 612532

Free House
Landlord Mr T. L. Lowe

BEDROOMS 11   Grade 1   £B
🍺 Flower's IPA; Whitbread Welsh Bitter,
Best Bitter; Stella Artois; Heineken; cider.
Real ale

The greeting is warm and friendly at this
popular town-centre hotel, whose red-brick
Georgian façade hides 800 years of history.
Comfortable accommodation is provided
in the well-kept bedrooms, where modern
pine units and tea-makers are standard. All
have neat bath or shower rooms. Public
areas include a TV lounge, snug little
writing room and spacious bar. Closed
Sunday.   **Family pub**

Wales

Cenarth *(Food)* — White Hart

Near Newcastle Emlyn · *Dyfed* · Map 7 B2
Newcastle Emlyn (0239) 710305

Free House
Landlords John & Anne Jones

Anglesey eggs £1.75 Teifi salmon £5.95
(Last order 10pm)
🍺 Whitbread Welsh Bitter, Mild; Buckley's
Best Bitter; Guinness; Heineken. *Real ale*

John Jones in the bar and his wife Anne in the kitchen make a splendid team at this agreeable old inn near the river Teifi. The menu shows a strong Welsh influence, with dishes such as Anglesey eggs, Teifi salmon and the splendid catrin pie – a light pastry case enclosing minced lamb with raisins and brown sugar. More familiar fare includes sandwiches and basket-type meals. **Family pub**

Chepstow *(Food, B & B)* — Castle View Inn

16 Bridge Street · *Gwent* · Map 7 D2
Chepstow (029 12) 70349

Free House
Landlords Mr & Mrs M. Gillett

BEDROOMS 10 Grade 1 £A
Aubergine & nut crumble £2.25 Rabbit pie &
vegetables £3 (Last order 9.30pm)
🍺 John Smith's Bitter; Simond's Bitter;
Kronenbourg.

The Gilletts' 300-year-old inn opposite the castle offers comfort, good food, friendly service and abundant period charm. Home-prepared bar snacks include omelettes, flavoursome pâtés, hearty pies and meaty casseroles, along with sandwiches, vegetarian dishes and nice sweets. Smartly modernised bedrooms have good-quality fitted furniture, TVs, tea-makers and well-equipped carpeted bathrooms. There's a lovely walled garden. **Family pub**

Crickhowell *(Food, B & B)* — Bear Hotel

Powys · Map 7 C2
Crickhowell (0873) 810408

Free House
Landlord Mrs Joan Hindmarsh
BEDROOMS 12 Grade 1 £B
Fresh salmon & prawn béchamel with salad
£4.95 Turkey américaine £4.50 (Last order
10pm)
🍺 Bass, Allbright; Whitbread Best Bitter;
Stella Artois; Taunton cider. *Real ale*

A charming 15th-century hostelry, with a warm, welcoming bar, a cobbled courtyard and an attractive enclosed garden. The snack menu offers something for most tastes and appetites, from super smoked salmon pâté to savoury pies and pancakes, steaks and turkey américaine. Bedrooms (most with private facilities) are neatly appointed, and there's a comfortably furnished residents' lounge with television. **Family pub**

Crickhowell *(Food)* — Nantyffin Cider Mill Inn

Powys · Map 7 C2
Crickhowell (0873) 810775

Free House
Landlord Mrs Barbara Ambrose

Smoked haddock kedgeree with salad £2.50
Cider syllabub £1.30 (Last order 10.30pm)
🍺 John Smith's Bitter; Marston's Pedigree;
Worthington Best Bitter; Guinness; Carlsberg
Export; cider. *Real ale*

Pork and cider pie and superb cider syllabub are two of Barbara Ambrose's specialities at this attractive pink-washed pub that was once a cider mill. Her smoked haddock kedgeree is another great favourite, along with flavoursome soups, cold meats and salads, quiches and treacle tart. The inn stands west of Crickhowell at the junction of the A40 and A479. Garden. **Family pub**

Dollgellau *(B & B)*   ## Gwernan Lake Hotel

Gwynedd · Map 7 C1
Dolgellau (0341) 422488

Free House
Landlords Mr & Mrs P. Hall

BEDROOMS 10 Grade 2 £B (No dogs)
🍺 Bass; Carling Black Label. *Real ale*

Trout-filled Lake Gwernan provides a
peaceful setting for this whitewashed inn
outside Dolgellau. There's a friendly little
bar and a panelled lounge adorned with a
fine collection of plates and pottery. Bright,
cheerful bedrooms, which share two public
bathrooms, are simply furnished. No
children under three overnight. Accommodation is closed between October and
Easter. Garden.

Felindre Farchog *(B & B)*   ## Old Salutation Inn

Near Cardigan · *Dyfed* · Map 7 B2
Newport (0239) 820564

Free House
Landlords Peter & Joan Voyce

BEDROOMS 8 Grade 1 £C
🍺 John Smith's Bitter; Sam Powell
Traditional; Courage Best Bitter; Ind Coope
Double Diamond; Hofmeister; cider.

Overnight accommodation is in a modern
annexe at this charming old whitewashed
inn, whose garden slopes down to the
banks of the river Nevern. All the bedrooms
have TVs, tea-makers and sparkling bathrooms and offer plenty of space and comfort. The two beamed bars are pleasant
spots for a drink and a chat and there's a
relaxing residents' lounge.   **Family pub**

Hay-on-Wye *(Food, B & B)*   ## Old Black Lion

26 Lion Street · *Powys* · Map 7 C2
Hay-on-Wye (0497) 820841

Free House
Landlords Mr & Mrs C. Vaughan
BEDROOMS 10 Grade 1 £A
Ploughman's £1.10 Steak & kidney
pudding £3.95 (Last order 10pm)
🍺 Flowers Best Bitter; Worthington Best
Bitter; Guinness; Carlsberg Export; cider.
Real ale

Low ceilings and creaking floors add to the
antique charm of this delightful hostelry in
a pleasant market town. Excellent bar fare
includes a tempting cold buffet and other
delights ranging from pasties and toasted
sandwiches to steak and kidney pudding
and home-pickled salmon. Delicious ice
cream to finish. Characterful bedrooms,
most with neat bath/shower rooms, have
handsome furnishings, TVs and tea-
makers.   **Family pub**

Henllan *(B & B)*   ## Henllan Falls Inn

Near Newcastle Emlyn · *Dyfed* · Map 7 B2
Velindre (0559) 370437

Free House
Landlords Mr & Mrs T. J. Revell

BEDROOMS 4 Grade 2 £C (No dogs)
🍺 Buckley's Bitter, Mild; John Smiths;
Guinness; Celtic; Hofmeister; Kronenbourg;
cider.

Close to the river Teifi, the Revells' agreeable little pub is a peaceful spot to spend
the night. Simply furnished bedrooms (one
suitable for families) have tea-makers and
washbasins, and share an up-to-date bathroom. Pool and darts are played in the
rustic public bar, and there's a quiet lounge
bar and pleasant TV room. Accommodation closed Christmas week. Pub closed
Sunday.   **Family pub**

Holywell   *(B & B)*   *Stamford Gate Hotel*

Halkyn Road · *Clwyd* · Map 3 B3
Holywell (0352) 712942

Free House
Landlords A. J. & K. L. Newell

BEDROOMS 12   Grade 1   £A   (No dogs)
🍺 Wilson's Great Northern Bitter; Watney's
Special Mild; Guinness; Carlsberg; cider.
Real ale

This go-ahead little hotel above the Dee
estuary offers spotlessly clean overnight
accommodation that appeals equally to
business visitors and holiday-makers. Bedroom decor is smartly cheerful, and TVs,
radio-alarms and well-supplied bathrooms
are standard throughout. Public rooms
include a comfortable reception lounge
and two bars, one with a nautical theme.
Breakfast is served in bedrooms.
Family pub

Llanarmon Dyffryn Ceiriog   *(B & B)*   *West Arms Hotel*

Near Llangollen · *Clwyd* · Map 3 B4
Llanarmon Dyffryn Ceiriog (069 176) 665

Free House
Landlords Mr & Mrs A. J. Edge

BEDROOMS 16   Grade 2   £A
🍺 Younger's Scotch Bitter, Mild; Harp;
McEwan's Export; Carlsberg Hof.

Situated in a little village at the head of a
lovely valley, this 400-year-old inn has
gardens running down to the river Ceiriog.
Trout fishing is available to guests, who can
swap anglers' tales in the charming bars or
catch a TV programme in the lounge. Bedrooms, some with splendid views, are
pleasantly furnished in cottage style. Six
have private facilities.   **Family pub**

Llanarthney   *(Food, B & B)*   *Golden Grove Arms*

Near Carmarthen · *Dyfed* · Map 7 B2
Dryslwyn (055 84) 551

Free House
Landlords Mr & Mrs R. J. Jones

BEDROOMS 7   Grade 2   £C
Barbecued spare ribs £2 King prawns in garlic
butter £3 (Last order 10pm)
🍺 Buckley's Bitter; Whitbread Welsh Bitter,
Tankard; Heineken; cider. *Real ale*

Evening snacks are a popular attraction at
this welcoming stone-built farmhouse,
which stands just off the B4300 about eight
miles from Carmarthen. The choice is
nicely varied, from soup and sandwiches to
local trout, spare ribs and speciality steaks.
Comfortable bedrooms of various sizes
have tea-makers and neat pine furnishings.
Closed lunch and Sun to non-residents,
also 14 January–1 March.   **Family pub**

Llandissilio   *(Food)*   *Bush Inn*

Near Clynderwen · *Dyfed* · Map 7 B2
Clynderwen (099 12) 626

Free House
Landlords K. J. & J. E. Honeker

Lasagne & salad £2.90 Cheese & onion
pie £2.20 (Last order 10.30pm)
🍺 Worthington Best Bitter; Harp; Double
Diamond; Guinness; Kronenbourg;
Whitbread Tankard. *Real ale*

This modest little roadside inn is a good
place to drop in and enjoy some very tasty
snacks. Cold meats and salads make a
tempting lunchtime and evening display in
the low-ceilinged bar, with locally reared
turkey one of the most popular choices.
There are also plenty of hot dishes, from
soup and lasagne to curries, casseroles and
delicious pies, both savoury and sweet.

Llandogo (B & B)   *Sloop Inn*

Near Monmouth · *Gwent* · Map 7 D2
Dean (0594) 530291

Free House
Landlords George Morgan & Grace Evans

BEDROOMS 4   Grade 1   £B
🍺 Smiles Best Bitter; Wadworth's 6X;
Worthington Best Bitter; Guinness; Harp;
Stella Artois; cider. *Real ale*

George Morgan is a most hospitable and
caring host at this carefully modernised
little inn in the heart of the Wye valley.
There are fine views from the panelled
lounge bar, while the pool table and fruit
machines are popular features of the front
bar. Accommodation is excellent: spotless
bedrooms (one with a four-poster) are very
attractively decorated and have colourful
modern bathrooms. Delicious breakfasts.
Garden.

Llandovery (B & B)   *King's Head Inn*

Market Square · *Dyfed* · Map 7 C2
Llandovery (0550) 20393

Free House
Landlords Mr & Mrs Madeira-Cole

BEDROOMS 4   Grades 1 & 2   £B
🍺 Worthington Dark Mild, Best Bitter;
Allbright; Hancock's Traditional Ale;
Guinness; Carling Black Label. *Real ale*

This pleasant little inn, parts of which date
back to the reign of Charles I, stands right
on the market square. The delightfully
rustic public bar is a popular place with the
locals, and there's a relaxing lounge bar as
well as spacious first-floor residents'
lounge. Bedrooms have a fresh, modern
appeal, with neat fitted furniture and sparkling tiled bathrooms.   **Family pub**

Llanfihangel Crucorney (Food, B & B)   ★   *Skirrid Inn*

Near Abergavenny · *Gwent* · Map 7 C2
Crucorney (087 382) 258

Free House
Landlords Mr & Mrs D. Foster
BEDROOMS 1   Grade 2   £B
Shrimp scramble £3.10 Casserole of wild
rabbit £3.95 (Last order 9.30pm)
🍺 Robinson's Bitter; Wadworth's 6X;
Felinfoel Bitter; Allbright; Guinness;
Carlsberg; Taunton cider. *Real ale*

The oldest pub in Wales, with a fascinating
history going back to the 12th century, is
renowned for the excellence of its food. In
the atmospheric flagstoned bars you can
tuck into Mr Foster's marvellous meat pies
or savour the delights of his splendid
soups, quiches and casseroles. Lovely old-
fashioned puds like figgy duff to finish.
There's one large, comfortable bedroom.
                                 Family pub

Llanfrynach (Food)   *White Swan*

Near Brecon · *Powys* · Map 7 C2
Llanfrynach (087 486) 276

Free House
Landlords Mr & Mrs David Bell
Range of curries from £2.75 Welsh-style trout
& bacon £4.95 (Last order 10.30pm. No bar
food Mon except Bank Holidays)
🍺 Brain's Bitter; Whitbread Traditional,
Best, Welsh Bitter; Guinness; Heineken; cider.
Real ale

You'll find this attractive, centuries-old pub
opposite the church boasting the largest
graveyard in Wales. The roomy, open-plan
beamed bar is full of character, and here
you can sample Mrs Bell's legendary pies,
baked to order, or tasty French onion soup.
Her careful cooking ranges from vegetable
goulash to baked crab, roasts and grills to
curries and casseroles. Closed Mon lunch &
last 3 weeks January.   **Family pub**

Wales

Llangollen   *(Food, B & B)*   *Britannia Inn*

Horseshoe Pass · *Clwyd* · Map 3 B4
Llangollen (0978) 860144

Free House
Landlords Cyril & Maureen Ashton

BEDROOMS 7   Grade 1   £B
Chicken & mushroom pie £2.50 Fresh fruit
pie 80p (Last order 10pm)
🍺 Border Bitter, Mild; Stones Bitter; Tetley's
Bitter; Guinness; Wrexham lager; cider.

Nestling at the foot of Horseshoe Pass, this
delightful old inn numbers prize-winning
gardens and fine mountain views among its
attractions. The rustic, spotlessly kept bars
are the setting for good simple snacks like
toasted sandwiches, salads, savoury pies
and chicken curry. Comfortable, homely
bedrooms with TVs and tea-makers share
three modern bath/shower rooms. Closed
Monday evenings in Jan and Feb.

Llangorse   *(B & B)*   *Red Lion*

Near Brecon · *Powys* · Map 7 C2
Llangorse (087 484) 238

Free House
Landlords Mr & Mrs C. Cocker

BEDROOMS 10   Grade 1   £B
🍺 Robinson's Best Bitter; Felinfoel Double
Dragon; Whitbread Best Bitter, Welsh Bitter;
Guinness; cider. *Real ale*

Occupying a picturesque position
complete with babbling stream, this
charming rose-clad inn in the village centre
is a cosy overnight stop for visitors to the
Brecon Beacons National Park. The stone-
walled bars are popular with the locals, and
the public bar features darts and pool. Neat,
bright bedrooms have cheerful floral wallpaper, simple white furniture and private
bathrooms or shower cubicles. Garden.
Family pub

Llangurig   *(B & B)*   *Blue Bell Inn*

Near Llanidloes · *Powys* · Map 7 C1
Llangurig (055 15) 254

Free House
Landlords Bill & Diana Mills

BEDROOMS 10   Grade 2   £C   (No dogs)
🍺 Whitbread Bitter, Welsh Bitter, Best Mild;
Banks's Traditional Bitter; Stella Artois;
Heineken. *Real ale*

Converted 16th-century farm cottages
make up this pink-washed roadside inn,
where landlords Bill and Diana Mills extend
a warm and friendly welcome. The rustic
bars are cosy and convivial, and there's a
traditionally furnished residents' lounge
with colour TV. Well-kept bedrooms (front
ones double-glazed) offer simple comforts,
and overnight guests can look forward to a
hearty cooked breakfast.

Llannefydd   *(Food, B & B)*   *Hawk & Buckle Inn*

Near Denbigh · *Clwyd* · Map 3 A4
Llannefydd (074 579) 249

Free House
Landlords K. C. & M. Johnson

BEDROOMS 10   Grade 1   £B
Steak & kidney pie £2.25 Chicken provençale
with rice £2.65 (Last order 10pm)
🍺 Wilson's Bitter, Special Mild; Carlsberg;
Foster's; cider.

Winding roads lead up to this remote stone
inn, which enjoys spectacular views from
its vantage point above the Vale of Clwyd.
Comfortable accommodation (no children
under eight) is provided in well-kept
bedrooms that range from traditional to
smartly modern; all rooms have excellent
private facilities. Splendid bar snacks
include home-made soups and pâtés,
steaks and fresh salmon. Closed weekday
lunchtime Nov–Easter.

Llanrug *(Food)*   *Glyntwrog*

Gwynedd · Map 3 A4
Caernarfon (0286) 2191

Brewery Lloyd & Trouncer
Landlords David & Gill Rochell

Local trout £2 Lamb kebabs £1.75 (Last
order 9pm. No bar food Sun lunch)
🍺 Ansells Bitter, Mild; Ind Coope Bitter,
Double Diamond; Guinness; Skol; cider.
Real ale

There's a lively local atmosphere in this
delightful whitewashed pub, whose two
traditionally furnished bars are the convivial setting for some excellent lunchtime
and evening snacks. Fresh fish, kebabs and
hamburgers are always in demand, along
with grills and cold cuts, casseroles and
roast chicken. A simple selection of sweets
includes ice cream and a delicious apple
pie. Garden.

Llantrissent *(B & B)*   *Royal Oak Inn*

Near Usk · Gwent · Map 7 D2
Usk (029 13) 2632

Free House
Landlords Mr & Mrs G. Rossiter

BEDROOMS 20 Grade 1 £B (No dogs)
🍺 Flower's Original; Felinfoel Double
Dragon; Whitbread Best Bitter, Welsh Bitter;
Heineken; cider. *Real ale*

Graham and Maureen Rossiter put out the
welcome mat for both old friends and new
arrivals at this charming old village inn.
Stone walls and oak beams give period
character to the cosy main bar, while
smartly furnished bedrooms (divided
between the original building, a converted
cottage and motel-style block) offer a more
modern appeal. All have colour TVs and
well-equipped shower rooms. Garden.

Llantilio Crossenny   *Hostry Inn*

'1459', proclaims the sign outside this attractive whitewashed inn a
few yards from the B4233. But it's certainly no museum piece, with
locals gathering nightly for a drink, a chat and a game of darts. The
place has considerable rustic charm, highlighted by the country prints
and paraphernalia that adorn the public bar. Patio.

Near Abergavenny · Gwent · Map 7 D2
Llantilio (060 085) 278
Free House   Landlord Douglas McAdam
🍺 Usher's Best Bitter, Triple Crown; Ben Truman; Carlsberg.
Real ale

Llowes *(Food)*   ★   *Radnor Arms*

Near Hay-on-Wye · Powys · Map 7 C2
Glasbury (049 74) 460

Free House
Landlords Brian & Tina Gorringe

Hot avocado £2.75 Fresh salmon & asparagus
quiche £3.50 (Last order 10pm)
🍺 Felinfoel Double Dragon; Marston's
Bitter; Guinness; Carlsberg Hof; cider.
Real ale

Prime local produce, from fruit and vegetables to lamb and Wye salmon, is put to
superb use in the marvellous bar fare
served in this delightful stone pub. Our
dark, rich mushroom soup was a master-
piece, the lamb hot pot simply delicious.
Other tempting dishes include quiches, hot
stuffed avocado, seafood omelette and
traditional faggots. The sweets are hard to
resist, too. Less choice Sunday evenings.
Garden.

Wales

Llyswen   *(Food, B & B)*   *Griffin Inn*

Near Brecon · *Powys* · Map 7 C2
Llyswen (087 485) 241
Free House
Landlords Richard & Di Stockton
BEDROOMS 6   Grade 1   £C
Fresh Wye Salmon salad £2.75 Fruit
crumble 75p (Last order 9pm)
🍺 Whitbread Welsh Bitter, Best Bitter;
Flower's Best Bitter; Brain's Draught Bitter;
Guinness; Stella Artois; Heineken; cider.
Real ale

Much changed since its coaching inn days,
this convivial inn is a good base for touring
Wales. Comfortable bedrooms, all with
private facilities, have practical modern
furnishings and tea-makers, and there's a
little upstairs lounge. Tasty snacks served
in the characterful bars include sandwiches, salads and hot specials like chicken
curry or beef in red wine. Less choice
Sunday.

Menai Bridge   *(B & B)*   *Gazelle Hotel*

Glyn Garth · *Gwynedd* · Map 3 A4
Menai Bridge (0248) 713364

Brewery Robinson
Landlords Kenneth & Barbara Moulton

BEDROOMS 13   Grade 2   £B
🍺 Robinson's Bitter, Mild, Cock Robin, Old
Tom; Guinness; Einhorn; cider. *Real ale*

Popular with fishermen and yachtsmen,
the Moultons' friendly quayside pub was
once the ferry house for the crossing to
Bangor Pier. There are fine views from
many of the bedrooms, which have neat
modern furnishings, TVs and tea-makers.
The spacious bar is a cheerful place for a
drink and a chat, and upstairs there's a
comfortable residents' lounge. Garden.
Family pub

Mold   *(B & B)*   *Arches Inn*

Alltami Road, New Brighton · *Clwyd* · Map 3 B4
Mold (0352) 58646

Free House
Landlords Mr & Mrs A. S. Meeton

BEDROOMS 14   Grade 1   £B   (No dogs)
🍺 Ansell's Bitter, Mild; Tetley's Bitter;
Guinness; Löwenbräu; Wrexham Lager; cider.
Real ale

Set back from the Mold–Flint road, this
attractive red-brick hotel offers modern
accommodation of a high standard. Well-
equipped bedrooms (no children overnight) are furnished in a modern style that
is both smart and practical, and all rooms
have spotless bathrooms with coloured
suites and shower units. The big lounge bar
is comfortable and elegant, with acres of
gold plush under its panelled ceiling.
Garden. **Family pub**

Monmouth   *(B & B)*   *Queen's Head Hotel*

St James' Street · *Gwent* · Map 7 D2
Monmouth (0600) 2767

Free House
Landlords Margaret & Alan Statham

BEDROOMS 5   Grade 1   £B
🍺 Piston Bitter, 1035 Bitter; Flower's Best
Bitter; Whitbread Welsh Bitter; Guinness;
cider. *Real ale*

Jovial landlords and cheerful staff create a
happy, relaxed atmosphere in this 350-
year-old black and white coaching inn.
Home-brewed beer brings a large local
clientele to the comfortable lounge bar
(note the ornate plasterwork ceiling), and
the pool table is a popular feature in the tiny
public bar. Accommodation comprises two
beamed singles sharing a shower room
and three larger rooms with modern
private facilities. **Family pub**

Morfa Nefyn   (Food)   *Bryncynan Inn*

Near Pwllheli · *Gwynedd* · Map 3 A4
Nefyn (0758) 720879

Brewery Lloyd & Trouncer
Landlord Mr A. Wilson

Leek & bacon soup 80p Cockle pie £2.75
(Last order 9.30pm)
📙 Ansells Mild, Bitter; Guinness; Double
Diamond; Wrexham Lager; Skol; Löwenbräu;
cider. *Real ale*

The bar snacks are fresh, tasty and satisfying at this neat little stone inn, which stands
at a crossroads on the outskirts of the town.
The menu extends to some 40 items, from
soup and spaghetti to salads and seafood,
pâtés and pies, curries and grills. Nice
sweets, too, including a tongue-tingling
lemon meringue pie. Closed Sunday.

Nottage   (B & B)   *Rose & Crown*

Near Porthcawl · *Mid Glamorgan* · Map 7 C2
Porthcawl (065 671) 4850

Brewery Usher
Landlords Mr & Mrs D. Parry

BEDROOMS 7   Grade 1   £B
📙 Usher's Best Bitter, Triple Crown;
Carlsberg; Ben Truman; Guinness; Foster's;
cider. *Real ale*

This cheery white-painted pub is a really
comfortable place to stay the night: seven
attractively furnished bedrooms, all with
TV and bathroom, are sparklingly clean,
with useful writing and cupboard space.
There's a TV lounge for residents and a
good hearty breakfast on rising. The three
little stone-walled bars with copper-topped
tables are hung with hunting cartoons, and
the Parrys make excellent hosts.
Family pub

Penallt   (Food)   *Bush Inn*

Near Monmouth · *Gwent* · Map 7 D2
Monmouth (0600) 2503

Free House
Landlords Mr & Mrs J. A. Wilson

8oz sirloin steak, chips & peas £4.75 Chicken
curry £2 (Last order 10.15pm)
📙 Hancocks Bitter; Bass; Hook Norton
Bitter; Worthington Dark; Carlsberg; Carling
Black Label; cider. *Real ale*

High above the beautiful Wye valley, this
sturdy, slate-roofed inn serves carefully
prepared bar snacks from a menu that
changes with the seasons. Smooth, creamy
chicken liver pâté makes a nice start to a
meal, followed perhaps by plaice or a steak,
home-cooked ham or chunky chicken
curry. Save some room for one of Mrs
Wilson's lovely puds. Enjoy it all outside in
summer.

Penmaenpool   (B & B)   *George III Hotel*

Near Dolgellau · *Gwynedd* · Map 3 A4
Dolgellau (0341) 422525

Free House
Landlord Gail Hall

BEDROOMS 13   Grade 1   £B
📙 Border Bitter; John Marston's Bitter;
Younger's Tartan; Guinness; Carlsberg Hof
Export, Pilsner; cider.

This attractive old inn overlooking a quaint
wooden tollbridge enjoys superb views
over the Mawddach estuary to the darkly
looming hills beyond. Two characterful
bars provide a choice for the thirsty, and
there's a delightfully cosy lounge. Best
bedrooms are those in the annexe, with
cheerful coordinated fabrics and good
modern bathrooms. Main-house rooms are
more traditionally appointed. Patio.
Family pub

Wales

Penybont (B & B)

Severn Arms

Near Llandrindod Wells · *Powys* · Map 7 C1
Penybont (059 787) 224

Free House
Landlords Mr & Mrs W. G. Lloyd

BEDROOMS 10 Grades 1 & 2 £C
🍺 Bass, Allbright; Worthington Best Bitter,
Dark Mild; Whitbread Welsh Bitter; Guinness;
Carling Black Label; cider. *Real ale*

The Lloyds extend a friendly welcome to
their pleasant whitewashed inn, which
dates back to about 1840. The two bars
retain a good deal of period character, and
there's also a games room and a large
residents' lounge with TV. The style is traditional, too, in the spacious bedrooms,
which all have tea-makers and good
modern bathrooms. Garden.
Family pub (lunchtime)

Raglan (Food, B & B)

Beaufort Arms Hotel

High Street · *Gwent* · Map 7 D2
Raglan (0291) 690412

Free House
Landlords Jeanes family
BEDROOMS 12 Grade 1 £B
Pâté-filled mushrooms £2.40 Beef
mexicaine £2.95 (Last order 10pm)
🍺 Ansell's Traditional Bitter; John Bull
Bitter; Double Diamond; Guinness;
Löwenbräu; cider. *Real ale*

Run in fine style by the Jeanes family, this
town-centre hostelry plays a dual role of
friendly local and comfortable hotel. The
well-furnished lounge bar is a refined and
relaxed setting for enjoying tasty snacks
that range from soup and stuffed mushrooms to seafood, coq au vin and a nice
spicy beef mexicaine. Warm bedrooms
(most with private facilities) have TVs,
radios and tea-makers. Patio. **Family pub**

Three Cocks (B & B)

Three Cocks Hotel

Near Brecon · *Powys* · Map 7 C2
Glasbury (049 74) 215

Free House
Landlords Barry & Jill Cole

BEDROOMS 7 Grade 1 £A
🍺 Worthington Best Bitter

South-west of Hay-on-Wye on the A438,
this family-run stone inn offers homely
comforts in peaceful surroundings. Heavy
beams and carved oak furniture give an
old-world charm to the pretty bedrooms,
which share three well-kept bathrooms.
There's a comfortable lounge and, across
the road, the cheerful Old Barn pub.
Overnight guests can look forward to a
well-cooked breakfast. Closed Jan–mid
Feb.

Trecastle (Food)

Castle Hotel

Near Brecon · *Powys* · Map 7 C2
Senny Bridge (087 482) 354

Free House
Landlords Dick & Joan Ward

Curried eggs £1.60 Lasagne & salad £2.95 (Last
order 9.45pm)
🍺 Usher's Best Bitter, Founders Ale; Ben
Truman; Webster's Yorkshire Bitter;
Guinness; Carlsberg; cider. *Real ale*

In the centre of a village on the A40, this
sturdy, grey-painted hostelry attracts a
sizable following with some good, wholesome snacks served in the traditionally
styled bar. Mushrooms in a crisp bread-
crumb coating make a tasty starter, and the
main-course choice could include salads,
lasagne or a richly flavoured lamb curry
served with carefully cooked saffron rice.
Simple sweets. Garden. **Family pub**

Whitebrook *(Food, B & B)* — *Crown at Whitebrook*

Near Monmouth · *Gwent* · Map 7 D2
Monmouth (0600) 860254

Free House
Landlords John & David Jackson

BEDROOMS 8 Grade 1 £A+
Pâté de truite £2.75 Coeur d'artichaut £3.25
(Last order 10pm)
Whitbread Bitter; Heineken; cider.
Real ale

The Jackson brothers set high standards at this remote 300-year old hostelry, where starters from the restaurant menu make up the very interesting snacks offered in the cocktail lounge: truffled duck terrine, perhaps, or tartlets filled with Gruyère and cream cheese. Finish with a sorbet or ice cream. Excellent bedrooms in cottage style have spotlessly clean shower rooms. Glorious breakfasts. Closed 2–20 January.
Family pub

Wolf's Castle *(Food)* — *Wolfe Inn*

Near Haverfordwest · *Dyfed* · Map 7 B2
Treffgarne (043 787) 662
Free House
Landlords Mr & Mrs Fritz Neumann
Smoked trout pâté £1.85 Sirloin steak chasseur £5.85 (Last order 10pm. No bar food Sun & Mon eves & all Mon in winter)
Felinfoel Double Dragon; George's Best Bitter; Worthington Best Bitter; Guinness; Carling Black Label; Carlsberg Hof; cider.
Real ale

Locals like to gather in the tiny public bar of this well-kept stone inn on the A40. Meanwhile, in the lounge and the charming conservatory-style dining area, a good choice of bar snacks is available, ranging from soup, prawns and home-made pâté to a huge and succulent sirloin steak with onion and mushroom sauce. Desserts like cheesecake, lemon mousse and gâteaux are a particular attraction. Closed Mon evening in winter.
Family pub

CHANNEL ISLANDS

Pleinmont   *(B & B)*   *Imperial Hotel*

Torteval · *Guernsey* · Map 8 C4
Guernsey (0481) 64044

Brewery Randall
Landlords Mr & Mrs J. W. Hobbs

BEDROOMS 12   Grade 1   £C
🍺 Randall's Bitter; Worthington 'E';
Guinness; Breda; Holsten; cider.

A popular base for family holidays, this
friendly, white-painted inn overlooks lovely
Rocquaine Bay with its clifftop walks and
sandy beaches. The views are particularly
fine from the picture-windowed lounge
bars, and the convivial public bar is a
popular local meeting place. Bedrooms are
bright and cheerful, with bold geometric-
patterned wallpaper, TVs and tea-makers.
Ten have private facilities. Excellent
housekeeping.   **Family pub**

St Aubin's Harbour   *(Food, B & B)*   *Old Court House Inn*

Jersey · Map 8 D4
Jersey (0534) 41156

Free House
Landlords Jonty & Vicky Sharp

BEDROOMS 9   Grade 2   £A
Lasagne £1.50   Moules marinière £2.30
(No bar food eves or Sun)
🍺 Mary Ann Special; John Smith's Bitter;
Harp; Taunton cider.

There's character aplenty about this
rambling harbourside inn, one of whose
bars is decked out in the style of an old
galleon. Lunchtime snacks announced on a
blackboard menu range from hearty,
flavoursome minestrone to well-presented
salads, spare ribs and outstanding moules
marinière. Ship-shape bedrooms are
homely, with antique furniture and colour
TVs. There's a cosy residents' lounge.
Patio.   **Family pub**

ISLE OF MAN

Andreas *(Food)* — Grosvenor

Isle of Man · Map 3 A2
Kirk Andreas (0624 88) 576

Brewery Heron & Brearly
Landlords Mr & Mrs B. Hamer

Steak & kidney pie £1.75 Fresh crab salad £2
(Last order 10.45pm. No bar food Sun eve)
Okells Bitter, Mild; Guinness; Harp;
Tennent's Lager; Taunton cider. *Real ale*

Lunchtime bar snacks bring the crowds to this well-kept modern pub not far from the sea. Toasted baps with grilled steak or gammon are very popular, as are black pudding, fishy things such as cockles and crab salad, and a good meaty steak and kidney pie served with super chips. To finish, a selection of familiar sweets from the trolley. Sandwiches only evenings and Sunday lunch. Terrace.

Peel *(Food)* — Creek Inn

The Quayside · *Isle of Man* · Map 3 A2
Peel (062 484) 2216

Brewery Okells
Landlords Robert & Jean McAleer

Open prawn sandwich £1.50 Lasagne & salad £1.45 (Last order 10.45pm)
Okells Bitter, Mild; Guinness; Harp;
Carlsberg; Taunton cider. *Real ale*

Down on the harbour amidst the bustle of the boats, this welcoming pub is a friendly and convivial place to meet for a drink and a snack at any time of day. Sandwiches, salads and pizzas are favourite choices, and an ever-changing blackboard menu announces specials like lasagne, scallops mornay and the popular Creek pie – a delicious concoction of sausage meat, onions, apples and potatoes. Terrace.

Family pub

AN OFFER FOR ANSWERS –
A DISCOUNT ON A GUIDE
NEXT YEAR

If you kindly complete the questionnaire below (your answers will be treated in confidence), we will offer you one of our next year's Guides before publication at a very substantial discount, as our readers' reactions are of invaluable help in planning for the future. *After you have made use of the Guide for a few weeks*, please tear out this page and post it to:

Egon Ronay's Pub Guide
Greencoat House, Francis Street
London SW1P 1DH

This offer is valid until 31 December 1985 and is limited to addresses within the United Kingdom.

1 Are you (*please tick*) ✓

				31–45	
male	☐	under 21	☐	46–65	☐
female	☐	21–30	☐	over 65	☐

2 Your occupation ....

3 Do you refer to this Guide (*please tick*)
   (a) four times a week?   (c) twice a week?   (e) once a fortnight?
   (b) three times a week?   (d) once a week?   (f) once a month?

   How many people, apart from yourself, refer to this Guide (including those in your home and place of work)?

   .... males .... females

4 Do you own our Pub Guide?   1983 ☐
                                                1984 ☐

5 Do you have our Egon Ronay's Lucas Guide to Hotels and Restaurants?
                        1983 ☐   1984 ☐   1985 ☐

6 Do you have our Just a Bite Guide?
                        1983 ☐   1984 ☐   1985 ☐

continued

7 Do you own the house you live in? [Yes | No]

8 Do you and members of your family residing with you possess
one car? [   ]   two cars? [   ]   three cars? [   ]

9 What year is your car? ....

10 What is your daily newspaper? ....

11 Which of the following credit cards do you use?
                  Access [   ]   Diners [   ]
    American Express [   ]   Visa [   ]

12 In a pub, do you usually drink
                      beer or cider? [   ]
                            wine? [   ]
    spirits, sherry or other short drinks? [   ]

13 Are you generally happy with the quality of wines served in pubs?
[Yes | No]

14 Are you in favour of accompanied children being served food
in pubs?   Yes, at any time [   ]
                      Lunchtimes only [   ]
                    No, not at all [   ]

Please *print* your name and address here if you would like us to
send you the order form according to our offer on the preceding
page.

Name ....

Address ....

....

....

Readers' comments

Please use this sheet to recommend bar snacks or inn accommodation of very high quality – *not* full restaurant or hotel facilities. Your complaints about any of the Guide's entries are also welcome.

Please post to:
PUB GUIDE 1985
Egon Ronay Organisation
Greencoat House, Francis Street, London SW1P 1DH

NB We regret that owing to the enormous volume of readers communications received each year, we will be unable to acknowledge these forms but they will certainly be seriously considered.

Name and address of establishment (*Please state whether food or accommodation*)

Your recommendation or complaint

Name of sender (in block letters)

Address of sender (in block letters)

Readers' comments

Please use this sheet to recommend bar snacks or inn accommodation of very high quality – *not* full restaurant or hotel facilities. Your complaints about any of the Guide's entries are also welcome.

Please post to:
PUB GUIDE 1985
Egon Ronay Organisation
Greencoat House, Francis Street, London SW1P 1DH

NB We regret that owing to the enormous volume of readers communications received each year, we will be unable to acknowledge these forms but they will certainly be seriously considered.

Name and address of establishment (*Please state whether food or accommodation*)

Your recommendation or complaint

Name of sender (in block letters) _____

Address of sender (in block letters) _____

Readers' comments

Please use this sheet to recommend bar snacks or inn accommodation of very high quality – *not* full restaurant or hotel facilities. Your complaints about any of the Guide's entries are also welcome.

Please post to:
PUB GUIDE 1985
Egon Ronay Organisation
Greencoat House, Francis Street, London SW1P 1DH

NB We regret that owing to the enormous volume of readers communications received each year, we will be unable to acknowledge these forms but they will certainly be seriously considered.

Name and address of establishment (*Please state whether food or accommodation*)

Your recommendation or complaint

Name of sender (in block letters) _____

Address of sender (in block letters) _____

Readers' comments

Please use this sheet to recommend bar snacks or inn accommodation of very high quality – *not* full restaurant or hotel facilities. Your complaints about any of the Guide's entries are also welcome.

Please post to:
PUB GUIDE 1985
Egon Ronay Organisation
Greencoat House, Francis Street, London SW1P 1DH

NB We regret that owing to the enormous volume of readers' communications received each year, we will be unable to acknowledge these forms but they will certainly be seriously considered.

Name and address of establishment (*Please state whether food or accommodation*)

Your recommendation or complaint

Name of sender (in block letters)

Address of sender (in block letters)

Readers' comments

Please use this sheet to recommend bar snacks or inn accommodation of very high quality – *not* full restaurant or hotel facilities. Your complaints about any of the Guide's entries are also welcome.

Please post to:
PUB GUIDE 1985
Egon Ronay Organisation
Greencoat House, Francis Street, London SW1P 1DH

NB We regret that owing to the enormous volume of readers' communications received each year, we will be unable to acknowledge these forms but they will certainly be seriously considered.

Name and address of establishment (*Please state whether food or accommodation*)

Your recommendation or complaint

Name of sender (in block letters)

Address of sender (in block letters)

Readers' comments

Please use this sheet to recommend bar snacks or inn accommodation of very high quality – *not* full restaurant or hotel facilities. Your complaints about any of the Guide's entries are also welcome.

Please post to:
PUB GUIDE 1985
Egon Ronay Organisation
Greencoat House, Francis Street, London SW1P 1DH

NB We regret that owing to the enormous volume of readers communications received each year, we will be unable to acknowledge these forms but they will certainly be seriously considered.

Name and address of establishment (*Please state whether food or accommodation*)

Your recommendation or complaint

Name of sender (in block letters)

Address of sender (in block letters)

ADVERTISERS' INDEX

English beers, Flemish settlers.
And probably the best lager in the world.

A Short Guide To What Goes Into Your Drink

Ale – Originally a liquor made from an infusion of malt by fermentation, as opposed to beer, which was made by the same process but flavoured with hops.

Beer – "Beer" and "Ale" were the words to describe all malt liquors until the 16th Century, when Flemish settlers re-introduced hops for flavouring. The hopped variety was then called "Beer" and the unhopped liquors were called "Ale."

Bitter – The driest and one of the most heavily hopped beers served on draught.

Burton – A strong ale, dark in colour, made with a proportion of highly dried or roasted malts. It is not necessarily brewed in Burton and a variety of strong or old ales were given the term.

Carlsberg – A Danish lager brewery, founded in 1847, based in Copenhagen and specialising solely in the production of lagers. The company has a major brewery at Northampton, England, where these lagers are produced by Danish brewers. Carlsberg is unique because it is owned by a philanthropic foundation which gives all its profits to art, scientific and medical research.

India Pale Ale – The name given to a fine pale ale first made for export to the troops in India. The term became popular with a number of brewers for their bottled pale ales.

Lager – Light coloured beer brewed principally on the Continent. Fewer hops are used than in English beer, and fermentation is carried out at a much lower temperature. Bottom fermentation is caused by special yeasts which descend to the bottom of the fermenting vessels, and character is achieved by the length of the fermentation and storage.

Mulled Ale – A hot drink for cold weather. Beer flavoured with sugar and spices and sometimes the yolk of an egg.

Pale Ale – Also known as light ale. Made of the highest quality malts, it is dry and highly hopped.

Pilsner – The German name for the Czechoslovakian town of Plzen which gave its name to Pilsner. Carlsberg first exported a pilsner type lager from Copenhagen to Scotland in 1868.

Special Brew – A strong, high quality lager produced by Carlsberg. First introduced to commemorate a visit by Winston Churchill to Copenhagen in 1950.

Stout – Heavy dark beer prepared with well roasted barley or malt, and sometimes caramel.

Carlsberg Brewery Ltd. Tel 0604 21621.